A Time To Rhyme

A collection of the best rhyming poetry from Anchor Books

Edited by Heather Killingray & Michelle Afford

Anchor Books - poetry by
the people, for the people

anchorbooks

anchorbooks

First published in Great Britain in 2006 by:
Anchor Books
Remus House
Coltsfoot Drive
Peterborough
PE2 9JX
Telephone: 01733 898102
Website: www.forwardpress.co.uk

HB ISBN 1 84418 423 4

Cover design by Spencer Hart

Foreword

A rhyming riot from Anchor Books!

This glossy hardback edition of rhyming verse was certainly one of the funniest and most challenging the Anchor Books team have been involved in putting together. From across the borders, thousands of entries were sent in and scoured. Scoured for the sparkle, wit, enthusiasm and poignancy that attach only to the best of poets.

Whittling down the entries from the thousands to the hundreds that made us 'aaah', giggle or gasp involved a concerted effort from the team (and much reading out loud!). From 'touching up' the not-quite rhymes and giving the authors a chance to correct and improve their piece, to the final product that appears before you, the satisfaction drawn was immense.

Rhyming poetry is probably the most recognised form of poetry in the world, yet many still pass it over as the simplest. However, the authors within this anthology heartily prove those critics wrong! It may be the simplest but it can also be the most effective way to emphasise, enchant and pontificate. As demonstrated on the pages that follow, rhythm and rhyme can be used to deliver laughter, emotion and the funniest of anecdotes . . .

Teaming up to encourage pen to paper, put paper to type and put type to book has been thoroughly enjoyable and we hope that you are as delighted with the finale of this project as we are. We can only hope that it will launch a new appreciation of the spirit and skill of rhyme and inspire you as much as it has us. We may even try our own hands . . . (but then we might just leave that to you!).

Heather Killingray & Michelle Afford

Editors

A-Z Contents of Authors

Carole Irene Jones	171	David Brown	93
Caroline Dean	285	David Cameron	307
Carol Kaye	344	David Charles	437
Carol Kaye	401	David Maidment	129
Carol Olson	52	David Pooley	340
Cassandra May Poultney	234	David Stuart	459
Catherine Blackett	462	David White	187
C B Price	23	David Whitney	55
Celia G Thomas	127	Davina-Aimée Guignard	219
Chantay Speed	414	Dawn Bennie	240
Charlotte Montgommery Mcmullen	228	Dawn Joyce	154
Cherry Hullock	281	Dawn Taylor	415
Cheryl Gordon	407	Dawn Taylor	459
Cheryl Nicholls	153	Deanna L Dixon	165
Chishimba Chisala	168	Debbie Storey	456
Chris Mann	96	Deborah Ayis	56
Christina Earl	300	Deborah Hall	145
Christina Maria Procter	110	Dee Dickens	259
Christine A Lee	106	Denise McDonald	116
Christine Crandon	339	Denise Winder	197
Christine Lawrence Estrella	31	Denis Martindale	46
Christine Nolan	279	Dennis Brockelbank	102
Christine Youd	403	Dereck Palmer	276
Christopher Head	387	Derek Harris	111
Christopher Higgins	242	Derek H Tanton	402
Christopher Mullin	39	Derek Norris	297
Christopher W Wolfe	409	Derrick C A Bright	435
Ciara McBrien	335	Des Beirne	341
Claire Pattison	110	D G W Garde	51
Clare Fairbairn	273	Dharminder Gill	220
Clive Goldsmith	294	Diana Blench	258
Clive W Macdonald	206	Diana Daley	150
C M Welch	352	Diana Price	265
Colin Allsop	47	Diane Beamish	210
Colin Beck	351	Diane Bowen	246
Colin Wallace	235	Diane Mundell	209
Constance I Roper	104	Dickon Springate	161
C R Slater	146	Dick Whitehouse	444
C Thornton	284	Dien Curtis (10)	213
C Wolstenholme	267	Dolly Harmer	366
Danielle Wills	167	Don Antcliff	264
Danny Harrison	154	Donato Genchi	236
Dan Pugh	232	Don Goodwin	112
Daphne Fryer	105	Donna Hardie	138
Daphne Fryer	448	Donna Salisbury	208
Darren Scott	308	Donna Wyles	289
Daryl Leslie	55	Don Woods	311
Dave Austin	230	Doreen Gardner	285
Dave Slade	117	Doreen Lawrence	74
David A Garside	317	Doreen P Damsell	260
David Barnett	280	Doreen Weller	346
David Bridgewater	357	Doris E Pullen	427

Doris Green	373	Garry Bedford	143
Dorothy M Mitchell	252	G B Mapes	170
D Sheasby	246	G E Bray	458
D Sherwood	319	Gemma Townsend	148
D Spence-Crawford	202	Geoffrey Elgar	333
D T Pendit	188	Geoffrey Pike	96
D Trow	328	George A Tanner	172
Duncan Robson	196	George Coombs	161
E B Holcombe	173	George D Conlon	438
Ed Hinsley	130	George Petrie	269
Edith Kinloch	348	George S Johnstone	278
Edmund Mooney	30	Geraldine McMullan Doherty	126
Edward Fursdon	238	GFB	395
Eileen Hope Hesselden	263	G Hall	233
Eileen M Pratt	308	Gillian Fisher	95
Eileen Tarr	296	Gillian Humphries	196
E J Fensome	347	Gillian Twaite	398
Elaine Fearn	301	Gilly Jones	344
Elizabeth McNeil	432	Ginny Rogers	98
Elizabeth Price	94	G K (Bill) Baker	244
Elizabeth Turner	115	Glanville Grey-Jones	72
Eliza Kokanova	316	Glenwyn Peter Evans	351
Ellen M Lock	107	Glenys Hannon	183
Ellen Spiring	279	Gordon Andrews	94
E Marjorie Bright	59	Gordon Andrews	439
E M Eagle	63	Gordon Forbes	120
Emily Woodhams	417	Gordon Gompers	186
Emily Woodhams	452	Grace Divine	118
Emma-Jane Lunt	118	Graham Connor	274
Emma Eliott	221	Graham Connor	457
Emmanuel Petrakis	24	Greeny	144
Emma Orlando (10)	298	Greta Forsyth	324
Emmeline Michelle Cambridge (14)	417	Greta Forsyth	460
E Riggott	101	Greta Gaskin	425
E S Peaford	324	Greta Solomon	426
Esta Taylor	217	G Steele	26
Eth Holmes	298	G Steele	452
Ethel Kirkpatrick	26	Gwladys Mills	282
Ethel Oates	453	Hamza Ismail	336
E Winifred Garland	350	Hannah Kate Willcock	152
F Buliciri	380	Hardeep Singh-Leader	412
Felicity Pigtails	388	Hardeep Singh-Leader	449
Frances Marie Cecelia Harvey	265	Harkanwalijit Kaur (12)	50
Francis Allen	359	Harold Hyman	247
Francis Arthur Rawlinson	126	Harry Cooper	332
Francis McGarry	219	Hasina Rahman	379
Francis Page	138	Hazell Dennison	372
Francis Xavier Farrugia	222	H Dormand	168
Frank Baggaley	446	H Dormand	462
Frank Howarth-Hynes	337	Helen-Elaine	190
F R Smith	286	Helen M Clarke	358
Gabrielle Gascoigne	425	Hilarie Grinnell	249

Hilary Ayling	314	Jerry Judge	160
H K Banks	75	Jessica Copland (14)	253
Ian Hardwick	293	Jessica Shakespeare	310
Ian Russell	243	J Hagen	145
Ida Jones	77	J H Bennetts	103
I D Welch	367	Jillian A Nagra	226
I Hood	117	Jillian Mounter	234
Irena Bunce	203	Jill Martin	79
Irene Kenny	188	Jim Lawes	89
Irene Reid	302	Jimmy Sinclair	156
Iris E Covell	125	Jim Pritchard	109
Iris I Glatz	21	Jim Tan	76
Ivana	108	J L Chapman	378
Jackie Davies	91	J L Preston	292
Jack Scrafton	338	J Millington	360
Jacqueline Bartlett	97	J Mitchell	142
James A Osteen	119	J M Redfern-Hayes	334
James Ayrey	39	Joan May Wills	135
James Blore	114	Joan M Wylde	43
James McIlhatton	365	Joanna Howstan-Clark	251
James Stephen Thompson	357	Joanna Maria John	401
Jan Cash	424	Joanne Hale	201
Jane Finlayson	238	Joan Prentice	433
Jane H M Hudson	329	Joan Thompson	261
Jane Johnson	342	Joan Winwood	156
Jane Limani	283	Joe Smith	137
Jane Somers	329	John Alan Davies	159
Janet Cavill	310	John Bagshaw	109
Janet Gomersall	374	John Benjamin Freestone	433
Janet N Hewitt	224	John Clarke	93
Janet Scrivens	220	John C Traynor	421
Janey Wiggins	436	John Eccles	262
Janey Wiggins	449	John Edward McBride	69
Jan Ford	287	John Freeth	131
Jan Hedger	375	John G Weeks	319
Janice Thorogood	176	John Knowles	157
J A Solly	378	John Lavan	315
Jay Smith	343	John Laver	59
J Collett	207	John Lee	189
J D Goodspeed	236	John L Pierrepont	112
Jean Bishop	194	John L Wright	47
Jean Bradbury	207	John Peaston	254
Jean C Pease	317	John Richardson	256
Jean Hendrie	268	John Robinson	385
Jeannie Ashplant	387	John Trinick	122
Jean Paisley	223	Jolanta Gradowicz	25
Jean Windle	125	Jondaniel Harris	76
Jennie Hope-Kirk	34	Jordan Hatch	340
Jennifer H Fox	83	Joseph Brough	381
Jennifer Smith	221	Josephine Luck	60
Jenny Bosworth	309	Josh Brittain	29
Jenny Parker	414	Josie Rawson	86

Joyce Walker	237	Lady H	273
Joy Saunders	97	L A G Butler	365
J Pepper	81	Laura Howarth-Kirke	263
J R Legg	191	Laura Jennings	426
Judith Arden	368	Laura Salmon	85
Judith Watts	257	Laura Todd	30
Judy Studd	228	Laura Urquhart	231
Julia Pegg	420	Lauren Elizabeth Rix	203
Julia Perren	227	Lauren McCarthy	408
Julia Sutton	334	Leanne Mizen	185
Julie Marie Francis	127	Lee Brooks	371
Julie Marie Laura Shearing	91	Leigh Crighton	424
Julie Marie Laura Shearing	441	Len Baynes	177
Julie Titchener	108	Len Hynds	289
Julie Trainor	392	Leon Oxenham	62
Julie Willis	142	Lesden Chance	286
June Coral Dye	288	Les Dernie	40
J W Whiteacre	355	Lesley Hartley	272
Kageni Pierce	407	Lesley Tuck	151
Karen Fedrick	399	Lesley White	274
Karen Langridge	164	Leslie de la Haye	65
Karl Hermanis	364	Liam Bailey	61
Karl Mercer	57	Lilian Perriman	326
Kate Williams	418	Linda Chenapa	36
Kathleen C White	139	Linda Howitt	261
Kathleen Furlong	380	Linsi Susannah Sanders	364
Kathleen Mary Scatchard	341	Lisa Alexandra Smith	275
Kathryn Atkin	260	Lisa Jane Mills	313
Kathy Johnson	303	Lisa Killeen	32
Kathy Rawstron	121	Loré Föst	105
K Cook	68	Lorna Lea	427
K D	75	Louis Dickens (11)	239
Keith Alan Deutch	447	Louise Chafer	384
Keith Alan Deutsch	56	Louise Mills	38
Keith L Powell	458	Louise Wheeler	102
Keith Tissington	376	Lynda Long	200
Kelly Earnshaw	63	Lynne Munn	250
Ken Lou	25	Lynne Saint	328
Ken Millar	370	Lynn Greer	306
Kevin Braid	187	Mac Stewart	92
Kevin Clark	411	Madeline Reade	325
Kevin Mytton (16)	143	Magdalen Ogundu	281
Kevin Whittington	231	Maggie Hickinbotham	190
Kimberly Harries	374	Mairtin K	249
Kim Davies	211	Mandy Ducksbury	65
Kim Kelly	377	Marc E Wright	103
Kiran Kaur Rana	277	Maree Teychenné	423
Kirk Blacker (12)	230	Margaret Ann Wheatley	406
K Jenkins	455	Margaret B Baguley	391
K Lake	295	Margaret Doherty	225
K M Brown	28	Margaret Kelly	224
Kryna Neil	269	Margaret Luckett	372

Margaret Ward	29	Miha Pintaric	28
Margaret Ward	192	Mike Hayes	186
Margery Rayson	144	Mike Tracey	321
Marina Smith	294	Mike Wenham	181
Marion Schoeberlein	270	Minerva Pinciu	24
Marj Busby	88	Miss Withakay	128
Marji Tomlinson	58	M J Banasko	92
Marjorie Brown	262	M McBride	282
Mark Cunliffe	353	Monica O'Sullivan	32
Mark Hutchines	383	M Rae	141
Mark L Moulds	68	M Sam Dixon	153
Mark Musgrave	233	Muriel Turner	395
Mark Spiller	165	M Watts	243
Marlana Edwards	42	M Wilcox	176
Marlene Allen	158	Nancy Elliott	244
Marlene Mullen	149	Nasur	119
Marlene Parmenter	349	Natalia Efimovna Carmona	18
Martin Colclough	18	N Carruthers	304
Martyn Leroy	31	Neil Outram	399
Mary Baird Hammond	304	Neil Warren	191
Mary Daines	172	Neville Saveall	290
Mary Frances Mooney	19	Nick Clifton	216
Mary Plumb	166	Nick Wright	19
Mary Skelton	169	Nicola Moreland	86
Mary Woolvin	121	Nigel Evans	36
Matthew Holloway	283	Nikki Jackson	349
Matthew Willbye (17)	385	Nikky Clay	133
Maureen Arnold	376	Nolan Maxie	22
Maureen Cox	85	Norman Bissett	367
Maureen Westwood O'Hara	43	Nyasha Musimwa	330
Mavis Gould	420	Olive Homer	78
M A Wiggin	35	Olive Young	296
May Rigby	299	Opal Innsbruk	354
Mbonisi P Ncube	79	Oritsegbemi Emmanuel Jakpa	84
M B Tucker	373	Oritsegbemi Emmanuel Jakpa	352
M C Armstrong	450	Owen Edwards	297
M C Barnes	371	Paff	455
M Damsell	204	Pamela Carder	166
Meg Lloyd	270	Pamela Popp	320
Melanie Martin	122	Pam Tucker	309
Melanie May	45	P Anderson	150
Melinda Penman	355	Paris Powell	436
Merl Bone	70	Pat Brown	155
M F James	400	Pat Heppel	290
Michael Popkey	20	Patricia Adele Draper	428
Michael Skerratt	113	Patricia Carter	227
Michelle Borrett	337	Patricia Herrod	264
Michelle Clancy	323	Patricia Lindsay	255
Michelle Harvey	235	Patricia Madden	404
Michelle Irving	184	Patricia Smith	98
Michelle Sims	208	Patricia Spear	278
Mick Gayfer	275	Patrick Daly	248

Patrick Folan	20	Roger N Taber	104
Paula Massey	180	Roger Tremethick	198
Paul Curtis	113	Roger Williams	377
Paul Gardner	307	Roland R Ruiz	90
Pauline Beames	298	Ronald Moore	232
Pauline Burton	419	Ron Beaumont	293
Pauline Pickin	81	Ron Martin	49
Pauline Vinters	443	Rose-Mary Gower	134
Paul Kelly	80	Rosemary Davies	429
Pearl Williams	363	Rosemary Yvonne Vandeldt	393
Perry James McLeod (11)	410	Rosie Hues	178
Persi-Vere	330	Ross Macmillan	64
Peter Mahoney	162	Roy A Millar	99
Peter Siggery	413	Royston Davies	345
Peter Vearncombe	87	Royston E Herbert	73
Philip Allen	37	R S Wayne Hughes	430
P Hoddinott	390	Rufaro Ruredzo	409
Pip	175	Russell Adams	394
P J Littlefield	189	Ruth Markinson	332
P M Stone	78	Ruth Martin	229
Poku Michael Kwadwo	173	Ruth Morris	21
P Phillimore	318	R Wiltshire	61
Rachel Gleavy (15)	453	Ryann Throckmorton	124
Rachelle Arlin Credo	41	Salmagundi	412
Rachel Mary Mills	100	Samantha Braum	134
Rachel McKie	397	Samantha Horton	141
Rachel Robins	116	Samina Nazish	129
Rachel Taylor	416	Sam Kelly	259
Rachel Van Den Bergen	54	Sammy Michael Davis	429
Rahela Begum	131	Sandie Smith	247
Ramandeep Kaur (17)	406	Sandra Garrod	454
Ramsha Sajjad	40	Sara Grice	326
Raymond A Uyok	271	Sarah Dixon	252
Raymond A Uyok	408	Sarah Heptinstall	299
Raymond Barber	120	Sarah Sidibeh	389
R Balaji (16)	123	Sarah Smeaton	331
R Bissett	185	S Ballantyne	338
Rebecca Herbert	82	S Beverly-Ruff	437
Rex Andrews	54	S Beverly-Ruff	439
Richard Charles Kennedy	64	S Cardy	53
Richard Marshall-Lanes	152	S Derbyshire	175
Richard Trowbridge	135	Sean James Olson	241
Rick Oak	443	Sean Kinsella	431
Rita Hardiman	95	Shabana Bi	34
Rita Palm	67	Sharon Grimer	198
Robert Basham	353	Sheila B Fry	411
Robert E Fraser	291	Sheila Jane Hobson	212
Robert Henry	301	Sheila Johanson	107
Robert Walker	74	Sheila Storr	177
Robin McGarry	305	Shelley Fairclough	194
Rodger Moir	82	Shireen Markham	331
Rod Trott	124	Shirley Pinnington	432

The Poems

Mountain Solitude

The sky darkens over the mountains,
and night falls silent and still;
The moon is hid behind the clouds,
as the mist forms on the hill.

The valley lies in quiet slumber,
sheep and cattle are not heard;
Not a soul to break the silence,
no one here to breathe a word.

Strange silhouette forms all around,
strike fear into my soul;
Images that are not really there,
some partial and some whole.

The cold night breeze sends a shiver,
to chill my blood and bone;
Heather damp beneath my feet,
as I stand here all alone.

Misty dewdrops form upon my hair,
like a diamond-studded cap;
Nature's night-time murky veil,
covers all in a nocturnal wrap.

Morning golden sunrise finds me,
lets the night-time gently pass;
Cattle low and sheep are bleating,
welcoming the dew-kissed grass.

Hilltop cairns and rocks stand boldly,
fearlessly watch the valleys below;
Easterly sun rises higher and brighter,
fills my veins with a warming glow.

Gentle warm air breathes across me,
buzzards soaring high above;
Sparkling streams dance over boulders,
nature's hand removes its glove.

The shepherd and his faithful friend,
round up a distant fleecy flock;
The buzzard swoops down on its prey,
takes the bloodied trophy to a rock.

I sit alone on a moss-cushioned rock,
amazed by the sights that I see;
All things wild and wonderful,
that God has given me.

Bryan Evans

Ana Laa Afham (I Don't Understand)

There's children on board
You're insane
There's children on board!
Don't crash this plane
There's children on board
What do you hope to gain?

Yes, there are children on board
But all of you will remain
Yes, there are children on board
Welcome to our domain
Yes, there are children on board
All will be slain.

In the name of God!
(We will not die this hour)
In the name of God
(Their faces seem so dour)
In the name of God
(I will not sit and cower).

Bismillah
Increase the engine power
Bismillah
Our flames will soon devour
Bismillah
Steer into the tower.

Oh my God!
Ya Allah!
Mon Dieu!
Mein Gott!

In any language
In every language …
Ana laa afham.

Martin Colclough

A Poet's Heart

It is uncovered, open and bare
It is made so to give, receive and care
Uncovered with self-interest, profit, caution
To care what it's set for in ardour and devotion
Open to tell us what it bears
To give its feelings fully it dares
Bare and touchy, tender and frail
To receive to the utmost of joy and pain
Will you prefer this heart or disdain?

Natalia Efimovna Carmona

A Debtor's Story

Oh God, am I in debt,
No easy way out, that's a safe bet,
Over my head,
Better off dead.
Cannot pay the bills,
Should run to the hills.
Presents for the kids,
At Xmas we'll hit the skids.
No food in my belly,
Knees shaking like jelly.
Robbing Peter to pay Paul,
Bank manager, not happy at all.
What to do, I do not know,
For help, where can I go?
Credit cards have finished me,
A way out I cannot see.
My caring bank has had enough,
They have started to play rough.
Nasty letters through the door,
The phone ringing, more and more.
The final nail was consolidation,
This has brought about total ruination.
Overdrawn, with many other creditors,
Get our story to lots of editors.
Offers of cash through the letter box,
No more shuffling debts like a wily old fox.
Winning the lottery is my last hope,
For not much longer, can I cope.
I have got religion, late in the day,
I am off to church to pray.

Any chance of a tenner?

Nick Wright

Jean

She brimmed over with joy
Never a cross word
Never a sharp reply
Always a ready smile
We never saw her cry
Tho' she'd many a grief
Her sorrows were brief
For the Bible had said it:
'Laughter is good for the soul'
And laughter makes one whole.

Mary Frances Mooney

Age . . .

When are we young: before we get old,
Is youth but a concept
which we tend not to hold?

Sublime? Is it merely an infinite word?
Defined; a life's cordial prime.
Although; is there no comprehensible definition,
to when it inevitably runs out of time?

Past 18; adulthood appears
but how young is an adult at 84?
They're still in their childhood, I tend to believe.
At least to those 90; and more.

Catches in youth; include the purpose of destiny;
however passionately meek.
Such as in later life; the yearning to retain one's youth.
An entirely hopeful wish; yet desperately bleak.

Up to, the ideal of youth?
It is a clandestine thought within one's own heart.
To decide when it ends, of one's personal essence,
it is a passionately resolute part.

Infinite words can be used in a prayer,
to provoke youth to forever remain.
Though I decide to fear, if youth did remain here,
with the ignorance of life; to its troubles and strife;
we'd all soon go insane.

Patrick Folan

11

Sweet youth consoles the weights and cares of age
Its fresh recourse unseats that plague of time
In blush and flame resumes the story's page
To write the scene anew, erase decline.

What portent's stage's script replay is cast
Combines the old with youth's more perfect form
To make new ways that of the old are passed
To realise potentials to inform.

That smile of promise craves ascendant view
Which intellect through study will achieve
To organise in agency anew
With powers bold created to conceive.

The threshold of release, repose, return
Projects an inverse pass through which we turn.

Michael Popkey

New Beginnings

Ticking eternally, the weeks run on,
Day follows day, another month gone.
Into the colder weather, summer far behind,
Winter's tendrils probe, taking hold, they wind
Around the country with tree bark bare,
Wizened branches droop, filled with despair.

Springing forward, time falls back,
Darkness everywhere, an abundant lack.
Running towards December, warmth depletes again,
Gone is the sunshine, to stay is the rain,
The shortest day approaches where light is at its least,
The season devours the world, a veritable feast.

Autumn is a memory, the seasons turn,
Winter's world grows weary, the sunshine infirm,
Underfoot the cold snaps and the leaves grate,
On the icy roads, cars are slaves to fate.
Wrapped in wool, scarves around faces,
The chill deepens and the wind braces.

But out of the fallen leaves comes new creation,
From lowly beginnings, a cycle of regeneration,
The promise of life lies dormant, anticipating,
Preparing for its burst and for the spring, waiting,
Directed by and subservient to Nature, our mother,
Out of the death of one year comes the birth of another.

Ruth Morris

The Year Of 1905

1905 was one of my darkest years
One cannot imagine my deepest fears!
Imperial Russia, beloved country of mine
How can I turn back the hands of time?

My people came
To bring their grievances to me
Imperial Guards, you put me to shame
When you killed them mercilessly.

Who gave you the order to kill?
Did you fire by my enemy's will?
Did you panic when the crowd came?
To whom do I give the blame?

Wherever I look, there are lies and deceit
How can I ensure the revolutionaries' defeat?
I speak to my God and silently await my fate
Hopefully help will not come too late . . .

Iris I Glatz

Another Man Condemned

Tonight, first time ever, I watched a condemned man die.
From this man's lips came words I do not believe; likely a lie.
To a few friends, relatives and media watching his final event,
Said he was not sure where eternity would be spent.

To his victim's family looking from a window nearby,
Said they seemed mighty cold just standing there to watch him die.
Sombre occasions like this seldom bring any joy or laughter.
None watching had any great concern for this man's hereafter.

From death chamber deep within prison walls, this man remained certain,
He was not the one to die for causing the fall of the victim's final curtain.
Others there were, he said, for this dastardly deed, never caught.
Putting him to death for a gruesome murder would only be for naught.

Circumstance all my life found me running with the wrong crowd.
That, he said, since my day in court, I have been shouting mighty loud.
Of such little evidence found, state prosecutors revealed plenty to throw in my face.
No one looking into my record would ever believe I was in another place.

In the news lately, said he heard of innocent men wrongly paying for crime.
Soon, frantically screaming we heard him yell *'Wrong man again this time'*.
In our nation today it seems many criminals remain at large, on the run.
But, remember, better to set 10 guilty men free, than to execute an innocent one.

To the very end loudly proclaiming innocence while deadly injections began to flow.
Innocence or guilt of this condemned man, no way for you and I to ever know.
Minutes later, taken lifeless from the gurney, love or remorse he did never show.
Deathbed denial is common and on final judgement day, only he and God will know.

Nolan Maxie

Car Park Caper

Two experienced drivers fail to see
What's going on behind them in the car park,
How can that be?
In reverse, in gear, on track.
Perfectly centred, hit or miss?
Bang on target, bumpers kiss,
Knock for knock, there's no insurance claim.
'Stupid women drivers are all the same!'
She steps out of her dented car,
Model driver, long legs, skimpy shirt, not wearing a bra.
Everything's fine, there's no harm done,
They exchange numbers and she has to run.
She seems well impressed by his flashy sports car,
Perhaps they could meet up sometime - she doesn't live that far.
She coyly smiles, drives away having given false details,
He tries but can't start up his motor, the engine totally fails.

Amelia Michael

Be Careful What You Wish For

Last night I had a wish come true, I woke up in your bed.
What should have been fantastic turned to travesty instead.
It started out quite promising, you snuggled in my arms.
But then your senses woke you up and set off your alarms.

I'd drifted off to sleep again, your scream got my attention.
I yelled myself, fell out of bed, this wasn't my intention.
You looked at me in horror, but at least you had stopped screaming.
How strange you were not reassured when I said I was dreaming.

'Are you all right?' your parents cried, they woke your sister too.
I hid behind the pillow, dread in fear of what you'd do.
You threw the duvet on my head, then opened up your door.
Explained you'd had a nightmare and had woken on the floor.
Your parents staggered back to bed, confused but satisfied.
I shook beneath your duvet, wondering why on earth you'd lied.

The duvet was pulled off my head, harsh sunlight struck my eyes.
I was naked in the coliseum, much to my surprise.
The lions were advancing while the band struck up a tune.
And the only weapon handy was an ancient wooden spoon.

I stood my ground, I wasn't brave, it's just I was surrounded.
My suspicion that my psyche hates me, seemed at last well founded.
A lustful dream concocted from a seething, bubbling broth.
Congratulations brain, I thought, *you're going to get bit off!*

A lion pounced, I gripped my … spoon, then woke up with a start.
At home in bed, intact and safe, the only sound my heart.
I wiped the sweat out of my eyes, relieved it wasn't true.
And as I fell asleep again began to think of … work; dead nuns . . . anything but you!

Alex de Suys

The Oak Tree

It has been standing for almost 500 years,
Seen many a season, shed many a tears.
Some people see it as only a joke,
The dark mottled bark of the mighty great oak.
The roots of the oak reach deep into the ground,
Provide shelter for creatures that greatly abound.
The trunk and its branches spread out high and wide,
To form a shape whose beauty cannot be denied.
The leaves from the tree exquisite in shape,
Hang down from the branches like a velvety drape.
Here I stand in front of the tree,
In all its glory and history.
Its mighty frame so strong to its core,
I hope that it sees 500 years more.

C B Price

I Am ...

I am the Master of Music,
I am the Lord of the Rings.
I reign over the muses,
The arts and many more things.

I bless you with such holy fire,
The maker of myriads of lives,
I fill your hearts with desire,
The core where reality thrives.

I am the harmony eternal,
The ebb and the flow of past lives,
I whisper in dreams most nocturnal,
From my essence all else derives.

I am the start and the ending
Of cycles through spirals of time,
I am the path you are wending,
The promise of realms so sublime.

I am the love all-embracing
That created all of mankind,
Connecting, linking, relating
All creatures of each kind.

I am the mind that is thinking,
The atom, the sun and the star,
The waters of truth you are drinking,
The door of all wisdom, ajar.

I am your spirit, true being,
Your mentor, your teacher and friend,
My plan and my pattern far-seeing,
Your guide till the exquisite end.

Emmanuel Petrakis

No One

You know what I think, I think
There's no love for me to bring,
There's no one who cares for me,
I'm not happy, do you see?

Now, there's no one by my side,
I'm alone, I cannot fight,
Here I'm staring at the wall,
There's no love, I've lost it all.

I don't know, what can I do?
I can't stop thinking of you.
How I loved you, how I cared,
But you didn't understand.

Minerva Pinciu

Getting There

You know that you're really getting old,
When animals come round to listen,
What looks like dead skin turns out to be mould,
And a slow walk feels like a marathon.

When you creak out of bed in the morning,
Everything smells worse than the day before,
All your bones and ligaments are aching,
While you keep discovering a new sore.

Crossing the road is a major event,
Every song you sing is out of tune,
Folks rush up to help when you start to pant,
Folks walk off whenever you start to croon.

You forget what you've just been saying,
Cannot remember what you had for lunch,
Half a flight of stairs will leave you gasping,
And intoxication has lost its punch.

Only thing going up is blood pressure,
Wearing the same old clothes for days on end,
Finding new cavities in your denture,
Forgetting the name of your closest friend.

Things you hate to do, things you just couldn't,
Come so easily even if you wouldn't,
Things you love to do, things that you shouldn't,
No matter how hard you try, you just couldn't.

And when you retire in the evening,
To unload your body parts one by one,
Just think, if life on Earth is a blessing,
Won't life in Heaven be even more fun?

Ken Lou

Anew

Thus, I begin my life anew -
New hopeful days with new chances,
New challenges and tasks to do.
I revel in this - the freshness …

I left my past behind - no pain!
The impossible became real.
I threw off the shackles - the chain.
My new life - joyful and simple.

I start over. I take a deep breath.
The air is clear - no mist!
I'm the happiest creature on Earth,
And strong enough - at last - to exist.

Jolanta Gradowicz

New Year's Resolution 2003 - 2004

A new year
A new start
Don't dwell
Or break a heart

Live life to the full
Be a good friend
Work hard in life
You never know when it will end

Don't feel guilt
It's not your fault
Don't feel hurt
Like wounds and salt

Be honest and truthful
And be as one
Do as you please
Life's not a con

Life is precious
Special and true
Life's for living
And not feeling blue

Remember, in the end
A broken heart can *always* mend.

G Steele

Fate

We two have met aeons ago,
'Twas fate that bade our love to grow,
From distant stars, we learned to fly,
Swooping, swirling in the sky,
To light upon a moonbeam glow.

We clung together in the flow,
And met again on Earth, below,
To cleave together with a sigh,
Of heartfelt love.

We live and love, have seeds to sow;
We light the path for them that go,
Onwards and upwards, hosts on high,
Nearing the stars as they draw nigh,
For each of them, a silent crow,
Of heartfelt love.

Ethel Kirkpatrick

The School Bully

I remember when you hit me
I remember how I cried
But when other people asked me
I remember how I lied

'Nothing's wrong' I used to say
I watched them walk away
Then you came back, it started again
Each and every day

For two years you did haunt me
I felt like I could die
Then this coward turned
And I asked myself why

Why do I let you hit me?
Why do I let you win?
My running days are over
It's time for me to begin

I hit you good, I hit you hard
I hit you on the jaw
You looked at me in disbelief
As your body hit the floor

No longer do I fear you
Your bullying days are done
No longer can you hurt me
My life has just begun.

Tony O'Sullivan

A Sonnet For A Lover

As I long to feel your delicate touch,
And as your fingertips caress the field.
You're breathing so softly, so softly such,
My body quivers, with your will I yield.
You arouse my soul, my senses will breeze,
One look in your eyes, I melt with desire.
To feel so tender, so tenderly tease,
My heartbeat flutters and now beats higher.
Our bodies joining and fluids entwine,
One heart beats, as we sexually peak.
Passion so lustful, so lustful divine,
To remain as one, our bodies so weak.
Floating from Heaven as we untether,
Cosy and warm, we snuggle together.

Anthay

Peace Tsunami

(A song)

Working for peace,
Working for peace every day,
So very easy to say,
So very easy to say.

But what do we do?
What must we do
To make this peace flow through,
To make this peace come true?

It is in our life,
In our everyday life,
If to ourselves we stay true,
If to ourselves we stay true.

Each of us feels it,
Most believe it,
It comes from the spirit within,
For we know that we're all the same kin.

What matters custom?
What matters spin?
When we are all equal within,
For we are all equal within.

Be still and think peace,
No harm will ensue,
If we love each other,
As we're meant to do.

K M Brown

A Lark

When under limpid southern sky
A lark soars up towards the sun,
Its heart goes melting into one
With sunshine flooding through its eye;

Transparent, light, and flying high,
As if from golden sun-web spun,
And free from all, all ties undone,
Forgets where earthly landscapes lie.

What sun will blind our eyes and set
Our souls ablaze and let them soar
To far-off skies, where we'll forget

The nonsense idols we adore;
In love, trust the Pascalian bet:
We'll only be when we're no more.

Miha Pintaric

My Dream Came True

This year 2006 will be so different
For a new home I now own
It's deep in the heart of the country
There are plenty of walks to roam
This was my last year's ambition
A permanent dream in my head
That dream has now come true
So it's the country for me instead
To live this new way of life
I had to leave my family behind
But they supported me all the way
For my future I needed to find
I had to say goodbye to my friends
So some new ones I shall make
It's all such a huge adventure
But the change that I needed to take
I didn't follow my head but my heart
And my heart said I must go
All life in itself is a gamble
If we don't take it we'll never know
So as the new year approaches fast
A different path has been given to me
I will take it without any worries
As in the country I wanted to be.

Margaret Ward

Sparkling Dust

Truth is faith,
That glimmer of truth,
An utter of confidence,
When others demand proof,
Nobody came - no one went,
Minutes were cast: none were spent,
Seconded, 'borrowing favours' for others,
Bludgeoned, the hammer fell,
Reaping goals, as the stars shone,
Glimmering: giving hope,
Trust is all we have,
Hope is desire,
Love is intangible,
Money is nowt,
Not even a sprinkle of dust,
On all the oceans' floors.

Josh Brittain

This Is Love

Through the wind,
Sun and rain,
Through the heartache and pain,
You are with me,
This could be love.

Through the good times
And the bad,
Through the hard times and the sad,
You are with me,
Is this love?

Through the torment and the tragic,
Through the danger and the magic,
You are with me,
This might be love.

Through the good and bad weather,
We will always be together,
You are with me,
This is love.

We're together,
Forever,
Until death do us part,
I will carry you forever,
You will live in my heart.

Laura Todd

The Smile

*(Dedicated to Christine Cardew, Wendy Mastin,
Rosemary Barnett, great loves of my short life)*

What smile endears thunder of the heart:
The world in beauty storms the raining:
Fire-crushed lips light up their training,
My heart, shining pitch of thought, love to start:
Into the deepness, bright, of love's art,
My lonely soul, love tears, complaining:
Be mine, be mine, radiant, restraining,
Loveliness, my soul cries out, far apart:
Oh let the sweetness of your gorgeous eyes,
Engulf my mortal being, forever:
Conquer me totally with soft replies,
With your comforting smile, release never:
My desire of you, love, is frightening:
I am struck by your smile, love's lightning.

Edmund Mooney

Trilogy Of A Mending Heart

Yesterday I said goodbye to tears
My heart is ready to face new fears
Time has healed the cold summer night
Still here I am keeping up the fight
Because now is a fresh new trial
Like the ending of a tormented self-denial

Time has ways to heal a broken heart
It will scar, bleed and fall apart
I do recall holding on so strong
For a right is nothing without a wrong
My love has endured the trilogy of time
Patiently I wait and hope for you to be mine

Today I bid yesterday adieu
Welcoming a life that is so new
Should I wait for you forever?
Should I give my heart a reminder?
Because tomorrow is yesterday gone
A new day spinning has just begun

Tomorrow I prepare for unwelcome sorrow
Like the moonlight the shining stars borrow
There is no challenge I dare fear to conquer
Because my love for you is eternity forever
Tomorrow I will treasure you like today
For you have never been my yesterday!

Christine Lawrence Estrella

Escapade To The Esplanade

When I desire time alone,
I go to a place I've always known
When I'm past my prime,
in the back of my mind
I visualise a coastal view,
known only to a chosen few
Who would dare to dream,
for a getaway scene
My old time radio tags along,
and plays me back a Beach Boys' song
Watch the palm trees sway,
at the dock of the bay
A single yacht comes sailing through;
the island girls are on-board too
The night brings on the surfer moon . . .
I hope I'm comatose.

Martyn Leroy

Refugees

Bewildered children, grieving wives,
Anguished parents, shattered lives,
Driftwood cast upon the shore.
Such is the aftermath of war.

The whole world teems with refugees;
Innocent victims swarm like bees
Into the villages, cities and towns;
Oft to be met with sneers and frowns.

What are they really fighting for,
Those who deliberately start a war?
Cannot they visualise the chaos and pain
As they tussle for power, prestige or gain?

How dare they ruin this planet of ours,
Forever conspiring to turn it sour?
God's wonderful gift, so rich and rare,
Has through Man's greed been rendered bare!

'Ere it's too late, Lord from above,
Teach this world's people once more to love;
Fill every heart with true compassion;
Bring *Faith, Hope, Love and Trust* back into fashion.

Monica O'Sullivan

If Only

If there was a world I could choose, I would fill it with peace
No hatred or pain, all fighting would cease
No shootings or murders or fears from the dark
No homeless people or tramps in the park
The sun would shine brighter in every way
The rain would be warmer when it came out to play
No more children abandoned and left all alone
All children would have parents and a warm friendly home
No starving people, plenty of food for us all
No difference between us, we all would stand tall
We would welcome our neighbours, ones near and afar
And let happiness surround us and shine like a star
No language barriers between us, all secrets would unfold
And the skin colour differences would blend and all mould
The world would come together, united as one
Escaping bad feelings like wild horses we'd run
Every bird would sing sweeter as they swiftly flew in the sky
And the grass would become greener as time passed by.

Lisa Killeen

Faltering Friendship

How long ago was it that I still believed
In your altruistic love?
How many years have fallen since
You became a raven from a dove?

I remember admiring your impartial kindness,
Respecting you in awe, with no room for doubt.
Yet I can no longer foster such feelings;
My mind has led me to another route.

Why did you change your supportive ways?
What reasons arose to lead you astray?
Or did my eyes simply grow wiser
And lead me to look to what games you play?

Now all I see is partiality:
Favouritism, special rights, privileges to the 'Selected'.
Where is that just, warm-hearted figure?
What have you done with her; why has she parted?

The grievance of truth; the harshness of reality;
I would rather return to my young, naïve state,
But merciless Time will not allow this,
For often, Time is almost as cruel as Fate.

Oh how I yearn for the Time way back when!
How I wish I could see you in innocence again!
Yet that has all passed, and will not return,
For blindness is bliss; enlightenment is pain.

Alice Chuang

The Eternal Struggle

Fossil fuel in heat consumed
Lends meagre light to dingy room
And hoarded near each darksome wall
Accumulated chattels sprawl
Through a chink in rich brocade
Corona of the moon displayed
And torpid on a veiled bed
Lies one from whom all life has fled
Metaphorically I speak
For still the tenuous spirit seeks
Purpose for this human state
And wiles with which to navigate
A kinder course to ride the waves
Upon the sea from crib to grave.

Andrew Carey

Calling For Truth

Please may I place the blame on you
It will ease the hate for me I feel?
I'll silently ask you not to cry
I'll preach, we'll cry, you'll heal.

Take confusion by the hand
I'm sure that you can handle that,
But please refrain from hiding
Wake up, face all the facts.

Truth, well that can seem daunting
I'm sure it's easier to hide,
But who is it you can turn to
When the troubles of today wake you with fright?

I have loved, I have lost
I have faced the fears of yesterday,
You have lied, you have
But you could never make it okay.

Give me just two reasons
That's all I ask of you,
One for your ignorance
The other, just to pull me through.

Do not turn away from me
You have done that too many a time,
Face the pain that only you have caused
Speak up … I can't read your mind.

Jennie Hope-Kirk

Shaken And Stirred

Shaken and stirred among the debris and rubble, a million voices unheard.
Then somewhere in the distance - I hear a call,
when I get there I wonder if I heard it at all.
At times it looks as though I see a hand,
but then it becomes a stone, a rock, a clump of cement and sand.
Only God can help us in our time of strife,
amidst this mortuary there must be a sign of life.
The twitching of a finger, the blinking of an eye
and the painful wail of a child's cry.
They are bruised, they are battered,
they are lost and they are scattered.
With the blurry visions of tearful eyes,
I notice a flame of hope flickers in the darkness of demise.
But for so many living and for so many dead
the remnants of an earthquake is for now, their bed.

Shabana Bi

They Say I Can Write

They say I can write, perhaps they are right,
But I haven't seen signs of it yet.
I sit with a page, get into a rage,
For it seems the words I can't get!

I know what to say, but can't find the way
Of making up things that will rhyme.
So I sit here for hours, my blood pressure towers,
All I'm doing is wasting my time!

But I'll struggle on, 'til my time be all gone,
I'll be blowed if I'll let this beat me.
What rhymes with contentment? Now I feel resentment,
And frustration just won't let me be!

Still I wrack my brain, 'tis really a strain,
And my feelings I just can't express.
Yet, wait, maybe tomorrow, or the day that will follow,
Will show me a way to success!

So I scribble away, in the hope that one day,
Pure genius I just might find.
And then if I'm lucky, go on being plucky,
I might write a verse of some kind!

Susan J Wilson

Bomb

Fast my eyes and you are gone without a word but softly kiss my brow
Clicks the latch and I awake but sadly no one now
Ne'er mind, this day will pass as others have passed too
Your toil will end and come the bell, again I'll be with you
But bereft I stand here broken now, my thoughts all yesterday
When I awoke as you did go and hear the words we say
Bye love
Bye love, take care
Not to worry, bus and tube, soon be there
Oh my love I could not know
Seconds, seconds, seconds to go
And now lifelong my heart will cry
Your being lifted me so high
Though memories will keep me sane
And time may help to ease the pain
Why? Oh why?
I wish, I wish, oh how I wish
Goodbye my love
Goodbye.

M A Wiggin

Mr D Scusting

He walks with a wobble, sometimes a wibble,
From the end of his chin hangs a big glob of dribble.
His clothes are all filthy, never clean,
Not once has he used a washing machine.

His hair is a mess, all greasy and dirty,
In there live nits, I think about thirty.
Never does he wash it or use a comb,
The nits are quite happy to call it their home.

The ears that he has each side of his head
Are both full of worms some people have said.
I've heard a tale, it's not only worms,
In one of his ears live a family of germs.

In his mouth are his teeth all covered in plaque,
The ones that are worse are green, sometimes black.
His toothbrush not used, still new and fresh,
Which is more than can be said 'bout the smell of his breath.

Next is his body all covered in fat,
His legs are like tree trunks, imagine that.
His tummy is huge, held in place by his clothes,
When he last saw his toes, nobody knows.

Last I will tell you the state of his feet,
All covered in grime, no way are they sweet.
If you thought yours were bad, a bit of a pong,
His are much worse, I know I'm not wrong.

So all in all he's not a pretty sight,
No way can I like him, try hard as I might.
His smell is much worse than a dustbin,
That's why his name is *Mr D Scusting!*

Linda Chenapa

Thoughts For Your Day

May the sun rise in the morning to greet you,
May the moon and stars keep you safe at night,
May the oval mystery of existence keep your tears from falling,
May the laughter of summer roses your heart be filling,
The embraces of loved ones be a constant feature,
Life and experience be a great teacher,
May water be your gift when no rain is falling,
May you be blessed with healing if God is willing.

Nigel Evans

Life: Chasing Poetry While Chasing Love

It all began as a simple rhyme,
So easy for the eyes to read ahead,
With protracted smiles he was flying,
Living life without knowing he was dead.

Began living when he first felt pain,
A hard slap on his heart from a young lass,
Tears along cheeks, poems on paper all in vain,
Her hand feeling another man's grasp.

'The Quill' suggested a way out: salvation,
Rush to the author's lumber yard,
Poem after poem, letter after letter: desperation,
A day in the life of the dead bard.

Again he writes, another rejection too,
And another poetry board to fill his cups,
Again he jumps, adjusts his boots,
Yet more verses to prove life is tough.

Tired from the constant trickery of flashing screens,
One more time he clicks on 'Contest',
Cash for silver and gold memberships such far-off dreams,
10 dollars per entry, the banner is on yes.

Rushing to yet another leaf of this vast tree,
Another poetry site, again he clicks 'Submit',
Two fake email IDs appended so quickly,
a@b.com and c@d.com, the form fits.

One more time he sees Preview/Submit too,
Drowsy eyes and tired beats of the heart agree,
One more attempt for his sweet love true,
Struggling to stand a bent knee.

The button's clicked; the time 'three past',
The Devil in codes too smiles.
Yet another try for his sweetheart,
Yet another time he cries.

S Venugopalan

Sex, Drugs, And Rock And Roll

Have you been to Hell and back for one who was so smitten?
Did you tell your friends and that about the latest 'kitten'?
Did you tell your friends and that, for one who was so smitten,
Or have you been to Hell and back about the latest 'kitten'?

Philip Allen

Memories

(Dedicated to my late husband William Dykes Cowper)

Memories are sweet, memories last forever,
Memories are pictures, memories are feelings,
Memories are fears, memories are tears,
And all these memories will last throughout the years.

As I clasp hold of all the sweet memories shared by us,
The feelings in my heart are always there,
Pictures on the walls to recall sweet memories,
When we both walked hand in hand,
Those were the days we walked so proudly and did understand.

Now all I am left with is our memories so deep and so far,
I know you're looking down on me from Heaven just like that shining star.

I feel your presence all around me day by day,
I prayed to God so hard to just let you stay with me for another day.

He said your life was slowly passing you by,
Even to this day I often sit and wonder *why?*
You had a heart of gold and this is something
Which could never be bought or sold,
It was something to me worth more than any mountain covered in gold.

They say you're my angel now in Heaven above,
Looking down on me, showering me with all your love.

I know you're always at my side,
Even when it's hard to take things in my stride.
I know there is one thing I can always say,
You loved me each and every day.

I no longer see you within my sight,
I pray to God, He is with me as I struggle to carry on life without you at my side.
I'm ever so proud you were mine and still are even from afar,
As you stand at my side out of sight,
I know you're my angel in Heaven above,
'Cause God took you out of love.

Anastasia Williams Cowper

Colour

Am I of fetish desire,
Who lusts without sexual aspire?
For I crave to be invisible to everyone's eyes,
To be that ever-changing chameleon under threatening skies.
And, if I desire something besides,
I shall be that cataract clouding everyone's eyes.

Louise Mills

Fighting The Fear

Why do I feel so alone in this world with people and friends all around?
Is it because I would rather be on my own, or is it something I haven't yet found?
Why don't I go out, what's wrong with me, why do I feel safer inside?
Don't want to go out without a mask, feel open, insecure and wide

Wide open to all the people around, the panic is starting to show
Can't cope anymore, the strain is too much, I really need to go
Go home, back inside where I am safe and secure, where I am happy
to be all locked away
I am settled and safe inside my house, tomorrow's another day

Confidence, confidence, where have you gone?
When you're not inside me, life isn't much fun
Life's not the same, when you are not here
Please return back and replace all this fear

The fear that's inside, is the fear that won't leave
To be happy again is what I'll achieve
To conquer and win and get back what I see
A nice smiling face looking straight back at me

Fighting the fear, is so hard to win
The feelings I get don't seem to give in
I will not be slave to the demons inside
No way will I run; no way will I hide

It sounds all so easy, but the strength that's required
Makes me feel weak, so sad and so tired
Yet still they're inside me year after year
Will I ever conquer this power of fear?

Please go away, please go away
And let me return back to the way
The way that I was many years ago
The person inside, the person I know

Christopher Mullin

Henpecked

Now I just thought that I'd tell you that my wife has gone away,
But I'm sure in my mind that she's coming back today.
I telephoned a lady in the paper, she started talking dirty talk to me,
But I think I'm going to get into a lot of trouble
When my wife finds out how much the phone bill's going to be!
I've never ever phoned so many ladies, but they all say similar things you see,
I'm really getting past that stage and sexy talk is not my cup of tea.
I'm going to pack my clothes into a suitcase, I'm going to stay at Billy's by the sea,
I'd better leave a note where she can find me.
She'll come there with her brolly and her hat,
But I hope she doesn't cause a lot of trouble, because of a thousand pound
Phone bill, or it might be more than that!

James Ayrey

Girls Vs Boys

The girls say:

Girls rule
Boys drool
Girls are pretty
Boys are witty
Girls think
Boys wink
Girls are gentle
Boys are mental
Girls work
Boys smirk!

The boys say:

Boys fight
Girls are light
Boys are fast
Girls come last
Boys are cool
Girls are nul
Boys are handsome
Girls are phantoms
Boys are wealthy
Girls are healthy

But it all comes to say both are needed and both are the best!

Ramsha Sajjad

Hard Times

Skimmers jump the stubble lumps
Clay cracks in the furrows
Seagulls dance, the worm has turned
And rabbits leave their burrows
No joy of sweet rain on the land
Though the grey clouds billow
Now harvest home has rung the bells
No sleep is on the pillow
Lake and river nearly dry
Fallen apples make a pie
Conkers drive the laddies wild
Death comes slow to one fell child
Bombers blow the Bali cafe
Proud man China, now they laugh
Christmas crackers, baubles, balls
Decorate the trees and walls
Gone the miner and the steel
Britain slips on orange peel.

Les Dernie

Aurora

Another wink of day creases
From the lofty dappled spaces
Glowing in twilight's splendour
Through the slightly opened door

The soft melancholy matures slowly
That once emblazoned the black immensity
When the dainty streaks of light
Herald the blue yonder's knight

The cold, hazy light dissolves the stars
Seeping in through the Earth's reservoirs
Into the ocean of green shrubs and trees
And a horde of butterflies and bees

The hills are drenched with crystal dew
They softly glow with flaming hue
When the first beams of dawn
Repaint the Earth's cocoon

The sleepy mountains' crests
Serenely swim out of blue mists
Greeting the royal sunbeams
With jolly birds' cheers

The morning beauty liquefies
Before my thirsty eyes
Catching me half a dream
As the splendid spectacle
Embraces my captivated soul

Rachelle Arlin Credo

Wild Bird

See the wild bird flying free,
taking on her destiny . . .

who can catch her
touch her
cage her?

Over mountains, skimming sea,
diving deep, the mystery . . .

who can soothe her
feed her
tame her?

. . . trills the wild bird flying free,
only he who sings to me.

Carol Ann Darling

The Worst Birthday Crash

It caused my heart a hunk of pain,
Tears fell from my eyes like rain.
Once again things didn't turn out right,
I have tried hard to be polite.

Relatives didn't even bother to call,
I wanted to fall.
All I had was a card and a cake,
There was much more pain that my heart couldn't take.

Birthday gifts are always late,
And I always have to wait.
My birthday month is totally cursed,
Because my exciting hopes always turn into a disappointed burst.

My water power was taken away,
It was a terrible and miserable day.
The tiny candles were still in the pack,
My birthday wish plan turned into a hunk of lack.

Three years is like a triple tie,
I wanted to lay down and die.

Marlana Edwards

Thanks For Being My Teacher

Autumn sees school terms begin,
And summer sees them end.
I never thought on my first day,
That you would be my friend!
But as the terms have shuffled by,
You've taught me to how to grow,
By helping me to understand,
That I can shine and glow.
It does not matter where I live,
Or what I make of life.
This time that I have spent with you,
Will help me smile at strife.
You aided me when I was sad,
Applauded me when good.
Brought out the very best in me,
Where others never could.
As far as teachers go I'd say,
Your gentleness and grace,
Has made this school turn out to be,
A safe and warmth-filled place.

Sid 'de' Knees

God's Grassy Knoll

Words show emotion, hearts feel a pain
Tears of confusion, dark nights remain

Rain everlasting, snow on the hills
Can't go out shopping, from these window sills

Will someone call? I can't see anyone
In the street - laughing, someone having fun

Should I have tea, what is the time?
Look again in the mirror, no reason or rhyme

Where is my post, where is my milk?
Many years ago I dressed in silk

Is it my bedtime? I've only just got up
Another cup of tea, in a chipped china cup

Where is my husband? He stayed out all night
I need to tell someone, it gave me a fright

The doctor arriving, there, with my son
They want me to move, I don't need anyone

A suitcase packed, understanding unknown
Moving home - to die, in an old folks' home

Don't take my key, I might come back
'Don't worry Mother,' says my son Jack

Will my husband be there, is he waiting for me?
He left yesterday and forgot his key

I now share a room, don't know anyone
When I was young, we all had such fun

Such is confusion - a curse on the old
Such lack of dignity, before you go cold

Life turns a corner, towards your end
Sometimes life is kind, in the arms of a friend

As you 'cross over' - confusion disappears
Your husband and family greet you, without tears

A glorious ending, for such a sweet soul
As she sits - dressed in silk, upon God's grassy knoll.

Maureen Westwood O'Hara

Half The Window

'You've washed half of my window, Mad Wayne
You should do double that,' said Jane.
So what did he do?
I'm telling you
He washed the same half all over again!

Joan M Wylde

Friendly Fire

Friendly fire like confetti
Falling all around
Friendly bombs exploding
No targets found

Snaking through the desert
Armoured patrol
Fighting for our country
Beats queuing for the dole

Shots across the river
Magnesium-lighted sky
Crackling on the radio
Talking while we die

Friendly little bullets
Cutting through my skin
Gentle falls the shrapnel
It's quite a mess we're in

Dear Mrs 'Insert Name'
I'm sorry to report
That your son 'Insert Name'
Was shot while he still fought

There's no one to blame
These things happen in a war
He was caught in friendly fire
And will return never more.

Ali Porter

Letting Go

They say that children are on loan
One day to say goodbye
That they will spread their wings and go
When time for them to fly

I know that I must hold the tears
Until you're out of sight
I'll wish you well, so you can't tell
My world's been robbed of light

At last I let you leave my arms
To board the waiting plane
A part of me will die today
But I toast you with champagne

Life was hard in years gone by
When you were young and small
But to go now from me, is easily
The hardest time of all

Ann Peat

The Fair Maids Of February

The earth lies cold and frozen, tight gripped in winter's thrall,
Sleeping, waiting silently for the day when the maids will call.
Accusing fingers, branches bare, point forlornly to the sky,
Pleading, sad, imploringly for winter to pass by.
Beneath the carpet of softening snow, nature's hand begins to show,
As myriad maids of February slowly, inexorably grow.
And as the sun rises higher, as if summoned to the dance,
Fair maids of February rise, wakened from their trance.
In woodland, forest, field and garden all across the land,
White heads of snowdrop gently nod, leaves entwined, hand in hand.
A vast cotillion of life, on spring's signal to emerge,
And soon the maids are joined in the dance as others feel the urge.
A host of fellows chase the maids, following in the dance,
Daffodil and tulip, and anemone perchance
Take their places for the great spring ball, each one in vibrant dress,
Each rising up to touch the sun, all eager to impress.
Glory of the snow sends swathes of purple heads on high,
And the heady scent of hyacinth drifts upwards to the sky.
All the while the tiny crocus, in colours myriad,
Fills the land with rainbows and suddenly, the earth is clad
With blooms and perfumes all around, with grasses lush and green,
As winter's fingers fast recede, spring reveals a rapturous scene.
All heralded by one so small, with flowers pure and white,
As fair maids of February dance their dance with such delight.
All the land is held in thrall by the sight of nature's ball,
Pastel visions greet the eye, never failing to enthral.
Where else on Earth can such delights of nature's hand be seen
Than here, in this pleasant land where the maid of February rules as queen?

Brian L Porter

Fragile As Glass

Leave me alone; I've done nothing wrong,
All you do is sing the same old song.
You wait for me to crack; I'm fragile as glass,
The torments, the torture, I'm the jokes, the laughs.
You want me to fail to humiliate me,
Why do you stop and stare at me?
I've suffered enough, your work here is done,
Look at yourself and what you've become.
You say you're my friend, who needs a foe,
You've hurt me so much that I want you to know.
As time passes slowly the scars will fade,
But it happens so much that I am afraid.
It's a cold-hearted world out there can't you see,
I'm really a great person, just take a look, it's me.

Melanie May

Batman Begins

Father and Mother I love you . . .
The loss is hard to bear!
Somehow I've managed, I got through,
Despite this dark nightmare!
The nights are lonely, thoughts are grave,
Yet duty calls all men . . .
Some nights I'll leave the Bat Cave
As Batman, now and then.

The Batmobile is fully stocked
To combat every crime.
Although at first the sight has shocked,
Acceptance comes with time.
Our Gotham has the right to peace -
The thugs won't gain control!
Such masterminds must not increase,
I've vowed this in my soul!

Tonight Bruce Wayne is put to rest -
As Batman takes the stage.
The Dark Knight flies from east to west
As if from page to page.
The battle's not to maim and kill . . .
It must not be that way.
The battle's not to claim some thrill . . .
This is no game I play.

I seek to overcome each foe
So justice is achieved,
Disarming them will somehow show,
My word must be believed.
I've trained to be the best defence
According to my plan . . .
The Dark Knight may not make new friends,
Yet here begins Batman!

Denis Martindale

Constant Chatter

You're always prepared to listen when things go wrong,
Attack your housework with merry quips and song.
You never seem to get blue or downhearted,
Phone me, make sure I'm home safe after we've parted.

I could listen to your constant chatter all day,
And a big thanks to you my mate, I need to say.
Closer to me than my siblings have ever been,
Having you for a friend, like a wonderful dream.

S Mullinger

Sitting Pretty!

Chatter, chatter, chatter - it is filling up the room,
It does not seem to matter that she does not have a groom,
Always flamin' talking, but what? I do not understand,
She will not stop the squawking but readily comes to hand,
She lazes in my kitchen, just eyeing up the scene,
I've tried to stop the twitching, fearing she might think me mean,
It's not that I'm complaining, I'm glad that she is there,
But it's almost like it is raining pieces scattered on my chair,
I always find her company when I am all alone,
You must think me a misery if about her I should moan,
To me she is a treasure, you will see what I mean,
She accepts me with some pleasure but fancies others who are green,
She is at me peering, so what can I now say,
Except that I am fearing she might sometime fly away,
I do love her dearly - I think she likes me too,
I am being honest - really - but I don't know what to do,
I am a lonely codger, I'd hate our being apart,
I could get another lodger - but that could break her heart,
I'll put up with her chatter as I'm a lonely sage,
The chatter will not matter, she's my budgie in her cage!

John L Wright

The Crimes Of Rhyme In Time

Lock all husbands in an institution
Marriage is just legal prostitution -
The Earth moves in an anti-clockwise revolution
So why bother with some stupid resolution.
Our nanny state makes more of a constitution
Back to the ape, thanks to evolution.

Your body rots with loads of infestation
Primitive man shows us days of aggravation.
Grass now grows where was our railway station
No working man can keep up with inflation.
The air full of animal and human fluctuation
No poem published now with rhyme or punctuation.

Call the police, send us an ambulance
We're charged with magic and clairvoyance.
The government give sick and old annoyance
If you refuse, they call that impudence -
Smoking and drinking just foolish indulgence
Where was the second coming, what consequence?

Colin Allsop

Land Poor

I have had another offer, wife. A twenty-acre more,
    of high and dry prairie land, level as a floor.
I thought I would wait and see you first, as Lawyer Brady said,
    to tell how things should turn out best, a woman is ahead.

And when this land is all paid for and we have gotten the deeds,
    I know that we can wait a while for less important needs.
Then we will see about the yard and fix the house up some,
    and manage in the course of time to have a better home.

Now there's no use of talking Charles. You buy that twenty acres more,
    we'll go scrimping all our lives and always be land poor.
For many years we have tugged and slaved, denying half our needs,
    and all we have to show for it are tax receipts and deeds.

That other farm we bought off Josh Wells, it took so many years
    of clearing up and fencing in, has cost us many tears.
I have grieved to think of the many months and days,
    and for it all we have never had one word of praise.

Men call us rich, but we are poor. Would we not freely give
    that land and all the fixtures for a better place to live?
If we had built a nice cosy house and took our pleasure as it come,
    our children, once so dear to us, would never have left our home.

I would sell the land if it were mine and have a better home,
    with broad-light rooms to front the street and take life as it come.
It is so sad, putting off enjoyment long after we enjoy.
    After all, too much wealth seems useless as a broken toy.

If we could live as others live and do what others do,
    we could live enough sight pleasanter and have plenty too.
While others have amusement, fine luxury and books,
    think how stingy we have lived and how this old place looks.

Were I to start my life again, I would take each separate day,
    never letting a single one pass unenjoyed away.
Don't think I am blaming you, Charles. You are not one bit to blame.
    I have pitied you these many years, to see you tired and lame.

It's just the way we started out, our plans too far ahead.
    Having worn the cream of life away, leaving too much when dead.
If there were things to envy, I would have them now and then.
    I would have a home that was a home, not a cage or pen.

With life passing through these years so fast, it makes me wonder,
    why we have not toiled harder for a life up yonder.
But, I have always thought and think so yet,
    small farms well-worked are the best bet.

Alice Virginia Lawrence

The Real Need

The sun was sinking slowly in the western sky,
The last few minutes of daylight ticked quickly by,
I was hoping that sleep would soon encompass me,
But my thoughts meant that this was not to be.

Those thoughts revolved about the news items of the day,
Of the political leaders and what they had to say,
I was searching for some hope or consolation,
But my thinking only added to my desolation.

I thought about the millions in Africa facing starvation,
Not really knowing what it was like to be in this situation,
I knew that there was something I should do,
I could not just leave it to a dedicated few.

My thoughts turned to the other places on the Earth,
Where wars and deprivation faced people from their birth,
I questioned if this could be part of God's master plan,
Until I realised that most of this was due to Man's inhumanity to Man.

What did the politicians say about the problems these people face?
People who should be respected as part of the human race,
It's not their fault that they are subjected to tyranny and poverty,
They have not had the chances life has afforded you and me.

For years politicians have debated how Third World debt could be reduced,
Gestures have been made but the situation is becoming more confused,
Because poverty is not the only problem that they face,
The tyranny imposed by their leaders is a positive disgrace.

Whilst the poor get poorer the rich get richer every day,
There is much evidence to show how much they have salted away,
The aid which has been provided for those in need,
Has been used to satisfy their leaders' greed.

Is this the excuse we need to withhold our aid,
Or do we believe that there is still a debt to be paid?
The answer we give will decide the future of millions on the Earth,
And will reflect what we think mankind is really worth.

There is no doubt that the future of others is in our hands,
To give them the chance we know that God has planned,
If you think that we have a debt that should be paid,
Remember that the burden of sacrifice on your heart is laid.

As individuals there is very little that we can do,
But the great powers of the world could if they wanted to,
History has shown that the spirit of apathy is everywhere,
If events do not affect them, most people do not really care.

Gifts of food and money will only answer the problems of the day,
We must ensure that tyranny does not continue to hold sway,
This will only be achieved if the great nations of the world intercede,
To give the poorer nations of the world what they really need.

Ron Martin

No One Noticed

Such a lonely existence,
When kept in secrets and lies,
And such a cliché,
For it to be at night,
Such a sad distance,
Between help and her cries.

No one noticed as
Tears of blood ran down her thighs,
And she became lost in the land of the wise,
Caught within everyone else's compromise,
Which finally led to her spirit's demise.

She now only exists,
Within her own mind.
And she's scared of life,
Of what she will find.
A world so distant,
Something she couldn't fight.

As no one noticed,
Tears of blood ran down her thighs,
Because she was ignored by those called wise,
And became everyone else's compromise,
This all led to her spirit's demise.

Angela Shortt

Dinnertime

Thin and fat, tall and small,
Those are the dinner ladies in my dinner hall,
Pouring beans and mashed up peas,
And I sometimes hope I don't find fleas.

Nobody ever dares to complain,
Or else they'll put us out in the rain,
Soggy chips and out-of-date pies,
If we tell our parents they say,
'What a complete bunch of lies.'

We have to eat it up or drink it up,
Or else they make us lick our cup,
Bubbling soup and wholemeal bread,
This is the meal I have always dreaded.

We feel hasty as dinnertime ends,
We all are cheerful, my friends and I,
A dinner lady says, 'I'll see you tomorrow kids,
I'll serve you kidney beans and fresh breads.'

Harkanwalijit Kaur (12)

Leah

Every cloud's lining is silver
And I'm gonna love her till the
Stars no longer shine!

I've always wanted to be a star
Sing my songs, play my guitar
Since I met Leah, I know I'll go far
For she means the world to me!

Leah means the world to me -
Her tender touch is ecstasy!
I know she will always be
The only girl for me!

Fondest feelings deep inside
Tender love that's hard to hide
Prevented by my foolish pride
From singing my love for you.

Darling how I love you so
You'll never know how deep
So let me whisper in your ear
The secret you must keep.

Every cloud's lining is silver
And I'm gonna love you
'Til the stars no longer shine.

Ben Wolfe

Frog

A young frog lost his leg one day,
it hurt a lot at first.
But then he felt much better,
and he was fit to burst.
He found it difficult to jump,
he went off to the right,
kept falling over, got the hump,
'twas such a funny sight.

One day he saw a female frog
seated by a pond.
He jumped an intervening bog
with an enormous bound.
He swam quite fast towards her,
but with a shock he found,
he could not reach the other side
although he tried, oh how he tried.
With only one leg on one side
he just swam round and round.

D G W Garde

Gender Rules (For The Rule Breakers)

The girl was told by her big sister to be sweet and tender.
Be sure to wear high heels on flat feet and
With some pretty pink wrapping and a name-brand label
She might even resemble Grade A meat.

Now the girl had something to prove to her mother,
Who said girls don't anger, fuss or fight,
To the young man who said, 'Her hair just doesn't look right.'
Her womanly mission was to be the symbol of beauty and serve him with good cheer.
If the girl didn't measure up, she'd learn to say, 'I'm sorry dear.'
'Look at me! I can do splits, the flip and that pretty twirl.'
He'd say, 'Don't forget to smile, show more teeth; that's a good girl!'

She learns that good girls only speak when spoken to,
They stay in the shallow end, away from those who question and seek.
A good girl doesn't worry her pretty little head,
She just relaxes and wonders, 'Do I look a little too well fed?'
So she puts more paint on her face. She puts on satin and lace.
She lives in fear that one day he will be displeased with her tacky taste.
'What about a little tuck here? A diamond in my ear or implants might look fine.'
She's a manufactured baby doll and her future's riding on his assembly line.

Venus Jones

The Storm Of The Century

The 'storm of the century'? *Katrina* was her name
Living through this hurricane
People would not ever be the same
Mandatory evacuations in a city of this size
In the celebrated city of New Orleans, water began to rise . . .

Katrina's fury was gaining strength . . .
This 'storm of the century' grew fast in width and length
Many had no place to go
They were sent to the large, Grand Superdome
The roof sprung a leak but for thousands it would be home . . .

The rains came down and the fierce winds blew
Many folks in shocked amazement couldn't believe it was true
Trees were ripped up and were laying down
America's most significant disaster, with floodwaters all around . . .

Many hurricanes through the years, have come and gone
Camille, Andrew, Ivan, Gilbert and then *Katrina* came along . . . !

Carol Olson

Festival Of Evil

Year after year, you're keeping all the little ones awake
Yet you parents, your sensible notions you forsake
Year after year you ignore the painful cries
Year after year there's always someone who dies.

Year after year, you're causing heartache for us thoughtful ones
Year after year, you're unnerving us peaceful, disgruntled ones
Year after year there's always someone who dies
It serves them right for not understanding why.

Year after year it happens
This mass euphoria, this 'celebration of a criminal's death'
Is Parliament that important to you?
Does the horrific end to an aspiring arsonist
Really justify the fun you enjoy, to fill us all with fear?

Year after year we can't stop the turmoil
Year after year we're forced to recoil
Year after year, you're keeping the future brainwashed
Influenced by this disruption, their own ideals quashed.

Year after year it happens
This mass euphoria, this 'celebration of a criminal's death'
Is Parliament that important to you?
Does the horrific end to an aspiring arsonist
Really justify the fun you enjoy, to fill us all with fear?

Year after year, we're powerless to escape the abhorrent waste
And the wretched, ugly taste
That all you mindless thugs leave
Will you still remember your happy times
When it's your turn to grieve?

Year after year, we hear the bellowing of the bangers
We see the culprits, the junkie street-hangers
Year after year we see in shops, these under age, drunken, insolent yobs
Shop assistants selling them these volatile toys
Too bored with their lives, too concerned with their jobs.

Year after year, we hear . . .
Fierce cracking, fizzing, popping, thudding, booming
Whooshing, screeching, rattling fury, howling chaos
Building up to its climax . . .
Then the fading of the echoes as the noise fades, not to be heard
The whole world rocks
Then the whole country turns back the clocks.

S Cardy

Bath Time

For the Swedes and the Finns
True hygiene begins
In the heat of a steaming-hot sauna.
Then they think it's quite nice
To jump in the ice
And take a cold swim round the corner.

A Yank who is choosy
Will take a jacuzzi
Or else he might dowse in the shower;
He likes his lustration
With lots of sensation
And plenty of pressure and power.

For the English, a scrub
In the scullery tub
Will eliminate most of the grime.
While the French on a free day
Can sample the bidet
Or maybe a douche if there's time.

You will find that the Turk
Has a penchant to lurk
In a sweltering bath of hot air.
The ideal solution
To purge the pollution
Providing you've got time to spare.

The resolute Roossians
Must make their ablutions
In water that's icy and numbing;
And the brave Eskimo
Simply rolls in the snow -
Which saves quite a lot on the plumbing.

Rex Andrews

The Hallowe'en Acrostic

H aunted houses stir and give you a fright.
A pple ducking.
L anterns shining in the night.
L uminous colours of orange, red, green, black and white.
O range pumpkins glowing.
W itches on broomsticks.
E vil lurks without showing.
E erie tunes playing.
N ight-time draws with treats and tricks.

Rachel Van Den Bergen

Looking For Rainbows

I just can't explain how I'm feeling
I can't seem to make myself clear
It's like my whole world's stopped revolving
Now my mother is no longer here
I try to pretend things are normal
Though the mask that I wear tends to slip
For a moment of time I'm in mourning
And it's then that I can't get a grip
If only I had the assurance
That my mother's OK where she's gone
I wouldn't need all this emotion
And the mask wouldn't have to go on
It's like a bad dream that's repeating
With too many demons in chase
And there's no point in looking for rainbows
To encourage a smile on my face
I'd just love a message from Mother
From the phone booth in 'Heaven's Arcade'
Just to tell me she's blissfully happy
With my dad in the new life she's made
Or to feel loving arms circling round me
Or to capture her kiss in the air
Would be more than enough to convince me
That my mother's eternally there
But till then I go on very slowly
With a burden of questions and doubt
It's a life in a maze of confusion
And I can't find the door to get out
But I know in the end I'll accept things
It's the way of the world and in time
I know that I'll find all the answers
And there will be reason and rhyme
Until then I keep praying and pleading
With the trust I've been prompted to hold
And her love to sustain and remind me
Of my fortune of memories gold

David Whitney

Llama Haggis

Haggis stole a circus llama and thought it would be funny
To leave it in his best friend's bed with its bum all brown and runny
Sirus yelled with all his might, 'A bloody llama! Where?'
'In your bed, but never mine, it could've been the bear.'

Daryl Leslie

Ain't It Just Like The Truth

Her cold mountain-stream kisses
My heartache still misses
In half-broken memories
And long-lost wishes.
Her silver spurs jangle,
Her hair's in a tangle
When she stands up on her buckboard whipping her team
With her cowgirl smile in some rodeo dream.

Her hot dusty trail tongue
Tastes of cactus and thistle.
Our minds in a whirl when we hear her lariat whistle
Round our dry spinnin' heads where it's hung.

I wanted her then and still want her now.
But the song, it is short and been sung.
She's gone up past the last bend
And the tale's near its end.

She left my heart tattered and tore up,
But that doesn't matter.
She may be buckin' some bronco,
On the run from the law
Or dealin' Faro in Reno
Or with a kid with no paw,
It's all just the same.

I loved her. She left me.
And ain't it just like the truth
I can't even remember her name.

Keith Alan Deutsch

Free

Even through the night
The fight still goes on
To survive in this life
To revive those trills
Of ever learning more skills
Feeding my yearning to be free
To flee from all aggression
As though it were depression
To free my mind and senses
And release myself from strain and tenseness
My spirit flows in endless time
But never do I mind
Knowing freedom is mine.

Deborah Ayis

The National

The ever grinding joints and limbs
Of virgin-white horses flying free
Through the breeze of mortal sins
And disappearing into oblivion
Of white-drowned foam on bitter death winds.

The horses falling at the gate
The traps are shutting, one by one
Ride the seas of pure black fate!
And dance to sinful merriment
And watch the apocalypse their actions create.

The lame ones get the wicked bolt
For freedom-flying nihilist gales
The withered nag or lame young colt
The pitied, punished, poor lost souls
They've no purchase. And in gaping wounds goes salt.

I bleed the blood of pure white hearts
As on dark waters the evil triumph
The horses never drawing carts
But bounding to their inevitable perish
Upon the philistine oceans that reject forgotten arts.

The coarse white waves of freedom true
Spill lightly across the naked eyesore
Of the thick, jet-colour ocean spew
And we cool our wits and raise our chins
Because we know full well what we have got to do.

Karl Mercer

Frosty

The dancing shadows of the night,
Created by the soft moonlight,
Give way to a crisp winter's dawn,
Where people awake and begin to yawn.

The frost lets go his icy grip,
Leaving behind the chance to slip.
Take care people, underfoot,
Or on your arm a plaster is put.

The daylight sun will be just right,
But Frosty will be back tonight
And as the sun begins to set,
Frosty won't be long, I'll bet.

Stephen Broadhead

On Hallowe'en Night

Pumpkins with faces carved into their heads,
Hardly anyone has got into their beds.
Trick-or-treaters everywhere
On Hallowe'en night.

'Trick or treat, smell our feet,
Give us something good to eat.'
This is the chant of the trick-or-treaters
On Hallowe'en night.

Ghosts and demons, spirits and ghouls,
A bloodcurdling scream comes from the swimming pools.
The younger children are having nightmares
On Hallowe'en night.

Inside the graveyard, the silence stirs,
A murderer, into the dark, his target he lures.
The slightest sound gives everyone a fright
On Hallowe'en night.

It's five to twelve, the hour is coming,
Sitting up in their beds, the children's hearts are drumming.
The clock strikes twelve; it's the rising of the dead,
On Hallowe'en night.

Thomas Cummings

Community Spirit

'Twas Saturday night in the underpass
Shoppers long since fled
There were bloodstains on the concrete
But who could say who'd bled

Who'd sniffed the barmaid's apron?
Who'd got more than tight?
Who'd looked at someone funny
And wound up in a fight?

Or does a body lie dismembered
On the local council tip
Or was it something silly
Like a nosebleed or split lip?

They called in the detectives
Pride of the local force
And after much deliberation they
Called out . . . tomato sauce!

Marji Tomlinson

Man's Last Conquest

Man's climbed the world's highest mountains
With teams of elite, brave men.
They have trekked the lengths of continents
And been in a lion's den.
Sailed all the oceans of the world
Even shipwrecked far from land,
Caught in many desert storms
And buried alive in sand.
Tunnelled into the bowels of the Earth
Through caves deep in the ground.
Explored the Earth's atmosphere and moon
Breathtaking but without sound.
Searched out both the Arctic Poles
Where the temperature drops sixty below.
Lowered himself into crevices
With walls, 300-feet deep in snow.
Survived thunderbolts and lightning
Earthquakes and a hurricane,
Whirlwinds, typhoons and tornadoes
But he came back again.
We can survive nature's worst
All round the world and more.
But we can't survive the toxic waste
That we permit to be dumped at our door.
It's taken Mother Nature millions of years
To carve out the world we enjoy,
But Man's been here for a blink of the eye
And his last conquest, the Earth to destroy.

John Laver

Shall We Dance?

She stands there waiting for the chance
Of that last dance.
Though it is late
She has no date.
A lad comes near who makes her heart
Wake with a start,
Beat really fast . . .
But he goes past.
Then suddenly he turns again;
Oh, what sharp pain!
She sees him bend . . .
To ask her friend.

E Marjorie Bright

To Celebrate A Life

Come and join the celebration
Shout aloud in acclamation
For the newborn baby born
His parents' pride and joy

Come and join the celebration
See a mother's dedication
Now this child has started school
Lunch in hand, textbook and rule

Come and join the celebration
He's passed exams with exulation
Looking handsome, strong and bold
Ready to meet the outside world

Come and join the celebration
The departing expectation
He is going off to war
Fighting on another shore

Come and join the celebration
Two hearts made one in consecration
See him standing with his bride
Their parents smiling either side

Come and join the celebration
Gaze in wonder, adulation
For the darling little girl
Has her grandparents in a whirl.

Josephine Luck

The Old Man And His Fly

(For Jannie Boon)

A toothless Turk once swallowed a fly
that irked him; therefore he ate a spider,
a faithful hound and its faithless rider,
to catch each other, and then a lion,
for a ruthless lion one might rely on . . .
        all doomed to die

till, one day, wait! He kissed a woman:
amen! An omen displaying acumen,
he kissed a woman, a beauty like you,
right here, one truthful, youthful and clever:
she cleared out the old man's private zoo . . .
        they lived forever.

Thomas Land

Global Warning

The world is permanently changed
by global warming.
Pollution has totally rearranged
the plates.
The way we live creates
this global storming.

In Pakistan the earth is quaking.
So many families die,
praying for real decision taking.
In his hands he holds their fate
because he is our head of state,
so why doesn't he try.

Upset about the country's wealth,
the pound's rate against the dollar,
forget about the country's health!
Remember no one likes terrible things,
the devastation disaster always brings.
The rope tightens around his collar.

How long will Britain be safe?
Is anywhere that safe now?
How long can Mr Blair save face?
Will the tectonic plates
outlast hectic mandates,
or make Mr B take a bow?

It's not 'if', it is 'when',
it'll happen and you'll be wishing
you'd listened to me then,
and so you see his name in print, suppose
you think he looks like a prince up close.
Remember, compassion is missing.

Liam Bailey

Uni-Blunkett

Blunkett's going to be a lecturer at a university,
to lecture on how politics doesn't mix with such as Kimberley.
This while he is a fat-salaried MP.
Another example of abuse by a politician who
should be giving it all to his constituency -
yet another argument for MPs having a job description.
To stop them using offices for their own perverse definition.
To make them accountable for all action and inaction
on constituents' problems and queries
and put an end to breeches.

R Wiltshire

Truth Of Fate

(Confessions to Ma)

I can't see for the blinding light
as it bursts and spreads throughout the night
beating upon the loser's plight
not giving up without a fight
Behind this wall of time
committed is a crime
between two lovers there is a sign
but it ain't on no one's tracks
hidden away within the sacks
are all these people's sins
discarded and thrown in the bins
These people shouldn't get the blame
with cruelty they all get the same
they all get to feel that pain
as if being locked down by chain
Don't believe those who say or do
things they say sound like you
for all they really know
is how to make their ego glow
so all they really show
is what they don't know
Tell me what you feel
the wounds you don't have to heal
roll your wave to my sky
without having to tell a lie
Let me know what you need
for it's making my mind bleed
Black crow sympathises the move
my wise men can't think how to improve
the situation I'm in
when I realise my sin
I can't get any hope
and it's making me choke
I don't wanna give up
it ain't the way to go
I don't want you to give up
but it's on my road
I don't want you to change
but it's outta range
for t'see the outcome
it's only in the mind of some
So knock on my door
show me some more
put me out of my war
get me off this floor
for it's wracking my brain
putting me on a strain

but it ain't a worry
'cause I'll never be sorry
'bout this act I've done
'bout the fruit tree I've taken from
'cause with all my decisions to date
I've followed with the truth of fate

Leon Oxenham

The Visit

They sit in high-backed chairs,
In a semi-circle row,
The ladies, clutching handbags,
All they have to show.
For eighty/ninety years of life,
All else was left behind,
When, in their time for help,
Themselves, in care homes, they find!
Losing their lifetime possessions,
With their dignity and choice,
They slowly submit to authority,
As if they have lost their voice.
Men don't seem to have that need,
For holding onto their home,
Happy just to be cared for,
Without the things of their own.
It is heartbreaking to visit
Then leave your loved ones behind.
Of course, it's not always possible,
Any other recourse to find.
So sad to live your active life,
Caring for others, or just yourself,
Only to find, in your hour of need,
You are quietly dumped upon the shelf.

E M Eagle

My Future

I'm scared of my future and what's in store
I don't want the pain and hurt anymore
I'm worried I won't be the one with a happy ending
I really wish now I could stop pretending
I would love a future with happiness and laughter
And to be held by a man who will love me ever after
I only hope he's in my future to be
So one day I will become a family of three.

Kelly Earnshaw

Music Can Move And Words Can Dance

Music should move and words should dance,
Meaning should enthuse, and at the same time romance,

With the effortless glow of an ambiguous phrase,
Expressing subtle elegance, leaving you in a daze;

Carrying a conventional wisdom that begs to be explored,
Through irony, or melancholy, intuition ensured.

A symbolic reference that inflates one's thoughts,
Flowing in emotion, hoping never to be caught;

A lascivious line that ignites one's desire,
A prelude to fantasy that should impulse to inspire.

It should begin in earnest, expressing expedition,
A journey unrivalled and steeped in premonition;

An evocative engagement, just one and one's will,
As the glass commenced half empty, you can feel it start to fill.

Simmering with colour and purity alike,
It remains infallibly infectious, as you tremor with delight.

But as the mist ascends, exposing an open trail,
The meaning is still there, but the feeling has set sail,

For now you feel lonely, but gracious for the chance,
That you can now provide the evidence,

That the music, really can move and the words, really can dance.

Ross Macmillan

Freedom

Let waves of warmth wash over her and better soothe her mood.
All at once her thoughts do lift, released from servitude.

For freedom finds its own silence and she shall hear no more.
Gone are the cold oppressions, renounced is daily thaw.

Sun in the sky now shines on she, rejuvenated beams.
And she, like I, has found new hope, for now at least it seems.

Is hurting 'par' for life's great course? If so this game she'll scoff.
Allow such things that pained you once to fall and just die off.

She'll heal the wounds with laughter and remedies of old.
And with soft hands, some lent by friends, she'll gently warm the cold.

For she is truly blessed, a gift from those on high.
Watch freedom course throughout her veins beyond her time to die.

And as the wind does softly sweep through fields of green and gold.
Freedom speaks, a voice within, be strong, be sweet, be bold.

Richard Charles Kennedy

Dieter's Dilemma

I've got a fat tummy and fat thighs
And regularly use sugar to get my highs
One piece of toast, three then four
Soon I won't be able to get through the door.

I've tried every diet under the sun
Eating now, no longer is fun
Weight Watchers, Slimming World, I've tried them all
After each meeting I'd have a ball
Chinese takeaways and Indians too
And fish and chips to name but a few.

I'd pile on the pounds again and again
After each binge I'd say 'Amen!'
I'll try harder tomorrow but that never comes
I'll count the points and do my sums.

To be successful, I'll have to change my way
Eating lettuce and carrots for many a day
Healthy eating is an option I've tried before
And to be honest I really find it a bore.

Cheese, chocolate, chips and ice cream
Are all friends of mine, we make a good team
But alas, New Year is here again
It's time to make another resolution; amen.

Mandy Ducksbury

Waterloo

High in cloudy skies, hangs the sun blood-red
Casting shadows dark on the field of dead
Against British squares, crash the French old guard
And in the distance ride the Prussians hard.

Again and again, hold Wellington's squares
Such men of valour fighting in pairs
Smoke of the rifles makes it hard to breathe
Many good soldiers will never leave.

The screams of the horses and dying cries
Why had they believed the many lies'?
That to die a hero is very fine
Not told; you are dead for such a long time.

As charge after charge the brave French troops make
Napoleon knows, no more can they take
The English are victors in battle of gore
Yet many have died: all brave men galore.

Leslie de la Haye

Football

The game of football in England:
Programme sellers, marching bands.
Turf which has graced famous feet,
Of men whose aim was to compete.
Mighty stands and motley crowd,
Chanting, singing, cheering loud.
Cup-tie fever, sweetness, pain,
Queuing for tickets in the rain.
Travelling and trains to catch,
Miss your breakfast, not the match.
Supporters from all walks of life,
Saturdays, don't see the wife.
Excitement as you await your team,
A surging roar of Wembley dream.
Defeated fans, dejected, mute,
Head home with no victory salute.
Winners dancing on the pitch,
Stronger still the Wembley itch.
Saturday night the pubs are full,
Wonder who'll draw Liverpool?
Papers scanned for shots of game,
Writers telling who's to blame.
Football's people wax and wane,
Till Saturday comes around again.

Terence Wrigglesworth

My Greenhouse And I

My greenhouse is not very big,
In fact, there's not enough room to swing a pig.
I only plant what I want for my needs,
But I haven't yet mastered how to sow seeds.
I have a needle and cotton, but it don't seem to work,
My wife says 'old man, you're a stupid old berk.
You don't do it like that, and that you should know,
You plant them in soil if you want them to grow'.
But I like being in there, my fingers turn green,
The glass is quite dirty, so I cannot be seen.
So I planted some seeds, and when they show through,
I'll have to ask her what next I must do.
She's quite good at telling me what I don't know,
And where to plant the things that I grow.
In the summer I'll have quite a nice display,
Of beautiful flowers, bright and gay.
It's been hard work, and back-breaking pain,
And next spring I'll have to start all over again.

William G Evans

This Long Journey

When I least expected it, you were there
 (Soothing my soul in a banter of riddle!)
Like a cat - curious I loosened my hair
 (And settled down somewhere in the middle.)

At ease, relaxed in the company of us
 (Laid down oft in the fragrance of your prattle!)
So easily won with every thrust
 (Word upon word building before the battle.)

Silence the aftermath of this long journey
 (And wearisome path of unexpected solitude!)
Not foreseen during the splendour of our flurry -
 (Perhaps fear gave way to unexpected moods.)

Unfinished melodies once blended, now discordant
 (Harsh, the reality of obscurities haunt!)
Hovering over me like a black cloud waiting to rant
 (Against the pull of my heart set in want.)

How chilled the once warmed casement of my soul
 (Weakened for lack of nourishment from you.)
Perhaps winter's chill, will be spring's console -
 (And the hearth of my heart will bud anew.)

Carla Iacovetti

A Great Bargain

Please listen up all you ladies out there
Does anyone have a husband to spare?
He needn't be handsome or rich or tall
In fact no special talents are needed at all
As long as he's kind and fairly polite
With a reasonable brain that works alright.

I don't want him for nothing; I'll pay you in kind
We'll just do a swap and you can have mine
Mine is tall and nice-looking and can cut quite a dash
Though his moods are uncertain and he's inclined to be rash.

He consistently always knows best what to do
As long as the one who's doing it is you
Whatever the task he's supportive and strong
Explaining precisely just where you go wrong.

He whinges a bit and does tend to whine
When things don't suit him which is most of the time
But all things considered he's really unique
And could very well prove to be just what you seek
So please stake your claim without further delay
Before this great bargain just slips away.

Rita Palm

Sodding Rain

The last few days
Have been tough
I have been feeling
Very rough
Tired and down
In no mood to clown
All I have done
Is cuss and frown
Scream and shout
Pace the room
Rage about
Become a madman

Where has all the sunshine gone
The warmth and the rays?
The things that make you feel good
From day-to-day
When I wake in the morning
It will not be the same
I am going to be positive
And laugh with the rain
I will walk with the clouds
Sing with the wind.

K Cook

A Good Old Moan

I'm told to let my hair down,
But there isn't any left.
I sit and wear this surly frown,
Of youth I am bereft.
My toes I can no longer see,
My eyes deceive my brain.
My waist has multiplied by three,
Bending down is such a strain.
'What's that you say? You'll have to shout,
My hearing's getting weak.'
My veins are growing inside out,
I mumble when I speak.
These teeth look better in a glass,
They roll around my mouth.
On spicy food I think I'll pass,
(Strange rumblings down south.)
So if you're young, be kind to me,
Being old is not so grand.
One day much older you will be,
Perhaps then you'll understand.

Mark L Moulds

Sorry

I shouldn't have hurt your feelings,
It seemed a good idea at the time,
In all my worldly dealings,
It now stands out a crime.

I was selfish and crude,
Your face expressed pain,
You know me, I'm not rude,
If only I could relive that moment again . . .

I'd give you due regard,
I'd put your feelings first,
My petulance I'd discard,
How for that replay I thirst!

Then I felt elation,
Now I feel only woe,
A moment's celebration
Led on for sadness to flow.

I ask you to pardon this fool,
Please don't ever show resentment,
For if you let small-mindedness rule,
Trust me, you'll never find contentment.

John Edward McBride

Look Around

We're all so busy driving around in our cars
No time to look at the sunshine and stars
There is beauty around us if only we could see
What God has given us to enjoy for free
Next time you go out for the day
Drive into the countryside, you don't have to pay
You can go for a walk and admire the view
Colours and beauty amazing, and you don't have to queue
And when the darkness comes there is still beauty to see
The moon and the stars shining down on you and me
The more quiet the place, the more beauty you'll spy
Nobody to take your money, trying to bleed you dry
Making money is more important to some
There are no pockets in shrouds so have some fun
The words of the song my dad sang to me
'What a wonderful world' if you would only see
So take the time and have a good look
Before your life becomes a closed book.

Teresa Smith (Holmes)

Watch For A Wonder

Hey you, why so sad in the eyes?
Cheer up my friend.
Just for a moment, stop, mute out all the lies,
Watch the rainbow's bend.
Watch for one wonder among the rabble,
Large or small.
Even if it's a tiny pebble,
It may soften your fall.
Along the world's black, comes a shade of white:
See it appear.
The sun comes up after a dark night,
It shines so clear.
The bad and good don't stand alone,
They come together.
Happiness accompanies a sad tone,
Warmth replaces the cold weather.
After a murderous winter, comes a healer:
Spring brings new life.
It stops the deeds of a heinous killer,
Of fresh and green it brings a rife.
An apology gives comfort to a wound,
Rain soothes a season dry,
A gentle hand dries a tear, and
A loving hold quiets a cry.
As long as there is good to balance evil,
As long as there is love to extinguish hate,
There has to be a reason for our being,
A purpose God has for us and our fate.

Yuliya Bulanova

Choosing Masks

Each day we wear a mask,
It doesn't have to be Hallowe'en.
In the sunlight we bask,
Hiding things yet to be seen.
Some day we're happy wearing a smile,
Some days we wear a frown.
The happy days seem so worthwhile,
And on sad days we're kind of down.
We can put on a lot of makeup,
When we go into town,
And each morning when we wake up,
We choose a mask with a smile or a frown.

Merl Bone

What Kind Of Animal Are You?

I met a snake - the other day;
Sitting lonely on the tube.
Around him people gave wide berth
To one so vicious, so cruel that no mirth
Would ever pass over his features.
Serpentine, savage, a voice that hissed -
Such is the lawyer and death is his kiss.

Justice is poison

I met a lion - the other day;
Battling home against the wind.
Her face was wrinkled and her hair was grey
But with iron - no force could make her stay
Or compel her to leave; she was monarch.
Lonely? Maybe, but do not forget
Her life is her own, she feels no regret.

Death can be beaten

I met a pelican - the other day;
Standing tall in front of his class.
He stood up straight, would not bow his head
To the thirty-nine hooligans who heard what he said -
And sometimes, acted upon it.
You say he was casting his pearls before swine?
Really . . . ? Ignorance is bliss - they were doing fine.

'Knowledge is power' corrupts

I met a dragon - the other day;
Still young, still unformed yet so wise.
Savage yet brave, clever yet strong -
He knew better than *they,* dark from light, bad from wrong.
So young, also timeless,
The child has it all
And round him the adults spin, held in his thrall.

Youth is innocence

But - we all leave our dragons
Behind, sooner or later
And become mighty beasts, or else fail.
Perhaps maybe some of us do see the light
But we still chose plain animals (wrong - but - what's right?)
Remember and try to be - *Dragon,*
Keeping your inner child alive.
They call it conscience
But you must let it drive
Your heart and your wandering feet where it will -

What manner of beast art thou?

Thomas Keefe

My Sleeping Beauty

Sleep my beauty, sleep; and dream of young love,
When you wake tell me all you were dreaming of,
In your dreams, if you dream of the things that you fear,
Don't be scared, for you know I will always be near,
If you cannot recall all your dreams when you wake,
Remember dreams are just wishes your heart wants to make,
So your heart will remember each dream that you keep,
And recall each sweet moment when once more you sleep.

Sleep my beauty, sleep and dream of the hills that we climb,
Of the wild flowers we see, foxgloves, violets and thyme,
Of the lanes that we walk down and rivers we pass,
All the birds in the hedgerows, and each blade of grass,
Dream of the bluebells, and sunny blue skies,
Hear the sounds of the meadow as a newborn lamb cries,
See the colours of rainbows and butterflies' wings,
Smell the fresh country air that each morning brings.

Sleep my beauty, sleep and dream of the good times we've had,
Of the pride that I feel when you call me 'my dad',
Dream of that time called *the rest of your life,*
When you fly from this nest to become someone's wife,
Though your eyes are both closed now, your laugh I still see,
Though your mouth is shut tight, your lips still smile to me,
You whisper, 'Goodnight Dad,' and drift off to sleep,
Back to your thoughts, private dreams; yours to keep.

Alan W Davis

On Bonfire Night

Precariously perched in a pathetic posture,
Sits the stuffed guy on his rickety throne;
No subjects below him, to witness his burning,
But mere spectators, this guy to disown.

There are broken-up boxes and tread-worn tyres,
Stacked very high, to encourage the flames;
Settees, once satin-smooth, mattresses, frayed carpets,
Newspapers, magazines, unwanted games.

The fireworks are stored well away from the 'pyre',
And with care, concealed, to avoid alarm,
Lest sparks should fly from the ensuing inferno,
Causing concern, deep distress, or great harm.

And now, this stuffed guy's fate is almost upon him,
As precariously he perches there alone;
The great 'pyre' soon lit, the flames leaped and they danced,
And children loud-cheered, when he fell from his throne.

Glanville Grey-Jones

The Forgotten Kitten

Mummy cat was feeling fine, washing all her kittens, nine
But hello, what is all this? Something here is quite amiss
For one small furry mite, is not exactly right
He's smaller than the other eight, poor mummy cat is in a state
'What shall I do?' she cries in woe? One kitten bad and I feel low.

The other kittens didn't mind, that's not to say they were unkind
They had all that they could wish for and did not want or need one more
Poor little kitten, small and weak, he had no strength his food to seek
So when it was time for all to lunch the others rushed forward in a bunch
Not caring that our small wee cat was left behind upon the mat.

Forgotten by his family, no breakfast lunch or even tea!
But wait a minute, who is this here to take away our kitten's fear?
A little boy has seen his plight and plans to rescue him from fright
'Look Dad,' he cries, 'oh can't you see, that's the pussycat for me
The other ones are all quite bad for making him so very sad!'

So Daddy takes the little lad into the shop for he's quite glad
That his darling, smallest boy wants a pet and not a toy
The shopkeeper takes them to the place where all the cats are in a case
He waits to see what the lad will choose and thinks he knows what he'll refuse
But wait a minute, he's chosen that, my smallest, weakest little cat.

'Upon my soul,' he says to Dad, 'your little boy must be quite mad!'
His father did not really mind because at heart he was quite kind
And secretly believed that all should have their chance, both big and small
So now there's no denying that our puss is quite the master cat
For he has caught up in height and weight since now all is his that's on his plate!

Royston E Herbert

Losing Count

200 magpies sitting on a wall,
Means many visitors will come to call.

300 ducks up the cut swimming round and round,
This surely indicates someone in need will surely be found.

400 chickens making a clucking call,
You can be sure the English nation is going to fall.

500 robins on a Christmas card,
Be on your guard there's a burglar in your backyard.

600 penguins standing by a pool,
The next person you meet will take you for a fool.

700 caravans on the golf course,
Plenty of work for the local police force.

Vann Scytere

St Christopher, Bearer Of Christ

Christopher, young man of great size and strength,
Vowed he would serve only a master
Stronger and braver than himself.
He chose Satan, who proved a disaster.

For when the Devil encountered a cross,
He halted and trembled with fear.
'Whose sign is this?' Christopher asked.
'Him I must find and stay near.'

He searched until he learned all about Christ,
Was baptised, and promised each day,
He would serve his Lord by helping folk
Cross a perilous waterway.

So Christopher used his physical strength
To ferry the fragile and weak,
And one stormy night he responded to help
A young boy who was gentle and meek.

On his shoulders he carried the lad through the gale,
Across waters treacherous and wild,
His burden grew heavier the further he went,
Far too heavy for such a young child.

He reached the bank and put the lad down,
Was amazed when the little boy said,
'You have just carried the weight of the world,
All the sins of mankind, on your head.'

Christopher then realised this was the Christ,
And by performing his everyday task,
He was helping his Saviour to bring love to Earth,
By aiding all who stopped to ask.

Dear saint of sailors and travellers too,
Help us follow Jesus in all that we do.

Doreen Lawrence

In Wine We Trust

'In vino veritas' was the cry,
Without my wine, I'll not get by,
I'll have a glass no matter what,
And frankly my dear, I do drink a lot,
I'll sup it here, I'll sup it there,
I'll sup it almost anywhere,
I'll sup it till I fall over,
And then my dear, I'll land in clover!

Robert Walker

Running Back To Pain

Running fast, running far
Hitching a ride in a friend's car
It feels so good to be free at last
It feels so bad to have to run from my past
Don't know where to run, don't know where to hide
Don't know how to face up to what is inside
I know it's daft and I know it's silly
And it starts to get cold, it starts to get chilly
I wanna come back but it's just too hard
From my past I am emotionally scarred
I want to get help, I want you to see
This is not the person I want to be

I can't let you in, you need to stay out
I can't let you see what my head is about
My boyfriend's too old for me but to that I say 'So?'
Because I am scared he will leave me, I am scared he will go
Like my mother did as you all know
But I will be strong when I find the strength to let him go

Now I am back and I will stay around
But I am so angry that I let you all down
I want to grow up to be the person in me
Just come to my world and I will let you see
It's not easy having to be me
Spread your wings across the sea
Let yourself soar, let yourself free
Look at me once, I am just a girl
Look at me twice, there's a hurting world.

K D

The Wedding

A society wedding, what a beautiful sight
The guests in their hired suits, the bride in all white
The bridesmaids delicious, a pageboy there too
Dressed like a miniature Gainsborough 'Boy Blue'
The organist playing 'Here Comes The Bride'
Parents all present with smiles oh so wide
Ushers are placing guests where they belong
But, something's amiss, something is wrong
The groom's done a runner, saying catch me if you can
Now the bride's left for London with the best man
The vicar, quite cross, hear him complain
'I could have been golfing now, I've missed a game
But the day is not wasted,' said he, shaking his head
'Next is a funeral, you can't flee when you're dead!'

H K Banks

Making Our Mark

Christmas is over, we are again at the year's end.
Will the palmistry clairvoyant lend a helping hand?
Read our palms for any leads or telltale signs.
Fame and fortune etched on the hand's lifelines.

Many will seek and find what the future holds,
Foretold for the young and old, weak and bold.
Accept our destiny, just wait and see?
Act right now, that might be the key.

Now is the time to make our new year resolutions,
Little by little, yet not enough to make revolutions.
Recycle paper and cut down any wastes,
Not the trees, don't let the forests blaze.

Logging onto computers, not logging for wood,
Electronic mail saves paper whenever we could.
Slashing down trees and burning clearings is not the only way.
Landslides and raging rivers will ruin the farmer's day.

We should all make a new beginning,
Before fossil fuel prices hit the ceiling.
Wind farm power is surely here to stay,
Nuclear energy should be kept at bay.

Nuclear proliferation to rogue nations,
One sure way to end all of civilisation.
Nuclear winters from fission materials will arise.
Will our green Earth be prepared to pay the price?

Gamble away one last throw of the loaded dice.
On the horizon, global warming and the melting of the ice.
The choice for mankind is clear and stark,
To be kept in the dark or make our mark.

Jim Tan

Revelations

Everything that was once of mine has now turned into past,
Only a long tomorrow left, to bring me hope at last,
I crave for all the feelings I've tried so hard to fight,
To close my eyes shut tightly and prepare to hold on tight.
I am falling steeply head first into a deeper underworld,
I glance to see beneath me, the path of my life unfurled.
Acidic thoughts of jealousy that had polluted my bitter mind,
An unhealthy mix of feelings, with violence and rage combined.
Time is of the essence on a slip road down to Hell,
Accusers shout your secrets, which no one should ever tell.
Fighting for someone else, a plagued and dying cause,
May you enjoy your eternity, with no time out for pause.

Jondaniel Harris

A Bargain Attraction

Out with the old, in with the new
It's great what a change of clothing can do
Off to the sales she went with a hop
Determined that she would shop, shop, shop

Bustling and jostling she joined in the throng
An odd-coloured T-shirt, a dazzling sarong

Pair of shoes that would give with wear
She hoped their bright colour would not cause a stare

A top and a skirt that would dazzle them all
When, down at the club, she'd be queen of the ball

Then she found a coat that was labelled 'classic'
So it must be good - well it cost a packet
No matter 'twas livid, a bright acid yellow
It would brighten her day when feeling mellow

She wasn't quite sure about shoes of puce
But they were a bargain at a great reduce

And the sarong was meant for hotter climes
Margate was cool at the best of times

She got home and spread them all on the bed
Got a headache and bagged them for charity instead.

Ida Jones

Foods We Should Eat

Foods we should eat and rarely do,
Are foods that should be good for you.
Lettuce, tomatoes, chicken and green beans,
Are items on plates that are hardly seen.

Instead we find fast foods that can be bad for you,
Such as pasta, pizzas and stir-fry to mention just a few.
Remember the oils and fats that go into these things,
Can be bad for your arteries, heart, lungs and things.

So go for a good old-fashioned stew,
That would be the right thing to do.
With water, carrots, parsnips, potatoes, peas and beans,
With a choice of meat that is within your means.

The gas or electric must be very low, once you have brought it to the boil,
One thing about this stew you won't need fat or oil.
Don't forget to add a little pepper and salt,
Then in two hours time you can call a halt.

Your stew is now ready to eat.
I hope your family enjoy the treat.

Zoe French

The Story Of Life

Life is but a story
If you look I'm sure you'll find
There are chapters still unwritten
Lots of pages left behind
It will all become much clearer
As you pass along your way
It's the story of your life
And every page another day

If we could just read ahead
When our lives are full of tears
Then we could see our own solutions
Perhaps the ending of our fears
Could you imagine all the fun
To read of when you were a tot
Remember how you learned to walk
And many other things forgot

The traumas that we go through
Like the losing of a friend
See it as it really is
Just another chapter's end
So when you have hard days
All the trouble and the strife
Look upon it as one page
In the story of your life.

P M Stone

Hallowe'en

This night holds such mystery,
shadows all around.
There's an eerie echo,
with each and every sound.

Trees groan and curtsy
like demented witches
on this ominous night
while clouds scudder
across the sky
and block the moon from sight.

Something rubs against my legs
and I let out a scream.
Could it be a black cat
or maybe a witch?
Who knows - this is Hallowe'en!

Olive Homer

The Way

I scratch my head
Start to bleed
Is this the lead
That I must heed?
Is this the way?

I start to cry
Then squash the fly
And dry the tears
To lullaby my fears
Is this the way?

I choke the tongue
Taste bile in my mouth
Then take the plunge
Is north south?
Or east west?

Is this the way?
Is this my life?
To stumble on a field;
Or beat the strife
Then see the way?

I stare at my shadow
Then strike out the light
The deep is shallow
The sun is not bright
Can I see the way?

I choose to go
Then close that door
And stare at the rope
My stomach gropes
Is this the way?

Mbonisi P Ncube

Treasured

Perfumed roses round a shed,
Robin's breast flits overhead,
Rich gazpacho keeps me fed,
Traffic lights that stop me dead,
Herrings that are falsely led,
Lazy redcoats still abed,
Angry mist within my head,
Blushing cheeks, sweet nothings said,
Such a bounty thus bespread,
Touches life with hints of red.

Jill Martin

Angels And Shepherds
(Luke Ch 2)

Christmas my friends has come once again,
but what is the truth, what's the tradition of men?
You've heard of those shepherds in fields nearby
and so many angels that appeared in the sky.
I ask read the scripture and see what is right,
an angel in the midst, on that wonderful night.
That one stood by them right there on the ground,
it says the Lord's glory as well shone around.
So understand now why they became terrified,
I guess you and I would, if one stood by our side.
'Do not be afraid, I bring news of great joy,
in Bethlehem's town there's the birth of a boy.
A Saviour, the Christ, the Lord's born to you,
you'll find him in swaddling in a stable, go view.'
Then suddenly to join them the heavenly host,
they stood with the angel and sang this riposte.
'Most glorious praise to our God upon high,
a word we must bring to you folk standing by.
Peace upon Earth, God gives of His best,
to those of mankind on whom His favour doth rest.'
They return to Heaven, the shepherds in awe,
look for a manger, find babe lain in straw.
Imagine the emotions of his mom and dad,
as shepherds tell story concerning their lad.
Then upon leaving they each spread the word,
of hundreds of angels and all they had heard.
We bless you dear shepherds for what you relate,
then off to their sheep, praising God who's so great.

Albert Watson

Fast Food

In summertime when days were ripe,
Mother served up ice-cold tripe.

Served on plates it looked a flop,
So she put tomato on the top.

If by chance cash flow was low,
That lone tomato had to go.

Mum stood firm, despite our moan,
Dished the tripe out on its own.

Mindset fixed, she simply glared,
So no one spoke another word.

Paul Kelly

Men Of DIY

What of the breed of men of DIY?
Of tradesmen to the wall.
They all but fail to do and try
Textbook experts, they all fall.

All but cowboys now remain
Craftsmen have long since gone.
Part-time men for ill-gotten gain
Jobs done for a pint and a song.

The botched-up job has come to pass
Of filling and mending and making do.
Experts shake their heads at the vast amass
The DIY man strikes again, you know the few.

Saturday collectors of paper and paste
Heads full of ideas, textbooks ready.
If only the jobs were not done in haste
Accidents many, if only they were steady.

Leave well alone if you are not able
Paint splattered heads and bandaged thumbs.
Using the cherished dining room table
As a workbench, convincing the mums.

I've made a mistake, but it will do for now
Gallons of turps on the carpet no less.
I know a man who will show me how
And help me out of this horrible mess.

Tasks patched up for another year
Sighs of relief from the rest.
If a job's worth doing, stay well clear
Of the DIY man in baggy trousers and vest.

Pauline Pickin

Stop Doom And Gloom

So you like a drink,
But let's be positive,
So what if someone important says,
'Stop now or you won't live'.

He may have had life easy,
And doesn't understand,
That putting on the pressure,
Is not a helping hand.

Important people are black and white,
With them it's cut and dried,
Could we have some grey please?
Someone already died.

J Pepper

Spooky Pills

Waiting for the train to go
She didn't seem to want to know
Take a spooky pill and chill
And let ghosts rage in my skull

I ache, so I bake a great big cake
To feed to the fishes that I see in the lake
Jake the hake is always there
With one of his scary songs to share
How he eats hooks
And gets thrown in the air

Spooky pills pop out the jar
Spooky pills I feel so hard
Spooky pills my brain is charred
Spooky pills they get me barred

When I float on spooky pills
Nobody speaks to me
'Don't end up like him'
They point me out and frown
I'm the laughing stock and shock
The nightmare of the town

A bell rings and doors shut, we must be on our way
I'll drop a couple of spooky pills
And bid you all a good day.

Rodger Moir

Untitled

This is the girl who says hello,
Who promises to never let you go,
That will help you when you're feeling down,
That will share her smile when you wear a frown.

This is the girl who is always dressed in black,
To hide her secrets and forget her past,
Who wonders about what the future may hold,
That waits for a new beginning to unfold.

This is the girl who once was shy,
Who lost herself when she would cry,
That once would never speak,
This is the girl who once was weak.

Rebecca Herbert

Sweet Dreams

I saw a sweet lady fall down a hole
Well, was she hurt? No, not at all
I pulled her out, and she gave a shrill shout
And I wondered what it was all about.

'Australia's fair dinkum,' she gaily said
'I saw the vision in my head'
I said, 'It wasn't that far to fall'
She said, 'Believe me, I saw it all.

I just went out to post a letter
To friends and family, they tell me it's better
There down under, I mean, it's a dream
So many sights that have got to be seen.

As I fell in the hole, I banged my head
Then I saw stars and a kangaroo red
Cuddly koalas came to my mind
Then just for a moment, I rubbed my behind.

I know there are creepies and crawlies and things
And one or two insects that have nasty stings
But I saw all the barbecues there in the sun
And on Bondi beach, all the kids having such fun.

Should I go home now and take to my bed?
Quite enough seen and quite enough said
But hey! I'm so old now, I don't give a jot
So I think I'll go visit, and to hell with the lot!'

Jennifer H Fox

A Runaway Car

A runaway car came rolling down the road,
It ran over a mouse, a weasel and a toad.
My Mazda estate was parked at the roadside,
It took a battering, now it's hurt my pride.

A runaway car came rolling down the lane,
It was a Peugeot driver who was to blame.
This careless chap is not getting away,
Because all this happened on Christmas day.

A runaway car with no driver rolled into mine,
It was while I was having a jolly good time.
He or his insurance are going to have to pay,
And it's surely going to be very soon one day.

William Jebb

Way Of Purposeful Love

Blessed is he that love is his true aim,
That will crush rocks for his claim,
And will not doubt to tread the unknown,
Nor fear to take a lot of his own;
Who is not afraid of contradictions;
Who does not hide from certain limitations;
Whose direction flickers subconsciously,
He actively follows consciously;
Who's brave to fall, still aspiring to fly;
Who knows the changing course of uncertainty;
Who lives still when proud love is slain,
And still dares to love again.
Whose love is like sun's golden rays
That fall on everything in their trails,
Whose love seeks not himself to please
But attend to another ease.
Whose love is beyond the state of law
And doles out an equal portion to all.
Who pricelessly loves but not for gain,
And never fears the proud disdain,
Who lives in the realm beyond faith,
Beyond law's layers of death,
Whose hands are the sceptre of mercy
And seek for higher recompense than justice.

Oritsegbemi Emmanuel Jakpa

The Window Of Friendship

The window of friendship
Is always open to you,
No matter what you say or do.
We have known each other
From the start of time,
I love you dearly,
Sweet friend of mine.
We have shared our sorrows
And laughed no end,
I love you dearly,
My dear, dear friend.
As time goes by
Our friendship stays true,
That's why the window of friendship
Is always open to you.

S L Teasdale

Gold Dust

I lay holding my nose in the trench
protecting my receptors from the stench
I look up at the gold dust, the home of my rotting-corpse friend
oh how I long for this war to end.

An everlasting bloody firework display
muddy coffee and measly pay
bodies decaying all over the floor
oh how I hate this goddamn war.

Every missile sound scratching the drum of my ears
and every command deepening our fears
sitting under the gold dust to wait
waiting for this war to deal my fate.

Each severed limb lying dead
fleshy parts, a blown-off head
it's not a place I like to be
why did this war bring this to me?

My inspiration, the gold dust, keeps me going
and keeps the bullets from my gun flowing
every time the sergeant speaks I fear he'll say
we're going over the top, we're going today.

I peer over into the enemy's ground
cannons fire a strangely beautiful sound
another man dead, his name was Seth
now this war brings me to the gold dust, it brings me to my death.

Laura Salmon

Seasons Of Time

Simple joys, simple treasures
take a stroll through life's pleasures
The tree that's bare and all forlorn
on this a crisp November morn
The wind is playing musical leaves
a scattered, mystical path they weave
The autumnal hues of golds and reds
lay softly on their forest beds
A robin searching for winter fuel
before the seasons become too cruel
The conkers that have all been taken
from up high they have been shaken
The fox that ravages for a mere morsel of food
whilst listening to the season's changing mood
Oh, how wonderful life can be
a life-sized masterpiece for all to see.

Maureen Cox

Bitter Taste

You smoke your cigarette
and sip your ale
each crease in your face
tells a different tale.
You hold the ash
wet with tear
a deeper crease
a salty beer.
Anger seething
glass goes down
head filled
with ingrained frown.
Fists fly
blood is spilt
who will help you
with your guilt?
Innocent eyes
blackened with pain
you say you'll
never drink again.
Without it
life's too tough
you have yourself
but is that enough?
You smoke your cigarette
and sip your ale
another crease
another tale.

Nicola Moreland

Flying Eggs

As I was just passing by.
An egg came flying from the sky.
Onward it travelled very far.
Flung from out of a passing car.
On it whizzed with no short cuts.
Until it landed in my nuts!
Down on my knees I fell.
I thought I'd died and gone to Hell.
So, you men, just beware.
Of eggs sailing through the air.
Protect your assets down below.
Because you may never know.
That after an egg impact.
You might find out you're not quite intact!

Josie Rawson

The Hilly Downs

I look upon the hilly downs,
They beckon me to go.
The day is cold and icy,
The sky is full of snow.
Shall I go to meet my girl,
And leave my fireside warm;
Go where the fields are white with frost,
Before onset of storm?
She promised me she'd meet me there,
Upon the hilly downs;
I now shall go there willingly,
Away from busy towns.
I go my way up grassy paths,
To meet her at the top.
I greet her on the hilly downs,
We walk a while, then stop.
The gathering twilight slowly falls,
The sun sinks in the west.
We rise up from our trysting place,
Freshened by our rest.
We kiss, part company and then
I wander down the hill.
I reach my home as darkness comes,
No breeze: for it is still.
I open up my painted door,
Enter my cosy home.
Then climb the stairway to my bed,
I'd earlier left to roam.

B J Webster

Part One

We find that we are running
Our feet blistered and thumping
Scramble we must, we must get away
Cannot look back, we cannot see
If it is gaining closer to you and me
Then *stop, shhh* and listen
I hear not a sound
No more footsteps on the ground
We look at each other, are we free?
Then we realise that us two have become three
We feel the eyes burning down
But too scared we are to turn around
We stand and wait to be handed our fate
Then snap goes a twig, around we turn
And then we see . . .

Peter Vearncombe

Angel Eyes

She walked into my home one day,
The best Christmas present for years.
She's a gorgeous curly blonde, big blue eyes,
Our granddaughter, we held back the tears.

Knee high to a goose, she stands so tall.
My son's daughter, he calls her Ollie.
A busy little girl, the world at her feet.
We went out and bought her a dolly.

She's nineteen months old, as good as gold.
She is now our 'Angel Eyes'.
Her parents have brought her up very well.
She will be gorgeous, clever and wise.

We hope she has a long and happy life,
She comes from that sort of stock.
God willing she will have lots of friends,
And peace and love en bloc.

We have always loved little children,
Spoilt our own a bit, I suppose.
Angel Eyes has come along,
We will love her 'til our eyes close.

Welcome to our home little one,
We love you lots you know.
Olivia, you give us happy hours,
Nice to meet you afore we go.

Grandad.

Brian Hurll

A Time For Rhythm And Rhyme

A time to rhyme is a good time
A response to one's inner heart's mime.
Feeling blue would be a good time,
Or even when happy, being a better mime.

So sway to the rhythm of a poem winging.
Dance to the music of a rhyme swinging
Its way into your soul, forever winging,
Making your feet do a dance, go swinging.

Catchy tunes and even adverts on the wireless
Make your mind feel full of joy, and timeless,
Tuneful, happy, merry even, on the wireless,
Making you remember that rhyme is timeless.

Marj Busby

In Times Of Conflict

How can I write a poem that tells the real story
Of heartache and fears, of pain, doubt and glory?
Those long days and nights that the people endured
Fighting for their country and losing their lives
The poppy fields that once were so lovely and green
With millions of poppies inflaming the scene
Were churned to a pulp in the fighting in the fields
The Christmas-time ceasefire that lasted till one
Then the gunfire resumed and hostilities began
Some were wounded and came home from the front

They were the lucky ones; 'They shall remember them'

The sounds of the gunfire so near and so far
Will always be there for the ones that came home
We should always remember of their humble distresses
As time is the healer of wounds and dilemmas
Soon there is quiet, no more gunfire and tears
Only the people that have lived through their fears
A generation of people that remember the war

An era that closes; 'We shall always remember'

We bow our heads and remember those times
Of conflict and bravery and camaraderie too
The devastation around this sorry world of ours
The bravery of the civilians remembered as well
Those were the days of losses profound
The highs and the lows of those terrible days
Standing at the cenotaph as we remember the dead
In horror and wonderment of those yesteryears
Bowed head and more tears we know we shall shed

Knowing, how can we ever; 'Lest we forget'.

Bryan Maloney

Have A Good Night!

3am and I can't sleep
Though I've counted countless sheep.
Body's tired; not so the brain,
Restless thoughts come in a train.
Might as well concede the fight -
Give in and switch on the light.
Squint to see the wall clock's face -
3.08, how slow the pace!
Put the light out. Try again.
Close my eyes, but all in vain;
I'm as wakeful as can be.
Damn it! Make a cup of tea!

Jim Lawes

Northern Lights

(Dedicated to Sarah Cardona)

In the silence of a winter's night
Lies a stillness of lasting thought
That gives a feeling of pure delight
To one who's seen the golden orb
In the shadow of the Northern Lights

As I drift upon the sea, without a soul to comfort me
I see the stars above the waves
that rock me to and fro

I wonder how I found myself, alone and
far from home. Somewhere
between Land's End and the coast of Newfoundland
It's been two weeks since we left the harbour of St John's Bay, in search of oil,
which drives us forth to catch the majestic whale

During the coldness of the tenth night, a gale pitched its eye on us
We rode the storm as best we could, but in the end
the storm won out, as the ship began to crack

I heard the captain yell out loud,
'abandon ship, save yourselves'
as the lifeboats were cut away

So quick the ship began to sink, I hardly had time to think
I remember jumping into the sea, reaching to grab the side
of a lifeboat floating by. With all my strength I pushed myself to get inside

Oh, how the waves did dance, between the cresting swells
As I looked out from the shell which protected me

In the coldness of the raging storm, the ship had slipped beneath the waves
Claiming the captain and the crew, in the blackness of the night

Finding myself all alone with only a prayer to remember them by
I lay back in exhaustion, in wait of the fate, that lies ahead of me

Two nights have passed since I boarded this craft
The gale that blew has gone its way, but the waves still crest with awe

I fear my time is closing in as the cold sets in my bones
As I look towards the northerly sky, a prayer forms in my heart

To God, I ask, please preserve my soul from the swirls of this relentless wake
With only the brilliance of the Northern Lights, to break the silence of the night

I peer in search of a ship, to save my mortal soul
I ask dear God to rescue me from the ravages of this domain

Or take me to Your golden orb, the one You call Your home.

Roland R Ruiz

The Spider In The Bath

It is the most dreaded of things and fills my heart with fright
I cannot move, I'm petrified, yet fight it as I might
I just can't seem to overcome the terror deep within
This tiny creature causes me and it bubbles up my skin
I go to bed the usual route, I tread the normal path
And then I freeze as I espy that spider in the bath
Just sitting there all brave and bold with me a shaking twit
I can't get in, it can't get out, I can't get rid of it!
I'm sweating now, I'm soaking wet yet I can't reach the door
It stares me out, I'm petrified, I'm transfixed to the floor
But if I leave the bathroom now it might just hide you see
And then I'd be too scared to look in case it crawled on me
Last time I managed to reach the tap and swilled it down the drain
But just before I grabbed the plug it just crawled up again
I have to get it out of there, this really is no laugh
I turn, I grab a towel, I lunge and fall into the bath
Panicking and screaming and flapping like a goose
The bathroom now a war zone as all hell has just let loose
Terrified and soaking wet, all I can do is yell
Can't see that dreaded spider, perhaps he's terrified as well
Did he go down the plughole? Did I push him down by chance?
If I can get the right way up I'll have another glance
At last I crawl out of the bath, splaying arms and legs wet through
And slam the door behind me as tonight a shower will do!

Jackie Davies

Guy Fawkes Night

Flash, bang, pop, there are such a lot,
Bonfire Night is here and the noise doesn't stop.
Whizz, squeal, as a firework flies high above a tree,
keeping those watching excited and happy.

Red, yellow, blue, green,
so many different colours not previously seen.
Sparklers are fun for young and old,
wrapped up warm to keep out the cold.

A huge guy on the bonfire,
he doesn't realise he's in such mire.
Organised displays don't last long,
but over many nights, fireworks go on and on.

Stories of old retold,
of a gunpowder plot that was very bold.
As we remember Guy Fawkes with bangs and bright lights,
we are glad he did not succeed on that fateful night.

Julie Marie Laura Shearing

Who?

Who is it who danced when the world was young?
Do you know who listened when the first song was sung?

Who heard the thunder and the roaring of the sea
In the untold ages before you and me?

Who saw the glory and the boredom and the pain?
Who felt the sword of death when you and I were slain?

Who is it who shivered in the bright cold dawn
When the circle turned from life to life and you and I were born?

Who is in the whispered prayer, the troubled heart's yearning
Who is it who rests in peace and whose desire is burning?

Tell me who's the dreaming one out of Heaven falling
Whose is the phantom voice from the long night calling?

Somewhere in the silence when the wild dreams die
The clouds will fade and show me the I behind my eye

When the light of darkness floods the quiet places of the mind
I will waken to discover that my rainbow sight was blind

I am the dancer and the child and the dying
I'm a joyful fallen leaf in the golden shadows lying

I'm an angel and a demon but my faces are a lie
I am you and you are me, but truly - *who am I?*

Mac Stewart

A Dream Come True

Once when I was thinking . . . upon the things I dream
My guardian whispered in my ear . . . . 'I'll paint another scene'
Wherein I owned all I would have . . . my every wish come true
And dying God did say to me . . . ''Tis yours to take with you'

All the property I'd own . . . as bonds and stocks and shares
With money, diamonds, bars of gold . . . and all my earthly wares
All given me beyond the grave to take to Heaven's gate
But laden I with all my wealth . . . I got there far too late

His door was closed upon my soul . . . my chance had passed me by
As another opened wide his door . . . on hearing me, my cry
'Come in,' he said, 'and join with me . . . and bring you all your gold
'Tis what I paid for you on Earth . . . to one day own your soul!'

Once when I was thinking . . . upon such things I dream
My guardian whispered in my ear . . . 'I'll paint you one last scene'
Wherein I owned but nothing . . . yet was a dream come true
For dying did I reach God's door . . . on time . . . uncluttered too!

M J Banasko

A Time Of Life

There comes a time in life when the easy chair becomes your friend.
You're more in tune with your body, especially when you bend.
It's harder and harder in a morning to eject yourself from bed.
Instead of fun and high jinks, it's a cup of tea instead.

Relaxing watching television, especially after a couple of drinks.
The end of programmes are never seen, you've just had forty winks.
The house reverberates with rasping, grating snores.
Put off until tomorrow, those awful boring chores.

When we go out now, for us fashion's a thing of the past.
We'd much rather be in favourite comfy clothes that last and last and last.
As for modern music, it's either some tuneless nameless group, or some awful gyrating teen.
It wasn't like that in our day, we had Elvis, and we had Queen.

When we used to go shopping, it was a pleasure, the owner knew your name.
Today it's impossible to get service. Everywhere's the same.
Now it's brightly lit musaked shopping malls, where acned hoodies roam free.
They say it's a shopping experience. Well it doesn't appeal to me.

In our day petty rare crime was curtailed with the birch.
Nowadays crime's everywhere and all you get's a smirk.
If the police arrive it's usually three days too late.
But credit where it's due. Their cars are clean and shiny, and always up to date.

David Brown

Humility

Humility be yours in thought and deed.
Feast on kindness and feel satisfied.
Go on your way, sprinkle love around like seed.
Give it blessing as it falls by the wayside.
Tarry not for it will grow, in friendship's hand.
Remember then, reapest thou what thou sow,
Then your harvest will be the one you planned,
But if destiny is what you intend to grow . . .
Be warned for the consequence of your intent.
Fellow Man calls retribution for foul intention.
In your god's name a pardon cannot be grant,
For crime against humanity, nor get you in despatches mention.
Follow the readings of your good book,
Then into your heart and soul do look.
Your faith does say, show your neighbour humility,
For hate in your heart and soul is futility.

John Clarke

Locked Feelings

Locked away from my life,
Locked away from my friends.
Pull the trigger,
And the nightmare ends.

Awkward silence,
Strangers present.
Not enough space to live,
Too much torment.

Telling them,
They don't understand.
Telling them all,
What I have planned.

Most professionals,
Have never felt this way.
So why take into hand,
Everything they say?

At a time I need friends most,
I get locked away from them more.
Crying again,
Dying behind this locked door.

Elizabeth Price

Making Music

I'm told that I am 'off-key'
When I break into song
It doesn't really bother me
I'm sure they must be wrong
Although I've not the timbre
Of an operatic man
I'm always keen to limber
Up, and let fly when I can
My wife gets very cross with me
And leaves me in no doubt
I only make my melody
Such times when she is out
So I confine my vocals
To singing in the shower
Don't care about the locals
This is my happy hour

Gordon Andrews

Acceptance

The student went for breakfast
And waited in the line,
The cafe was quite busy
As it was ten to nine.

Suddenly a hush came down
And people backed away,
She looked around to find out
What was happening that day.

A smell then enveloped her
And she saw a homeless man,
With tousled hair and dirty face
Down which the sweat ran.

He had come in for a drink
And ordered some strong tea,
It was all he could afford
As everyone could see.

As the student stood by him
He looked up in her face,
And searched it with his big blue eyes,
Would she help his case?

She ordered him a sandwich
And quietly shook his hand,
He thanked her very warmly
And thought that it was grand.

The student had accepted him
As a sad and lonely man,
We should take people as they are
And do all we can.

Rita Hardiman

Noisy, Blazing Nuisances

A private member's bill could become law before
This year's fifth of November, to curb private
Firework displays, so neighbours won't feel the roar

Of the loudest rockets, whose after-bangs rivet
Clouds together. They have been grey as ship-metal
Just lately. Dousing-time's eleven, so be it.

Regulations put shopkeepers on their mettle.
It isn't only pretty fireworks we're thinking
Of; but bangers, whose bodies then settle
On every lawn, above which they had been twinkling.

Gillian Fisher

Atollic Follies

Will Man's manic quest for fission wrest the fish life from the sea?
Will eclectic, strident colours transpose less vibrantly?
Will sea horses and sea cucumbers be solely hued green pea?

Will uranium's proclivity unfold a seething, sick event
'Neath the atoll's beauty mask and rent each black, basaltic vent?
Or will coral, mollusc, squid and kelp rekindle colour's bent?

Will Earth's slow-creeping mantle be pressed to speed its plan
To stretch its hot, tectonic plates like crusty porridge in the pan?
Will each radioactive ridge clam colour from crustacean?

Will bustling, scuttling cuttlefish be culled to uniformity
To nucleonically transmute through thorium's activity
To a funnelled, unique hue - to a funless, half-life entity?

If you go down this decayed track
You'll find a poisson cul de sac.
Meet mal de mer: you can't go back.

Will perpetrators offer sops to this isotopic topic
And mollify and fob us off to make us soporific?
Will each plutonium-tainted test genuflect our ethic?

It's facile to fashion nuclides and let Earth fissile out.
Don't let atomic glibness strike its convulsing, slow knockout.
Take this time bomb off the plan; let's make up and not fall-out.

Let sense illuminate the dark and black out nuclear distress.
Put nuclides on the chopping block - blast atomic mindlessness.
Let fishes' iridescence flash to rescue Man from the abyss.

Geoffrey Pike

No Bravado

What can I do that will not break my heart?
My soul is in the autumn of its years,
I cannot play, I cannot sing or dance,
I sit alone and contemplate my fears.
My life, it is an ever-bloodied scar
That feels the rage and power of the sea;
It is the mark which drives old friends afar,
O Lord, I ask You what death cannot be.
I am to die, of that I can be sure,
Though I am boy and have not seen the sun,
In wealth I'm rich, yet life has left me poor,
If I could wish, I'd wish to beat love's drum.
My time is up and now I must depart,
My mind is struck by fate's uncaring dart.

Chris Mann

A Nonsense Poem

Wilkie the wheelchair had a wobbly wheel
So when you pushed it, it gave a loud squeal.
You turned to the left but it went to the right
And poor old Joseph the occupant received a horrid fright.

His false teeth leapt out, they fell to the ground
He spluttered and splattered but they couldn't be found,
So for a long time he was gummy and couldn't eat peas
He had to make do with a lump of soft cheese.

The trouble was, it made the poor chap have a recurring dream
And every night he felt he was swimming in cream,
When it came to a meal he'd push away the spoon
He'd look at the food and then he would swoon.

He would fall on his head and go out like a light
All because of this dream he kept having each night,
But Charlie, his son, only made things worse
The cream he changed into beer of course.

It started Joseph singing, *not* in tune but right off-key
So loud they all decided to stop him you see.
Anything was better than that dreadful din
So they pushed him and the chair into the old dustbin.
And the dustman wheeled the bin out that very week
The wobbly wheel let out its loudest squeak.
'What's that noise?' one dustman said.
'Don't worry,' the second one shouted, 'it's that cat, it's not quite dead.
By the way, what happened to that old chap in the chair?'
'Oh, he found a gun and went dotty but he's around so beware.'

Jacqueline Bartlett

Tsunami

We viewed through tears, scenes of vast devastation
each day another tragic episode.
Such unbelievable annihilation
left pain and suffering on overload.
We wept to see sweet innocent young faces
with nothing and no one to call their own
the horror of death's final resting places
the destitution we have never known.

If there's a God, omnipotent and caring,
could He not calm a tumultuous sea?
Would He inflict such anguish and despairing
on any nation or community?
We doubt Him yet, in moments of concern
we need to feel we have somewhere to turn.

Joy Saunders

The Kissing Culture

The Swiss just won't miss the occasion to kiss
In saying, 'Hi! How are you?' 'Bye-bye' or 'Thank you'
By cultural habit, they simply must have it
Three kisses each time; this is almost a crime
On the road, the dance floor, as you rush through the door
So earrings entangle and bracelets they jangle.
While spectacles crash, or lenses are lost
I'm all for Swiss culture - but this is at some cost.

In France they make do, by dishing out two
For a 'Hi! How are you?' 'Bye-bye' or 'Thank you'
This has to be done even though it's not fun.
And it's hard to endure but there still is no cure
As I spend time each day and kiss the French way
If I do not hobnob I'd be labelled a snob
So - I try to act French and do it with flair
As I smudge all my make-up and mess up my hair.

Just one, say the British, so that they can finish
With the 'Hi! How are you?' 'Bye-bye' or 'Thank you'
But they do change their stance when living in France
Or when mingling with Swiss, as they learn how Swiss kiss
Then they find it is nice to kiss twice, even thrice
And they'd stand in a queue to kiss 'How do you do?'
So the world becomes small while we kiss one and all
As the European Union responds to its call

Now I think the smile can go the whole mile
For that 'Hi! How are you?' 'Bye-bye' or 'Thank you'
You can embrace a hall with just one smile for all
And the smile is returned without energy burned
Your glass you can fill without fearing to spill
And you maintain your poise without smacks full of noise.
But - if on occasion you do hesitate
Just go on and kiss - as your heart does dictate.

Ginny Rogers

Limerick

There was a young girl from Berlin
Who wanted to be very thin
To further her aim
She bathed in champagne
Less fattening than taking it in.

Patricia Smith

Tam The Water Gypsy
(For Mary MacFetteridge)

Tam the water gypsy, he now is dead and gone,
He left this Earth a while ago, his memory lives on,
His houseboat moored on Leven water, at Dalquorn Point,
I always found a welcome there, back on his cosy joint.

Tam collected bric-a-brac then sold it off for cash,
To buy some sweeties for the weans, or buy a bit of hash,
His patter was convincing, not easy to resist,
He sold a man his ain bike back, when the guy was pissed.

I'd take my fiddle with me, and visit gypsy Tam,
He always made me welcome, with tea and bread and jam,
Warm and cosy in the boat, the weans at play outside,
We'd roll a joint and have a smoke, down by the Levenside.

We'd have a little tune together, Tam on his guitar,
I'd play the fiddle with him, the notes rose up afar,
Down along the Levenside you'd hear a gentle tune,
Folk would smile when passing by, beneath a pleasant moon.

The council they would offer to try and house his crew,
The water gypsy said, 'No thanks, I like just what I do,'
Down here by the river bank, I watch the clouds fly by,
I'm free as any bird you know, down here I'll gladly die.

Roy A Millar

The Debut

Today will be the day I see
The face of those who conceived me
To look upon this big, wide world
Bring joy beyond compare.
The time has come for me to leave
My comfortable surroundings
Though now a little cramped
And take my first breath of air.
For those who look upon 'a wait'
Patiently for sight,
For me a stark environment
Clinical and bright
I leave behind for just a moment
The gentle calming echo of a strong beating heart
Having lost already the warm blanket of water
That has enveloped me and protected me.
I am alone, but for seconds,
Then to nestle safely at my mother's breast.

V Aggett

It's November

It's one of those days in November,
Dark nights and fireside days,
But in between the sun shines,
And sends down welcome rays.

It's one of those days in November,
When the fireworks light up the sky,
But please remember your animals,
Keep them warm and cosy inside.

It's one of those days in November,
When we think of Christmas cards,
Holly and mistletoe puddings and fir trees,
Goodies to resist, it's so hard.

It's one of those days in November,
When the year's nearly over and done,
And a new year will soon be dawning,
May you have a happy one.

It's one of those days in November,
When I think, *will we have snow or not?*
But winter will not be forever,
And I'll soon see my first snowdrop.

Rachel Mary Mills

Life's Lesson

The wind of change blows through your life,
And leaves a state of disarray,
The tears will flow and people grieve,
For those who can no longer stay.

Life's vast array of pleasures sweet,
Is but a banquet spread before,
The hungry eyes of those whose lives
Enjoy the gifts of nature's store!

The pleasant ways of daily life,
Have stretched ahead for many years,
And then the sudden rocky path,
Leads only to a vale of tears.

With passing time, the sorrows heal,
The pain subsides, new hope is born,
The tears run dry, sweet memories bloom,
Regret remains the only thorn.

So, as we journey through our lives,
To family, friends, our love display,
Each moment must be made to count,
For mortal men, with feet of clay.

A Pickering

Endless Love

You came into my life when I was sad,
Everything in my life was bad.
All my friends they seemed to have gone,
They had lives, families all of their own.
You had warmth in your smile,
Something I had not seen for a while.
You took away all my pain,
You taught me how to laugh again.
I'd always liked you from afar,
Then you became my guiding star.
You helped me through my hurt and pain,
You taught me to trust again.
One day you said you loved me true,
Then I told you I loved you too.
We laugh and cry, tears we spill,
But I want you to know I love you still.
I could not ever love you more,
I hope you will be mine for evermore.
I'll try my best for you, just wait and see,
Because you mean the world to me.
Man and wife we became,
Our love for each other is still the same.

E Riggott

Superman

Wham! Zam! Bam! I'm Superman.
I'm every girl's delight.
I heed the call and bring my all
On supersonic flight.
So here I stand all tall and butch
Among this brood that cluck too much,
To wish yon hen, the bride so dear,
All starry-eyed for wedding near,
The best of luck; much joy and health,
And fruitfulness of love's great wealth.
Making the bridegroom constantly
Scratch and scrape contentedly;
And may this girl bright blushing now
Fill his life with *pow!* and *wow!*
Pow! and *wow!* and lots of zip
Every time they make love's trip.

Yes, *Wham! Zam! Bam!* I'm Superman,
The guy men love to hate,
But I must zoom to Macholand,
Mum scolds me if I'm late.

Violet M Corlett

My Rainbow Will Return

This life I live, so lacking in hue,
Never as me, but the other half of you
I need to be yellow, dance like a daisy
Not tired and grey, driven almost crazy
My rainbow will return one day
My rainbow will return.

I may be purple-striped with pink
Beneath monotone I will not sink
I'll tiptoe through stars, silver and gold
I will not settle for ashen and cold
My rainbow will return one day
My rainbow will return.

With scarlet and crimson I will adorn
To be pallid or pale I was not born
In lime and citrus I'll skip in the rain
My spirit in mud you cannot stain
My rainbow will return one day
My rainbow will return.

I'll colour my nails with marigold
And break away from your dismal hold
It matters not what you do
My colour will always come shining through
My rainbow will return one day
My rainbow will return!

Louise Wheeler

The Donkey's Reply

As a horseman travelled on the dusty road,
He came upon a donkey with such a heavy load,
The horseman shouted, 'Donkey, please tell me if you may,
Why you walk so slowly that you block my way?'
The donkey replied, 'Because, Sir, you are on a horse,
So you can travel so much faster than this ass of course.
But I will tell you this, Sir, because I know it's true,
Upon a donkey's back rode a greater man than you.'

'What is that you're saying?' the rider then replied,
'Who was that famous person, and where did He abide?'
''Twas long ago in time, Sir, for when this man was born,
It was in a stable upon a winter's morn.
A donkey was there too, Sir, and they also say,
The baby's cradle was a manger nestled in the hay.'
So if you see a donkey when homeward bound you plod,
Just think, it could be a descendant of the one that carried God!

Dennis Brockelbank

A Night Not To Remember

Down a path beneath shaded trees of green
over a wooden bridge, that crosses a trickling stream.
There stands a little thatched cottage with honeysuckle around the door
inside lives an old lady who does not welcome visitors anymore.
Children think she is a witch and go there to make fun
throw stones at her door, when she comes out they run.

A witch is far from the truth, a recluse she may be
but her life was all destroyed working in Africa as a missionary.
For years she worked with the children, the dying and the sick
bringing them to our Saviour's arms, so caring and sympathetic.

That fatal night they came, white women were their prey
she offered her own life, so most could get away.
She was dragged into the bush, left for dead three nights and days
they found her in a clearing, giving God all her praise.

The pastor of that mission, all those years ago
watching with others in the undergrowth, her torture evil and slow.
Like David confronting Goliath, the love of God in her soul
she would not tell that others were hiding in a hole.
They were fortunate to have come out of that hole covered by leaves
but Sister Mary never has, she is still frightened by the wind in the trees.

J H Bennetts

Celebrity

I saw it in her pretty eyes,
That her make-up was just a disguise,
Even after her success,
She's still plagued by loneliness,
She sings a song of teenage dreams,
In a skinny corset bursting at the seams,
She co-writes a tale about first love,
Forgetting all the things above,
It's not commercial, it's not the thing,
To express the pain, when she goes to sing.

I saw it in his best-selling book,
That his voice was coached as was his look,
Even after his success,
All he wants is a girl to possess,
He sings a song of a teenage crush,
In baggy jeans bought in a Top Shop rush,
He co-writes a tale about lost years,
Forgetting all his human fears,
It's not commercial, it's not the way,
To talk of commitment, and of an uneasy lay.

Marc E Wright

Age Concern

I have read in books
About old people's looks
That their ears and their nose
Still grows!
That the ears grow so
That the hearing won't go
But it does go you know
So it just can't be so!
Now a nose that starts small
Won't change much at all
But a nose that starts longer
Leaves something to ponder.
If it just grows and grows
Would it soon reach the toes?
And if the old back is bent
And the nose still has scent,
That again is something to ponder
With a nose growing yonder and yonder
Long ears you can hide in a big woolly hat
But a mile-a-minute nose! What's to do about that?
A hanging basket sounds fine
With pretty flowers and vine
And as it reaches the feet
Would keep the feet sweet.
'Til they close down the casket
Then the preacher can relate
She made a great hanging basket
But was a martyr to her fate.

Constance I Roper

Tsunami

In the bowels of an ocean, Nature's rage
lashes out at Man's wanton destruction
of his own, crams history's subtler page
with stark images of insurrection

O cruel aftermath of grief, loss, pain!
A divided world unites in horror
without (immediate) thought of self-gain
but only to save, bury, restructure

Prayers, dollars, aid, flood in to assist
severed lives, livelihoods, whose simple joys
of a paradise once by angels kissed
now thrown by tsunamis into chaos . . .

Though paradise regained, only in part;
as feisty waves breaking, so too, its heart

Roger N Taber

After The Rain

A leaden sky, for a storm it looks set
As the raindrops come tap-tapping down.
Without an umbrella you're sure to get wet
As the grey road is turning to brown.

Tap-tapping grows faster, p'raps rain's here to stay
So, button up your collar and run,
To those tall plants there, over the way
Very useful till rain has all gone.

Bright green leaves nearly three feet across
Rhubarb-like of the wild butterbur.
Growing between earth and damp moss
Couch grass, the wild oats and cockspur.

As umbrellas, use the wide-spreading leaves
Till the storm eases off and soon stops.
Then repetitive sound which no one believes
Is the echo of returning raindrops?

The noise seems to come from under a leaf
But not one which was used in the rain.
Now everyone's list'ning in disbelief
Because the tapping has started again.

So you lift the leaf from where the sound came
And it was the correct one to choose.
For what should you see, which made you exclaim?
It was a leprechaun mending some shoes!

Under the butterbur leaf he sat
With a boot he had recently soled.
You took your glance from him - quickly as that -
He disappeared! So, there's no crock of gold!

Loré Föst

What Am I?

I hobnob with nobility
And mix with the very poor
Once folk have seen me
They certainly want more
I'm rich in every aspect
But not to everyone's taste
So to let them see and touch me
Really is a waste
I like to think that I am special
In fact I think I should
Have you guessed yet what I am?
Of course, I'm the Christmas pud.

Daphne Fryer

Welcome To My World

A small gift of treasures
Packed in a pretty jam jar
A collection of small finds
Beachcombed from near and far.

Breast feathers from a seagull
Green glass sandblasted by the sea
Pieces of blue and white china
A conker from a chestnut tree.

Ammonites and fossils
Washed up after millions of years
Petrified extinct creatures
For which we shed no tears.

Golden marble pebbles
A tiny, plastic cartoon lamb
Seashells, cockles and mussels
This is me, it's who I am.

Welcome to my world of
Endless skies, beaches and sea
These souvenirs of my life
A simple gift to you from me.

Christine A Lee

Daphne's Dilemma

'These are not lamb cutlets my dear,'
Whispers dear Daphne in my ear.
'Leg chops maybe - cutlets, never
And overdone in this hot weather!'
Maltese Joe, his dark eyes blazing
Zooms in on Daphne complaining.
Smiling, growls, 'Why you not liking?'
Daphne shrugs, her blue eyes widening.
As cook is summoned from his lair
Tanned, tattooed arms; grey greasy hair.
Retrieves the chops - then reappears
'Forget mint sauce - so sorry dear!'
Soon her companions, hunger sated
Ignore burnt chops, mint-sauced, plated.
Spot gambling den immediate right
But cook - and kitchen? Not in sight!
Just then Daphne, polite as ever
Vows to herself she will never
Climb a staircase - metal or wood
To lunch on lamb in a Labour club!

Betty Lightfoot

My Sister

She's five feet tall and quite petite
She really is quite small and sweet
But in her heart she's ten feet tall
She has much love for one and all

Her day first starts at the crack of dawn
Her doors are open to all forlorn
The down and out, the just plain weary
She takes them in and still stays cheery

Her time is yours, she gives her best
Leaving little time to rest
From early morning to late at night
She never will give up the fight

To help those people less fortunate than her
That's what makes her such a special girl
A willing heart, a heart of grace
So in my heart she has a special place

When God gave us her no one could know
The love and comfort she'd always show
So thank you dear sister for all you have done
From me and all the others
You're God's special one.

Sheila Johanson

When A Child Is Ill

Our firstborn son - just two years old
A little angel, good as gold -
Went to bed quite happily
Then in the morning, suddenly
Our little boy was taken ill
Maybe it was just a chill
But it was plain that he was sickly
So we called the doctor quickly
His condition was so critical
She sent him into hospital
I le was too ill to even cry
They operated or he'd die
We knelt in prayer, *Oh Holy One*
Please God save our little son
He cannot die, it cannot be
He means so much to his daddy and me
The nurses tended him with care
His life with tenderness to spare
Till we brought home our little boy
To be again our pride and joy.

Ellen M Lock

107

One Wish

One wish is all I'd need
To help me to sow the seed
Everyone would be free of pain
The world would become sane
Sickness would disappear in the dead of night
The blind would regain their precious sight
If only I had but one wish, how magic
To waste it would be crazy and tragic
But, if I had only one wish
I would wish
For endless wishes
And then for just one more
I'd wish for suffering to cease
With endless wishes for world peace
Perhaps for us to really care
To love each other, if we dare
To show our hearts and open our souls
There are endless possibilities with achievable goals
A world full of peace, of love and kindness
Where wondrous things endlessly astound us
Where every day is a joy to behold
More precious than silver, more iridescent than gold
Should I ever be so lucky to have but one wish
That's how I'd like the world to be, just like this
Where hunger and thirst are things of the past
Pain and suffering has gone at last
Where work is a pleasure and not a pain
Free time is enjoyed again and again
This to me sounds just like Nirvana
Meditate enough and I'll get there

Ivana

You're Perfect
(Dedicated to Phillip Lee)

You make me feel happy, you make me smile,
You make me feel, that everything's worthwhile,
I miss you when, you're not around,
You're perfect for me, and you're really sound,
I love it when I am, cuddled up with you,
Having loads of kisses, they feel really true,
Listening to, your voice every day,
Keeps a smile on my face, you know what to say,
I want you to know, how special you are
Even though I am here, and you are so far.

Julie Titchener

I Wanna Be A Banker

I wanna be a banker and lend money by the ton,
then when I know that it's all gone I really will have fun,
I'll send polite reminders that the *time is overdue* -
for us to meet and talk about the *'annual review'*.

We'll arrange a time convenient, your problem to discuss -
well, a time to suit me really, because as yet *'we'* are not *'us'*.
I'll ask about market research and cash flow for the year -
and 'what does your accountant think - and why is he not here?'

Before I hand a penny out I'll ask questions by the score,
and examine your life history, plus birthmarks and much more;
'The project that you have in mind, are you sure that it won't fail?
I know the sailing's steady now but what if there's a gale?'

'Do you *really need* all that at once - at insurance we must look,
I'll ring through to my colleague to bring the other book;
You say you have a house and car, and a first-class guarantor,
you've proved that you don't need it, so what about much more?'

I don't wanna be a banker now, I've followed banking rules,
I drove my Skoda to his house - six bedrooms and two pools.
Two Rollers were parked in the drive - I'd called to tell him *no* -
So why am I the money expert but he's made all the dough?

Jim Pritchard

They Are . . . My Children

They are the warmth of day's first light
They are the ones, given the chance, just might
They are the ones we'll grow to see
Consume the life, of you and me.

They are the ones that have spirits free
They are the ones that we used to be
They are the ones who will tell a white lie
And live inside us till the day we die.

They are the ones who will play with your heart
They are the ones who one day will part
They are the ones who will stand so tall
And leave you and me, loving their all.

They are the ones who we can't live without
They are the ones we should leave with no doubt
They are the ones we protect from sorrow
And love so strong, today and tomorrow.

John Bagshaw

One Wish

If I could have one wish
Which one would it be?
I'll have to write them down
So you can judge for me

I wish I could be a film star and live the lives they do
I wish I could be a pop star and sing a song or two
I wish I could be a millionaire and give to the poor and needy
I wish I could own that big mansion but does that make me greedy?

I wish I could stop the war and make peace
I wish I could feed the starving and give them a huge feast
I wish everyone could love and learn not to hate
I wish we could all live forever, wouldn't that be great?

I wish I could stop the abuse of children young and old
I wish you would just listen to the story they have told
I wish I could stop the cruelty of the animals in pain
I wish I could stop the elderly from going insane

I wish we could all stay healthy and not suffer like we do
So now you have heard my wishes let me grant this one to you
I wish you all to be happy with this one life you have got
And treasure every moment until it has to stop.

Claire Pattison

Cakes And Kindness

It is not often I find someone so kind,
Looking all around us it's very hard to find.
From the first time I met you, you really appealed to me,
Representing someone special and pleasant for eyes to see.
Your baking is so like you I could hardly believe
'Twas the tastiest piece of kindness a man could ever receive.
The taste will last a lifetime, your hands they do you credit,
I'd be most satisfied if your heart I could inherit.
Please don't misunderstand me, I'm being honest to you,
Although we're very different, my feelings are so true.
Our earth blossoms with ladies each made a different way,
A man has to make a good choice for survival day-to-day.
Your lovely personality is a very good quality,
I would like to share my life with you until eternity.
I'm really saying thank you, I hope in a special way,
I would share your goodies forever, even if I had to pay.
Continue this homely practice, you sure are a delight,
It would sure encourage any man to be with you day and night.

Christina Maria Procter

Up In Flames

He sits alone, at the top of the pile
His clothes resemble those of a tramp
Hair is unkempt, not been cut for a while
His legs are stretched, like he has cramp.

He has finally reached the end of the road
His life will come to the end of its span
For his short existence, he's had no fixed abode
And he cannot work out any escape plan.

He has no emotions, he cannot weep
Though possessing a mouth, he cannot speak
He cannot close his eyes to obtain any sleep
His immediate future is totally bleak.

His arms cannot function by his side, they are still
He has no vision, though stares straight ahead
He cannot feel warmth, does not feel the chill
And flying creatures keep picking at his head.

He has no descendants, he was not born
Pairs of hands put him together in one day
Already he appears tired and forlorn
As his time comes to slowly fade away.

He has never enjoyed eating a good meal
He knows not of thirst, unable to drink
To very small people, he makes great appeal
He has no brain and is unable to think.

He is unable to comprehend the meaning of time
He does not know light is beginning to fade
Because of one man who committed a crime
On top of a bonfire he is now displayed.

Bangers and rockets he will not hear, within hours his body will be gone
Flames reach out and people will cheer, Bonfire Night must be carried on.

B W Ballard

Musical Muse

I asked a violin player,
At King's Cross underground,
The reason why he did it -
His reply seemed very sound.

'I don't pay any tax,' he said.
'So don't have any arrears.
What I make is what I get to keep . . .
I've been on the fiddle for years!'

Derek Harris

An Ode To The Sun And Moon

Oh! Shining sun of golden light
Keep my love safe tonight
Far away though he may be
Bring him safely soon to me.

He's been away so many days
Let me be knowing of his ways
Running, swimming, happily playing
Listening to his children saying,

'When will we be going home?
Is our lovely pet alone?'
'Time will come for you to pack
All your bags for coming back.'

Back to here, and we wonder, where?
Is there only me to care?
Care what you will have to do
Where you go, but safe from foe.

We've been together lots this year
There's only one thing that I fear
Fear that you will be alone
Far from me, and far from home.

Where'er you go, let's hope you'll be
Always true, a friend to me
I would not want to lose your love
I'll always be there, like a dove.

Fly to you when you're in need
A true friend is a friend indeed
I've said before, we must never part
I'll always keep you in my heart.

Oh! Wondrous moon, help his flight
Coming home on Thursday night
Keep him safe whilst homeward bound
Safe, secure till touches ground.

John L Pierrepont

My Dream Woman

Her hair was long and blonde, her eyes were vivid blue,
She was the prettiest girl I had ever seen, too good to be true.
She had the perfect body, with not a trace of fat,
She walked by and smiled, as on the bench I sat.
This calibre of woman I thought I would never find,
Then I did wake up and I found she was only in my mind.

Don Goodwin

The Depth Of Night

Long in the night, of places unseen.
Far down in the depths, the untenable dream.
Sight and sound, the visions of sleep.
Eternal thoughts of the strong and the weak.
A path to be taken, that road long and hard,
To seek out the truth of perfection unmarred.
Keeping a balance with all that is said,
Sanity, reality, it's all in the head.
Being a liar, with all of the shame,
Telling home truths, no difference again.
Living a life, every day just the same,
Missing the meaning, only ourselves to blame.
Woman gives life that men take away,
War after war as the scenes of a play.
Science, religion, politics or greed,
Stupidity en masse is all that we need!
A moment to stop and a moment to think,
Then do we realise how lowly we sink.
A moment of glory, a moment of pain,
A circle unbroken lest he become whole again.
Looking inside you may find a truth,
Staring right back, the reflection of youth!
Beware though the path, that takes you this way,
If you wish to return to see a new day,
Presuming to know, is the danger to face.
Understanding we know little, is to be in the wise place.
Lost in the hustle and bustle of life,
An Eastern way may rid us of strife.
The answers are there, for the seeker of all,
Though long is the road and so is the fall!

Michael Skerratt

Hair

Some men love them red
Others love them brown
Some men like it up
Others like it down
Some men love them mousy
Others love them black
Some men like it forward
Others like it back
Some men love it ginger
Others love it blonde
I don't care about their hair
It's of girls themselves I'm fond

Paul Curtis

If I Loved A Woman

If I loved a woman I would be free,
I could sit and talk with her upon my knee,
What about? We will see . . .

Love, marriage, sex, what can they be?
An evil veil over our face to not let us see?
What can we do about this strange love?
Love each other like God would from above?
Or let us see the truth behind the veil,
And one day, I hope, love will prevail.
All of our hopes, our dreams come true,
But for those three magical words of:
'I love you'.

Happiness, sin, what life's about?
Trapped in your life,
You must die or get out.
There's only one way to escape this sin,
You must kill the love within.
Once out of the world,
Then you can see,
'What's what' and 'who's who',
Therefore you are free.
But without this love to drive you on,
You find yourself on your own, and then gone.
Without this precious motivation,
You soon will die without the levitation,
And your heart that should fly,
Will very soon die.

One day,
Many days away,
If you should still live in trapped harmony,
Out of the blue and just for you,
Shall come your love.
They shall come from Heaven,
Flying through the sky,
And the lights of Earth shall shine on them,
For they, among with many others rejoice;
Because you have found your love.

James Blore

All In A Night Shift

It was a quiet night in casualty,
Six beds made up and all empty.
Suddenly! The bell rang and doors flew open,
In rushed nurses, with a locum.
Up jumped Rachael, at the ready,
All calm, and nerves quite steady,
Into crash, the nurses raced,
The doctor called, and in he paced.

Rachael stood at the bedhead,
Patient white and almost dead,
'All stand back,' the sister shouted,
The electric shock, patient clouted.
The poor chap, open-eyed,
Actually nearly died.
Now laid back, in dazed reaction,
Heart now belted into action.
Bed made up and porters called,
Off to the intensive care ward.

In a side room on ward eleven,
A flicker of life and a shout, 'Am I in Heaven?'
Nurse Rachael, now all serene,
Appeared, calm just like the Queen,
Said, 'No dear, don't you know?
It just wasn't time for you to go.'
The chap laid back, now in relief,
Uttering, 'It must have been the beef!'
Eyes now closed and gently sleeping,
Rachael tiptoed, and quietly creeping,
Pulled the curtain and left him sleeping.

Now off to the smoke room, she did race,
Nothing stopping her in her haste.
Quickly lighting up and puffing,
Stifled a yawn and did some coughing.
Look out for Sister, she could be coming,
Oh Lord, it's her! She is a-coming.
With a twinkling eye and a grin on her face,
The other nurse giggled and took her place.
'It's alright my dear, I'm having you on,
The Sister went home, and is long gone.'
Back on the ward, after the break,
It's surprising the difference a puff can make.
Lights dimmed low and all things put away,
Rachael nods her head, until break of day.

Elizabeth Turner

Winter Shivers

I awoke one morning
Couldn't stop yawning
The world looked
Dull and grey
And shivers arose in
My body all throughout
The day
Sneezing, coughing
Shivering, tired
Feeling grey
I knew the winter
Flu was at bay
I arrived home feeling
As weak as can be
Under my duvet
All alone
Feeling weak as can be
Downing my medicine
As could be
Woke the next day
Feeling a lot better
The next day I woke
Feeling as fresh as a rose
And happiness was wherever I went!

Denise McDonald

Twins

You're counting stars
In a forest tonight,
I see your face
Turned up to the sky.
Miles are between us,
The light may be dim,
I know I've succeeded
In finding my twin.
No doubt in my mind
I will stand by your side,
Turning our faces
Up to the sky.
We're specks of dust
In the light of the moon,
So I promise my twin
I will join him soon.

Rachel Robins

Blue Eyes Cry

(Dedicated to Wendy Lacey-Williams)

I wanted our love
To last forever.
I knew you were
The one for me.

I was the one
Who made your blue
Eyes cry.
I turned the blue
Skies grey.

I never wanted to
Break your heart.
I never meant to
Make your blue eyes cry.

It was me who made
Your blue eyes cry.
Yes it was me,
It was me
Who made your blue eyes blue.
Your blue eyes must
Never cry again.

I Hood

Happiness

This is a very individual thing
But oh! what joy it does bring
This is what it means to me
But you might see it differently
Being with someone who puts you at ease
Talking in depth on any topic you please
The smell of cut grass on a fine day
Makes me feel this way.
A sunset by the Mediterranean Sea
Surrounded by beautiful scenery
Lost in love, just Helen and me
Saturday afternoons playing cricket
Team doing well, me taking wickets
Winning as well is just the ticket!
Each new day watching the sun rise up
Cacophony of birdsong, a barking pup
Strolling along in misty rain
Thoughts developing in your brain
Being fulfilled is what it's about
Feeling great and wanting to shout.

Dave Slade

You Broke Me

You sat there just watching me
then suddenly . . .
you got up and grabbed my hair,
you called me names like you didn't care,
you pushed and pulled and made me fall,
you kicked my head against the wall,
you made me scream out in pain,
you made me feel small and lame,
I tried to get up . . .
'Oh no you don't,' you laughed and tutted
you climbed on me and pushed me down.
I screamed in pain as I hit the ground,
'You stupid freak,' you screamed and shouted,
you grabbed my head as I passed out,
when I woke you laughed and sneered,
my eyes welled up with masses of tears,
I was lying bleeding on the floor,
you laughed again and headed out the door,
in agonising pain I started to cry,
you left me alone . . . in pain to die,
I was still lying there when you came back
ready for a second attack
which I did not survive,
it's all your fault I'm not alive.

Emma-Jane Lunt

One Wish

If I could have one wish then it would be
That everyone be treated equally
The black and white in every country
Would all have equality
No one to go hungry in the land
Everyone would give a helping hand
There'd be medicines for everywhere
We'd pull together to show we care
The goods of every country would be used
And little children would not be abused
There would be no begging in the street
For everyone would have enough to eat
Water would be free on every shore
And children not afraid to ask for more
Instead of all the power used in the West
We'd share everything we had with the rest
It would be like Heaven on Earth
The first time we all shared since Jesus' birth.

Grace Divine

Taking Time

It's that time of year again
for us to celebrate
by piling extra helpings
upon our dinner plate.

A time to get together
with all of those we love
and rest for just a moment
from all the push and shove.

A time to be forgetting
if only for a while
all the many trying things
that take away our smile.

A time for reminiscing
the other times that we
have gathered all together
around the Christmas tree.

It's that time of year again
so let us all be glad
and make our Christmas this year
the best we ever had.

James A Osteen

Dreams

I ponder as life passes by my window
Dreams running wild in my mind
Blurry thoughts, those once clear though
Remind me of the lost times unkind

Memories cut deep - my delicate skin
Dissipate the dreams I once saw
To reveal the forgotten pain deep within
I've forgotten how to dream anymore

Captured, I sit in this moment of time
Masking the pain as remembered so raw
On recalling dreams - forgotten mind
I stare numb in time out of the window

Reminiscing in those fallen years
I watch the world pass by in awe
Giving weight to my standing tears
To dreams which will be no more

Nasur

Guy Fawkes Rocks

A fire burns, oh so bright
On this Bonfire Night
Sparks crackle and glow
Let's get on with the show
A rocket flies up to the sky
It zooms up, my oh my
It bursts open with a bang
Stars sparkle in the sky
As others shoot on by
Catherine wheels dance around
What a lovely sight
Roman candles shine and glow
As the guy on the fire
Is burning, we know
This is a wonderful show
A banger goes off as well
Sparklers shine in the dark
Jumping Jacks bang about
As kids run around
A wonderful night
They have found
So many happy faces all around

Gordon Forbes

Lifetime

And on we go - high then low,
Never stop - that's life you know.

If we complain - don't like this game,
Our time will come - as we move on.

The scene will change before our eyes,
Present itself to our surprise.

'Do you like this now?' 'Oh yes, that's fine,
Just hold it there' - 'Sorry no time.'

Moving on and on and on,
Yes that feels good but that's all wrong.

This constant change confuses me,
My ideal state is totally happy.

Well sorry mate, that don't equate,
Each fraction of a second of every day,
Life's in control of your chaotic fate.

Raymond Barber

Bonfire Night

Bonfire Night is one day out of the year,
Baked potatoes and cans of beer.
Roasted chestnuts on the fire,
Looking at coloured fireworks,
With my heart's desire.

Reds, purples, blues and greens,
What a wonderful Bonfire Night this has been,
Catherine wheels, rockets and Jumping Jacks galore,
Sparklers of many colours,
And lots, lots more.

Logs burning, Guy Fawkes on the top,
I'm so excited I just can't stop.
Sparks are jumping off the ground,
Burnt logs falling to the ground,
Everyone standing all around.
Orange flames, jumping to and fro,
Warming our hands,
It's so cold you know!
Children's faces all aglow,
Fireworks so high and away they fly,
So you see, it's so exciting,
Once a year, the 5th November,
(What a happy night for everyone to remember!)

Mary Woolvin

O For The Wings Of A Dove
(With apologies to King David and Felix Mendelssohn)

O for the wings of a dove,
That I could rise up and soar
Into the sky, above
The traffic jams and the lorries' roar;
Above the drivers just sitting in a trance,
Denying the rest of us a sporting chance
Of getting to work without being late,
Having worked ourselves up into a terrible state.

I would fly to where a light breeze blows,
Through the trees, the grass and flowers,
Where no bosses deign their pressure to impose
Upon us from their ivory towers;
Where birdsong and gushing waterfalls
Replace the sound of the telephones' ring,
Where the pace of life virtually stalls,
And stress-related illness is an unknown thing.

Kathy Rawstron

You Are

You are the glowing light,
that illuminates my way,
you are the sunshine in the morning,
which warms up each day.

You are my food that I eat,
the water that I drink,
you are the safety net beneath me,
that stops me falling to the brink.

You are the vitamins I take,
that I need for good health,
you are the money that I earn,
that brings me my wealth.

You are the sky over my head,
and earth beneath my feet,
you are the little tasty nibble,
when I fancy something sweet.

You are the glue that I use,
when I have something to mend,
you are the one I always turn to,
when I really need a friend.

You are the air that I breathe,
that gives me my life,
you are the one I want to marry,
the one to be my wife.

I've tried to put in verse,
the way I feel about you,
but as I told you long ago,
it's simply that *I love you!*

John Trinick

Love For Our Family

Love for our family,
It goes a long way.
We care for one another,
Each and every day.

We learn by our mistakes,
From our parents support.
They guide us through life,
With good intentions.

Love for our family
Love for our friends

Love goes a long way . . .

Melanie Martin

Carnival

Carnival in Rio,
Carnival in Spain,
Carnival in our town,
Bridgwater's claim to fame.
One night in November,
Folk come from all around
To see a festival
Of colour, light and sound.
People wait for hours,
Despite rain or freezing cold,
To have a prime position,
Worth its weight in gold.
At last comes the procession,
Huge floats taking part,
Each one in construction
A brilliant work of art.
All the clubs competing,
Members working thro' the year,
To win the premier trophy
They strive and persevere.
Each year it's more impressive
Than the one before,
The spectators are delighted,
Their approval they roar.
All the cash collected
Goes to charity,
A grand and helpful enterprise,
A dedicated community.

Sue Cann

Arduous Examinations

Here come the examinations,
With their many new innovations,
There's chemistry, by reactions,
Physics is the law of actions,
Biology is reproduction,
Civics, the constitution,
Geography is identification,
Mathematics is equations,
Economics, urbanisation,
English is communication,
Computers is information,
History, our civilisation,
O! All these for an examination,
Although ensued by sheer relaxation.

R Balaji (16)

2006 Is Our Year

Two thousand and six has arrived my friends,
Although those long classes seemed as though they'd never end.

September snuck up suddenly, the summer faded quickly,
Applications are now our priorities, acceptances our goals.

Senior-itis is the contagious disease,
Which we must all overcome with ease.

Exams are not a worry this year, for if we work to our potentials,
The faculty and staff will accept our exemptions.

As the months pass by, we anticipate our graduation,
After all is over, we will wish the year had gone slower.

Our ultimate summer of freedom has come at last,
Let us make this a memorable one, just as those from the past.

Long walks on the beach, partying every weekend,
These are the times we much cherish my friends.

When August rolls around, it is soon to be found,
We are ready for college, so distinguished and proud.

Two thousand and six has arrived my friends,
Let us make a promise, a pact till the end,
For 2006 is our year.

Ryann Throckmorton

Whistler

Whistler
Oh you whistler please
Bring the cynics
To their knees
Break the silence
With your song
When all the peace
On Earth is gone
Whistler
Oh you whistler now
Save us from ourselves
Somehow
Lift our spirits
To the stars
And help us heal
These battle scars
Whistler
Oh you whistler please
Bring the cynics
To their knees

Rod Trott

My Grandma

It was so many years ago
when I was only three,
I had a lovely grandma
who bounced me on her knee.

She used to sing me lullabies
and many other songs.
I still believe she's with us
where I know that she belongs.

I don't know why my grandma
came to stay with us,
my mum had five more children,
but she never made a fuss.

One day my dear old grandma
had to go away,
I was too young to understand
she could no longer stay.

For years I thought she would come back
and bounce me on her knee,
but I still hear those lullabies
my grandma sang to me.

Jean Windle

New Beginnings

Another new year, another new day,
Each hour is the start of the rest of your life,
With all its ambitions, its hopes and its dreams,
And also its times of troubles and strife.

We all have our dreams of hope and success,
Dreams of what we would do.
If only life were different,
And all those dreams could come true.

Each day is a new beginning,
When we open our eyes at dawn.
Like turning a brand new page in a book,
Leaving behind the ones that are worn.

But those old pages in a book,
Much useful information hold,
To give us guidance for the future,
With the stories that have been told.

And so as we look forward in life,
To another brand new day,
We also need to look back to the things,
That can help us on our way.

Iris E Covell

Deep Waters!

These waters whisper secrets
That no one else can hear
Telling me of bygone days
I gently brush away each tear

A little boat lies within
This water deep yet still
Grandparents lie peacefully
Somewhere here at God's own will

Whispers of tranquillity
Soft voices calm and sweet
I feel their presence engulf me
From my head right to my feet

Sitting here I see each face
Standing on that little boat
They gently wave and blow a kiss
For a few seconds they are afloat

Are they watching over me
Sending me their love?
Letting me know that they still care
As from deep water they come above?

Disappearing into the depths
The whispers fade, they're gone
There's just the ripples of gentle waves
At the breaking of this dawn!

Geraldine McMullan Doherty

Thorn

Thorn was a whippet just twelve months old
He had just started to do as he was told
On the journey home from a night in the pub
We were accosted by a group thirsting for blood
'Get it that will kill 'em,' one was heard to say
What they referred to I don't know to this day
When I resisted I was grabbed from the back
I was overpowered in my inebriate state
Breaking free I ran with an unsteady gait
Whistling and calling my faithful young hound
It let out a blood-curdling dying sound
A dog so young did not deserve to die
With a home and a warm fireside in which to lie
Only felons so heinous and cruel
With the inept actions of a drunken fool
If the truth were out about that night abroad
Thorn saved my life and deserved the Dicken bravery award

Francis Arthur Rawlinson

Fergus In The Snow

Disdainfully he pats the snow
And gingerly he treads,
Shaking the bright, faceted flakes
On frosty crocus heads.

His small, unbooted paws are chilled
And frozen is his tail.
His disapproval he declares
In every mournful wail.

He plunges through the pliant drifts,
Burrowing like a mole,
And what a transformation when
He dons an ermine stole!

He's quite bemused because this rain
Is creamy just like milk,
Tipped out from heavenly churns that pour
A topping smooth as silk.

He is bewildered by a world
Where paths are lost to sight,
Where boundaries have disappeared
Beneath a cloak of white.

No need to wear his hunting pink,
No sport for him today.
Dormice can sleep because they know
He'd never find the way.

Celia G Thomas

A Bit Like Life

Blossom falling off a tree
is a bit like life, you see.
First we grow, then we blossom,
each petal that falls is like a year
of our lives gone by.

But the tree doesn't worry
or complain and says, 'Stick
that petal back on again.'
It's dead.
Forgotten.
Why can't we be like that,
at the end of each year?
Just forget all the bad and
hurtful things that have happened,
and start again.
Life would be so much simpler
if we were like a tree, you see.

Julie Marie Francis

Christmas Virtues

Christmas morning had just dawned as the jury assembled to assess the year.
Lord Anger roared, 'From what I observed, mankind brought forth nothing but fear.'
'They do believe in fair treatment for all,' Master Justice brandished his sword and cried,
'I have watched them for centuries and their compassion cannot be denied.'

Mistress Pride sniffed haughtily, 'Compassion! Take off your blindfold and see.
For Man is arrogant and self-absorbed and their sins are obvious to me.'
Master Avarice vehemently concurred, 'Most have it all, but still demand more.
Insatiable; only desire holds their attention on this destructive path to war.'

'Please test me on their gluttony for I am a true expert on this matter.
The only factor that inspires them,' groaned General Greed, 'is how to get fatter!'
Lady Lust laughed long and low, her eyes radiant with passionate fire.
'My experience of them has left me curious; Man cannot control his desire.'

'I am jealous of your love of Man; I begrudge your waste of passion,'
Sobbed Master Envy, 'your continual adoration is becoming an obsession.'
Master Fortitude was fervent, 'Look at the determination shown in their lives.
They have endured much over the ages and mankind still survives.'

'An easy life with little effort,' Master Sloth yawned from where he lay.
'A 'give me now society' and 'I'll do it another day'.'
Madam Temperance raised a slender arm, 'Not all mankind are trite.
Most adhere to my call for moderation and restrain their appetite.'

Mistress Prudence agreed with her words, 'I believe their judgement is sound.
The mankind I know demonstrates common sense; your comments are ill-found.'
'The jury appears to be hung yet again,' roared Lord Anger, 'this cannot be,
Bring forward the last three jurors, the Mistresses Faith, Hope and Charity.'

Faith rose gently to her feet, her voice did not betray her fear.
'I judge them to be steadfast, the majority to be loyal and sincere.
My Lord you should spend time on Earth and walk within each nation.
Perhaps you would better understand their beliefs and motivation.'

Hope agreed, 'We have to trust that they have the ability to live in peace.
For if they do not, then mankind and their time on Earth, will cease.'
'Please Lord Anger and fellow jury members, your compassion is all I seek,'
Begged Charity, 'give them the opportunity to show that mankind is not weak.'

Silence until Lord Anger sighed, 'We have heard the words against and for.
Man must learn to cherish his world and vow to abide by our law.
Be respectful, value one another; seek forgiveness before it is too late.
Hear my words once more, mankind, else our judgement will seal your fate.'

Miss Withakay

Timeless Consternation

Here I lie in pensive thought, pond'ring lore to children taught -
That they won't be by evil caught, amidst the blackened midnight toll.
My son I scarcely had but told to think not what terror night might hold,
And head to slumber, brave and bold, to quell the fears within his soul . . .
Fears of untold, unseen things, nightmares to which my child's fear sings,
Legions from Hell and church-bell rings to warn of plagues upon us all.
In childlike bliss I ne'er have seen such morbid sights that plague Man's dreams,
Nor questioned if such truths should mean that e'ry sight that doth appall
Holds no sway outside my mind - such things, to think, seem awfully kind -
And further, what would I truly find were I to stray from out my door?
Would e'ery spook to haunt this shore, that chills men to the very core,
Then plague my thoughts for evermore as I confront these beasts of lore?
And so I lie in silent thought, questioning lore to children taught,
Terrified to soon be caught treading through the blackened halls.
And thus, with several seconds gone, my dressing gown I idly don -
'To prove a point,' my mind does con, as 'pon the door my shadow falls.
Then creeping forth with this brave dare, receiving soon a startling scare,
I ask in fright, 'Pray tell, who's there?' as from out the door I hear a moan.
And from my mind spring countless thoughts of godless ghouls and savage sorts;
Upon me such fear's freely wrought, and such woes so swiftly sewn.
Then comes a knocking, sharp and loud, and from my mind, a stirring crowd
Doth gather - numbering fierce and proud - within my dread fit to delight.
I hear again the knocking - louder still! - a tapped-out threat to maim and kill,
Expositions of the vilest will; Der Führer of the darkest night.
My heart within my chest does soar as comes then forth a mighty roar;
And I can do nought but implore; to beg that I not meet my doom.
And then, in fear, as lightning strikes - my son and I now both alike
In cowering quick from evil's Reich - the door swings forth into the room.
Swiftly then sweeps in my fear, and in my heart, a feeling queer.
No death nor doom comes even near, but ghoulish wailings still persist.
In peeking from behind a chair, myself exposed (a trifle bare),
I glance to find - and o', despair! - 'tis but my son with sleep 'a-missed'.

David Maidment

Relax

Leap years, light years and eclipses
Sound like creations of the gypsies
Dates, times, let's stop using all of these
Come and go as we please.

I tried it once as an excuse to skive
But I was quickly handed my P-45
Sat here now with nothing to do
Night or day I haven't a clue!

Samina Nazish

The Breeze

As the breeze ruffled up my hair
It went for the nearby trees
It swayed the grass on the ground
And then the twigs and the leaves

Playfully it swooped into the dale
I followed it all around
It quavered the pretty cherry tree
And the cherries till they broke down

The water on the lake
Was no more all smooth
It went on now darting
Something beneath it moved

The fish turned their faces
Out of the water and gazed
The breeze that went on dodging
The trout and geese as they played

The breeze now headed
Towards a nearby bush
It quaked all the branches
And then scooped into the woods

Lurking from tree to tree
Swaying and whistling
The breeze went on and on
While I followed it listening

Abeera Wali (17)

Iambic Arrest

Little by little at my homework I whittle
From dawn till the midnight hour.
I go on and on till my nerves are quite brittle
And my patience begins to turn sour.

I battle with triolet and trochee
Till I can't see the wood for the trees.
In despair I dance hokey-cokey,
Then my A4 takes off in the breeze.

In pursuit I trip over the milkman,
Finish up in a heap on the street.
'Hello, hello,' says a policeman,
'I've picked up your work on my beat

And reading it through, sort of quick,
Blushed with shame at the revelations.
So come along with me to the 'nick',
Cos they're obscene publications!'

Ed Hinsley

Napoleon's Secret

His fate was sealed by Wellington.
A prisoner on a distant isle,
He was dejected for a while,
And then he had a change of style.
Away from all the cares of state
And petty military hate,
Away from all the strains of war,
He found his happiness once more.

After the long Moscow retreat,
And Waterloo, the sad defeat,
The quiet life was one long treat,
And after all the stress and strife,
Now was the best time of his life.
He met a native on the shore,
A lovely girl of twenty-four.
A life of pleasure now he saw,
He now had happiness galore.

Historians were not aware
Of this romantic love affair,
Where all his other plans had failed,
This time alone success prevailed,
And history was not to know
A baby girl would steal the show.
This secret of Napoleon
Was hidden then from everyone.
The mistress of Napoleon,
She was the perfect paragon.

John Freeth

Untitled

As he ran down the street,
to escape what he wished he had not seen,
he felt all his weight rushing down to his feet.

He stopped to take a long hard look,
at all the pain and suffering he had left behind,
and all those things he had mistook.

He suddenly felt the urge to look up high,
and through all the dark clouds,
he could see the bluest sky.

There was hope for him yet,
he began to raise his arms and reach,
for a whole new world that he never met.

Rahela Begum

Santa's Beard

Santa's beard had grown this year, long and white and curly.
He combed it down and donned his hat on Christmas Eve quite early.
He packed the sleigh with toys for all as quick as he was able,
Kissed Mrs Santa, then he went for Rudolph from the stable.

Some time later Mrs Santa looked out of the window,
Stars were shining in the sky, the wind began to blow.
Then to her great surprise she saw Santa in a tangle,
Rudolph tossing his head in fright and all his bells a-jangle.

The wind had caught that curly beard, with Rudolph's reins entwined it,
No matter how he struggled then, no way could he unwind it.
Mrs Santa to the rescue came, with scissors sharp she hurried,
Cut that beard right off his chin; then to the sleigh he scurried.

Poor Santa looked an awful sight, but had no time to worry,
The sleigh soared upwards through the night. Dear Rudolph had to hurry.
Each stocking must be filled before the light of day was breaking.
They knew they must be home before the children started waking.

At length the task was finished and no one ever knew
How very funny Santa looked without the beard he grew.
He hid from sight all summer long, and now you know the reason,
He had to grow that long white beard before next Christmas season.

Barbara Dunning

Life In A Material World

L ook around and tell me what you see
I n this world that we live in, a world for you and me
F ocus if you can on the joy and the shame
E ach of us is given, the pleasure and the pain

I magine for a moment how it feels to be free
N ow think of what it could be like if you were just 'me'

A nd if you can just think beyond the wants you think you need

M aybe you can rise above and recognise the greed
A ffect the way you live your life by changing one small thing
T houghts - and the changes they can bring
E ach and every one of us can recognise our blame
R ealisation is all we need to start a tiny flame
I can see it in your heart, though you may not see it too
A nd I'm sure that if you stop and feel, your humanity will shine through
L ook around and tell me what you see

W hat changes can you make, changes for you and me?
O pen the door, we each hold a special key, where
R iches can be found, riches for you and me
L et your life become a chance to show what you can do
D on't allow materialism to overcome you too.

Sue Rogers

The USA And Us . . .

We live in the land of welly boots, the ones you call galoshes,
Morning and it's ham and eggs, to us it's plain old sausages.
We shop in the shopping precinct, the one that you call the mall,
In England it is autumn, the season you call the fall.
When I soak in my hot bath, the thing that you call a tub,
If you go for a drink in a bar, I'll be at the pub.
You drive a massive pickup truck, mine is a simple van,
When I need to use the loo, you're sitting on the can.
I pop out to the chip shop for some fish 'n' chips, whilst you have French fries,
I go out and see my mates, you visit with the guys.
Whilst I will have a chocolate bar, you'll be eating candy,
You may have an ice-cold beer, I'll stick to the shandy.
I work out in training shoes, the ones that you call sneakers,
You'll drink from a Thermos, I'll stick to flask and beakers.
Oh and what about where you park your car, the place you call garage?
Your chiefs of police are sheriffs, we have a nice ole sarge.
At school you went to junior high, we do good ole grammar,
We brush our teeth with Colgate gel, you have the Arm and Hammer.
So when you're next in Rodeo Drive looking at the clothing in posh shops,
I will be in Oxford Street perusing all the frocks.
If ever I go to Uncle Sam and ask for tea and buns,
I'd best beware 'cause you may come out with someone's pert, tight bum.
When I had my baby boy I put him in a nappy,
But diapers are the things to use on your dear little chappy.
At Christmas time we have Father Christmas, you have Santa Claus,
You go up and down the elevator, I take lifts to upper floors.
And then there's trousers you call pants, we call pants our knickers,
We used to have a Marathon bar until you changed it to sad old Snickers.
You put your money in a purse, to me it's called a bag,
And if I need a cigarette, I won't ask for a fag!
So this is where the poem ends and I shall say ta-ta,
So have a nice day my Yankee friend, good bye, farewell, au revoir!

Nikky Clay

The City

People are rushing from here to over there,
The city is now bustling; a single motion blur.
Hundreds of different people walk along the street,
They all must see each other, yet none of them meet.
This world is just so hectic; so little time to talk,
Along they plod, with their dreams, like drones, along they walk.
They all walk straight yet no one will collide,
Am I the only man who has to step aside?

A Wilkinson

Unholy Love Story

The young girl was flattered and courted
Their clandestine liaison illicit and wrong
In secret they cavorted and cuddled
Blinded by a love and desire so strong.

Before long the inevitable happened
A swollen belly the proclamation of shame
The debased monk returned to his monastery
Her furious parents demanded his name.

Worn down by threats and coercion
The girl was at last forced to confess
Her angry father ran to the monastery
To confront the miscreant, seeking redress.

Satisfaction was demanded and granted
A merciless beating before being cast out
The abbot deaf to the penitent monk's pleading
Warned his chances of Heaven were in doubt.

The girl's labour was agonisingly bloody
Unresponsive she looked at her son
Slowly her life force drained from her body
With a sigh her existence was over and done.

Buried hastily in the garden
The Church not wanting to know
Her restless spirit is now Earth-bound
Aimlessly wandering with nowhere to go.

Centuries later, aware of her presence
The householders muse on her fate
The tombstone's inscription withholding the story
Of Jane Jones, Aged 15, 1778.

Rose-Mary Gower

The Poets' Creed

I believe in my existence.
I'm the mistress of my own fate.
I believe in the beat of my drum.
I am the cause of my own mental state.
I believe I wield my own sword.
I am my own lady, and lord.
This pen is mine!
I am the writer!
I believe in me!
I am the maker!

Samantha Braum

Helpers

We each have an angel
I'm sure that you know.
Without them beside us
We never would grow.

They're there when we're good
And they're there when we're bad.
But when we defy them
They're ever so sad.

They stay there beside us
In good times, and sad,
And give us support
Even though we are bad.

No wings do they have
So their life's very hard.
And they don't get a day off
Cos days off are barred.

Angels tell us the right way
To speak and to think.
But we each go our own way
Even though we may sink.

There's no complaining
When we get it wrong,
Just stay there beside us
To make us feel strong.

They send us some help
In the guise of a friend,
You'd never believe
The people they send.

So be kind to your angel
For on them we depend,
Cos they're always beside us
Right to the end.

Joan May Wills

Giggle

Cups of coffee, cups of tea
Doesn't do a lot for me,
But after a few glasses of wine
Weee, giggle, hic, giggle, hic, I feel fine.

Richard Trowbridge

Desire

In the early summer days
Of a year that time forgot
Screams and cries and brilliant rays
Silence and darkness broke

And the rising brilliant sun
Ripped the night and unveiled
A heroic holy land
Where new life was being revealed

And the newborn in its cry
Brought around too much joy
But the stars upon the sky
Spoke the words that it would die

For the newborn had a twin
Death its name and with a face
That with eyes cannot be seen
And it wouldn't act for days

And for weeks, for months and years
This new life would grow and seek
Answers to its questions, remedy for all its fears
Pain and joy would alternate, day by day, week by week

And in this life one would find
Satisfaction and needs, nightmares as well as dreams
Appetites for soul and mind
Challenges to give you smiles or screams

And with hunger comes a feast
And with pleasure comes a need
And with angel comes a beast
Appetites that you should feed

But most vicious of all games
Pretty maidens, warm as fire
And every time they'd say their names
All you'd hear is the word desire

And the ones you thought were angels
The ones for which you hide a fire
Will remain forever strangers
As they share the name Desire

And with hunger comes a feast
And with pleasure comes a need
And with angel comes a beast
Appetites that you should feed

Till one day the twin would show
Uninvited but expected
In the form of dove or crow
And your birth with him connected

And he'd ask you about your life
Pose a question about your past
If the scales you weigh your life
Show for him your hate or lust

On that moment and that land
Time and Earth don't know yet
Dark and silence will return
Laugh and cry will reach the end

Spiros Kitsinelis

The Bully

You're ever so demanding,
you drain me to the max.
If you don't believe me,
let's go over all the facts.

If ever I want to help myself,
you're always close at hand.
Think, you brute, you're not so cute,
you give me hell like a swollen gland.

I never have a penny in my hand,
it goes straight from mc to you.
Whenever I decide to get my pay,
you're there again, always right on cue.

I want to have some friendship,
invite my friends around for tea.
Once they know you're on the scene,
you've even seen them flee.

I always like to dress up nice,
lovely, clean and tidy.
I turn around, you're there again,
glaring, very snidy.

Whenever I try to better myself,
you always pull me down.
I'm your wife, I've got a life,
so please, stop pulling me down.

You're just a nasty bully,
you treat me ever so bad.
Why don't you treat me equal,
and make me ever so glad.

Joe Smith

Island Of Mine

Reach to an island
within the fringes
of time,

bathe in coconut
oil, sea salt
and lime.

Sing with a guitar
to the stars of
the night,

sleep in a hammock
until the early
light.

Make a house up
a palm tree,
fish and dive for
oysters in the sea.

Season, after season,
of endless sunshine,
it's in my dreams that
island of mine.

Francis Page

Free ...

Let me be
So safe and free
Let me sail
Amidst a calm blue sea

Free from lies and hypocrisy
Is there anyone here
Who understands me
Who yearns also to be free?

To fly like a bird
And hum like a bee

A chance at last may
Come my way
Freedom, happiness
All in one day

Donna Hardie

As We Were

Red penny stamps,
No meter clamps,
And Sunday schools
Taught moral rules.

No sloppy dress,
No roadside mess,
Our wholesome food
Tasted so good.

No indoor screen,
No sordid scene
Of scanty clothes -
Or crooked toes.

No fast food shop -
The village cop
Who wore a beard
Was greatly feared.

No shaped tea bags,
Cheap Woodbine fags,
Men still wore smocks
When tending their flocks.

No probing space -
Much slower pace,
Roads full of bumps,
Few petrol pumps.

The village shops
Held useful stocks
Of sugar and spice
And all things nice!

Street lights were gas
In cone-shaped glass,
Lit by a pole
Pushed through a hole.

Kathleen C White

Luck

I stood beside a fallen tree
'Twas my lucky day, it had just missed me
With arms raised high I cheered my luck
That's when the bloody lightning struck

Steve Thompson

Into A Bar - Whitby

Into a bar - Whitby;
Out of the rain;
Looking at old photographs of women
Gutting herring;
And mussels being weighed on the docks;
And old men in smocks;
And merchants setting the grade
And the sound of gulls circling and screaming
Where the fish are displayed;
At so much a box.

Into a bar - Whitby;
Where weathered cliffs find the sea;
And on the point a lighthouse beams -
And a full moon waxes free;
Sending a strange light across the waves;
Pulling white horses on to the shore
Like thunder on to the near black cliffs;
And the taste of sea spray by the ocean door;
And the feel of snow in your face
Blowing sideward in the gale.

Into a bar - Whitby;
After out on the wall;
Where a lighthouse beams far out
And boats come in with the swell
Making for the dock;
There tall masts silhouette a wet, red sky;
And the horizon looks greenish-jade;
And the ocean looks dark silver lead,
Like a huge molten cauldron;
And above the sea the light of a blue star . . .

Into a bar - Whitby;
Where cormorants beat the waves;
And grebes surface nearby;
And a square rigger whistles in the wind;
And on the slopes the shadows
Move round the cove;
And the tiny lit-up cottages - Baltic style
Slowly changing colour in the soft mellow light;
And the smell of fish and chips nearby.

T Ritchie

I Am

I'm the one that called out your name
You turned your back on me
This is the place; my greatest shame
Where I don't want to be
You pushed me deeper

Where is the one that called out your name?
Nowhere to be seen
Recently she hasn't looked the same
The young troubled teen

Here is the one that called out your name
Lying on the floor
You see now how you are to blame
You could have done much more

I see the one that called out your name
In nightmares, so obscene
I see the one that couldn't last
The one wrenched violently into the past
You pushed her deeper

I see the guilt that lies in your face
The one you tried to hide
The feelings you refuse to place
The ones that know you lied

Samantha Horton

My Child

I close my eyes, and search my mind,
For something I don't understand,
It's as if I have left something behind,
Now I'm searching for salt through sand.

Mother Nature has led her course,
And took me this long, weary path,
I tried to fight with all my force,
But now, my past is past.

As I looked on, I couldn't see stars,
Or the roses I thought there should be,
All I could see were my darkened scars,
And they may always shadow me.

Then a child I brought into my world,
And now this is what I see,
Sunshine, stars and an endless path,
My daughter gave this to me.

M Rae

Work Out

Come on girl, new year, new start.
Get on that treadmill, it's good for your heart.
Take the plunge, get it done,
run five miles - just for fun.
At three quid a time, you can go - if you like,
and do some aerobics or pedal a bike,
down at the centre where the 'slimmies' all go,
parading in skimpies, it's all just for show!
Miss Perfect is there, all titters and frills,
and young Mr Muscles who works on the tills,
biceps all bulging, a chest full of hair -
poor Polly, the cleaner, can't help but stare.
Some go twice weekly and know all the ropes,
the rest just sit laughing, discussing the soaps.
If you don't fancy that, why not visit the pool,
where the newcomers sink, but try to look cool?
Cos instead of on swimming, their minds are elsewhere,
eavesdropping and learning of someone's affair!
Or just stay at home in front of TV,
and jiggle about with that new DVD,
the one by that young, well-known, fit singer -
who makes you feel like you might just be a dead ringer
for ET dressed in tights or a hippo's rear end,
oh and don't let cholesterol become your best friend!
'Too much excitement,' I'm hearing you say,
well, give me a call and I'm on my way.
I'll pick up the choccies and wine from the shop,
we'll keep fit next week and work out till we drop!

J Mitchell

Abandoned

I stroll along the cobbled streets alone,
Blistering feet, no shoes to wear - all outgrown,
Heavy rain pounding against my sensitive skin,
No warmth of clothing to keep me protected from within,
Feeling abandoned like a sinking ship,
Life being swallowed up by the sea's grip,
The love within my heart going to waste,
Leaving behind but an empty trace,
Yearn, how I yearn to be fulfilled,
Instead of feeling like I've been killed,
How wicked is life to strip happiness from the soul,
Never to achieve any one goal,
I continue to live in this empty world,
Abandoned, yet existing, hoping one day again to be held.

Julie Willis

Adam

Your journey has just begun
The course of life it must run
From a child you always had a wanderlust
To go with your heart and instincts you must trust.

I have watched you grow from child to man
I have tried to give you honesty, integrity, as much as I can
You have always filled me with pride
Even before when my emotions I did hide.

So do not be like me
Just say what you see
Sometimes you have to be hard to be kind
Think with your heart and mind.

I hope you find your true love
With a little help from above
Then the journey will be complete
With a loved one, and family running round your feet.

Adam, words are sometimes hard to say,
So all I can do is write and say, 'I love you, this is my way.'

Dad Garry

Garry Bedford

Life ... What?

To where am I heading, I do not know,
The feelings I'm feeling I want to show.
To feel how I'm feeling, you need to see,
The things that matter most to me.

To understand my weird speech,
My weird words I will need to teach.
My life is simple, but so complex,
The reason for this is not just sex,
The girls I meet are funny and fine,
But when it matters, they're a waste of time!

To see what I mean, and how I feel,
You need to know such a great deal.
When you know most of it all,
Look me up, give me a call.

To me you can speak and tell me why,
I'm so frustrated and want to cry,
The only reason it's worth the stress,
Is because it's *my life*, no more, no less.

Kevin Mytton (16)

Thank You

thank you true
my lifelong love
for the care you give
as each hour we live

the days have passed
into years
I will treasure you
my love forever

your work-worn hands
and your greying hair
those thoughtful moments
for us to share

to give and take
to love and care
to trust each other
cherished and blessed

we have lived our lives
through each other's eyes
the time has come to realise
love has a heart
tender and true
an abundance of love
to last with you

Margery Rayson

Yesterdays' Heroes

Yesterdays' heroes
Never to be forgotten
Distant vivid memories
Of many a victory gotten

Yesterdays' heroes
Oh so many of them
Everyday women
Everyday men

Yesterdays' heroes
Not one died in vain
Remembered for always
Etched on the brain

Yesterdays' heroes
To them I write this poem
For all of the heroes
Who never came home

Greeny

Untitled
(For Matthew with love)

Blackbird bathed and quenched her thirst
Always at the table first
When Robin followed Chaffinch came
Even Wren joined in the game
Until one day we put out nuts
The birds stood back and said, 'Tut, tut
Who is this stranger sat aloft?
All the nuts have now been scoffed!'

Cheeky Charlie named was he
This squirrel coming round for tea
Feeding morning, noon and night
His fluffy tail a familiar sight
Used as a brolly in the rain
To keep him dry while munching again

A lady squirrel soon appeared
Smaller, redder, pointy-eared
They set about burying nuts
Just in case the larder shut
With no need to find them all
Until the silence of snowfall

A busy winter to and fro
Telltale footprints in the snow
Across the lawn to flower pots
Their gathering just never stopped
When springtime came we were to find
Three more strangers of their kind
These were small, oh could it be?
Charlie raised a family

Deborah Hall

The Power Within

Dig deep within your brain,
Who knows what you will find.
You might surprise yourself,
Discover you have a mind
For there within the mystery,
Of who and what, you are,
You can make a better place,
Or just prop up the bar.
Power must be harnessed,
They call it self-control.
You can wreck it with drink and drugs,
Or aim for a higher goal.

J Hagen

Fight For Freedom

I heard sweet Highland music drift across the glens
from a lonely Highland piper, who from the hills appeared and then
the mist it slowly rose up from the heather on the ground
and the skies were brightly lit up by an old familiar sound
of bagpipes and drummers marching homewards from the war,
once more victorious, although pools of blood I saw,
with faces, they were grieving for brothers, sons and friends,
and for those who had fought for freedom until the bitter end.
Their eyes were fixed like bayonets, they were stained and smeared with death,
bellies were full of hunger, but there was no time to rest,
as the enemy had gathered, regrouped with new-laid plans
to regain the advantage that was taken from their hands,
by those men in kilts and tartans whose allegiance to the cause
could not be broken by the mighty English swords
or the longbows that were aimed and fired to foil these fearless men
who were led by the Highland piper through the mist-enshrouded glen,
where the battle roared and English sword may have won favour for a while,
but there was no calculation in their plans that Scottish guile
would foil and thrice outwit them, as they stood and faced defeat,
they had no other option but to turn and then retreat
back to the Lowlands; to the homelands that they knew,
to rethink how those bagpipes and their tunes could be subdued.
To live and breathe, to never leave, from the cradle to the grave,
to breed a strength of character that still today is on parade,
as if a mighty peacock as it spreads its coloured tail,
the Scotsman's fight for freedom will never be derailed.
It will always be a part of life in times of war or peace,
it will be written as the epilogue when life on Earth has ceased.
When bricks and stone are all that are left, when oxygen has gone,
the eerie sound of the bagpipes will forever linger on . . .

Alan Glendinning

The Meaning Of A Single Red Rose

A red rose my love, one that I purchased for you today
Caught a thorn on my nose, turned my whole world grey
One single rose is special, has more meaning than three
But this one has spoiled our date as you'll surely agree
A plaster on my nose and a bandage about my hand
It's not funny my love, yet I know you'll understand
Cutting the plaster, the scissors slipped across my palm
Cutting at my vein, hence, also the sling now on my arm
Getting up to phone for an ambulance, my love this is true
I slipped upon that rose love, my leg's in plaster, broken too
One single rose may well have more meaning than three
I think this maybe now shows that you're bad luck for me!

C R Slater

A Nervous Breakdown

After years and years of stress and anxiety
I'm from now on number one priority
I remember those times, deaf, dumb and mute
I sat in the chair as bold as a coot

I would never go out or open the door
Just lie in bed with the curtains drawn
Day after day, sit in the same old room
Look out of the window at the flowers in bloom

Often watch the cars pass me by
With my head in the clouds way up in the sky
Caught in a daydream, in some sort of trance
No real regrets, I was never given a chance

A person with no confidence, low self-esteem
When I was a small boy I used to have dreams
I feel like a misfit, like a child neglected
Left out in the cold totally dejected

I think about the years, of verbal and physical abuse
I sit in this chair now a recluse
Years and years of mental torture
Day after day, continually being slaughtered

I've suffered for long enough, once too often
It seems I am left with two different options
Once upon a time, I would curl and die
I realise now you have to fight to survive.

Andrew Nokes

Darren
(A special gift)

When I think of you, my heart still feels the pain,
My only consolation, that your life was not in vain,
I wonder how you'd look, if you grew into a man,
Time it does not heal, however long the span,
To me the time stands still, always you will be,
My child so cruelly taken, from sight away from me,
The hardest thing of all was to say my last goodbye,
Remove the tubes, switch off machines, break the final ties,
My precious little angel, how could you leave so soon,
The hardest thing I've ever done to leave you in the room,
Your eyes to give to someone else, a precious gift of sight,
Organs all to strangers, to forever shine your light,
I never will forget you, my heart still torn in two,
To wrap my arms around you, hold onto only you.

Winifred Curran

Tired Of Waiting . . .

When you smile, I smile,
When you laugh, I laugh too,
When you're upset I want to hold you,
When you're not with me I miss you.

I think of my life without you there,
The things I could achieve and do,
But all the highs and all the lows would be more exciting shared with you.

I'm not a poem person; the words are usually hard to find,
With you it all flows easily, as you are always on my mind.
Your every action, every move is leading me to say,
The reason for my poetry . . .
I love you in every way.

It's hard to watch you pass me by, unable to make you see,
I feel as if it's a waiting game, waiting for you to accept me.
When all I want is to be loved like crazy, for someone to be so sure,
To wake up happy every day, not running for the door.

A life with someone you love so much, in the knowledge it will last forever,
A feeling of complete content and excitement for the future.

But . . .
In your mind you're still debating . . .
Between the two of us . . .
I fold, I lose, I'll never win . . . I can't wait around for your rating!

I think you put a percentage on just how sure you were,
50 for her, 50 for me, well she's welcome . . . I'm worth more.

Gemma Townsend

Prison Cell

In the eerie silence of my grim, darkened cell
My mind is a fermenting emotional hell
With visions of my kids crying out for their dad
It tears at my heart and makes me feel sad
I have so many thoughts that run through my head
That they make me so weary and so full of dread
When I close my eyes, they are in my thoughts
When open in the morning, my stomach it's in knots
I cannot control all this emotional pain
As it continues to create so much untold strain
With all my resistance becoming so poor
How much more pain do I have to endure?
I'm forever hanging on by a fingertip
Cos I know should I fall that my head will dip
I put on a front and I hide it so well
All those peering eyes, they can never tell.

Steven Wilson

Mind And Emotions

That dreaded morning feeling, you wake and it's still there
The churning in your stomach, you feel the mind despair
Even though you're trying - yes trying really hard
You wish you had the answer, that it was written on a card

Depression is an illness, something we cannot see
No one understands - it's only happening to me
Believe me, it can heal, like a broken toe
A light is through that tunnel, one day you'll see it glow

Take the time to 'think a bit', is it really this bad?
To yourself be positive, these feelings before you've had
Never say 'I cannot' - start saying 'I can, I can'
Think *it's just a little problem*, make yourself a plan

I know you feel it's difficult for you to occupy your mind
You believe it's out of the question, but something you can find
Never try to fight it - let it come, then let it go
Relax a little when you can, the benefits will show

That mountain you see, you feel you cannot climb
Will slowly get easy - if you do a little at a time
A few steps a day is all you need to make
Does it matter how long it really does take?

Accept it's only 'feelings' sensitised beyond compare
One day you will realise, that is all that was there
Never underestimate the strength we all can find
For there is nothing more complicated, than the 'human mind'

Veronica Buckby

The Most Important Love Of All

Love yourself each and every cell, please love yourself today,
Nurture and care for yourself as this is your healing way.
Only by respecting and realising your inner sacred light,
Can you find total peace in your long and dark night.

Cherish the spirit inside, truly God loves you as you are,
He values you unconditionally, His brilliant shining star.
As we travel life's journey our hearts may break in two,
But He will always be there to lift our spirit and renow.

Love yourself as you love those closest to your heart,
Then you will be centred, calm and whole, never come apart.
So I pray you find spirit and treasure it within forever,
There is nothing more important as we sail life's turbulent river.

Marlene Mullen

The Fat Ballerina

Our Marilyn was born to dance,
From an early age she would skip and prance.
She twirled around so gracefully
And her pas de deux was a joy to see.

Then there came that dreadful day
When cream cake and chocolates came her way.
As the years rolled by poor Marilyn
Grew older, heavier and far from thin.

With waning ambition and not so wise,
Marilyn grew to enormous size.
Her frilly tutu was far too tight
As she strained into it with all her might.

To find a partner was proving hard
And in Swan Lake her performance was marred,
Her dying swan looked all forlorn,
Like a dying duck in a thunderstorm.

So alas, poor Marilyn had to retire
And leave the ballet complete with spare tyre.

P Anderson

First Aid

The dog was barking in the yard
When I went to knock on your door
No one answered, so I went to the window
Looked in, and saw you on the floor
Luckily the window was open
So I climbed in and came over to you
But as I knelt down on the floor
I saw that you were blue
After dialling for the paramedics
I didn't know what else to do
So I just prayed and held your hand
And thought I wasn't much help to you
They came and put you in an ambulance
And with speed drove you away
I watched you go, but couldn't remember
What made me call on you that day
You are well and back home again
And have thanked me for the call I made
But here's something I forgot to tell you
I'm going to learn first aid

Diana Daley

Lord, Make Me

Lord, make me beautiful
But not in body or face
Make me ugly, Lord
Make my beauty into grace

Take it all, Lord
Make my spirit radiate with hope
Make my soul glow with peace

Lord, make me wealthy
Make me rich beyond all measure
Make me affluent in mercy
Let forgiveness be my treasure

Please Lord, make me smart
Give me intelligence beyond compare
But not in science, not in sums
Please deny me business sense

Take away my witty comments
Make me say the most stupid things
But Lord, when someone is hurting
Give me the wisdom to know what to say

Take away my strength, take away my courage
Take my power and my worth
Take everything, Lord
Please just let me love.

Lesley Tuck

Who's Old?

Elderly? Me?
No, not I
Can't you see?
Not a day over . . .
Oh, dear me!

I'm still a young thing
Though like an old comfy sofa
My body has lost its spring
The spirit is yet young
It has a sparkle and a zing

So, elderly?
You can't mean me
Old is not in my vocabulary

Teejay

The Solitary Dreamer

Everyone gone from around him
His world between these walls
Solitary dreams, living life on a whim
No one is here to heed his calls

Inside the doors locked away
Terraced house he once called home
Behind the windows dusty grey
Here he sits, he lies alone

He hides the wounds upon his wrists
He hides the anger behind his fists
Which are embedded in his head
Crazy thoughts, wishing he was dead

Inside the doors locked away
Terraced house he once called home
Behind the windows dusty grey
Here he sits, he lies alone

Out in the world, manic, humour, extreme
Bosses criticise his every move
Others just see him as just being mean
Sorry the word he can only say to disprove

So inside the doors locked away
The terraced house he still calls home
Cleaned the windows, no more dusty grey
Yet still he sits, he lies alone . . .

Richard Marshall-Lanes

The Snow Globe

Sometimes I wish I could get inside
Another world, a place to hide.
Somewhere protected that cannot be touched
No noise, no pollution, no dirt, no dust.

Nobody enters and nobody leaves
A world built entirely for you and me.
It never rains, there is never a storm
We never feel cold, it is never too warm.

Sometimes we get shaken or turned on our head
But here that's no disaster, it's magical instead.
This is when the snow falls down
It flurries around us, then settles on the ground.

We are just two people standing together
Undisturbed, alone forever.
Living inside a bubble of dreams . . .
Until it gets smashed into smithereens.

Hannah Kate Willcock

Bats' Bow'r

Lo, how the dreadul vault unfolds
Dark, sinist'r and hung with cobwebs old,
A crest'd crypt of mournful stone
An altar o'er which sighs are thrown;

Yet, slumb'ring lie the bats in bow'rs
Awaiting patiently their sunset hours,
Until the porches of the night
Hail tiny hearts and wings to flight;

Thence, quiet'r than the sheet'd ghost
Departs the velvet-wing'd host,
Out happy 'neath the mystic moon
Exultant in the silver'd gloom;

Conscious as the wanton air
With owl they shall the silver share,
Round tree, through gard'n to curtain bright
Only the shrewdest eye may glimpse their flight;

Yet, their sweetest song defies our ear
As their intentions court both myth and fear,
They, the children of the night
Yield no concern for shock or fright;

As night declines the hour shows
The blushing flush of dawn's first glow,
The silver'd moon again retires
And with it too the bats to bow'rs.

M Sam Dixon

Friend

Walk with me friend, through the forest and glen
As we contemplate theories, discuss now and then,

Talk about the beginning, the end and the middle,
The greatest of stories, the poem and riddle.

We will cover the planet, our thoughts and our feelings,
And all that surrounds us, it's place and their meanings,

We can talk about anything, at any cost,
The hardships we've faced, the things that we've lost

And as we grow older, I still need times when,
I need to talk through with you theories again.

So walk with me friend, through the forest and glen,
And we'll once again speak of the now and the then.

Cheryl Nicholls

Time

Time swirls turbulently around me;
Harshly he ticks away.
And I am still left wanting
Identical to the story of yesterday.

My mind is surely not shameful
My thoughts clearly not weak
But the mask remains on my face
And these words are not yet in print.

Courage shines sometimes upon me
Perhaps it is actually my fears.
Brave to let people enter my heart
Afraid of my hidden tears.

Clock, soul and body tell me he's drifting far
The jury is coming out
And I am the one on trial.
Time is my ultimate enemy
That I am unable to destroy.
My task is to beat his fast hands
And begin my long journey to the confident lands.

Dawn Joyce

Love Tonic

Is love a tonic?
Then how does it taste?
Could be

Like gin maybe
Or just Jack D
Or just Coke

Mmm let's see
How would you want it?
With ice and lemon?

Don't be absurd
Of course no lemon
It leaves a bitter taste

In your mouth
You want it sweet
Not shaken or stirred

Just still and cool
With some added heat
As you taste it so sweet

Danny Harrison

Words

What can I say
what words will you heed?
Of news to you given
not good words indeed
Words I should impart
although you know
that somehow my words
won't easily flow
I feel your pain
but words cannot tell
I feel the stress
of your personal hell
I think of the words
they don't come out right
Can I put into words
your biggest fight?
Perhaps words are a folly
a need for them not there
Perhaps thoughts
are the things to share
I give you my thoughts
use them as you will
I give you my dreams
my hopes for you still
I counsel my fears
never to be laid bare
I give you no words
but you know I care

Pat Brown

Food For Thought

A graduate's first line in business chat,
Is 'Sir, do you want fries with that?'

Out in the real world, in the raw,
Not always doing what they have studied for.

Their career has gone as far
As the well-known local burger bar.

They have shed a private tear,
At this enforced catering career.

At least this enterprising girl or chap,
Can avoid a year called 'Gap'.

Look around your town, this may seem crude,
But where there is money, there is food.

Trevor Napper

The Things We Meant To Do

We meant to put our faith in God, we promised to go straight,
We trust You will forgive us, but perhaps it is too late,
So we could go through life again, oh Lord we'd promise You,
That we would do all those things, those things we meant to do.

We meant to help 'The Down and Outs',
Good intentions went astray,
We just went by 'The Other Side',
Put kind thoughts 'Out The Way'.

We meant to help those in 'Distress',
Folk who were 'Out of luck',
But things for us were going right,
So somehow we got stuck.

We meant to help 'The Coloured Folk',
But where would we begin?
Their hearts are just the same as ours,
They cannot help their skin.

We meant to help 'The Beggar Man',
With his heavy load,
Good intentions did not help,
We passed him on the road.

Oh Lord, You've waited long enough,
Our prayers have been so few,
If it's Your will please help us,
Do 'The Things We Meant To Do'.

Jimmy Sinclair

So - What Now?

So you think that you are old now
That your life is spent, gone by
So you spend your time in dreaming
All you do is sit and sigh
Tho' the people all around you
Pass by on the other side
And to ask for small attentions
Is so hard it hurts your pride
At one time you needed no one
No one's help, you walked alone
Now each hour, so quickly passes
As each day, you call your own -
You're not old, you're just maturing
Now you're senior - now you're free
You've got years until you're wrinkly
And Jurassic - just like me!

Joan Winwood

Balancing Act

Across the ether spider fingers dance
A query ventured, a message sent
A rustle, a crunch, a sidelong glance
A journal is open, waiting

A galleon is spied, and becomes the past
Four eyes stare through rounded globe
She drums her fingers, they corner the mast
She sits there, singing

As daylight bleeds she tries once more
A balancing act with endless toil
A once joyful game that turns to chore
They hear the splash, calling

When shadows win she turns and sighs
They peek from hull and tattered line
A chair pushed back, she starts to rise
Today declines, belated

In early hours a gasp of breath
Sheets pulled back and feet on rug
To face the foe in dance of death
Two guardian angels, praying

The final step, the final push
To equilibrium and success
Holding back she dare not rush
Airless mouths cry, willing

And suddenly she knows she's won
Last piece in place it gently rocks
She smiles at last, salutes the sun
They spin and roll, applauding

John Knowles

My Harp

I never thought there would come a day
When I would sit and learn to play
My harp, an instrument of my dreams
It looks so elegant and so it seems
My dream has now at last come true
My harp I own and play I do.

This special instrument, my heart's desire
Can kindle a flame to spark a fire
God's greatest gift was heaven-sent
The love for my harp was truly meant.

Susan Bamford

My Mother-In-Law

I'll tell you a story, sad but true,
Of a father, mother and children two;
These were a baby and a girl of eight,
When a tragic accident sealed their fate.

They lived in a cottage; father was employed
In a boilerhouse, a situation all enjoyed.
They took Dad's tea daily, but one day while there
The boiler burst, scalding fat flew everywhere.

The baby was scalded and died that awful day;
Her dad, who'd taken the brunt, also passed away.
Mother and daughter were scalded to a lesser degree;
The plant owner, though burned, made a good recovery.

This was years ago, no chance of compensation;
The survivors, very traumatised, got little consideration,
Though court officials gave the widow their fees,
These wouldn't amount to much, consciences to appease.

That little girl became my mother-in-law,
The kindest lady that you ever saw.
Despite everything she lived to seventy-five.
I thank God that she came into my life.

Marlene Allen

Execution

I see him always up and down
Scrounging about for bits of bite
Or slouching about in this bustling town
Not one of those who spoil for a fight.

Now I see him dart like a mouse
Pursued by mob with stick and knife
He's pilfered some fellow's food from house
So they have to snuff out his life.

The boy blindly bounds for a nearby cop
Who turns his face and quickens pace
Cop sees no need to make them stop
He affords them space to finish the race.

The waif sees me and fast he flies
His hands outstretched for help to draw
A piteous appeal in his feral eyes
The drowning youth is clutching at straw.

Not wishing to be a spoilsport - no!
I draw my knife and end the show.

Sospeter Mwakio Shake

Centre Of Arrogance

I'll build a Centre of Excellence around my vision,
I'll act very fast while others are in decision.

I'll talk loud about all the wonderful things I've done,
That put me ahead of all men, the new king of the sun.

I'll trample on those who get in my way,
Those cleverer than me I'll disdainfully disarray.

We had the Centre of Competence but that was just for good talk,
It's excellence that I promise, I'll make the politicians balk.

I've promised the cure for death, and the elixir of life too,
And with my vision, I can conjure up fallen angels anew.

Just put the money in that box over there,
Royal honours and medals too, I'll take all you can spare.

How can you call me the greatest conman of all time?
For what I promise you, all that I want should be mine.

I even sold God His immortality for a price,
Tell me what you want, if you learn to be nice.

For what I offer, can you afford to take a chance?
Think of all you can lose if you choose not to dance!

For what bigger stake is there if I promise all?
Dare you doubt? For all that you dream might fall.

Alan Bruce Thompson

You Minus Me Equals Blue

Take away the sky above, there's nowhere for clouds to roam
Take away the earth and trees and birds would have no home
Everything has a reason, an equation that is true
And you - minus me - equals blue.

The hour needs a minute, the willow needs to cry
A question needs an answer and that's the reason why
We need to be together, one becoming two
And you - minus me - equals blue.

Blue is never being free, it's a heart that feels no pound
A concert without sound, a watch that's never wound
A ship that's run aground
Blue is surely the result of never having you around
Love that's lost not found.

Winter works with red and white like berries in the snow
Summer is an artist's dream, with her colours all on show
And autumn would be bleak and strange without her leaves to view
And you - minus me - equals blue.

John Alan Davies

Living

Have you sailed a tropic sea
a sea like molten glass
rippling softly in the wind
as the waves so softly pass?
Or have you seen the albatross
living its life on high
wheeling, riding the heavenly winds
in his kingdom in the sky?
Have you been in the eyes of a ship
watching the dolphins at play
leaving a web of creamy wakes
to show the ship its way?
Have you seen the flying fish
gliding on shimmering wing
bouncing along from wave to wave
a truly wondrous thing?
And have you seen the giant ray
leap, reaching for the sky
leaving a rainbow in the spray
as it goes drifting by?
Have you seen the thunderhead clouds
build up in banks of grey
like a devil in evil shrouds
sweeping the clouds away;
whipping the placid, dozing sea
to great walls of raging foam
racing to envelop all before
in a tumbling, watery tomb?
But then the violence of the storm
gradually fades away
then comes the silence of the night
at the end of the threatening day.
Then again you sail a calming sea
marvelling at the sight
of the gently swaying mastheads dance
'gainst the moon's soft, shining light.
And in the sparkling spangle of the Milky Way
in the darkness of the night . . .
If these things you have never seen
or these things you deny
then; my friend you have not lived
and life has passed you by.

Jerry Judge

Egypt In Twilight

They'll flock round you from every side,
no matter where you stand.
And with fake goods try to divide,
your cash and closed hand.

If you want Nefertiti's bust,
but at a price that's fair.
Rejecting their first bid's a must,
try half price if you dare.

And when one makes a firm approach,
remember to stay calm.
You'll never wear that scarab broach,
that's sitting on their palm.

Some think them sly and wonder how,
they even sleep at night.
It's just their way of coping now,
for Egypt's in twilight.

Its wealth and gold's all lost in time,
the power's almost spent.
Relying now on foreign dime,
with which to pay the rent.

The last ditch change to raise some cash,
by every man and boy.
Is hawk a trade with tongues that lash,
the grave's for those too coy.

So spare a thought and go one day,
to this dry land of awe.
By going there on holiday,
you'll also help the poor.

Dickon Springate

House Of Roses

There is a house of roses
Deep in the sunflower wood
Where sunbeams live and play
As little sunbeams should.

Sometimes sunbeams leave the wood
And return when it's dark outside.
It's never dark in the sunflower wood,
There's no dark place to hide.

The house of roses always shines
In the sunflower wood of light
And all the sunbeams live there
When the world is full of night.

George Coombs

Bed

(Dedicated to Pat)

'Do you misuse your bed?'
That's right, you've heard what I said.
Let me explain: lest you refrain,
wondering, what exactly my game!

Would you serve dinner - on bed
Play cards, feed the pets; that's not cred.
So let me divulge what's on my mind,
not wishing to be cruel but - rather, kind.

A bed is made - the length that it is,
to lie prone, outstretched and at ease.
For years it's evolved, got better than old,
and now it is there to please,

to 'please', for the purpose of *sleep!*
Certainly no place to eat,
but over the years - I certainly fear,
misuse, has become a false 'treat'.

What more, the true use of our beds,
(other than when we are dead!)
Sex is the name, and this is no shame;
no matter what else may be said.

Illness, confines us to bed,
in home, hospital; most dread.
But the greatest 'sin', I profess,
is those who *read* - in their beds!

Peter Mahoney

Manners Of A Louse

A slippery snake
Slides along the ground
Goes into a hole that he has found
But in the hole's a little mouse
Who tells the snake, 'Get *out* my house'
The slippery snake is none too happy
In fact becomes a little snappy
'Where are your manners?' he asks the mouse
'You have the manners of a louse'
'Manners?' said the little mouse
'It's *you* who slid into *my* house
I did *not* invite you that's for sure'
At this the snake opened wide his jaw
And gobbled up the little mouse
Who had the manners of a louse.

Trudy Simpson

Magick

Magick spelt with a k, is deeper than most
Some might say

Than pulling a rabbit out a hat
Vanishing silks, then saying 'Howzat!'

Magick goes deeper and flows through souls
Magick is practised outside of shows
And spectacles cheapen magick's power
And magick changes from hour to hour

For every moment a new soul's born
Wiccans grow strong with every one
The balance is fixed from those who die
Eternal souls allowed to fly

For some are punished and some are blessed
Yet some remain trapped, distressed
These pull the Wiccan deeper still
And some believe can cure the ill

A conjuror has no real power
His charm will last at most an hour
His flock dispersed into the night
Reality's slave by morning's light.

Andrew Blundell

E621

Meaty flavour enhancer that makes you want more.
Only now, in the twenty-first century, it's used like never before.
Never-ending lists, of the processed food we buy.
One to make food tastier, the manufacturers cry.
Some foods contain it naturally, others are produced by Man.
On the labelling it will say what's used in any can.
Devastating disorders are linked, southern scientists claim.
It's not true, western science says this substance is not to blame.
Until it's proven safe, should it be used at all?
Mental health, will it get better, if our use begins to fall?
Great research should be taken, until it's proved who's right.
Let's campaign to stop its use, it is a credible fight.
Understand the natural stuff, is different from the industrial sort.
These are the facts, Australia and New Zealand are taught.
Alleged reports of its safety, flawed and possibly untrue.
Make an informed decision, it's something you must do.
Avoid anxiety, schizophrenia, Alzheimer's and depression.
This neurotoxin kills brain cells, its use we should now lessen.
Everyone deserves a healthier life!

Annette Smith

Reborn

Ted, my husband, died a year ago, almost to the day,
He was killed in a huge crash on the motorway.
The day he was killed, I remember well,
The police called and rang my front doorbell.

When I opened the door and saw the officer, I felt unwell,
Instinctively I knew the terrible news this messenger had to tell.
I invited her in, felt sick, fearing what she was going to say,
She told me of a pile-up on the M25 motorway.

Sixteen slain including my beloved Ted,
No more will he be returning to our homestead.
It was after the funeral I really felt alone,
To me our house suddenly became a cold and empty home.

The nights to me never seemed to end,
His warmth, his love, his caresses, never again will he send.
In the garden the flower beds and roses were in my care,
He cut the grass, the shrubs, everything else, as I am aware.

Yes, I miss him, we had a happy life together,
Those past days and memories I could never forget or sever.
I am just over sixty and in a healthy condition,
No financial worries, not needing a highly paid position.

Ted and I were never blessed with children of our own,
When we considered adoption, too old, our chance had flown.
Now I am going to work with children in a special home,
I feel Ted would smile down on me with an approving tone.

I feel warmth, happiness, in helping children in need,
I feel reborn, I know I am going to succeed.
A month has passed; I know I have chosen right,
Seeing children's happy faces is always a wonderful sight.

Terry Godwin

The End

Light a candle for me and watch it flicker
And know that I am that flame
Raise a glass to your lips and sip the wine
As I will be tasting the same

I lived, loved and came to know
That not without reason it was time to go
Hold onto your thoughts, cherish what's dear
I will be watching, so hold onto your tear

No point in refusing to carry on in hope
That's not what your life has been for
No more to be said, no reason to mope
So see you soon, all my love, now and for evermore

Karen Langridge

The Joy Of Sunshine

With a twist of the key, and the engine revving,
The grey cloud of smoke, 'It's Thunderbird seven'
Its smooth straight lines, with aqua on its roof,
Who cares about fancy! With speed from the hoof.

The hot tarmac road, slow caress of wind,
Up goes Radio 2, as Mark begins to grin.
He veers slowly to the right, closing to the middle,
Distraught cars behind, trying to solve the riddle.

Call it blinding innocence, Mark looks in the mirror,
Flicks the ash from his roll up, 'My what a picture!'
Speed stretching to thirty, their impatience going wild,
Mark eases off the pedal, enjoying being the child.

With the perfect Fakenham straight, yellow speed camera in sight,
The foot slams to the floor, showing 'Thunderbird's true might'
With the first of the few, accelerating to pace,
Parallel with Mark, head high, vibrating grace.

With an evil mind, and humour of a clown,
A swift turn to the lay-by, brake hard, slowing down!
With a sliding halt, the dust cloud disappears,
The impatient car, races past, showing no cheer.

Mark's sly face showing real smirk,
The cars slow down, too quick to lurk.
With the flash of light, like a lost gold mine,
Mark's hand straight out . . . 'Up yours Sunshine!'

With a loud laugh and a cackle intense,
He looks at the camera, 'That's quite a few pence.'
He turns the volume up, loud through and through,
Roaring Thunderbird seven, 'Mean machine coloured blue'.

Mark Spiller

Don't Go Where I Can't Follow

Don't close your eyes forever,
It's not your time to sleep.
You said that you would stay with me,
That's a promise you should keep.

Don't give up on this day,
And slip into the night.
Our time is just beginning,
Stay with me and fight.

Don't you leave me here alone,
Not now you have my heart.
Don't go where I can't follow,
We're not meant to be apart.

Deanna L Dixon

My Two Fidgety Feet

Oh! Why can't I get comfy?
Where can I put my feet?
Shall I stretch them right the way out
or tuck them up into my seat?
All I want to do is sit and have a rest,
but my two fidgety feet think they know what's best!
I started my spring cleaning
very early this morning, you see,
and now my new-found energy has got the better of me.
So I have sat down on the sofa
to pass an hour away,
but my two fidgety feet, on my legs
they don't want to stay.
I close my eyes for a few minutes it seems,
and my mind drifts away into a fantasy dream.
My feet have little hands and they are running to and fro,
dusting and cleaning in places I couldn't reach or go.
Everything is spic and span and so very sparkling clean,
I couldn't even imagine I was sitting here in a dream.
I opened my eyes so suddenly and looked straight down to see,
yes, my two fidgety feet were looking straight at me!
Is it my imagination, but does everything look so clean?
Was it my own doing, or was it true, my fantasy dream?

Mary Plumb

Dreams

Close your eyes, give in, succumb to sleep.
Relax, let your eyelids droop, the body rest.
But while we sleep the mind is probing, deep,
Within the brain, its every small recess.

Its findings are portrayed in dreams and words.
Bubble to the surface, inner self expose.
Showing what lies within, often the absurd,
How bare the naked soul in sweet repose.

No control over speech and words we do choose,
Within sleep's pattern, dreams become reality.
Our alter ego speaks, gives its views,
Frustrations, fears and longings are freed.

So beware, that, deep within the cells,
Our brain observes us, conscious and unconscious.
The revelations made in dreams will tell,
That what we reap, we sow, 'twas ever thus.

Pamela Carder

The Policeman

Have you ever thought about the policeman
Who walks along the street
Trying hard to keep the peace
As he strolls along his beat?

Some people call them rats or pigs
Yet they are the first to yelp
When attacked or broken into
And who do they want to help?

Of course it is the policeman
A good job he is at hand
Just what would we do without them
If they didn't patrol our land?

Just think what they have to solve
Murder, rape and such
I'm afraid I couldn't stand it
For me it's far too much

Truthfully, could you fancy his job
And tackle it with pride?
No chance, I'm afraid to say
Some would rather hide

So when you see a policeman
Walking along his beat
Just think what could happen
As he walks along your street.

Ted Bage

The One Child Limit

My baby I have is alive and well,
But now I feel I have to tell.
The bump is small; I know it's wrong,
But the journey I've started is hard and long.

The limit is one but I'll have two,
I don't want to be told what to do.
We need a boy to keep the family name,
I'm not trying to bring it any shame.

I know we'll manage with the money we've saved.
Now we have to keep being brave.
The workers will try and persuade me to have an abortion,
But I'm not getting rid of the baby,
You order the meal you get the whole portion.

Danielle Wills

Frustration

It has been debated worldwide
How children should be reared
Parents' patience is well tried
And then they feel a-feared.

Are we doing right
Or are we doing wrong?
We weren't taught to be parents
So how do we go along?

You must do this, you mustn't do that
There seem to be so many rules
That rule wasn't there when I was a child
Parents sometimes feel a thousand fools.

Common sense helps a lot
And knowing right from wrong
It's all very confusing
We just hope as we go along.

When offspring don't turn out right
Is it always the parents' fault?
Some just have this quirk
No matter what they have been taught.

So we try our best
Should we really judge?
Because other parents' best isn't the same as ours
Even though we find it hard to budge.

On the whole parents do very well
What we must remember, is to exist
If parents hadn't been there
Children would desist.

H Dormand

Holding Me In Place

Hold the door for me.
Hold my hand.
Check that I'm behind you,
and then frown where I stand.

I don't need another.
I know you hear this voice.
Check that I'm breathing,
and then cut down the choice.

Above and beyond you,
above and beyond.
Not a parallel universe,
watch as I respond.

Chishimba Chisala

Lost Will

(An aspiring poet's contradiction)

Too old is he to stir and make his mark or bust
In poetry or some other wordsmith's game
For as a nation's migrants spread like global dust
His thoughts traversed the realms of mind and brain

Where once a theme did capture message clear
Now road-blocks loom to falter verbals race
As resignation's comfort reigns to smother cheer
His wearied soul repels the mental chase

There was a time wherein his memory kindled fire
And blazing up enveloped words and phrase
But now there's naught save inexpressive ire
At how the years have flown to this accursed phase

Alas his journey yields no raptured wilful plan
Nor thought-extrapolated text to ponder on
Only the blankness of a palsied, brain-dead man
Confronts him with the ghost of yester gone

And now this brief-writ ode must gently fade away
Lest coaxed to tarry on whilst mindless foes assail
Perchance some motive may one day retain a sway
And bestir his abject soul with reason to prevail.

William A Mack

The Emigrants

I scan the years that long past flown
Memories like melodies flood the heart
I travel far to many a zone

I call New Zealand on the phone
What do I say, where do I start?
I scan the years that long past flown

O my darlings, how you must have grown
Remember when we kept a chart?
I travel far to many a zone

Your accent's changed, you've different tone
How long now since we've been apart?
I scan the years that long past flown

Let's make the most, I must not drone
Love's laughter paints a work of art
I travel far to many a zone

Remember, give my love to Joan
So glad to hear of Cupid's dart
I scan the years that long past flown
I travel far to many a zone

Mary Skelton

The Children's Visits

All the children decided to meet
At the sweet shop down the street
The year was nineteen-hundred and ten
Not much money for children then.

The windows were large with a good display
How many pennies do you have today?
Old Mrs Brown saw them near
She had kept the shop for many a year.

The shop was old and rather quaint
Lots of chipped flakes from the paint
Large shelves that held so many jars
Toffee, sugar mice and chocolate bars.

The sweets she weighed upon her scales
And knew her eyesight often fails
But kindness and love were her many joys
And she could not resist the girls and boys
Their excited faces gave her pleasure
A sense of devotion beyond all measure.

She had no family of her own
Into a working life was thrown
But now she would not change it all
Because the children came to call
Her life was enriched much more each day
When the children came her way.

G B Mapes

Marking Time

As the old man in a circle treads,
The path around the flower beds,
Obscenities fall from his withered lips,
Once traced by loving fingertips.

Vacant eyes for an instant flare,
Reveal the soul imprisoned there.
Such rage, such passion, quickly gone,
He bends to the treadmill, on and on.

The communal lounge is filled with light,
Dispelling the long and empty night.
In their unease, the frail, the castaways,
Are shadows chasing 'yesterdays'.

Hold this thought, shall we be there,
Sitting in a regimented chair,
Drifting, lost on a tideless sea,
And the past our only reality?

W H Billington

Tractor Man

Little Alec couldn't sleep
because of dreams of cows and sheep.
His mummy thought it wouldn't harm
to send him to Ireland, to work on a farm!

A few years elapsed,
but now, at long last,
it was time for Alec to sail.
He boarded a ferry
which was bound for Derry
and arrived on the wings of a gale!

Delighted and expectant to realise his vision,
when told to his cousins was met with derision!

No sloe-eyed cows or grazing sheep - instead machines of every hue,
well, what on earth could Alec do?
He climbed aboard a sturdy tractor,
amidst his cousins' hearty laughter.

From then on he was completely hooked,
driving everywhere, he'd not be brooked.
Through loamy fields and grainy dust,
stopping a minute to chew a crust.

The end of summer now is here, time to board the evening ferry.
The cousins cry, 'See you next year,' whilst Alec waves goodbye to Derry.

Hands in pockets, he paces the deck,
suddenly realises he'll get it in the neck.
There's a girl called Miss Lees, he should have contacted,
with all the excitement he'd become distracted.

This lovely girl, Miss Lees,
Alec tries really hard to please.
With a rush of emotion
to his mind comes the notion,
no longer will he tarry,
but ask her to marry -
if he has to fall to his knees!

Now nearly 40 years wed to Miss Lees,
Alec is feeling rather pleased.
He has his own farm
and life without qualm
and what's more - a final factor -
he's the proud owner of a green and yellow tractor!

Carole Irene Jones

Inside Me

Inside me there's a joy
To see my family live and grow
Inside me there's a soul
I still have to come to know
Inside me there's a person
Full of fear and doubt
Inside me there's a victim
Who cannot scream or shout

Inside me there's a past
That's best left far behind
Inside me there's a calmness
A gentle peace of mind
Inside me there's a knowing
Of the path I have to take
Inside me there's a forgiveness
For the mistakes I make

Inside me there's a reason
For everything I do
Inside me there's a belonging
But who do I belong to?
Inside me there's a hopefulness
For what is yet to be
Inside me there's a strength
And that strength is me.

Mary Daines

The Wee Folk

Look closely if you think you see
A fairy on the lawn . . .
Cos it may not be a fairy
But a blinkin' leprechaun!

How to tell the difference?
Here's a little clue . . .
A fairy is delightful,
But - a leprechaun's like you!

On the other hand, if it's got wings
Coloured lightly blue . . .
It's not because you've had a drink
- more like - quite a few!

But, don't despair, cos miracles
Can happen any day . . .
The trouble is, by morning,
They've always gone away!

George A Tanner

Just Phone

When, you are far
             From home
And, you think
             You're on your own
Just phone.

When you find that
         No one's there
And your heart
         Is in despair
Just phone.

But, then you think
         Who loves you
All the family
         That you knew
They are waiting
         Just for you
So . . .
Just phone!
(And make
Them happy.)

E B Holcombe

Dreams

In this present atmosphere
one wonders whether we
can write like Shakespeare
We would like to be powerful like The States
and be rich like Bill Gates
to think like Einstein
and not like Goliath the Philistine
To be holy and obey the Bible wholly.

This is one of my dreams
to sing like Jim Reeves
It is said that it's costly
to preach like John Wesley
Even someone with a malady
wants to speak like J F Kennedy
No one wants to be clothed in tattered
penury
but in Burberry.

Poku Michael Kwadwo

If Only

I love you more than he,
Because I love you endlessly,
And if only this love could be,
I'd let this feeling fly free.
If only you could truly see,
The way I think and the way I feel,
Maybe you wouldn't walk over me,
And realise that I am real.
If only I could truly see,
The way you think and feel,
Maybe I wouldn't feel this way,
And realise my fate is sealed.
I no longer want to feel this way,
Because you can't feel the same,
I no longer want to know of your existence,
And I want to forget your name.
But no matter how much I do this,
And try to push away,
I take one look at your gleaming face,
And your beauty is making me stay.
I want to go, I want to forget,
I want to fully live out my dreams.
Then that one sweet word rolls off your tongue,
And makes my heart burst at the seams.
But I can no longer sit here and wait,
I've weighed up options and made a fool of me,
It's all hurting me too much deep inside,
In a place that no man can see.
But why did God do it?
Why did he set this girl I love apart
And make her by far too perfect for me?
She has now destroyed me at the heart.

Stephen James Hulme

Evening

The day folds its wings
And settles into night,
The last traces of light
Vanish from sight,
The last bird call
That held us in thrall
Fades into silence.

The first faint stars
Peep from behind
The velvet curtain of the sky.

Ann Clifton

174

Mower Mania

My husband has a mania for mowing all the lawn
He's out there mowing merrily as soon as it is dawn
I expect you think well after all that's really not too bad
But you haven't heard the worst of it, it's really rather sad
He'll buy a brand new mower, then out he'll go to mow
Humming along quite happily, cutting down each row
I sit indoors and listen, waiting for the groan
You see I know it's going to happen. Silence! He's hit a stone
'Don't worry,' he says every time, smiling sweet at me
'I'll mend it.' *Mend it?* thinks I, *this I've got to see*
Soon there are bolts and nuts and screws, piled up everywhere
'I think I'll put it in the shed,' says he, 'it must be wear and tear'
And so into the shed it goes, in with all the others
Oh yes there's lots of them, lined up just like an army
And if I go near that shed, I'm sure they glare at me
I had a dream the other night, they were marching side by side
Getting ever closer, I had nowhere to hide
I tried to run, my legs were weak, I thought, *they're going to get me*
I woke up just in time, oh it did upset me
I'm going to move into a flat, a flat with a window box
He can't surely mow without a lawn, however much it shocks
And if somebody buys this house, remember what I've said
Whatever else you do, just don't go in the shed!

S Derbyshire

Bouncing Baby On The Way

Now you are a manager
Let us make a start
Now you are successful
Give me what's on my heart!

Now you are a manager
You need a brand new car
For commuting and taking me to the hospital
In safety we have to travel far.

Now you are a manager
We'll need a bigger flat
Or better still, a house
No room here to swing a cat.

Now you are a manager
You must not waste a day
The extra money is needed now
With a bouncy baby on the way!

Pip

Poets' Corner

I'd like to write 'verse' for a living,
I wonder how could I start?
Perhaps getting pens and some paper,
And writing to follow my heart.

I'm not bad at being creative,
Though must admit I cannot draw,
But my friends like to call me a 'wordsmith',
As that's what I have talent for.

I like to write verse, it's expressive,
Relaxing, creative (it's true!),
I find that it's really a pleasure,
To sit down and do what I do.

So if you hear of an offer,
Where one seeks a poet for pay,
Give a call in my general direction,
As you might just be making my day.

As a kindness, a few lines I'll write you,
On whatever you'd like me to pen,
For life is too short not to thank you,
In my quest to write verse now and then.

So please keep your eyes and ears open,
When travelling local and far,
And when I am rich (even famous),
I'll fetch you a drink from the bar!

M Wilcox

Who?

Who irons my shirt when I'm tired at night
Who holds my hand and says everything is all right
Who gives me comfort when I seem alone
Who makes me laugh with jokes on the phone?

Who does dinner, Chinese sometimes
Who, when work becomes tiresome, says everything's fine
Who finds my good points, when I feel I have none
Who lends me money, when I don't have some?

Who shares their time each day as it comes
Who puts pen to paper and sorts out my sums
Who, in the morning helps shape my days
Who is my rock in so many ways?

Who brings me sunshine, when there is rain
Who rubs in ointment, when I have a pain
Who finds a smile over silly things?
Why it's you, who makes my heart feel it has wings.

Janice Thorogood

My Dream

Worlds beyond worlds, far out of sight,
An endless journey of day and night,
Where stars appear, a twinkling boon,
Far beyond the mountains of the moon,
Toward the sun, I travel on, in my dream our Earth, our land,
Is but a dot, in a sea of cosmic sand,
In my dream I travel on, long after
The dot, my Earth has gone,
Beyond the deserts that are Mars,
Beyond a million twinkling stars,
In my dream my mind is free,
To go beyond all things I see,
The planets known in my Earth's own sky,
Get a fleeting glance as I pass by,
I see so many, many things,
As I pass Saturn's sparkling rings,
On past Uranus, Neptune, Pluto too,
My dream will ask, can I pass through?
Beyond the knowledgeable realm of Man,
My dream will tell me that I can,
To pass beyond, and then beyond,
It will seem, can only ever be in dream,
For what is beyond?
Will Man ever know, will Man ever get to go,
To see the millions of stars unknown,
That scatter the heavens, as seeds are sown,
Or will those countless twinkling gleams,
Be only ever seen in dreams?

Len Baynes

Dreaming

Dream not of today, but of the past or future yet to come.
Fond memories of people past and present, there are some.

Mother, Father, gone but still they linger on in reminiscences
of joy and sorrow as life still goes on.

Where do all the nightmares go as with the night comes dawn?
Swept away by sweet dreams when another day is born.

Ambitions it is said are dreams, but ambitions I have none,
except maybe to say that all my dreams I've done.

But time is only borrowed and ambitions and dreams change,
so maybe one day when the time is right my future I can arrange.

And so I keep on dreaming, the past is far behind.
I look forward to the future and the joy of life I find.

Sheila Storr

Danny

We have a very young Great Dane and, though he's just a pup,
He's big enough to make you think he's really quite grown up.

The other day, when the garden was wet from the rain the night before,
This dog (we call him Danny) made us laugh, he made us roar!

He'd found a paper cup and in his daft and lanky way,
He was bounding around with the cup in his teeth, dropping it and running away.

Then he'd pick it up again - it all seemed very tame,
Until the cup got stuck on his nose, and this was a different game.

Trying to look at the stuck-on cup and going quite cross-eyed,
He ran around, growling, and madly shaking his head from side to side.

'Oh very amusing, Danny!' I laughed as he passed for the second time,
But in blind panic, to free himself, he ran through the washing line.

This cross-eyed, cup-nosed, muddy dog, wrapped up in shirts and vests,
Went hurtling in through the open back door - a whimpering, pitiful mess!

Legs akimbo, Danny skidded across the kitchen floor,
And scrambling frantic'ly, trying to stop, crashed into the larder door.

He lay there in a tangled heap - a really funny sight,
We sorted him out, he slumped onto his blanket - and he didn't move all night.

Bill Eden

I've Decommissioned The Major

I could be called a squaddy in a regimental sort of way.
Only capable of menial tasks and criticised in all she had to say.
Held no permit for the kitchen, apparently I couldn't boil water.
The fault-finder was the mother, I had thought I was the daughter.
Took my orders from the major, I questioned not a word.
Really had me brainwashed as I took in all I heard.
At last I'm not so stupid, learned that to her I don't belong.
She treated me with such contempt which I now know was so wrong.
I had given her a label, it suited her so well.
Major Fault-Finder was her title and it was right as I could tell.
Finally I am in recovery and from orders now I'm free.
When I became aware she was destructive I was glad to leave her be.
Had never known a mother so never questioned what she did.
Now know how much she has hurt me, so bad - I can't forgive.
Now I no longer see her, my mind is very scarred.
In my mind she still shouts orders and glares with eyes so hard.
She has been decommissioned, neither major nor mother to me.
I no longer march in time with her, and one day I shall be free.

Please?

Rosie Hues

To Be Blind And Deaf

To be healthy, wealthy and wise would be great,
Sadly, however, life is not like that, no mistake,
Often we inherit our lifestyle via our parents,
Many times all is well and there are no variants.

But life can be hard and exacting, say from birth,
A person might be born deaf and not know any mirth,
Whilst if blind at birth, one would know little else,
Then again, to be blind and deaf must make life seem false.

To the average person, handicaps are really unknown,
In later life, with knowledge, it might raise a frown,
Sadly ignorance can even cause some dissent,
However, few would fail to help in any event.

What a boon it is that we have help for the blind,
No one can really know blindness, but still, will mind,
Some say it's worse to be deaf than to be blind,
Others will know that not to see is very unkind.

So how can we help our folk, so very in need?
By making sure that loving assurance is theirs indeed,
Also with love when times are really tough,
Blessings from our Lord above should be enough.

W R Burkitt

With Arms Outstretched

They nailed Him to the rugged Cross hewn from a lowly tree
On Golgotha Hill, with arms outstretched, Jesus died for you and me
Mankind's transgressions upon his back, He gave up His 'perfect life'
Our ransom He did pay in full, God's Son was the sacrifice
The power of Satan duly snapped on that momentous day
For each drop of blood that Jesus shed, washed all our sins away
Man was reconciled with God, the atonement for us complete
Then Christ's resurrection showed to all that death we can defeat
The Cross, a sparkling beacon, has shone for two thousand years
Lifting us up from deep despair and banishing our fears
If we try to follow Jesus and take the rocky road He trod
We will live again in Heaven and meet with our Redeemer Lord.

When the earthly curtain drops, and I leave this ageing shell
I know a place will be prepared where I can go to dwell.
His outstretched arms will welcome me, and to them I will run
I pray to hear those lovely words, 'Well done, My child, well done'.

Vyna Broom

A Funny Thing

A funny thing happened on my way to work
it happened like this one day
I had started my journey quite sedately
walking slowly on my way
whilst passing a house that stood near the road
I slowly glanced around
and to my surprise I noticed a black cat
on a mat, just sitting down
wearing a red collar and a silver bell
it looked so pretty there
that I felt compelled to stop and stroke it
it nuzzled my hand with care
then it looked at me so strangely at first
trying to talk so low
it opened its mouth and guess what came out
twas a distinctive, *Bow-wow*.
I stood there amazed, not believing my ears
and waited for an encore
but it wasn't repeated I'm sad to say
and so I continued once more
just around the corner of the little house
I saw another odd sight
a white fluffy dog was patiently waiting
as if claiming his own right
it was some time later when I realised
'twas a strange but true fact
I had witnessed such a clever performance
from a ventriloquist act
named 'Fido and Fluff' who just lie in wait
to astound us on their date.

Terry Daley

Sorrow

In another country, in another place,
Everywhere got flooded,
It's quite a disgrace.
No food around, and the babies cry,
They all lost loved ones,
Why did they die?
God works in a mysterious way,
If only we knew what He had to say.
It doesn't matter what colour you are,
People send food and gifts and travel afar.
They help each other in their time of need,
If that's what He meant, we will all succeed.

Paula Massey

Ode To Richard - Our Gardener

He turned up one day on a tatty old bike,
and an old baseball cap on his head.
Politely he asked if we needed some help
with the lawn, or the odd flower bed.

He looked fairly harmless, and had a nice face,
so we found him a few little jobs.
We'd give him a nice cup of tea later on
and he'd scoff half a dozen HobNobs.

The garden got better as each year went by,
and the young man became a good friend.
More people would ask him to help them as well,
he did most of the street in the end!

Mowing lawns, pulling weeds, planting numerous shrubs,
his devotion to gardening grew stronger.
I must say the only thing I've noticed lately;
his tea breaks are getting much longer!

But that doesn't matter; the job still gets done
and now he's clocked up *twenty* years.
Richard, I thank you for all that you've done,
your devotion has moved me to tears.

Mike Wenham

Jumping Puddles

Jumping puddles is great fun
But wait until I see my mum!
I came out all nice and clean
And my shoes had a sheen.

But now they're wet, and so am I
To school I go like this, oh my!
Was it worth the fun and laughter,
To be like this all day after?

I've kicked cans and stripped sweets
Left my rubbish in the streets,
Instead of putting it in a bin
I've littered gardens; what a sin!

But jumping puddles is the best
And for this I have a zest!
Never mind being wet -
Simple fun is hard to get.

Susan Green

The White Palace

On soft and gentle scenic view
The sky hangs in clear blue
Against the texture of warm and golden beach
As the tropical sea brushes against the shore's reach
On the land stands a regal palace in glimmering white
Statues of beauty stand either side and greet stairs' flight
As I climb the easy stair
I am greeted by a Garden of Eden there
Walking barefoot on tepid marble floor
I go through the garden door
A long courtyard stands before me with a fountain and pool
Shade and columns stand in rows, shadows fresh and cool
The sweet perfume of honeysuckle fills my nose
And flora and foliage fill my eyes with sweet repose
Birds of colour sing their song
Insects and bees go about their business and buzz along
And as I wonder at this marvel
Walking on black-veined and crisp white marble
Music in the distance greets my ear
The sound of flute, harp and mandolin as I draw near
Laughter and song fill the air
Those inside this palace, without a care
I draw closer to the sound
I see through the curtains, young ladies dance around
As I brush away the silky coloured hanging frieze
That seems to be dancing to the breeze
There she stood like a goddess in chiffon white
Her dress flowing soft and transparent in the light
A jewel (a bindi) on her forehead shining bright
Dazzling as caught by sunlight
Her hair, long and shiny black
That flowed down her long and slender back
Her coffee skin of radiated complexion
Dark brown eyes burn and meet perfection
And the silhouette of her perfect body seen through the dress
Took my breath away I must confess
She turned and smiled, and with a gesture beckoned me
Held her arms out to greet and welcome so sweetly
And took both my hands to gently dance
As if to know me by chance
We talked, laughed and ate
Had many things in common to relate
And as the day turned to twilight
I told her I had to go as it's nearly night
She turned and we kissed
Told me I would be missed
And to come another day
But inside I think I really wanted to stay

As we walked across that marble floor
Our last kiss on the sandy shore
We bid goodnight as I walked away
I returned the following day
There was no palace on that plot of land
No stairs to greet me at hand
Just an empty space
And an expression of shock on my face.

Terry J Powell

The Price Of Coal

When I was a child I loved to sit
By a fire of coal from our pits
There were a number of pits in South Wales
The men that mined them were very brave

They went down into the depths of the earth
Were they ever paid what they were worth?
I remember my uncle coming home all black
And thinking *why would he want to go back?*

They were proud men these diggers of coal
To earn a wage was their only goal
Work was scarce, they had no choice
It helped them when they sang out in full voice

Across the valleys a wonderful sound
Men joining in as they did underground
Now nearly all our pits have closed down
But choirs live on in valleys and towns

The sound of Welsh voices is heard far and wide
When they sing about Wales they do so with pride
When I think of those days so long ago
A lovely red fire to toast my toes

I remember those who gave their all to keep their homes together
With lungs filled with black dust that haunted them forever
The women who nursed them with undying love
Until they passed into Heaven above

People pulled together in so many ways
Helping each other day by day
Times have changed, pits are closed down
Instead of communities we have rolling towns

The personal touch, the sense of comradeship
Seems to have been left behind with the pits
But when we sing about our homeland we do so with pride
Still the same kind of people, loving and caring with big hearts inside

Glenys Hannon

And Still The Swing . . .

Raucous laughter
and high-pitched giggles.
The one on the rope and stick
fidgets and wiggles.
The boys can't stop laughing,
the little girls scream.
One false move
and you're into the stream!

And still the swing goes higher . . .

Now, to get off . . .
brother makes this look easy.
But really, deep down,
you feel shaky and queasy.
You stare at the spot
on the bank where you aim . . .
then launch
and the time crawls frame by frame.

And still the swing goes higher . . .

As the years pass
you look back and smile.
The fun you all had
in true 'Coe-Burn' style.

Now the seasons speed by
with a fast exclamation.
The stream is awaiting
the next generation.

And still the swing . . .

Vivienne C Wiggins

Are You A True Christian?

So you claim to be a Christian, honest, kind and fair,
You give generously to charity to let people know you care.
You say all men are equal in the sight of our dear Lord,
Unless he is a foreigner, for him you have no good word.

So you claim to be a Christian and care for all mankind,
But only if his skin is white, white skin is the best kind.
You go to church each Sunday in your very best attire,
You stand there in the House of God, a hypocrite and liar.

So you claim to be a Christian, I would ask you, think again,
Remember Jesus Christ our Lord died to save all men.
If you really were a Christian, it would come from deep within,
And you would not judge a man by the colour of his skin.

Michelle Irving

Deceptive Reasoning

Holding to conceptual notions,
    Being convinced of righteous ways;
Living with intense emotions,
    Devastates the best of days!

Beyond the pale of common sense,
    Where night brings no relief;
When little things - may seem immense,
    And logic - past belief!

If fear becomes the rational,
    And thinking is obscene;
Then what of the traditional?
    The things which might have been!

Bravely facing confrontation,
    Courage filling every nerve;
Challenging hallucination,
    With degrees of sudden verve!

Within the grasp of understanding,
    Lies a world of disbelief;
As hidden by the brain's demanding,
    Solace, in its hour of grief!

Then living with imagination,
    Awakening the ripened state;
To the hour of provocation,
    Bowing to the hand of fate!

R Bissett

Children Seem To Know Much More

Children don't find pointless problems,
They don't need to live by a law
And though they don't have as much knowledge,
They always seem to know much more.

Children are pleased by simple blessings,
It's love they're looking for,
They're not obsessed with making money,
They always seem to know much more.

Children don't care much for power,
They don't undermine the poor,
They do not live in competition,
They always seem to know much more.

Inside every person's a young child,
That learnt by what it saw,
To appreciate life's simple pleasures,
Think like a child and love much more.

Leanne Mizen

Coity Castle

No regal Rhuddlan or Caernarvon might,
No roof here, a few stout walls, columns there,
Arched Norman voids leak light and wet Welsh air,
A limestone pile, an orphaned film set site.

To these delicate remains no tourists throng,
Among the best kept secrets, past so unknown.
Assaulted, raked and pillaged for cut stone,
In heyday to great names it did belong.

Scant records show six hundred years or more,
So many violent acts of war-like bands.
This silent sentinel must hold in store,
Sometimes proud Celt; not all from foreign lands.

Not content to dig for dead men or gold,
Please thaw the frozen voices locked in stone.
Liberate past chat and tall stories told,
By common folk who never sat a-throne.

No coastal view or river to defend,
On flat terrain, without commanding height,
Was it ever so, no stomach for a fight,
Just a grand dwelling, gift of royal friend?

No strategic worth or military might,
Dim tallow lamps replaced by searching lights,
You wince at grown-up friendly fights less gory,
While *'choirs on the lawn'* praise another's glory.

Support is crumbling, how can you endure
More centuries of frontal full attack
By shopping mall, rat-run or red-brick shack,
As contempt and greed snatch the profit lure?

Civil wars, science slalom, acid rain,
What next to cause you grief and pain?

Mike Hayes

There Ain't No Justice

The law of the land is most unjust
The poor and the rich go naked ev'ry day
The poor because they must
The rich because they may.

Gordon Gompers

Four Minutes

This morning I woke in a dreadful state,
Severe cold, and a bad headache.
Into the bathroom the quickest of shaves,
Spray-on deodorant speedily waved.
I'm still getting dressed as I fly down the stair,
Check the change in my pocket for my exact fare.
The clock on my wall says three minutes to eight,
Not to worry for my bus is usually late.

A sip of coffee, a breakfast bar,
I need to hurry, so good so far.
The bus passes me as I leave my gate,
And I have to sprint or arrive at work late.
People are waiting at the bus stop,
They'll hold the bus up, and I slow to a trot.
There's a dreadful explosion,
And I'm blown to the ground,
Carnage from my bus is strewn all around.

It takes a second or two, to understand this thing,
Then I'm sifting through wreckage, bodies and limbs.
I do my best for the people inside,
But my tears for humanity, I cannot hide.
The rescuers come, one leads me aside,
And I'm covered in blood, yet none of it's mine.
A trip to the hospital, a statement or two,
I'm on my way home; I'm all black and blue.
I arrive home in a sadly shocked state,
And the clock on my wall is just four minutes late.

David White

In Clover

There's been a storm brewing in my mind,
it has been for some time now,
but one day you will find,
there's more to me than meets the eye.
You cannot read me,
you cannot see behind these glib words,
they make me feel in clover.
But please don't step into my world,
cos your days are just about over.
Hey idiot, with all your decibels,
it's the empty vessel that makes all the noise,
and I'm the one with all the poise,
to make you burn in Hell
and people will say 'Oh well'
a decrease of the surplus population.

Kevin Braid

Anguish

Loneliness surrounds me like the darkness of the night
Everything seems wrong, nothing seems right.
There's emptiness about me, I can't understand,
It's as if I'm lost in a strange foreign land.

Nothing enters my mind, I'm cocooned in a trance
I'm floating, I'm sinking, seemingly without a chance,
Twisting and turning, whirling around in space
Lost from reality, a human being without a face.

A numbing darkness envelops my being
My eyes are open yet blind, not seeing.
A cloud of devastation appears to control my mind
Blocking out sanity, leaving common sense behind.

Yet sometime, somewhere, I must search and find
A solution to the upheaval that befuddles my mind.
Surely hidden away, buried deep in my head
Lies an answer for survival, for living instead.

Hidden deep in my brain, a spasm, a glimmer of light
So small in the darkness, like the dawn after night
Then growing, the realisation of the horror untold
The agonising wretchedness there to behold.

Flashing lights, screeching tyres, the tearing of steel,
Screaming your name, an awful dread I can feel
A smashed doll-like body, covered in bright red blood
I wanted to rebuild you. I just wish I could.

But alas, I'm no creator, I cannot make you well.
There's one thing I can do. To the world I can tell
Of the love that was true that none can impair,
Wait for me darling, I'll join you up there.

D T Pendit

Self-Portrait

I look through my mirror and what do I see
A familiar lady looking at me
She isn't very tall - blue eyes and dark brown hair
Her face is rather serious but I'm sure there's laughter there
The skin is unlined, hair shiny and bright
Her blue eyes shine clear and her figure is slight
No wrinkles as yet on the very fair skin
Peace and contentment shine from within
She's an ordinary lady, she isn't clever or bright
Has always done her best in life and tried to do what's right.
You would like this lady, she seems so young and free
As I look through my rose-tinted glasses, I remember me.

Irene Kenny

Wishful Day

One wish only, to put things right,
One wish only, to ease my plight,
With my one wish, I could be selfish or greedy,
Think only of myself, ignore my better judgement and the needy,
I suppose I could wish for a million pounds,
Then go on a permanent holiday, strut my stuff, do the rounds,
Or my one wish could transport me and mine,
Back to a distant place way off in time,
A place where troubles and worry,
Were not on the itinerary, nor were chaos or hurry,
A place, a utopia so bright and clean,
A place where joy and happiness were only ever seen.

One wish only, you say,
What to wish for on this wishful day,
Perhaps I could return to when Man landed on the moon,
Or to my childhood, when the dish ran away with the spoon,
Or to some great historic moments of our past,
To when Nelson was triumphant at Trafalgar, or poor Diana breathed her last,
I could have been there when Albert Einstein's theories were put to bed,
Or shook the tree when the apple fell onto Newton's head,
Or I could have hung Leonardo Da Vinci's paintings on the wall,
As the doors to his last exhibition were opened to one and all,
Maybe I'd have run round Wembley with Bobby and the boys with the cup aloft,
Or been present at the birth of my children, nestling in their mother's arms, so safe,
so warm and soft.

I could wish for a cure for cancer, and I do,
Not one more human being that pain and heartbreak should have to go through,
I might wish that one day, when I die, I go to Heaven not Hell,
Or if I'd been very bad, perhaps a little taste of both for a spell,
Wishfulness is already a harmless trait of mine,
Endlessly searching through my life, my subconscious, wishing for a glint, a crack of
light, a sign.

P J Littlefield

Sense Of A Dream

What beauty does the blind man see?
Touching pictures with imagination his reality
Never do people's voices age
In his ears he only sees youth
Reflection he can smell by looking back through music
The eras of beauty he can live, but not see.

John Lee

Thoughts Of You

When I think
Of losing you
I wish there was something
I could do

To stop the tears
Sliding down my cheek
I can't fight them
I'm feeling weak.

You say you love me
But will it last?
I can't stand the thought
Of us being in the past.

The mere thought of you
Not being by my side
It stops all time
And it turns the tide.

Here I am
Laying in my bed
Sweet memories rolling
Inside my head.

Thoughts of you
Send me to a special place
I gaze in the distance
While my mind is off in space.

I can't help the feelings
Being this strong
That is why I'm here
Singing my song.

Helen-Elaine

The Dying Rose

I am a rosebush standing so tall,
I grow and cling to every wall,
Climbing high to reach the light,
All my colours could be very bright.

I am a rose so soft and blue,
Unusual but very true,
My scented aroma is a powerful smell,
If fed, I will grow very well.

I am a rose about to wilt and die,
Covered in blight and blackfly,
Once I was a beautiful rose,
Elegant and with pose.

Maggie Hickinbotham

Balloon Ride

I settled in the basket
Waited anxiously for the lift
Suddenly we were up
And the balloon began to drift

A wonderful sensation
Floating on the breeze
The anxiety and tension
Had now begun to ease

Things were getting smaller
Below me on the ground
The view was quite breathtaking
I could see for miles around

The thing that I most noticed
Was the silence in my ears
Just floating in the evening sky
Beneath a multicoloured sphere

Different coloured fields
Like a patchwork knitted quilt
Ancient old farm buildings
And houses newly built

Monuments of mystery
I never knew were there
So many things of interest
All I could do was stare

An experience of a lifetime
Another one complete
An ambition I have now fulfilled
And would be happy to repeat.

Neil Warren

Porthcawl Of Yore

We're in Porthcawl on the small steam train;
In an open carriage, hope there's no rain!
We chug along on the narrow track,
Through the tunnel, clickety-clack.

We laugh and shriek on the Waltzer at the fair.
We scream on the Figure Eight, but with care.
We sail 'Around The World', it's quiet and cool.
Then on the 'dodgem cars' and dodge the boys from school.

But soon our happy day is ended,
We say goodbye to all that's splendid.
Adieu Porthcawl, farewell my friend,
The day has come to another end.

J R Legg

Extinct

And so the great debate began
Controversy as to the best benefit to Man
Should he be allowed to live his span
Or to be prime specimen, mounted in a glass-domed can?
Genetic printing he could scorn
His species would never again be born
He soared high above a sheep-grazed glen
Swooped over a crofter's hut and ben
Free as free, he could be
Protected till finality
A legend for eons to come
Extinct, to be entered in a tome
Shot by lens, zoom and clear
Or hounded by hunters, whose fear
Of being the last to see
This species who could never be
Protected, collectors would with each other vie
To secure his mounting, he must die.
A famous national character he would be
In a great glass dome for all to see
With outspread wings, talons gripping prey
Labelled: *this species, extinct, 1988, 21st May*.

A Quinn

I Can Only Tell You

The love that I have for you just grows and grows
How can I explain what you already know?
I can tell you one hundred times of that I'm sure
That I miss you so much and want you some more
I can tell you again and again that I love you so
Words don't seem enough, but how can I show
I can be there for you to let you know that I care
But we can't be together yet for it wouldn't be fair
How can I hold on to you? I have nothing I can give
I can tell you again that I want you with me to live
You might not stay around or wait that long
Someone might come along who wouldn't be wrong
I can only tell you again that I want you so much
But words are inadequate, they don't seem enough
What more can I say or do so that you see
That you are everything I want and all that I need?
I can't ask you to wait, for it wouldn't be right
I can only tell you again, I want you in my sight.

Margaret Ward

Stolen Kiss

A maiden resting in a fragrant bower
Her hair entwined with scented flowers
Mischievous sprites who attend their queen
Scatter as our hero approaches the scene

A knight in armour, bold and brave
Seeks the sweet maiden to save
He dreams the reward of grateful embrace
When he leads her from this enchanted place

He gazes on her, his soul is lost
To the beauty immobile, cold as frost
Her raven hair, her dewy skin, the perfect circle of her arms
She's bound him with her sleeping charms

Who is she? This faerie's child
That stokes desire till love burns wild
He leans close to lips petal-soft, rose-pink
Like a dying man to an offered drink

And with one kiss he is ensnared
Steel armour left him unprepared
To be trapped forever in guilty bliss
By the promise of a stolen kiss.

Aaminah Haq

Bedtime

The room is filled with winter air,
A tiny girl with long brown hair
Climbs up high upon a bed.
With achy feet and heavy head,
Her weary eyes and tired mind
Need nothing more than rest.

She pulls the covers up around,
And squirms about until she's found
The perfect way in which to sleep,
Across the bed, piled in a heap.
Eyelids shut and then she yawns,
The day is nearly over.

The sheets are soft, the blanket snug,
She drifts away, no toy to hug.
The bedside nightlight gently glows,
A stretch of legs, a wiggle of toes.
With dreams of what tomorrow brings,
And thoughts of nothing else.

Victoria Barron

A Chance Meeting

As I was walking down the lane
I met a woman in great pain
She said to me what can I do
When all that's here is me and you?

I walked up to her in surprise
For in each hand she held two pies
Both steaming hot and very brown
She said she'd bought them in the town

I realised this wasn't wise
And asked the question, 'Why the pies?'
She answered quickly with a frown
The thick, brown gravy dripping down

'Oh my!' she said, 'oh my! oh my!'
I stepped away and gave a sigh
Then down the lane there came such sounds
Of horses, pigs and goats and hounds

'They want my pies,' she cried in fear
'Then let them go, they're nearly here'
And up she went into the air
The creatures having not a care

And so my story ends just there
I really do not think it fair
The pies no more, the woman too
I wonder where, don't you?

Shelley Fairclough

Perfection

Of muted passions, cry to me
To levels now of winged high
The soul to rise for all to see
As birds soar in a mackerel sky.

Elected sorrow dance for me
Like curdled clouds on silver feet
The bustling steps humanity
Shape joy, another day to greet.

Of laughter speak, the you to me
As pathos draws its wavering line
From birth to all eternity
Rain-spotted days, to sunsets fine.

Elected promise, call to me
On double doubt and times before
When hope was lost, no light to see
Perfection waits the open door.

Jean Bishop

Untitled

A bright little star
Shining high in the sky
So distant and far
Yet so near to our hearts

Each night that goes by
Our eyes wander to the sky
With sadness in our hearts
We always say goodnight

But time slowly moves on
And the pain will always linger
But slowly smiles will conquer
Our nightly star ritual

For somewhere high above us
You sit shining down on us
Our little star in the sky
Somewhere to the north

No matter where we go in life
We'll see you shine each night
Our beacon through the years
Our little star shining bright

Brandon Barr Jamieson
Your star shall shine forever bright
High in the sky above us.
Ni ni Sweetpea.

Agnes Neeson

Missing

Three years ago on this day
Three years ago I last saw your face
Three years ago I never thought
To cherish your last embrace.

They said they'd do all they could
But nothing ever came
Nothing to say 'ha, got you this time'
And prove you were playing a game.

Sometimes I feel down
But others I get mad
At how you could leave us
And make us all so sad.

But really we know it wasn't your fault
It was something we couldn't prevent
But all we can do now is hope
And live with what we've been sent.

Sophie Hall

Stop Struggling My Precious Child

My child, the life before you now is full of dreams and hopes,
So many choices you can see, some up, some downward slopes,
What should you do, who should you trust? It's all up in the air,
The world is full of bright allure, it drives you to despair.

I sense the restlessness within, and long to meet your need,
Because you have free will you see, all I can do is plead,
Please let Me in to touch the parts that ache with pain so deep,
You've reached the point of no return, so you can hardly sleep.

You're asking questions all the time, *what is life all about?*
Why is the path so fraught with pain, and you're so full of doubt?
Decision time is here, My friend, it really has arrived,
Because you have no real peace, what you know is all contrived.

Without forgiveness, there's no peace, all searching is in vain,
I have to tell you I am here, to turn your loss to gain,
I died to set you free and came to wash away your sin,
And only through Me you can come, please won't you let Me in?

The needle is on empty, so life's journey is on hold,
For everything you've touched My friend, can never turn to gold,
Because the calling on your life is one to follow Me,
I've touched you and anointed you, the path is clear you see!

The gifting that you have is one, which I'll use mightily,
You'll play and sing and bless My name, and folks will be set free,
I'll speak to you via a dream and tell you what to do,
My precious child, new life is just about to start, it's true.

Come near and listen to My voice and I will share with you,
So many precious promises; I'm doing all things new,
Your life will never be the same; I'm going to show you how,
Just kneel before Me, precious one, for I am with you now!

Gillian Humphries

The Fisherman's Prayer

God grant that we may live to fish
Until our dying day
When comes our last catch
We shall most humbly pray
When in God's safe landing net
We'll be peacefully asleep
That within His mercy
We'll all be judged as good enough to keep.

Duncan Robson

Christmas Cheer!

We deck the halls with boughs of holly, adorn the tree with fairy dolly,
'Tis the season to be jolly . . . so why do I dread Christmas?
We trek for miles round every shop, we search for gifts until we drop,
We're all possessed, we just can't stop . . . my feet are sore at Christmas!
We clean the house, dust every stair, we wash the curtains, every pair,
We do our roots, we perm our hair . . . why? Because it's Christmas!
We send our cards to kith and kin, they send one back with kisses in,
On January 5th they're in the bin . . . sincerely yours at Christmas!
We visit friends for old times' sake, we make mince pies, we bake a cake,
Oh what a lot of fuss we make . . . every year at Christmas!
We get dressed up for the office do, insult the boss when we've had a few,
Next day at work oh how we rue . . . the demon drink at Christmas!
We do a final shopping dash, tempers fray and trolleys crash,
We've now spent all our hard-earned cash . . . at the superstore at Christmas!
It's 5am, I'm still worn out, 'Santa's been,' the children shout,
This is what it's all about . . . I tell myself at Christmas.
We find our gifts beneath the tree, tear off the wrapping, keen to see,
We look surprised and shout with glee . . . then change them after Christmas!
We roast the bird to feed the brood, for days it's offered minced or stewed,
But no one's really in the mood . . . we all feel stuffed at Christmas!
On Boxing Day we have a do, more beer and lager, trifle too,
Next day we stay close by the loo . . . recovering from Christmas!
It wrecks our minds and costs us dear, we moan and grumble, yet I fear,
We'll do it all again next year . . . *so merry flippin' Christmas!*

Denise Winder

The Warmth Of A Smile

A smile can make somebody's day,
Take all their fears and sadness away.
A hug can say, 'I understand';
So can the touching of a hand.
Our eyes, the mirrors of our soul
Can show compassion when life takes its toll.
If we can take the time to spare
In showing others that we care . . .
To 'lend an ear' when there is need,
Who can tell where this could lead?
For what does it cost to extend a smile,
To give of our time for a little while?
To raise the spirits of one in despair
By listening to problems they may wish to share.
So give a smile freely - so little to impart . . .
But means so much when it comes from the heart!

Vivienne Vale

The Night Visitors

In the dark of a night
As quiet as the mice,
Some gypsy folk came camping
On ground as cold as ice.

Below the slope of the field
Their caravans were stood.
A pinto horse just beyond
As still as painted wood.

When the morning sun arose
And spread its rays around,
The dewdrops shone like diamonds
Upon the thawing ground.

Before the world was awake
At the calling of a bird,
There was life around the camp
With children's voices heard.

The horse continued grazing
By the motorway,
Among the weeds and towering grass
As dry as any hay.

There was no sign of hurry
In the travellers' pace.
Just a scene of contentment
All around the place.

Then, one day the village woke
To find the gypsies gone.
For they were just like wandering souls
Forever moving on.

Roger Tremethick

Lacy Whispers

Lacy whispers from a dove
Mountain grandeur tells of love
Spicy sonnet speaks so true
Out of darkness comes the blue
Flame on wings of brightest green
Comes the rarest rose ever seen.

Sharon Grimer

Not Mine

I read the news, I hear the views.
I laugh aloud as others muse.
The song and dance, majestic prance,
we struggle to our soul enhance.
It's not for me, don't put it here.
Don't bring the men that children fear.
Rest him there and I won't care.
Perhaps their child is unaware.
Not mine.

How can they let the killer feed
from words about her evil deed.
It's morally wrong but some will pay.
My newspaper is out today.
They publish lines that pass the guilt,
the victims' lives will ne'er be built.
Who will buy this awful book,
into the mind of Satan look?
Maybe this is what all need,
sickness that will slake our greed.
Not mine.

A bullet for a cup of grain.
A rifle to relieve the pain.
Across the sands the children die
their mothers have no tear to cry.
Flies around their faces small.
Camera crews around them crawl.
Away from here the menfolk fight,
heroes as day turns to night.
When will they stop? Where is the peace?
What price to make this madness cease?
Not mine.

Who sells the guns to feed the foe?
Who buys the guns that cause such woe?
Can we wash our hands and say,
we played no part in this sad day?
And in our palms along life's line,
does the blood of others shine?
And when the pointed fingers near,
can we speak, our conscience clear?
Not mine, not mine.

Bill Surman

The Tale Of Louisa Rafferty

On a cold winter's day
Louisa Rafferty was born
She lay swaddled in a blanket
That was tattered and torn

Her lungs were hail and hearty
Her locks were flaming red
A real bonnie little baby
Placed in a box by the bed

Alas her mother did not make it
Although she gave a good fight
So her father had to raise her
Working day and night

Poor Louisa she was bullied
As she walked to school each day
The children picked her out
With her they did not play

She had one dear friend called Charlie
He was skinny, dark and tall
Charlie was her unsung hero
Waiting around for fear she'd fall

She left home to work in service
A new life she had to find
She bid farewell to all she knew
Leaving Father and Charlie behind

At work she scrubbed and polished
Her tiny hands were sore and red
Long hours of thankless servitude
At night she collapsed into bed

She continued her weary lot
'Til one day a messenger arrived
To inform her of very bad news
That her father had suddenly died

With sadness and sorrow she grieved
Feeling lost and so alone
A wealthy inheritance was left her
And she sold the family home

She acted very wisely
A small guest house she had found
Determined to succeed
She'd make it the best around

By chance Charlie travelled by
He needed a place to stay
The door opened to reveal Louisa
And the years just melted away

They courted and wedded in haste
A baby soon to follow on
She was blissfully happy at last
Bad memories were now gone

But life was never that simple
Her Charlie was taken away
His first wife caught up with him
For bigamy he had to pay

Louisa was broken-hearted
She vowed never to love again
Her son James kept her mind busy
And his love eased her pain

Together they were happy
Louisa was again content
She may not have had her Charlie
But her son was heaven-sent

James was a man of some standing
He married a beautiful wife
Louisa became a proud grandmother
And lived a long and joyful life

This tale must now be over
Louisa's days are at a close
At her graveside each week
Lies a tear-stained red rose

When asked who lays it there
A tall, thin man was to be seen
It was Charlie who stood alone
Thinking of what could have been.

Lynda Long

Why?

Why does the grass make my feet wet as I walk in the morn just begun
And why is it green, not blue or pink or golden like the sun?
Why do the waves on the river make patterns as they flow
And why do swans float against the tide, when the other way's easier to go?
What makes a squirrel climb a tree and why do birds learn to fly
And why do crabs walk sideways and not get sand in their eye?
Why do fish swim together, instead of swimming alone
And why don't they bump one another, why don't they shout or groan?
What makes the sea so salty? What makes the sun so bright?
What makes the sun shine for me today and the moon come out at night?
Why do the stars twinkle and what makes a baby smile
And why must I ask *why* all the while?

Joanne Hale

Moods

The human race consists of a complexity of moods,
as varied and interesting as the selection of foods.

In fact, the latter may have some bearing on the first,
as indeed must the liquid intake have on thirst.

If correct meals are chosen and the right drinks selected
(unfortunately, more often than not, they are neglected).

People would be healthy, wise and happy,
less reason to be moody and 'snappy' . . .

One day cheerful, loving and bright;
the next day 'almost' wanting to fight?

However, of course, there is the artistic mood,
which has no bearing at all on food . . .

The dancer, writer, painter and clown,
have ways of 'uplifting' when a person feels 'down'!

Those talents - gifts bestowed by 'the powers above' -
bring their own special kind of love.

An expression in song, has been known from time beginning;
such enjoyment can be found from music and singing.

Then, there are sports of all descriptions and kind,
which please many a person's mind.

D Spence-Crawford

Nasty Village

We were few, the village's back of beyond
Close to the cesspit, near the junk pond
Truth was, there wasn't any bond
We would often dislike each other
Fierce fighting, all hot and bother
Curse me, I threw stones at my brother

Village life wasn't at all idyllic
A so-called pal giving you a kick
Or being picked on till you felt sick
Johnny Holliday, big nasty lout
Older than me, but I punched his snout
Bully Jimmy Clark still deserves my clout

That's where I learnt to be on my own
Think quietly, away from moan and groan
Realising words hurt, not just stick and stone
Reach out to the bad ghosts of that past?
Never! Rage and resentment last!
Out of the village those demons be cast!

Terence Magee

Society In Bondage

The delicious fruit of the vine
- fermented and misused -
has led to social decline.
An alcoholic force raping human mentality,
barring the way to wisdom and moral reality.
A force rampant through generations,
enslaving people of many nations.
Presenting itself as a social prop
and many drink until they drop.
It holds under compulsion the ruling classes,
who helplessly struggle to control the masses.
The Church's communion holds no power
since grapes were fermented and turned sour.
The Devil's brew has this world in a trance,
leading society a wild, merry dance.
Claiming victims as young as nine and ten,
addicted before they become women and men.
On the way to the downward slope
of degradation, crime and loss of hope.
A painful tug of war between evil and good,
started by the misuse of grapes, meant to serve as fresh food.

Irena Bunce

War

The war is here and I will fight,
Remember me, both day and night.

The world's at war, I'll die for you,
I'll bring you peace, that's what I'll do.

The battle starts, they've kind of won,
Remember me for who I am.

My blood will spill, my grave will keep,
Watch over me and you will weep.

Remember us, who've fought a battle, killed at war
And will stand tall for evermore.

Poppies will grow, memories will stay,
Soldiers in Heaven, watch over you each day.

Many killed in battle, many wounded and ill,
Many soldiers fighting, many laying still.

The war will last for many years,
Many soldiers never come back, many shed their tears.

Please don't cry, please don't fear,
Wherever you are, I'll be near.

Lauren Elizabeth Rix

Love Is Like

Love is like a red, red rose
an expensive well earned treat,
but when the bloom is over
it's the bills you have to meet . . .

Love is like a luxury car
expensive, fast and sleek,
but as the mileage it builds up
the way ahead looks bleak . . .

Love is like a new mattress
soft and full of bounce,
but when the springs begin to wear
you do not dare to pounce . . .

Love is like a telephone
it's good to talk for hours,
but when the line cuts off at source
you then say it with flowers . . .

Love is like the roaring sea
surging full of passion,
unlike the constancy of tides
it gets to go on ration . . .

Love is like a pig in muck
loving every minute,
comes the time you get bogged down
not so good then is it?

Love is like a butterfly
fluttering here and there,
you get scooped up into a net
use your wings then, if you dare!

M Damsell

Strangers Inside

It's such a shame when it comes to this,
Minds put forward to a ten-year kiss;
When no one knows what will happen next -
No working script or prompting text.

No understanding of how it's been,
Pain and terror, felt and seen,
With no appreciation, how can you say -
That such and such must be this way?

The things that I have been left feeling,
So much hurt and anger, a deep, dark reeling;
Knots and stress, I *will* explode -
Tension, fear, too great a load.

I find it hard to see past this,
When all these feelings still exist;
Bought to the forefront of my mind,
With no escape, no way to find -
Of dealing with them finally;
When I'm still trying to deal with me.

Things get rocky and have been hard,
But you work at them and don't get marred -
By angry feelings or defensive ways,
No angry words will help today.

To say it was good, but now it is not -
You know that's how to hit the spot!
But then how do you explain away -
So much laughing, how much we play?

It feels like a knife you know to turn,
Insecurity heightened, as you will learn.
So let's try and keep it above the belt;
Every hit, is a hard hit dealt.

Victoria Tagg

Foodstuff

In days of medieval wrath
And monasterial tax
When knights in oath were honour bound
To stretch the foe on racks

A common man was but a pawn
Upon the board of life
Longevity a luxury
And minimal his life

His oaty gruel was pitiful
And scabrous in the bowl
With leaven bread or meagre stew
Sustaining heart and soul

On scarred and howling battlements
With banquetings beneath
The lutenists in tabards plucked
Above the spitting beef

The chicken legs in unison
Were sucked to viscous bone
As peasantry and serf alike
Made do with what was thrown

It was not nice to treat them so
But power was with the king
And like the ones with money now
Do almost anything

And so, as centuries pass by
In virilescent doom
Still breakfasting, we stir and scoop
Our porridge from the spoon

Within the sharp commuter belt
The worsted suited crush
Consuming plastic sandwiches
To catch the morning rush

Those weekend eateries are sought
With fry-ups on the hop
From motorways to burger bars
Or filling-station shop

Reflecting on the certain course
Of overflow and waste
Will food be but a memory
To cellophane or taste?

Clive W Macdonald

Much Ado About Nothing?

Changing times and signs and climes,
New-found beats and rules and rhymes,
To set the pace, invading space,
Repelling grace. A frenzied race,
To stumble to the finish line.

And ringing, singing, drilling drones,
Technology's resounding tones,
To ease and please and thrill and kill,
And laud Man's undisputed skill,
He now can calculate and clone.

And jar and jangle, tease and tangle,
Frenzied minds to weep and wrangle,
And still the beat marks out the time,
Keeping hopelessness in line,
With fiery darts from every angle.

And dragging, flagging, sagging forces,
Sapping all required resources,
Nothing left, bereft, for pride,
Has sought to cover up and hide,
And measure out its own dark course.

J Collett

Living With Nature

I feel at home in my garden
With nature all around
I hope God will pardon
The way I use his ground.

There are trees large and tall
Beside them the flowers look small
In spring all the birds appear
It makes you feel God is near.

Many of God's creatures visit to see
What there is for a feed
Different kinds of birds arrive
Swooping down from the skies.

A starling stops to have a bath
His antics really make you laugh
The garden is a refuge for all
Creatures both large and small.

It is quite true
The peace of a garden is good for you
Enjoy your garden when you can
Because that's where nature lends a hand.

Jean Bradbury

Somehow Knowing

My husband Paul, with my life I share,
a love so deep without despair,
I said these words so long ago,
when this man I did not know.
Deep inside though, always knowing,
in which direction I was going,
to his heart and far beyond,
but I never saw such a holding bond.
There had to be such a love this true,
just didn't know it would be you,
I saw your face a million years before,
the day we met I was so sure.
My strength and energy all in one,
and a magical feeling had begun,
the world was sad before we met,
but now I can face it without regret.
A love so true, a love so strong,
that can only last for all life long,
one moment's glance and time stood still,
the pause, the hope, the fear, the thrill.
There has never been a love like this,
together we are strong and life is bliss,
could not go on without you here,
you're my world, my life and to me so dear.

Michelle Sims

Earth's Destruction

Tampering with nature's plans
Who do we think we are?
Altering the world and its plans
Just for the sake of our cars.

Polluting the oceans and the rivers
With all our toxic waste
Dumping without thinking
Causing chaos in our haste.

Cutting down the forests
Making animal species extinct
What on earth are we doing?
It's time to stop and think.

Time to save the planet
To help Mother Nature bloom
Time is of the essence
Do something to help soon.

Donna Salisbury

Stuff

This stuff, this stuff
Once it was useful
But now it is duff.
We take it from here
And move it to there
But it's got to be sorted
So please take a care.

More stuff, more stuff
Clothes, shoes and odd bits
All covered in fluff.
Stuff packed into cases
And some in a sack
Maybe there's treasure
But at most bric-a-brac.

Enough, enough
It's no longer a laugh
Our landscapes are filled
Our cities defiled.
Soon it will fill every space
Then we'll be buried alive
And none will survive
It's the end of the whole human race.

Diane Mundell

Seeds Of Time

Live life within your limits.
Don't judge time by the passing of minutes.
Time is of no concern.
Think only of life and the lessons you'll learn.
Each day will pass, as is the way.
And all your problems will fade away.
Life is more than the passing of hours.
Think of it, if you will, as a plant that flowers.
It blossoms, it grows, it comes to seed.
It does not question the time that it needs.
Time is of no concern.
Don't think of life as an amount of years.
Don't burden yourself with guilt and fears.
Life is for living, love for giving.
Start with yourself, let your feelings flow.
Then like the flower, your love will grow.
And before you know it, there are no limits.
Time is of no concern.

Andy Peek

A Mother's Love

She bears down to give birth,
To a son that takes her heart.
A new life is born on Earth
And a love you cannot part.

Caring for him through his infant years,
And protecting him with all her might,
Wiping away his innocent tears,
And keeping him safe at night.

She tolerates his cantankerous ways,
And wipes his dirty nose,
Lapping up his childhood days,
While his curiosity grows.

Then comes the teenager from Hell,
With his temper ever flaring,
But she won't give up as she can tell,
He still needs her caring.

Her little boy is now a man
And he's ready to fly the nest,
She knows she's done the best she can,
But still her heart won't rest.

She whispers the words 'I love you',
As she watches her young man leave,
She's knows it's what he now must do,
But still she can't help but grieve.

A new beginning, a new life,
As he moves to pastures new.
A first job, a beautiful wife,
But a mother who'll always love him too!

Diane Beamish

Collaboration

Why can't governments collaborate
and majorly elaborate,
on the plan,
the yearly ban?

The big man
should stand on the stand,
he should explain the theory, expand,
make sure it's clear,
the people understand,

what the country's going to do,
what, where, when, why and to who.

Instead of Mr Blair,
giving the authoritative stare,
to the journalist who asked the
question he couldn't answer.

Doing the conference makes him a chancer,
there's always the chance of that question.
Why are we in this war?
What are we fighting for?
What are these soldiers dying for?

Put the evidence on my door,
I might agree and support your campaign,
but then again,
I might disagree,
would you then listen to me?

Why can't we collaborate?
It's our country!

Kim Davies

The Rainbow

Seated in the car one afternoon,
The rain ended our picnic, all too soon.
A flash of lightning struck and the thunder came,
And the road was filled with flashes of rain.

Our pleasant afternoon had soon come to an end,
Quite soon we would make our homeward trend.
But wait, let the worst of the storm go by,
We may somewhere see, a brighter sky.

Five, ten, fifteen minutes, time did not race,
The storm decided to seek another place.
And as it left, our joys rose high,
A beautiful rainbow filled the sky.

It was the brightest, clearest rainbow I ever did see,
A magnificent sight and it was something free.
The clear beautiful colours of this wondrous dome,
I'll never see a better one, wherever I may roam.

An architect with the finest compass set,
Could never make a better curve than that.
Much more to our delight, there was a second one too,
Its reflection completed, a most thrilling view.

Think of old Noah and his anguish of forty nights,
In his ark, defying the storm at its might.
And the promise God made, that never again,
Would He think of destroying His fellow men.

Albert E Bird

My Life

As I sit in my chair
And reflect on my life
My duty as mother
My role as a wife

I can't help but wonder
Did I make the right choice?
Did I make myself heard?
Did I have a voice?

Did my life really count
In God's great scheme?
Are my memories important,
As real as they seem?

If I wasn't here
Would anyone care?
These thoughts surround me
As I sit in my chair.

Sheila Jane Hobson

The Night Makes Me Think

The night makes me think
Of horrible nightmares
Of demons, of monsters
But nobody cares

This isn't nice
It's actually mean
It treats me like a slave
And night is the Queen

I want something to kill it
The moon maybe
Or the sun, or the stars
Or even the sea

It's bedtime now
Another scary night
This won't be good
But a horrible fright

The moon is nicer
Shows us night has begun
It feels so safe
Another *day* will come!

The moon will kill
That would be great
Then I wouldn't feel so
Scared at night.

The night is now
No longer scary
Not frightful and mean
And not even hairy!

Because now I know
It's all in my head
So I won't be scared
When I jump into bed.

Dien Curtis (10)

Love Is ...

Love is a beautiful, rambling rose,
That seeks not want, nor yearns repose.

Love is faithful, sweet, secure,
Innocent, laughing, gay, demure.

Love is the look between a man and his wife,
The unsaid word that breathes of life.

Love is the warmth of a baby's smile,
Pure and sweet, without any guile.

Love is the laughter of children sweet,
Who play together in a happy street.

Love is the joyous abandon rare,
Of sports-car thrill of youth who care.

Love is the strength of a church-filled hour,
That renews lost hope 'neath a belfry tower.

Love is passionate, grand and strange,
The thrill of fulfilment in a wondrous range.

Love is the beauty of a nodding flower,
Telling the bee of its hidden power.

Love is the chatter of lovebirds sweet,
That perch together in their tiny retreat.

Love is the cuddling of a kitten soft,
In chubby hands now held aloft.

Love is a newborn baby's cry,
The birth of love, not born to die.

Love brings contentment, sweet and serene -
The vision of hope in God's hidden machine.

Valma Streatfield

Interview

Sleek suits stare back at you
from across a shiny mirrored desk
they do not take their eyes off you
putting your nerves to the test

You do not know how to move
every blink betrays your calm unease
- just a matter of confidence -
a chair scrapes towards your destiny

The first question nails you to the floor
and you dredge your mind for a sharp reply
bottled water unopenable
and all the time your mouth's gone dry

Halfway through you know you've lost
but the game continues
inexorable
grilled and turned on a mental spit
and your voice sounds uncomfortable

And then it's over and they smile
and politely lead you to the door
- a shake of hands, an eye contact
that you've seen somewhere before . . .

Thin envelope lying on the mat
blights all hope you held on to
you know its contents all so well -
another folded interview

'We were most impressed with your skills
but on this occasion we regret . . . '

so another charade comes to a close
best of luck . . .

unemployed!

Steve Gunning

Death Cheater

This time my poet shall begin the show!
This time of mine is up, I have to go,
This time my dance of life came to its end,
This time from life to death I did transcend.

This time of death deals me such sweet sorrow,
This time for me there will be no tomorrow,
I crouched upon the ridge of roof so high,
Held up my head and touched the naked sky.

That was, but now my body's bent and dead,
That was before when I could see the shed,
A big brown cat thought he could hide from me,
A big brown cat on shed was plain to see.

That's when the worst of all gave out its call,
That's when my toes turned straight so I should fall,
My corpse which no longer saw for miles,
My corpse cascaded down those sloping tiles.

One simple bounce saw me pass grey gutter,
One simple drop to stop with no flutter,
Then *thump!* Big brown cat can't believe its eyes,
A non-flapping dinner, what a free prize!

From shed the leap across the garden sky
Meant nowt to me and no past life flew by,
Extended claws dug deep to hold me firm,
Extended claws made sure I should not squirm.

Gently in its mouth and carried with stealth,
Gently whisked away my nutritious self,
My feathers that made me look ever so fat,
My feathers were spat by that big brown cat.

In cat's quiet place there seemed no real haste,
To place a fine napkin around a fat waist,
That big brown cat was a sloppy eater,
That big brown cat was in fact a cheater.

Nick Clifton

Untitled

Scared to love, scared to trust
Am I just company with an element of lust?
A victim again, I'm scared to become
My feelings emerge slightly, then again they fall numb
I say the words yet I fear they fall on deaf ears
Been searching for that unconditional love for far too many years
Just when I think I've found it, it shatters like precious glass
And I wonder why I feel that I'm forever living in my past!
I make people see the person I want them to see
Yet they never know the depth of pain within the *real* me
Too scared to tell the story, the horrid, sordid truth
Would anyone really believe me without solid, given proof?
I've never known what it's like to live, just what it's like to survive
And I still keep at bay that girl inside who wants to come alive
I know she's still there within me but she's just too afraid
To trust another person for fear of being betrayed
Do you really love me? is always my question
Needing constant reassurance for fear of that rejection
I always feel I'm never good enough, yet I yearn for that acceptance
Is it possible for someone to love me, without so much subjection?
I feel sorry for some of the people I meet along my way
The ones I always push away, when really I want them to stay
I'm not sure how to solve that, it's like it's terminal with me
A cancer slowly killing me, deep inside that you cannot see
I'm looking for a way out, so it doesn't hurt me anymore
How to trust that someone that my heart wants to adore
Yet, it's just too hard for me to believe life can be kind
It's all life's cruel lessons and how they just won't leave my mind
But if I'm writing this to you, then I guess it shows I am willing to try
How I really want to believe that you won't ever say goodbye
I feel very lost at the minute, but I don't know how to make you understand
Of how I feel inside and my fears of what future life has planned
I'm just asking for your patience and endurance of my insecure ways
And just a little reassurance at times, that would bring sunshine to my days
It's not the big things that matter to me, it's the little ones you see
I'm sure that is all that's needed to heal the real me.

Esta Taylor

Mum, I Love You

Mum I love you, I really do.
Everything I am, I am because of you.

You taught me compassion at an early age.
And you've been there for me through every stage.

School was a nightmare, I didn't fit in.
I was so tall and they were all thin.

I wanted to be special, Daddy's little girl.
I hated my straight hair, I wanted a curl.

I loved you, Mum, while I was growing up.
And I really meant the words written on your cup.

You're always there to listen, you never say I told you so.
When there's something I don't understand, you say 'Ask and I will show'.

We always laugh and giggle, I hate to see you cry.
And I'm dreading the day we have to say goodbye.

Oh Mum . . . how will I go on without my best friend?
All your hugs and kisses up to Heaven I will send.

I'll talk to you every day, I know you'll be close by.
I'll miss you so very much, this is the reason why.

Mum you've always loved me, you've held me as I've cried.
Every time I failed, you've smiled and said 'At least you tried'.

We've walked along the path of life, you've always held my hand.
You told me that no matter what, by me you'd always stand.

You've never let me down, go hungry or feel the cold.
And I hope God lets you stay with me until you're very old.

I'll become the one who will never let you down.
I'll make sure you always smile, I couldn't bear to see a frown.

The years of love you've given me, the hours that you spent.
The arms to always hold me, the shoulder you always lent.

All the love invested, the hours, minutes too.
Now it's time dear Mummy that I gave it back to you.

Angie Kesteven

Fifty Million Years Ago

What fine leaders the world has got
They will lead us to the Promised Land
Even if we wish them to or not
They will take us there by force or hand
They erect status of themselves that say
Such great men they were that day
What great heroes they were fighting with a gun
As our people lay dying in the blazing sun
I now want to tell them one and all
Your very fine status will one day fall
We don't want you to bury our name
Still nothing changes, it remains the same
History has shown what we have always known
Different gods come, different ones go
Always Man who is left to sow
Cast no blame, it was our fault
Time for all men to call a halt
We did not believe way back then
Leave the statues and guns, take up a pen
Mankind has so little time to see
If you don't, no more history will there be
Guns are not toys for you to play
Man must raise his voice, have his say
Erect no status, they will be lost in history
Then who is left, just you and me?
I tell you, time for all mankind to talk
Or we will be alone, as upon this Earth we walk
And all mankind has had to leave
Then only 'I' am left with 'Eve'.

Francis McGarry

When I Need You

Feeling totally used
So completely confused
Lost and alone
I just want to come home

All I want is you here
Telling me to be strong
Telling me you were right
And how he was so wrong

But you're not here
And I am so scared
Because when I need you
No one else compares.

Davina-Aimée Guignard

Landlady's Lament

It's coming up to Christmas
And the students will be gone
I'll have my house for me alone
Just me myself
And no one else
To share what is my home

The bathroom will stay tidy and clean
No funny smells, no residue
I'll have to stop the curries
And feed them all on goo
The toothpaste will last twice as long
My toothbrush can come out of hiding
The shower gel can grace a shelf
Cos there'll be no one to help themselves
To anything that's there

I'll have a gay old Christmas
With family and friends
But afterwards when things go flat
I'll smile to myself knowing that
In just a week or so from now
The place will buzz with familiar row
Of students clattering around

No matter what the future's storing
It'll be anything but bloody boring.

Janet Scrivens

Gods In The Sky

Astronomy is known as the oldest science
The oldest telescope used as the appliance
To explore the sky on a very clear, dark night
In a place where there are no city lights
And to behold an absolute, amazing sight

It consists of thousands of stars
Some near to the eye, some very far
Some much brighter than others
A beautiful unexplained mystery that discovers

The moon changing from a thin crescent
To a full circle then back again
As one of the stars starts their great descent
Something to see to the time's end

In days of old in ancient times
People back then used to think of a sign
From the sun, moon and stars as godlike
A magnificent scene to enjoy by mankind.

Dharminder Gill

Help Wanted (Apply Within)

Why are things not the way they seem?
Cut wrists not seen as a silent scream
And crying is seen as crocodile tears
Not the emerging of your innermost fears!

The pain in your head caused by tension
And pills being popped for attention.
How many doors need to slam
Before you realise they don't give a damn?

How many times we try to please
So we can feel at total ease.
And many times we stop to look
At broken hearts and the time it took.

What started as a little tiff
Nasty words come fast and swift.
And how many lives will it take
To part true love with the fake.

Why do the good always die young
When only half their time is done?
Sitting at night all alone
No one to talk to on the phone.

Other people sit alone with their strife
Praying for someone to sort out their life.
Sitting alone they slash their wrist
Add another suicide to the list.

Jennifer Smith

A Friend Like You

Your promise to me was a simple one,
I didn't believe it would hold true.
But you never failed, you kept your word,
That trust to me is new.

Thank you Jo, for your steadfast care,
Your peace and logic and calm.
You could have taken my fragile self
And crushed me in your palm.

Belief in my ability, to change my life,
A happier year, no bitter strife.
No expectation or weight from you,
I love you Jo, hope you love me too.

Emma Eliott

To My Firstborn On Her 51st Birthday

Oh child with heavenly wings
flying overhead happily sings

Reminding me of those pleasures
that I always kept as treasures

I remember when you were born
your mother moaning, with pain torn

Seeing you for the first time
holding you, life felt sublime

How time runs fast
but memory still lasts

Never shall I forget our first meeting
your mother with joy weeping

With you I have conquered death
that I have loved you, no regret

But, being proud that I fathered you
forever and ever, I keep loving you.

Francis Xavier Farrugia

Ending Zellaniy

Lofty heights, some might say,
Loft it was in which she sway,
Head held high, toes to the ground,
Plumbers pendulum, gently round and round.

Bobby-pinned hair, very sweet,
Pleated skirt, cardigan worn neat,
Pressed shirt, even the striped school tie,
No hint of planning to die.

Recoil from the suffocating hell,
From the torture, despair that collar yells,
Scramble, stumble frantically far away,
Pleading our lives never meet so devastating a day.

Tracy Woodberry

Britain
(At the end of her empire)

A country full of poets where the love of God was strong,
whose energy and industry was admired by the throng.
Great men of honour stood their ground and fought for what was right,
and everywhere the people fought their corner full of might.
New things were made and buildings built to last a thousand years,
on Sunday they would go to church to pray for any fears.
They had such pride and standards then from the great to the small,
everyone did send someone out when England, she did call.
Their drum beats matched their hearts of oak, not many ran away,
the streets were full of happy folk when they had won the day.

But now a cold wind blows within and the curtains they stay drawn,
a greyness settles all around, everyone is forlorn.
Buildings are neglected, the machinery is still
and people never smile at all, it's as though they've lost the will.
Houses are just burgled and everything is lost,
the police are too short of men to add up all the cost.
Rich folk burn their British boats and sail off to the sun
as streets are ruled by drug dealers backed up by their own gun.
What an end for an empire that once ruled half the world,
whose banners went everywhere and were proudly unfurled.
Had we not bent our knees so low before the fatted calf,
we may have noticed that our God did not do things by half.

Jean Paisley

Leo

She always knew some random day she'd have to face this news,
But how could she prepare to hear that she now had to lose,
The most precious gift that life could lend to anyone on Earth,
This treasured son to whom she had the honour of giving birth.

What game is this You're playing God? Oh why should she have trust
In You who's made her face this thing, so cruel and so unjust?
Her focus has been poured away in a spiral of pure sorrow.
How can she ever believe there'll be a brighter, tearless morrow?

Because her son was Leo, he's still with her every day,
Cloaking her in comfort and knowing what to say,
I le hopes that she'll remember to always be his mum,
He's privileged that he's the one who got to be her son.

Leo wants to thank you for all you've done again,
For everything you give to life despite your hurt and pain.
He's walking in your footprints and he'll never leave your side,
And he's often smiling at you and he's always full of pride.

Alison Adams

Sacrificial Love

Such sacrificial love only a mother can give,
To give up much of her life so her offspring can live
A better, more fulfilled life than was her destiny,
To nurture her child and then set him or her free.

She is taken for granted and mostly neglected,
Because her caring role in this life is expected.
Not for her are special treats or bouquets of flowers:
It is her duty to sacrifice thousands of hours.

She has to make the decision to let her child go,
Knowing sadness and utter rejection will follow.
Yet, if she holds on, protests, wrenches her hands and cries,
Her precious baby's choice of future life she denies.

So then, after all those many years of tending,
She has the freedom at last to pursue her 'own thing'.
Trying to find her self-esteem, sense of worthiness,
She cannot convert to being selfish from selfless.

The fruits of her womb presume she will always be there,
Whenever she is called upon, especially for childcare.
They know she will, because she adores her grandchildren,
She will childmind for them over and over again.

The day will surely come when her child will realise,
As time takes its toll, he or she becomes worldly wise,
How much his or her mother gave sacrificial love,
Maybe when she has gone to live in Heaven above.

Janet N Hewitt

My First Tap Shoes

To be a dancer I want to be,
For I've been dancing, since I was three.
My first tap shoes were a joy to me,
Tap, tap, tap, I just loved the sound,
As my first tap shoes touched the ground.

When I was four I did my first show,
I felt all excited, and all aglow.
The stage, the lights, the thrill of it,
I did feel nervous, well just a bit.

Now that I'm six, it's ballet for me,
As I gracefully pirouette across the floor,
The freedom I feel I cannot ignore
And when I'm older you just might see me
Perhaps? if I'm lucky, dance on TV.

Margaret Kelly

Catherine

Following the sunbeams
As they waltz across the floor
Trying hard to catch them
Wondering what they're for

Sunbeams change to rainbows
Glistening through the glass
Transfixed by their colours
You watch them as they pass

Grabbing at your toes now
But they're too far away
Rolling on your tummy
Another game to play

Time now for your bottle
Your face shines with delight
Learning how to hold things
You hold the bottle tight

Then the dreaded nappy
A job that must be done
It's another game for you
Wriggling is such fun

Tired out by your playing
You settle down to sleep
Such innocence, such beauty
Such memories to keep.

Margaret Doherty

Never Say Never

I'm never going to . . .
Never going to what?
How can you say never?
You may, or may not.

How long is never?
Never can be a day,
A week, a month,
Or until the sun goes away.

Never say never,
You might change your mind,
Then, it's no longer never,
You've left never behind.

Anne Logan

If It Should Be . . .

If I grow frail and weak
And pain should keep me from sleep,
Then you must do what must be done,
For this, my last battle, cannot be won.
You will be sad - I understand,
But then don't let grief stay your hand,
For this day more than all the rest,
Your love and friendship must stand the test.
We've had so many happy years,
What is to come holds no fears.
Please take me where my needs they'll tend
But stay with me until the end.
Hold me close and speak to me
Until my eyes no longer see.

I know in time you too will see
It is a kindness that you did for me
Although my tail, its last has waved,
From pain and suffering I've been saved.
Don't grieve in thought that it must be you
Who has decided the right thing to do,
We've been so close for so many years,
Please don't let your heart hold any tears.

I love you so with all my heart
And though we now at last must part,
Be strong, remember too . . .
Look after yourself for me . . .
. . . for you.

Jillian A Nagra

Normality

I have good days and bad
Some happy, some sad
I get depressed and excited
I have thin days as well as dieted
I can be conceited, can be kind
Can be calm or out of my mind
I can be irritable, can be happy
Can be nice, sometimes snappy
I can be arrogant and vain
Can be beautiful, can be plain
I am normal in what I feel and do
I am ordinary, just like you
I can be whatever you want me to be
But most of all I just want to be me.

Angela C Oldroyd

Under The Azure Blue Sky

On our planet lies Asia,
Where paradise islands lie,
Under the searing solar,
Cloaked with an azure blue sky.

Nestle yield bound shores,
Shrouded, radiant, golden sand,
Calm marine-blue sea,
Spirit, hypnotic, alluring land.

Hustles crowds of blissful visitors
In ceremonies vacations enjoy,
The earnest, friendly natives,
Hospitality and blessings employ.

On 26th December 2004
Emerged nature's furious course,
From beneath the Indian Ocean
An earthquake of terrible force.

The rushing, tempestuous tsunami
Conquered violently on shore,
Engulfing the entire landscape
With towering, destructive roar.

All now is sheer devastation,
No panoramic beauty lies,
Only despair and suffering,
Beneath the azure blue skies.

To all who lost their lives,
Angels guard in peace,
God bless the brave survivors,
World unity never cease.

Patricia Carter

Sad Reminder

I wince at the sun's glare
Speckling the water under pale skies.
This vivid sea has a liquid stare,
Like the fierce blue of your eyes
That was later rinsed through,
With the sun descending,
To a puzzled blue
As your life was ending.

Julia Perren

Carousel

Searching for existence in the puzzle that is me
I try to find reality; a reason just to be
Do I wear a smile today; do I wear a frown?
Shall I scream and shout today or shall I be a clown?

Will I have some purpose to take me through the day
In this meaningless existence will I find my way?
I want to show my anger; I want to show my pain
When I try to *be* myself, I'm knocked down once again.

The maze of life's confusion leaves me right out on a limb
A search for true identity has made my vision dim
This crazy world we love to hate has left me standing still
There must be meaning somewhere, this aching void to fill.

I need to search for answers, but where do I begin?
A creature of captivity, securely bolted in
The people who are close to me say my soul is well
Is there a key to turn this lock; release me from my cell?

So; it's either on a soapbox or turn the other cheek
Would that make me strong as steel; would it make me weak?
Truth and confrontation might get me through the fight
But ships on alien courses float aimlessly through night.

There is one conflict left to choose - silence or speech
Both contained within my grasp but simply out of reach
Silence could be golden but I will face the truth
I will discard my mask today; risk it and be bold.

Judy Studd

When We Meet Again

Let's meet up in Heaven when my time on Earth is through
Let's talk about the good times as sisters should do
Let's laugh together and talk from the heart
Let's paint all the missed years that we have been apart
Let's colour in the dark days that once we both knew
Let's pretend that nothing happened, to change our worldly view
Let's say our lives were normal right through to the end
Let's fly along with angels and love and light we'll send
Let's leave all our sorrows to melt into space
Let's pray together lovingly and ask for God's grace
We'll ask why things happen to innocents on Earth
We'll ask why some children are stripped of their worth
We'll get all the answers then carefully we'll plan
Our next reincarnation as sisters to return.

Charlotte Montgommery Mcmullen

Yellow

Yellow on bees that buzz and fly,
Yellow on butterflies fluttering by,
Yellow on daffodils' frilly crowns,
Yellow on buttercups covering the downs,
Yellow on rape flowers carpets in May,
Yellow on clouds of a dawning day,
Yellow on canaries that sweetly sing,
Yellow on primroses found in the spring,
Yellow on sunflowers growing so tall,
Yellow on leaves dropping down in the fall,
Yellow on roses with fragrances sweet,
Yellow on ripe fruits ready to eat,
Yellow on sunshine dazzling bright,
Yellow on moonlight's soft glow in the night,
Yellow on corn that sways in the breeze,
Yellow on sand that borders the seas.
Yellow is found on so many things,
From lofty trees, to butterflies' wings,
Yellow is bright; yellow is mellow,
How dull the world, without any yellow.

Ruth Martin

Fall From The High Wire

(Sketch by E J Lewis (1863))

Poised high above the trapeze,
tinsel reflecting the light;
born to the circus ring's call,
trained to perform at a height
sixty dread feet from the ground;
dedicated aerial sprite.

Nerveless and wholly engrossed,
warily testing the tension;
keyed up to venture on wire,
sensing the crowd's apprehension;
grasping her balancing pole,
weighing each pliant extension.

Drum roll! Portentous tattoo.
Silence! Expectancy's lull;
death with percussive éclat,
youth in her heyday to cull,
drubs with a skeletal wrist;
top hat askew on his skull.

T C Hudson

Santorini

Sun-held alleys of whitewashed stone -
Dark cliffs topped white as burnished bone,
Cubist dwellings reflecting light,
Seem to sway on a dizzy height
And depths of dream in sky's soft haze,
Unravel thoughts of halcyon days,
Where seabirds wheel beneath the sun:
On crumbling walls quick lizards run;
Now, like a hawk, descends the night
And foam-flecked waves fade out of sight:
Where countless galaxies above
Are mirrored in a sea of love:
From Delphi fair Apollo flies,
Gives back to men their youthful eyes -
To scan the whole horizon's arc
For stars like holes in velvet dark
And where volcanic beaches lie,
Beneath a moon about to die,
Small twinkling towns wedged into night,
Are luminous with spectral light;
Their ghostly glow pervades blue domes,
Whose crosses protect human homes:
The moon-held alley's soft-lit stone
Hems me in lamplight, all alone.

Dave Austin

My Grandad Pete

Grandad's cool, Grandad's great,
He's the one that no one will hate.
Grandad's loving, Grandad's loveable,
But most of all Grandad's cuddlyable.

He's my pal and spoils me rotten,
But under the skin he is as soft as cotton.
I love him to bits, he is a god,
But when I'm bad, he thinks I'm a sod.

Grandad's funny, he is a good chap,
When I was younger I sat on his lap.
He tells me stories from the war,
After he says it once, I hear it twice more.

He's travelled the world with the marines,
He tells me what it is like, living on beans.
I love my grandad; I wouldn't swap him at all,
He is really clever, my grandad knows it all.

Kirk Blacker (12)

Vicky

When I was but a teenage boy
my sister gave me a wonderful gift.
But when I found it wasn't a toy,
I really was rather miffed!

The gift, you see, was a baby girl
and I really wasn't impressed.
She threw my mind into a whirl,
and her crying made me distressed.

For many years I viewed the babe
with nothing but disdain.
With all the noise that she made
she really was a pain.

So much time has passed since then,
we each have gone a different way.
Now we're back together again,
and there is something I must say.

For that noisy babe has now grown,
she's beautiful and tall.
I really wish back then I'd known
she was the greatest gift of all.

Kevin Whittington

Wisdom In The Wilderness

Thank you for helping me
To be myself again
For reeling in the sunshine
And letting go of rain
For the calm and quiet sanctuary
Of an understanding ear
For making safe the present
And banishing the fear.
When all around seemed chaos
Thank you for the core
For giving me the will
To hope and dream of more
For wisdom in the wilderness
And the courage to evolve
Once more to put my faith in love
And its magical resolve.

Laura Urquhart

Hidden Charms

Hello Jenny, I'm here - but you really look bad,
You're all bandaged up, what a time you have had.
I miss you so much - it must be grim to be here,
But they will keep you awhile - they've made that quite clear.

I can just see your eyes - I can't see your face.
That car was caught speeding - it was quite a disgrace.
He tried to escape but the police caught his car.
He was caught in the traffic. He didn't get far.

I'd never have guessed your eyes were so blue,
And I wish you could speak - I bet you do too.
You look ever so worried by the look in your eyes.
That's all I can see - it's like a disguise!

But Jenny I know you - you do worry so much,
You've just got some bad bruising - not a lot - just a touch.
The nurses have told me you are getting on well.
We'll soon see your face, so then we can tell.

They're taking off your bandages - oh, I'm so glad about that.
I'll wait till it's done, then there'll be time for a chat.
Bye Jenny for now - how I long for a talk,
I'll not leave the hospital, I'll just go for a walk.

. . . Oh Jenny - oh my goodness it's *not* Jenny I see -
I don't even know you - where can she be?
Who was I talking to when I sat here before?
Heavens - there's Jenny! She's just come through the door!

Ronald Moore

Start Of The Dance

Somewhat belatedly I rose, belatedly,
And asked for just one dance;
Gave a shy, honest glance -
Somehow appealing, somehow revealing -
Said in every weather we belonged together!

Our eyes meeting, our hearts beating
To the music's rhythm and drumbeat's time
Through all of our days
In all of life's ways
Back and forth with delight together -
Our feet as light
As a wind-blown feather
Like we danced last night!

Dan Pugh

Life

Travelling on this journey called Life
Through aeons of darkness and strife
Putting aside the real life within
Not knowing where it all begins.

To travel this life is wearying
Not knowing of love and caring
Loneliness is the downward spiral
That leads to the loveless environs.

Picking up threads day after day
Trying to knit a web of happy affray
Watching the sunrise as the stars fade
Another long day has been made.

Waves beat on shingle and sand
Never-ending as time in a different land
A far-off land that remains in dreams
Utopic is the description it seems.

This place is where there are zephyrs warm
Where inspiration, love and light are born
No hatred, darkness or sickness there
Only recognition and where people care.

This is where Life is free, is where to be
When Life is plunged to bended knee
A place to go when hungry and cold
To be loved and cared for when we grow old.

G Hall

Soul Doubt

what's on the path, what lies ahead
bramble, bracken, leaves been shed
coated macadam, smooth and solid
gentle streams crossing, or rivers torrid
inclined to aim, for higher ground
a beautiful view, is there to be found
at the summit, all is yours
loneliness, enters the pause
climbing down, to allow another
to find themselves, pinnacle discover
life's work achieved, pearl in the shell
best-selling author, tales to tell

Mark Musgrave

Cornwall

The light is so pure,
It dazzles the eye.
Distance seems nearer
Where earth meets the sky.
Flowers bloom early,
And palm trees grow high,
Where artists have tried
With many a sigh,
To capture on canvas
The colours that lie,
In those lush green fields
That touch the sky.

Our southern peninsula
That reaches out west,
Is the place called home
I'll always love best,
Where the light's so elusive
It amazes us all
In our magic land . . .
Cornwall.

Cassandra May Poultney

Enid

She was my mother's bridesmaid.
A district nurse she'd been;
Before that at my mum's school,
As a prefect she was seen.

When I was born she used me
As if I was her niece.
She gave me lovely presents
And lots of love and peace.

She talked to Mummy and me
But I never heard
Her talk about anyone
With scandal - not a word.

She was a lovely person,
Was always just the same.
She died not long ago, you know,
And Enid was her name.

Jillian Mounter

You Can Run

You can keep quiet
Or you can run away
It will catch up with you though
You know that, one day
Keep laughing and joking
Pretend that it's a lie
But people will notice
And they will wonder why
Don't stutter or shake
In case people see
That you're not in control
But afraid, unlike me
The clock is now ticking
Your time has run out
Soon everyone will know
What my life was about
What you did to me
Will soon be heard
It doesn't take much
Just a few little words

Michelle Harvey

Au Revoir

As we move through our lives,
This world keeps on turning.
We search in our hearts,
For the love, that we're yearning.

Goodbye seems so long,
Adieu seems so sad.
Our memories are full
Of the times, we once had.

Fresh tears well our eyes,
Hearts ache at the strain.
Our memories to hold,
Until we meet again.

Colin Wallace

Landmines

Landmines lurk low in war-torn lands,
Waiting, anticipating the unwary tread.
Cunningly hid beneath the sands
To add their quota to the grim toll of the dead.

The battle has long departed.
Who tells a landmine that it's no longer needed?
Set to explode now it's started,
It lies till its fell purpose has succeeded.

No maps were kept to the minefields,
Yet there were many thousands of landmines planted,
They've proved a steady crop that yields
New victims, although their fate is now unwanted.

Have you ever seen a maimed child?
An arm, or leg, or both, blown off with bloody stump?
With this I can't be reconciled;
Compassion and outrage both make the heart strings jump.

If the world cared enough perhaps,
If the richer countries were just for once aligned,
Seeking to remove these death traps,
Not just leaving them for local poor souls to 'find'.

Why, little children could run free,
And farmers in safety could cultivate their land.
Alas! this seems a fantasy.
Landmines still lurk, and children still don't understand . . .

J D Goodspeed

The Old Gate

As an old gate I stand where people pass
And I swing on hinges made of brass,
All tattered and worn as wood never lasts
Ancient and old I feel the bitter cold - from rain and wind blasts,
Unlike the time I was new when sold
Now I feel all tatty and old,
And because my wood is rotten
At times I'm neglected and forgotten,
And so I feel happy and gay
When people pass through me on a summer or winter's day,
Yes though I'm old I'm still proud as can be
Waiting for the time when people pass through me.

Donato Genchi

Thank You For Nothing

Thank you for spurning me when I needed you
Thank you for not being my friend.
Thank you for not sharing problems
And the olive branch you didn't extend.

One day you'll find someone you care for
With feelings so deep and so true.
And I hope and I pray, God forgive me,
That they'll do the same thing to you.

And you'll thank them for not being with you,
And thank them for not being a friend,
And thank them for not sharing problems,
And the olive branch they don't extend.

And you'll wish that they'll find one they care for
With feelings so deep and so true
And you'll hope and you'll pray, just like I did,
That they'll do the same thing, like you.

Joyce Walker

My Mini

M y last Mini and I, we had to part.
 I took it to the scrapyard, it broke my heart.
'N o, I will not have another,' I said, 'definitely no more.'
 I am now the proud owner of Mini number four.

M inis have characters all of their own.
 A nd when I own one, I'm like a dog with a bone.
 N ow this little gem is sixteen years old.
 I took one look, and it was sold.
 A ny other car doesn't have the same appeal.
'C ause I love my Mini, I'm proud to be at the wheel.

Barbara Russell

On The Death Of My Husband

Damp, sweaty sheets, feverish brow,
Eyes pierced by the light,
We'll use candlelight now.

I hold your hand gently,
I keep my voice low -
There's so much to say, love,
Before you let go.

We have much to remember,
Down the years we have shared -
Children and laughter
And joy uncompared.

There's been sadness and sorrow
But our love has been true -
We've faced problems together
And always won through.

And now you are drifting -
You've nothing to fear,
Your pain will soon vanish -
Angel wings hover near.

In the midst of this anguish,
I ask You, 'Lord why?'
But ask not *who* is dying, love,
I know that it is I.

Jane Finlayson

My Wife

The most important thing in my life
is the love and support of my wonderful wife -
She's always my Sun, my Moon and my Stars -
my Jupiter, Saturn, my Pluto and Mars.

So you can imagine my joy on a brilliant clear night
to see my wife spread through a brocade of pure light -
and know that for us, just everything's right.

Edward Fursdon

A Question Of Love

'Will you marry me?' she asked.
Her eyes filled with adoration.
He was caught unawares
by the boldness of her question.
'But I'm forty years old
and you're just a child of twenty.
Is it my money you want?
I admit there's plenty.'
She gazed up at him with affection
like a puppy in awe of his master.
'I don't care about your money,
it's you I'm after.'
He took her in his arms,
she had awoken his sleeping heart.
'If what you say is true,' he said,
'then we shall never be apart.'
'Oh I love you,' she whispered,
'don't you ever doubt me.
I'll never be unkind
just you wait and see.'
Even then he felt unsure
but decided not to worry unduly,
for he fancied she'd have no objection
to starting the honeymoon prematurely.

Anne Palmer

Grampy

Grampy, Grampy you're the one,
I'm so sorry now you're gone.
Times are gone and times have passed,
Now I realise you're not fast.

Grampy, Grampy please come back,
Oh come to your habitat.
This is where you belong,
Something terrible has gone wrong.

Now I know that you are dead,
Something now has to be said.

Louis Dickens (11)

My Boy

A rescued dog you were
Long gangly legs and thin
A beautiful face for sure
You became as good as kin

Young and full of life
Discarded, streetwise and vulnerable
A life brimming with strife
I thought you were adorable

Faith didn't take long to arrive
Your trust in me never faltered
Our love would always survive
As through the fields we sauntered

Those big brown eyes watched me
When I brushed your wiry fur
Then you'd lie across my knee
To sleep, snore and purr

My companion protector you became
It was plain for all to see
Benson was your given name
My treasure so dear to me

Illness came one dreadful day
You struggled and strained for breath
I was filled with utter dismay
As I faced your certain death

Still I love and miss you so
My son, my mate, my treasure
Thoughts, memories and your photo
Now make me smile with pleasure

Dawn Bennie

A Lonely Man

A man alone sits in a crowd,
People talking, voices loud,
Silent thoughts but none to share,
This loneliness that's hard to bear.

I wonder through this life of mine,
Searching often for a sign,
A place apart for peace of mind,
Is such a thing so hard to find?

Regrets are many, wishes few,
Little dreams that ne'er come true,
Life that runs from day-to-day,
But should I go or should I stay?

Wanderings that ought to cease,
But still I search, I search for peace,
Restless feet that seek a rest,
A mind that doesn't know what's best.

Family mine and friends they are,
But those I miss, away, too far,
For these I don't know how to reach,
Although I need and long for each.

Shall I search for evermore,
Or do I stop and close the door?
Fade the memories, close them away,
Ne'er to see the light of day.

I do not know what I should choose,
Little to gain but lots to lose,
My mind is blank, a sheet of white,
Tell me what is wrong or right.

Sean James Olson

My Inspiration

(Sir Paul McCartney)

My inspiration is a lovely man,
A very famous gentleman.
I can always remember being a fan,
And still am today,
In my own special way.

I love this famous hero of mine,
I wish I could be with him,
Yes, that would be fine.

The songs he sings,
And the sound of his voice,
Cheers me up,
When I feel blue,
He's my own special choice,
Yes, beautiful Paul I think of you.

I dream that one day,
We can be very good friends,
From an early age,
My love never ends.

So, you see,
Beautiful man,
Now the whole world knows,
That I'm your number one fan.

S Longford

Watch Over Me

Please watch over my sleepy head,
as I lie here, in my nice warm bed.
I know you can hear me, when I pray,
keep all the bad dreams far away.
Keep us all healthy, and safe please,
help me, as I pray here, on my knees.
Watch over my family, my mum and dad,
if you will do, then I shall be *so* glad,
and if you *can't* watch over me, as I say,
will you keep an eye on me anyway?

Christopher Higgins

To Ruth

Five and forty years have passed
Since the day that we were wed
And still together side by side
We face the years ahead

The love we pledged upon that day
Stronger still has grown
The good times that we both have shared
The memories we own

As we look around and see
The family we've raised
The memories of their childhood
Their achievements that we praised

The sad times now we set aside
Retain the memories that are good
The changes that we could have made
And wonder if we should

But still we share together
The good times and the bad
Knowing that our love will last
Will always make me glad

Now as they years fly quickly past
As they seem to do
One binding fact will never change
The love I bear for you

Ian Russell

Myself

Someone's put a mask on me
I don't look like I used to be
There's silver highlights in my hair
My hairdresser didn't put them there
There was a time my waist was thin
But now I've got a double chin
Shoe heels once high, have now gone flat
Could it be possible, my feet are fat
I used to dance to rock 'n' roll
I've also done the twist
But if I went on the dance floor now
No doubt I'd slip a disc
So I'll sit down and watch TV
And think of how life used to be
When I was young and fancy free
As I was then, I still am me.

M Watts

243

Timmy

He acquired us one day as a teeny, tatty kitten,
As unkempt and scruffy as a cast-off, woollen mitten,
His half-wild tabby mother squatted ruins from a bomb,
His father was disreputable, a 'love and leave them' tom.

He blossomed and he bloomed with our tender loving care,
His thin frame filled out, and he no longer looked so spare,
His tiger-striped coat shone and gleamed in sun-reflected light,
His eyes glinted emerald-green in darkness of the night.

He started to repay us, using his inherent skills,
By laying at our feet, his stalked and hard-won kills,
A rat, a mouse, a frog, a vole, a little feathered bird,
He looked so proudly at them all and literally purred.

As he reached maturity, he'd go out on the tiles,
And woo the local talent with all his cat-like wiles,
Fighting off the opposition became a nightly chore,
He attacked them so ferociously, he always held the floor.

Now he's old and battle-scarred, his ears all torn and tattered,
He lays and sleeps, his whiskers twitch, and dreams of toms he's battered,
He thinks of all the kits he's sired, and inwardly he groans,
'Cause now he only stirs himself for milk and meat and bones.

G K (Bill) Baker

For Someone Special

There is so much in my heart that I'd really like to say,
Yet no matter how I try I just cannot find a way.
For you see, you are always there even when clouds are grey,
You make everyone you see have joy in a very special way.
The kindness in your heart, words could never convey,
For you make this world so beautiful in such a special way.
And people will always love you no matter what you say.
So remember that you are very special in everything you say and do.

Nancy Elliott

Earth Mother

Earth mother is nature
An ambassador to God
To every living creature
She is their rod

Controlling the four divisions of the year
Known as the season
Mistress of the atmosphere
Synchronised in union

Sometimes she is cruel
In a sombre world
But when she does refuel
She does it in a positive attitude

At times when she is good
She is calm and tranquil
Very much understood
Because she has an iron will

For God in His wisdom
Has given her the power to act
In her own way she bids you welcome
In His name she is precise and exact

This powerful ambassador
Is unique like no other
Having the key to Heaven's door
The one and only earth mother.

Walter Mottram

A Dying Child

I want you all close to me, to hold my hand,
When I start my journey to the unknown land,
Though I feel so happy and I have no fear,
I just like you round me, to know you are there.
I don't wish you to cry or mourn over me,
I'll still be with you but at last I'll be free.
While you're in the garden among the flowers,
Think of me then, and the many happy hours.
When you walk on the sands beside the wild sea,
I'll be walking there too, so remember me.
When you gaze up at night at the brightest star,
I'll be shining on you, yet I won't be far.
When you sit outside in the hot summer sun,
You will feel my warmth, for we all are one.
Keep on holding my hand, it won't be too long,
Like a bird I will soar to eternal song.

U Johnson

Golden Wedding

My dad said what's all the fuss
It's surely not 'cause of us
But the family you see
Well we all agreed

That occasions like this are quite rare
As everyone here is aware
Fifty years is a milestone in time
So we're celebrating with wine

And I call for a toast
To whom I can boast
Are both now the genuine thing
Fifty years ago sealed with a ring

Golden oldies I think that is the phrase
How they did it will always amaze

The ups and the downs
The smiles or the frowns
Through good times and bad
Both happy not sad

So raise up your glasses with me
I wish them the best there can be
From all of us here in this room
A toast now to Ron and June

D Sheasby

Self-Portrait

Hair of gold and ochre skin.
Lips of pink, neck long and thin.
Cheekbones blushed with rosy hue.
Eyes quite small and cobalt-blue.
Ears just pert and neat straight nose,
Wrinkles, some (forget all those).

Diane Bowen

Colours

Colour is all around us,
Even though we may not know.
The sun is gold and yellow,
When it is all aglow.

The trees are green, the grass is too,
The sky is white and blue.
The buildings are all different colours,
And as people we are too.

We have flowers of red and purple,
And pink and orange too.
Bees of black and gold,
Even birds of brown and blue.

So life is not as dull as we think,
With colours like this to see.
We should be glad to be alive,
To see these colours for free.

Sandie Smith

Precious Moments

Precious moments in a life
When we became a man and wife
Days of course that have much worth . . .
The miracle of a baby's birth.
Those times of joy and ecstasy
Embracing one you love
Moments we feel we've received . . .
Great blessings from above.
Seeing nature at its best
In glorious hues and shades
Knowing that our own true love
Is love that never fades.
Those special days we toast with wine . . .
When told our problems are benign.
Silver, ruby, golden days
We celebrate in joyful ways.
And happy moments as we age . . .
Enough to fill another page!

Harold Hyman

The Ghost In The Machine

Unaware that there would be strife
Faith and reason started the quest
For value and purpose
And meaning to human life

From an early start in Greece
One has been to the moon and back
The other cannot safely cross the street
And Euripides can still put bums on seats

In the divided house - a schizophrenic split
With instinct based belief o'eruling wit
And still we find war drums
The oldest sound in history
Serve again to perpetuate the mystery

Beirut, Bosnia, Belfast, they know
Value, purpose, meaning have little relevance
And it is useless for his eminence
To pray 'De profundis clamavi'
For soon the flawed engineering
Of the triune brain will prove
That it is always somewhere
Darkness at noon

Patrick Daly

A Child's Tale

This hollow tree
Made just for me
Hides secrets in its roots to see
Of fairy tales from childhood times
And nightmares I so quietly spied
I climb the branches of this tree and memorise my route for safety
The trunk of it I name my mind
Where in my journey I hope to find
The answers to my future tasks
And if and how long they'll last
Before my tale comes to an end
I trust this tree and then descend

Bryony Freeman

Sensuality

On the wings of a dove
Are carried messages of love.

How do I think of you?
As I recall.
Like the touch of Angels' wings,
Do you ignite my soul?
As the Sun lights up the sky,
So do you bring warmth to me.
When I hear the sound of the Ocean,
It is Sensuality.

How could I forget you?
As I recall.
Your image is printed in my mind,
Forever in my Soul.
Sometimes it fades and is not clear,
At other times it is bright.
Occasionally, you seem so very near,
And then you're out of sight.

How do I remember you?
As I recall.
An ever constant image in the memory,
Always in my Soul.
As music makes me think of love,
The climb of ecstasy.
When I think of your touch, your kiss,
This is Sensuality.

Hilarie Grinnell

A Past Mind

I know my mind is there somewhere,
though I can't explain why it is there. . . ?
These surreal ideas hit me high and low,
wild of the past many years ago.
My memory's dying and flickering in the light
but there's still a glow, though not very bright,
I'm standing old and below a shade
and the glow will shortly begin to fade.
Though I can't explain why it's there,
I know my mind is there, somewhere . . . ?

Mairtin K

For Pity's Sake

How could I, fairly defined as ordinary,
Dare to harbour the timorous hope that you,
Loving nature as you do with such intensity,
Could ever have any left to spare for me?

So deeply do I envy the bees and flowers
That rouse you to such delight,
The birds, bumblebees and butterflies,
Shooting stars, and a slipper-moon at night.

With your entire being, so it seems,
You respond to nature in all its forms,
In your eyes the unfolding of a ladybird's enamelled wings
Is magical, you even look most tenderly on worms.

O look! look on me as you do them,
If not with joy, then pity.
I too, however ordinary, am part of nature,
Would I were loved with such intensity.

Lynne Munn

A Man Amongst Men

(For Ken Duxbury, a loving husband, dad and grandad - sleep well my love - your Sylvia)

My darling Ken, I love you
There is no one above you
I cry such tears of sadness
Together we shared gladness

Our lives were so entwined
A love like ours so hard to find
It's of the very rarest kind
I miss you so with heart and soul
Without you here I'm half not whole

My lifelong love, my dearest friend
Until the day we meet again
My deepest love is yours till then
I'm proud to say my husband Ken
Was simply the best, a 'man' amongst 'men'

Angela Maria Wilson

Amber-Jade

I am a young beautician - my name is Amber-Jade
Nails my speciality - package tailor-made
In readiness for weddings - or romantic date
Fashioning 'extensions' - lovingly create.

I am based in Suffolk - a sleepy market town
Once took the title (and the mantle/crown)
A carnival in summer - waving from my throne
Surrounded by attendants - I was not alone.

Ambitions I have plenty - saving for a car
Or working on a cruise ship - travelling very far
There I'll be dealing with facials every day
Therapies (aroma), keeping stress at bay.

I *will* have my salon - I am very sure
Advising my clientele how to find a cure
Of smoothing out the wrinkles with expensive creams
But that, maybe, in pipeline - beyond my wildest dreams.

I am very happy with the hours I do
NVQ from college - Stages One and Two
So here's to the future - still learning at my trade
The world is now my oyster - look out! - Amber-Jade!

Steve Glason

The Break-Up

I gave you my heart
You ripped it apart
And left me to pick up the pieces
I'm now all alone
With nowhere to turn
Just memories of fading, cold kisses

I miss you so much
Your warm, secure touch
And laughter I'll treasure forever
If only you knew
And understood too
I'd have loved you forever and ever

But it was not meant to be
You were not meant for me
And in time my heart will recover
I just long for the day
When I don't hide away
And maybe that day I'll find my true lover!

Joanna Howstan-Clark

Trusting

We have a pair of blackbirds
Sort of like to call our own,
How wonderful, they deemed our garden,
Safe to build their home.

Every day through early spring,
They searched our haven fair,
Chose at last the holly tree
Fashioned a nest with care.

Within its density of bough,
Away from prying eyes,
Amidst barbed leaves for safety
To begin their family lives.

Holly tree stands in our secret garden,
Beyond a rustic gate,
Fairies and gnomes keep vigil,
With bated breath they wait.

To hear chirruping of chicks, new born,
For so devoted a pair,
Blackbird and the Mrs,
Their joy of new life to share.

Then one day, oh joyous morn,
Two baby blackbirds fair,
She looked like Mum, he favoured his dad,
Oh what a handsome pair.

Did parents tell them, 'You are quite safe here'?
I feel sure they do understand,
For when it comes round to feeding times
This pair almost eat from my hand.

Dorothy M Mitchell

To Mary

You anchored me through desperate days,
You never ceased to give, amaze,
Your light, a beacon in a storm,
Your dazzling kindness caring, warm.
What little I had left you held,
In safety while my life was felled.

I love the way you're blonde and dizzy,
Always get in such a tizzy,
Snorting giggles while we're bitching,
Pleasure in our perfect witching,
Pity they will never be,
As wonderful as you and me.

Sarah Dixon

Garden Of Ashes

I could not cry at your funeral
And to this day I don't know why
Maybe teenage incomprehension
That a loved one could actually die
The father I had taken for granted
Too young to appreciate
How much you underpinned my life
Until now, many years too late

I've shed so many since that day
In frustration and anger but when
Shed over those who mean nothing to me
Why could I not cry for you then?
I wanted each tear, a word I never said
A conversation we never had
When it was never the time for a youthful male
To say 'I love you Dad'

It's a guilt that will rest with me now
Through showers of future tears
Until I can finally tell you how
I've missed you in these years
For now I'll pace the Garden of Ashes
The place we had to part
And talk to you as if by my side
Crying within my heart

Simon Pennicott

A Christmas Poem

(For Jonny)

This Christmas is way different,
Than it's ever been before,
Now I'll have a great Christmas just with you,
After this I'll be wanting more.

A kiss under the mistletoe,
A smile from you would do,
Material things mean nothing,
Than to know that I've got you

And for my baby this Christmas,
This card is to say,
I love you more and more,
Each and every single day!

Jessica Copland (14)

Once A Friend

Over many a year and for many a day,
Our friendship was close as the mist and the breeze,
But now have the feelings that were, gone away,
And now has the aura, the touch of a freeze,
For now seems the pleasure all seeping away,
And what was once now has the ring of the past,
Whilst the warmness that was is the cold today,
And the closeness that was to the distance is cast.

But if you should no longer give thought for my name
Nor a tinge of regret for the warmth that has gone,
Yet I may be allowed to remember the same
As the sun was recalled though it no longer shone,
For for some what has gone has a value today
Neither time nor regret can extinguish the flame,
For for me what not said is the better I say
And the feelings that were, and today's, are the same.

So I shall not be cursed by the burden of years
Nor troubled in sleep by the dreams of the cold,
Nor ever be frightened by motiveless fears
Nor suffer with rancour the scorn of the old,
But will seek to subdue what rejection cannot -
The laughter that was and the friendship that's gone -
And recall in its stead that life's pleasureful lot
Was a still summer day when life's sunshine still shone.

John Peaston

Starburst Number One

Way up in the skies tonight
    Two stars are burning bright,
One shines as my lover
    The other's my guiding light.
The guiding gleam pulls me so close
    To the jewel I need for me,
Alongside Starburst Number One
    Is the only place to be.
This star is one of the female species
    I can't miss her, she's electric
As soon as I get close to her
    My heartbeat's epileptic.
I don't need a rocket in my pocket
    To link up with her light,
My guiding star leads me to her
    Every morning, noon and night.

Andrew Hobbs

My Faith

My faith it means so much to me,
It helps me through each day.
It's always there, you will agree,
Especially when I pray.

Sometimes when I'm feeling low
And also when I'm sad.
My faith is there to clearly show,
That things are not so bad.

He shines down on all of us,
Our dear God in Heaven above.
In Him there never is a fuss,
He just fills us with His love.

To prove this is so very true,
Dear Jesus Christ, His Son.
Lived, died and rose again too,
And now His work is done.

This was to save us from our sin,
And all our selfish ways.
To make us good and be like Him,
And serve Him all our days.

So just to say that never fear,
Your faith won't let you down.
Because you know God is always near,
Right here and all around.

Teresa Street

Grandma

I sit here in this armchair
Encased in body frail.
Thank God for one great mercy -
My mind is not in jail.

Outside I'm bent and wrinkled,
My eyesight's very poor.
I need a little help of course,
I hope I'm not a bore.

Inside I'm in my twenties,
My mind's alert and keen
On likely conversation
I'm not an old has-been.

Strength and health are low now,
And wealth was never mine,
And all I really want today
Is a little of your time.

Patricia Lindsay

By The Cliffs Of Magho

How often Magho's cliffs would make me gasp
In wonder at the beauty there displayed!
How oft in speechless awe I would survey
The islands in Erne's waters there arrayed!
And if those sights had failed
My childlike wonder to instil,
A glassy lake, no ripples there
Sweet birdsong on misty air,
Would surely then my senses fill!

But her hair was wafting in the breeze
Her laughter filled the air with song,
No time had I to see Fermanagh's lake
Or trace the line of Magho's top along.
Brown eyes gleamed 'neath her ashen locks
I traced contours of her laughing face,
Were all Earth's valleys mine to roam
I'd ask to be in no other place.

Boa Island lay in pool of blue
Inniskeragh's wooded shores at attention stood,
The glimpse of winding road through fields and trees
Before it was lost in Castle Caldwell's wood.
I pointed to Belleek
Then motioned where Atlantic breakers roar,
The beaches of sand that crown the land
With hues like golden ore.

Fermanagh's lake and rock were dimming 'fore my eyes
They could no longer hold my thoughtful gaze,
Before her feminine touch and radiant glow
The rest of God's creation lost in haze.
Silently she wandered to my side, I held her tight
She gazed across the lake,
O Creator, thank You that You share with men
The beauty of all that You make!

I ran my fingers through her hair
Explored the texture of her skin,
Ignored Atlantic breeze blow strong
Heard nothing of the stormy din.
The cliff top sight, the view from shore
But all I saw was in her eyes,
All other views could not contend
With her hair, still wafting in the breeze.

John Richardson

Our Family Of Four

Wondering when we first married
About what the future held in store
As we became older and wiser
Reality came right to the fore.
We then looked at life differently
Grateful for things we've achieved
Not looking for the impossible
Made it this far, just relieved.
We will never be millionaires
One day own a mansion or yacht
We hold something more precious
A loving family, we have got.
We no longer all live together
The children have flown the nest
But we can rely on each other
To sort out any crisis.
We've had our share of worries
Not always had an easy ride
Yet somehow we've come through
Standing together side by side.
Never taking each other for granted
But knowing we're surrounded by love
Thankful for the family life we have
And sure our gift was sent from above.

Judith Watts

Parents' Message

Yesterday's a memory,
That's lived, then filed away,
Tomorrow's still a mystery,
And that's how it must stay.

Days come along like all the rest,
So live life to the full,
Keep smiling love and do your best,
Then things never will be dull.

We don't love you 'cause you're clever,
(Although we know you are),
We would rather know you're happy,
And love you just the way you are.

You'll always be the same to us,
Whether near us or afar,
For nothing will ever change the fact,
That you're just our little *star.*

Susan Geldard

Introducing 'Percival P'

Portly Percival had a brother,
And another and another,
Also of sisters he had three,
'And then of course,' he said, 'there's me.'

Percival's father was rather big,
From snout to tail, a very fine pig.
His mother she was kind and stout,
She spent her time foraging about.

Percival's sisters took after their mother,
Thoughtful and kind, they looked after their brothers.
Four boisterous boy piglets played together,
In the farmer's yard, whatever the weather.

Father and Mother pig watched their brood,
Heads down in the trough, enjoying their food.
Seven curly tails in a row so neat,
Seven sets of trotters instead of feet.

Old Farmer George was very proud,
Of his pigs, and often said aloud,
'My Lincolnshire pigs are the finest you'll see.'
Percival grunted, 'Especially me.'

One day young Percival cut his snout,
On a piece of glass left lying about.
It was very sharp and Percival cried,
Tears trickled down his cheeks on either side.

His brothers ran squealing to the farmer's door.
'Percy's crying,' they said. 'Whatever for?'
When the farmer's wife saw the state he was in,
She fetched some water and bathed his chin.

The farmer's boy slunk off in disgrace,
Guilt was written across his face.
His father swore and walloped him hard,
'I'll teach you to leave broken glass in my yard.'

Said the farmer, 'I've plans for this family,
Annual Pig Show comes first, then pig rally.
We stand a good chance of awards, two or three.'
'I'm bound to get one,' snuffled Percival P.

Diana Blench

Generation Gap

You light up the dark days
You chase away the gloom
You let me know my failings
You never clean your room

I hate it when you hurt me
I love it when you care
I worry when you're out late
I never like your hair

We argue every other hour
We seldom chat or speak
We share nothing in common
We live in worlds unique

They say it's just a phase
They tell me not to mope
They call it part of growing up
They give me cause to hope

They think you are an angel
You have this charm and grace
We know we are so much alike
I see me in your face

When will *we* bond again
When will *they* see us touch
Will *you* never be once more
The child *I* miss so much?

Sam Kelly

My Special Grampy

Grampy you are special to me,
although it may be hard to see.
I love you always with all my heart,
I always have done from the start.

You make me happy, you make me sad,
but most of all I'm really glad
cos you are my grampy for evermore,
this we both know this for sure.

Your smiling face lights up my heart,
I see you in my dreams at dark.
You are with me all the time,
it makes me happy cos you are mine.

Dee Dickens

To My Grandchildren

Find happiness in simple things,
The joy that every sunrise brings,
View the world through different eyes,
The starry studded winter skies.
No diamond ever could replace
The smile upon a baby's face.
Try to see that every tree
Is fashioned for eternity.
The hum of bees,
The butterfly,
The blueness of a summer sky.
The rainbow after April rain,
The earth has been refreshed again.
The sweetest song you'll ever hear
Is when a bird sings loud and clear.
If ever you have been denied,
Some peace of mind,
Then look outside,
And you will see,
That all these things are yours
For free . . .

Doreen P Damsell

Being Beautiful

It's hard work being beautiful
I wouldn't mind some tips
just let me mix the concrete up
and slap some on my lips

It's murder being glamorous
the things a poor girl does
the aches and pains and varicose veins
from four-inch high-heeled shoes

It's not cheap looking natural
these false nails cost the earth
it takes hard cash to look like trash
perhaps that's all I'm worth

You'd hardly recognise me
without the painted face
the deathly white would look a sight
and seem quite out of place

You don't know what I go through
to look a doll divine
you only see the finished me
not the bride of Frankenstein . . .

Kathryn Atkin

You
(For Paul)

In all my days I see your smile
In little things and all the while
I wonder at the life we've led
The times we've laughed; the things we've said
Despite the times we found it hard
And meanly fought, our friendship scarred
Still we stayed together, just
We learned again to love and trust
And build new days together that
Are scrapbooked here beneath my hat
So many memories safe and strong
Of summer evenings warm and long
Of walks and talks; discussions, heated;
Special days and times entreated;
Of autumn, spring and winter too
So many thoughts and all of you
Reminiscence close to heart
Moulded into memory art
It's hard to say just what you've meant
The phone calls made; the letters sent
The touch; the nod; the wink; a smile;
Each moment stored in memory file
And each a message to my soul
You are the half that makes me whole

Linda Howitt

Memories And Thoughts

Dear Jenny I've not forgotten you,
You're in my thoughts every day.
I remember the many happy times;
How you loved to run and play.

It's six years since you left us,
Then another little friend came to stay;
Sally, so gentle and loving,
She too, will break our hearts one day.

Joan Thompson

Sophie

My nanny made me a cape of purple brocade,
she said it was the stuff from what dreams were made.
So in bed every night, as I snuggled under cover,
into my life came this most wonderful colour.

Purple was the colour of my every dream.
Purple the colour I wore when I was queen.
Purple the cushion where I laid my golden crown.
Purple was the colour of my wedding gown.
Purple-cloaked was the prince who woke me from sleep.
Purple his coat he laid so not to wet my feet.
Purple was the dragon who carried me away.
Purple plumes wore the knight as the monster he slay.
Purple hearts and purple flowers.
Purple ribbon in my hair.
Purple paints and purple patches for my purple teddy bear.
Purple wings had the fairies who came to me at night.
Purple sails of the ship that brought morning's early light.

But now I'm very old I don't dream anymore,
and a purple-cloaked prince never knocked at my door.
Now the memories of childhood have started to fade,
but I still have my nanny's cape of purple brocade.

John Eccles

Growing Up

I fastened a bonnet on that tiny head,
To protect and keep her warm.
Before long I was tying ponytails instead,
Fashion was blue jeans, tattered and torn.
Next was school uniform - what a bore,
She rebelled at everyone wearing the same.
Then came designer labels, but what for?
Back to uniform as they all wore the 'in' name.
Career move brought about a new flair,
From chrysalis came delicate butterfly.
She spread her wings and took to the air,
The world looked different when viewed from the sky.
But eventually butterflies come back to earth,
It's not much fun flying all alone.
They come seeking that which is of great worth,
Keeping themselves for that special one.
Now I fasten a veil on her graceful head,
A vision of loveliness dressed in white.
To the one who now will protect, soon to be wed.
I feel happy to know we got it right.

Marjorie Brown

Ode To Amy Claire

Amy dear Amy
Your moment has come
And nobody's prouder
Than your dad and mum
We watch and we cherish
Each day of your life
From baby to woman
You've shone clear and bright
The gates of your future
Are now open wide
So gather your dreams dear
And walk through with pride
The joys and the sorrows
The laughter and tears
The pleasure of sharing
Dispelled all the fears
So now that you're eighteen
And you've come of age
We offer our love and support
Through each stage
The joy that you bring us
No words can express
From Mum, Dad and Lucy
We wish you success.

Eileen Hope Hesselden

Mum And Dad - On Your Anniversary

One special day, twelve years ago,
In warm September sun,
True love to last eternally,
Two were bound as one.

Throughout the years, the good and bad,
The things that made you cry,
Your problems and your differences,
You let them all fly by.

Despite those things, that made you strong,
Your love created me,
Such happiness from each good time,
Made countless memories.

One special day, in years to come,
Sun shining from above,
Your golden anniversary,
For everlasting love.

Laura Howarth-Kirke

Family

'They're family' I always say
To people who visit or come to stay.
There are some rules I try to keep
Not to jump on chairs and go to sleep.

Brothers they are, but not alike,
One is placid, the other a tyke.
One obeys, the other does not
But wagging tail tells a lot.

Glen knows he should 'down' or 'sit',
He doesn't care one little bit.
Brett his brother, tries hard to please,
And stands with head upon one's knees.
He whinges, whines and asks for more
With soulful eyes and lifted paw.
Glen stands and waits, head held high
With tongue stuck out and eager eye.

They keep me company when times are bad
And comfort me when I feel sad.
They sense the slightest little thing
Love and loyalty to me they bring.

I sleep soundly as I well know
To an intruder their teeth they'd show.
My 'family', my collies bright
Keep me safe throughout the night.

Patricia Herrod

Our Jim

My uncle Jim never had any side,
Just wore his red beret with a good deal of pride.
The paras took him quietly away,
On that far-off September day,
Soon after the telegram came, shattering the dreams,
Of all the things that might have been.
Arnhem was the venue, we heard afterwards,
Uncle Jim was mown down as he crossed the greensward.
We look near the window, that was his chair,
Now there is no one to sit over there.
If only he could walk in saying, 'Hello Mum and Dad,'
We'd all laugh and cry and be so very glad.
What madness is it that makes some have this horrible craze,
To send others to an early grave?

Don Antcliff

Dog Daisies

The dog daisies are pure delight
Bowing and nodding in the sun
Tall, straight and comely, every one
They thrill my heart and please my sight.

They fill the verge for mile on mile
A sea of green and pearly white
Their yellow centre shining bright
A scene to cheer and bring a smile.

Their scent is musky on the breeze
And here and there a poppy red
Nestles in the cool clean bed
And flowers with them in cushioned ease.

They take me back to childhood years
When we picked them long and wandered far
Then home to place them in a jar
And never prey to any fears.

For life was sweet and days were long
And every year the daisies came
Tall, straight and comely just the same
Like a pure white clean unspoken song.

Frances Marie Cecelia Harvey

Listen To The Grass Grow

Lie in the grass
And listen to it grow,
Up in the fields
Where everyone can go.

Long grass, sweet-smelling,
So cool and green,
Sprinkled with flowers,
A countryside scene.

Grass just grows naturally,
Everyone knows,
But how many people
Can hear how it grows?

Lie in the grass
And hear the sweet sound
Of grass, just green grass,
Coming out of the ground.

Diana Price

A Mother's Cry

My heart is heavy and aching
It seems too tired to beat,
The world is upon my shoulders
And I am weary for sleep.

Just after tea came a knock at the door
'It's Jim,' I cried hurrying through,
But no son stood there just the form of a man
A policeman in uniform blue.

'I've some bad news for you,' he started to say
'Your son won't be home today.'
Then very gently he sat me down
And quietly began to say.

'Your boy died in the line of duty'
The voice droned on and on,
I didn't hear much more than that
All I knew that my son was gone.

He'd been such a good baby, so full of life
As I sat, I could picture him there.
His twinkling eyes and squat little nose
His head covered with dark curly hair.

I was seeing him growing through childhood
In his uniform, going to school.
No longer a baby but a growing man
The years hurry by all too soon.

Can it be just a year when he came home to say
A soldier I will be, to protect the meek,
Maintain the strong
To keep the people free?

Why should our young men have to fight
For the ignorance of others?
Why can't we learn to live in peace
All races and creeds like brothers?

I felt an arm round my shoulders
I realised my husband was there.
God grant us strength and help us through
This darkness and despair.

Betty Jenkins

A Mother's Love

A mother's love is a special love,
It knows no bounds or end,
And I am not just your mother, love,
I also am your friend.

I'll be with you through thick and thin,
I'll be right by your side,
I'll always do my best for you,
My love I will not hide.

I'll hold your hand and comfort you,
From bad dreams in the night,
If anyone tries to hurt you,
I'll protect you, that's my right.

So don't you fret, my little one,
I've a mother's love to share,
Our lifetime's journey's just begun,
And I promise you I'll be there.

Andrea Ashmore

Accident Black Spot - Another Fatality

No tears fall for you, Mother, though you cried
For those other mothers whose children died
Slain by random bullet or madman's knife
Or grim victims of genocidal strife.

Loud voices in anger for them complain
Wracked by guilt and the vicarious pain
Wrought by the images of brutal death.
They scream compassion, but with vengeful breath.

But you, Mother, are left alone to weep
For your child run down to an endless sleep,
Sacrifice to the god we hold in awe,
The speeding car we worship and adore.

C Wolstenholme

A Rattling Good Ditty

I wonder if all the tablets
That I take every day,
Know their destination
Or ever get lost on their way.
Cos for my arthritic knees
I have to take a few,
And the water pills I have to take
Mean I'm never off the loo.
I take some for angina
Also bowel problems as well,
And I sometimes have to take other ones
If I have a dizzy spell.
I have one for my cholesterol
Also one to thin my blood too.
Then I often get antibiotics
For chest infection or the flu.
So sometimes when I hear
A great big rattling sound,
I know it's only my tablets
Trying to find their way around.

Jean Hendrie

Madame S

War or peace between the sheets
Talk cheap, eat late
Meet your mate
Madam S - Irish way or British stay

Much ado, still shacking up
Tuck good at Maggie's Farm
Severed head also read
Poet's news out of harm

Talking about you
Certain it's new
Madame S offer true, always true
Perfect ending for Madame S - untold success!

Stella Thompson

Taste Life - Taste Death

The petals of all the flowers around
I picked and gathered by the pound
Spread them all onto my bed
The quilt I pulled over my head.

Slept away, slept all night
The aroma left me drunk that night
Fragrant roses, carnations too
Danced around in the morning dew.

The clean air awoke me refreshed this day
Salt and sugar do not mix, you see
Nor does ash and fragrant flowers
One or the other, you've got to ask.

Morning dew or stale smoke
Two personalities; which are you?
Headstone small, or head up high
Packet of fags I lay by your graveside.

George Petrie

Transmitting

Communications broken down
Situations dire
Tense with desperation
Adjusting to the wire
Connecting lines
Defences unspoken
Imaginative whispers
A fortunate token
Casting eyes upon
The oceanic sea
Dreading the warning
To you and me
Burning embers
Creating a sting
Illuminated signs
Always transmitting

Kryna Neil

The Dream

There's a dream I used to have and thought never true,
That I would one day mean a little something to you.
And when the day came that you took me in your arms
The world moved from under me, so stirred by your charms.

And I knew happiness and I felt love
And I felt the blessed grace from God above.

But then we died by my own hand
From all the images I could not stand.
Of unrequited love, your feelings bid adieu.
You turned your back on me for someone new.

And I felt pain and I felt hurt
From the nightmares I had conjured up.
Never content, never without fear
Always feeling hopelessly inferior.

Never believing your heart so tender
I broke our love beyond all render.

And now on reflection, the truth shines through
Of the impossible expectations I put on you.
But to this day I cannot see
What someone like you saw in me.

So from our tryst I set you free
To save you from my killing spree.
Before I destroy the memories too
Of what I might have meant to you.

Meg Lloyd

March Dance

The wind is dancing in the trees,
Look! there's a paper butterfly,
It's so much fun to have a kite
That you can sail up in the sky.

One day the sun shines, then it rains,
The cold wind pushes us along,
March is a temperamental month,
Singing her windy, rainy song!

Marion Schoeberlein

The Supernal Advice

God's men be it ever so shiny as gold,
Together yourself hold and as well mould,
Till it is seen when young and old.

Though men in life must so much cherish
Somebody or something; though their special relish,
Beware! oh men, lest you should in it perish.

Though men in life may grow so hard and brave,
When in love, somehow to it become slaves,
Beware! oh men before love digs your grave.

Though men in life must have some friends and foes,
Never cheer only friends and to foes rain woes,
For some friends are your foes; some foes your rose.

Though some men's successes are preceded by strains,
Persist and persevere, never mind the pains,
For you'll be in your success shelter when it rains.

Though in this life; it's very certain and clear,
That men must have severe or little pains to bear,
Don't live in fear; for pains come and go my dear.

Raymond A Uyok

Did You Stray From The Path?

Did you stray from the path, stop seeing the people who care?
Did I drop my guard for a while, become remiss, unaware?

Did you lose faith in the love that surrounds you?
Did life, in fact, start to astound and confound you?

Did your eyes become blind to the gifts you were given?
Did you let go of the things for which you had striven?

Come back to the path, start seeing people who care,
no, they haven't dropped their guard and they're not unaware.

Don't lose faith in the love that most certainly surrounds you,
and don't let life both astound and confound you.

Please don't be blind to the gifts you were given
and take hold of the things for which you have striven.

Hold out your arms and please know that I care,
that you'll always be loved and I'll always be there.

Annie Morrice

Shaun

You saw a lot in your growing years
The arguments and all the tears
A quiet boy, whose thoughts ran deep
Some things inside you'll always keep
Hidden away from those who care
Those younger years weren't always fair
Got into trouble, like most boys do
And I worried more than you ever knew
Back when I had you, I was young
Resentment took the place of fun
There wasn't time for things for me
This perfect mother, I was meant to be
But I was far from that, it's true
Back then when it was me and you
For I cared more than you will know
With deep down pride, I watch you grow
And even now I wonder how
You've survived from then to now
The baggage of unhappy years
Held together by hurt and tears
Was I too busy to notice how
This little boy with furrowed brow
Who quietly witnessed all he saw
Would retreat behind his bedroom door?
If looking back I could undo
All the things we did to you
Erase it like a pencil mark
To spare your tears, shed in the dark
For it's only now I realise
That firstborns have a special tie
A place inside a mother's heart
A bond no one can tear apart
Now I'm older and looking on
I watch you righting every wrong
A better parent you will be
Much better than your dad and me
You've grown into a nice young man
And I couldn't be prouder than I am
And now I know you'll be okay
And me, I'm just a thought away.

Lesley Hartley

Perfect Day

All I ask
Is the perfect day
In the perfect school
In the perfect May.

With a perfect breeze
And a perfect sunrise
In the perfect morning
On a perfect moonrise.

In the perfect twilight
With the perfect moon
On the perfect day
With a perfect lagoon.

On a perfect beach
Under a perfect coconut tree
In the perfect light
Of the morning sea.

Score the perfect try
On the perfect pitch
Put the perfect ball
In the perfect ditch

See the perfect clouds
In the perfect sky
Feel the perfect breeze
Feel like I could fly.

In an almost perfect house
With a perfect lawn to tend
Bring this perfect day
To a perfect end.

Clare Fairbairn

Constant

I will be right by your side,
With you I will always abide.
I would travel any tide,
To hear your sweet laughter.
I will be your constant friend,
And your faithful partner,
With you till our lifetime's end
And my love, forever after.

Lady H

A Child

I see a child who is aggressive and sad,
This child has only heard that he is bad,
I see a child who kicks and throws,
Perhaps this is all he knows.

I see a child who's silent and still,
Eyes full of innocence and trust,
I see a child who challenges and denies,
Perhaps he's always been told lies.

I see a child, resilient and bold,
Who rarely does as he's told,
I see a child living day by day,
Perhaps this is his only way.

I see a child seeking attention in every way,
Who's excluded from others' play,
I see a child who's lost all hope,
Perhaps he wants to be loved one day.

Positive poetry 2005,
This poem looks inside,
What little faces often hide,
So others, too, may see,
Who the child really wants to be.

Lesley White

Easy For You

I'm not so lucky, my eyes grieve
That explains my tear-stained sleeve
And why I dare not walk alone
In this world that's a life of my own
Full of pain I can't leave behind
Without losing a piece of my mind
I drink to pass the night away
But it inspires the words I have to say
Listening to the ballad that was our song
I have to wonder what you're running from
Or to; if that is what you wish
But I shall never forget your tender kiss
It may seem easy for you to leave
But for me, I shall forever grieve.

Graham Connor

Remembering

It's my birthday today and looking back
I still see the faint old track
of who I used to be.
So in my mind I turn around
and once again I walk the ground
of happy memories.
A snapshot here, a glimmer there
the warm soft feel of teddy bear
o' days of comfort gone.
The kiss I gave in lover's lane
was it truly worth the weight of pain
it brought throughout the years?
But that was then and now is now
I managed to get by somehow
but what experience gained!
Yes, thinking of the days gone by
I gave my all, I had to try
but oh the price I paid.
So here and now I'm forty-six
both good and bad I've had the mix
of life's rich tapestry.
O' special day, what wish for me
if dream fulfilled what would it be?
What sweeping changes make?
Would I begin to turn back time
relive the age that once was mine?
No, not for wealth of gold.
For I am rich by dint of years
my road well paved by joy and tears
I'm where I need to be.

Lisa Alexandra Smith

The Wife

In times of trouble and sometimes despair,
I can always count on you to be there.
A cheeky grin or maybe a smile,
Or just to sit and talk a while.
A friend and lover for the rest of my life,
You put the effort into being my wife.
I love you dearly with all of my heart,
And let us just hope that we never part.
So when life drops all those things from above,
I'll buy us a crash hat so we'll stay in love.

Mick Gayfer

That Fateful Day
(26.12.2004)

An earthquake beneath the Indonesian sea,
Is what caused the great tsunami!

There was no warning, there was no sound,
About the earthquake deep underground!
Thousands of people would soon die,
And thousands more wondering why!

The birds flew, the animals ran,
Almost as if they had a plan!
The sea rolled in without a care,
And caused devastation everywhere!

White or black, young or old,
The final death toll may never be told!
Thousands dead, and thousands dying,
And thousands more we saw crying!

Friends and families just swept away,
On that fateful December's day!
Lying on the beaches or sleeping in their bed,
Thousands of those people are now dead!

They did nothing to anger the sea,
But, angry the sea got as we can see!
So many bodies still to be identified.
And so many people needlessly died!

Thousands of families and friends torn apart,
While thousands more now have a broken heart!
From around the world, aid is slowly arriving,
To help those poor people, homeless and starving!

Broken-hearted and with no hope,
With all our help, we can help them cope!
Rebuilding their lives, reclaiming their land,
From around the world, they are receiving a helping hand!

Dereck Palmer

Charles

A courage; strength and
Faithful friend
'Tis such the man that
Did me send

Care and compassion
Loving heart
Dear Charles doth hate it when we part

A healing presence, sprightly ways
Hath coloured heavy cloudy days
A help to sow the seeds - for way
Of light of dreams - see light of day

Thus inspiration, warmth and light
Thereto succeeds one; starring bright
Close, nearby, thus ones troubles fade
Charles as a comfort and an aid

Charles Binham as are peace and grace
A gentleman
A grateful face
For me thy truly represent
The greatest friendships
Ever sent

Kiran Kaur Rana

Sister Dear

The meat and potato pie
My sister Margaret made
A culinary delight
It really made the grade

Over lunch we chatted
About times long ago
Through which our family struggled
In toil and strife and woe

Photographs and letters
Brought memories flooding back
Of holidays and weddings
With Mam and Dad and Jack

This memory I will always keep
As long as I'm around
The pleasure of a lovely meal
The warm welcome that I found.

Terence Leslie

Asian Tsunami, December 2004

The earth cracked beneath the ocean
Sending a tidal wave to shore
Where once people lived in harmony
Alas, they exist no more.

What force of nature expounded thus
Sending that deluge to shore
Causing mass destruction and terror
From the deep ocean floor.

So great the expanse of water emitted
That rampaged upon the shore
Thousands perished in an instant
Drowned by the sea's furore.

We will never forget the sea's ferocity
As she raced violently to shore
Her strength and volume unequalled
By anything witnessed before.

No time will heal the scars borne
By the survivors on the shore
They'll grieve as one for humanity
Today, tomorrow, for evermore.

George S Johnstone

A Prayer Of Hope

Autumn leaves tumbling, tumbling . . .
Winter's world crumbling, crumbling . . .

Lord:
Send us the green that comes with the spring.
Help us repair and renew everything.
Send us the power that comes with Your love.
Send us the help that we need from above.
Help us to join in a circle of hope.
Help us to free all the slaves from the yoke.

Let's see the people smiling, smiling . . .
Hear our Earth breathing, breathing . . .

Those of us who care, are joining as one.
To send out a light as bright as the sun.
We'll banish the darkness from the loneliest soul.
To fill mankind with joy is our ultimate goal.
We'll start over again - repair the mistakes.
Oh help us, dear Lord, we'll do whatever it takes.

For hearts full of gladness, gladness . . .
Can cure the madness . . . madness . . . !

Patricia Spear

Family Ties

We were at school, two chums together,
We braved the weather be it fair or stormy weather.
We thought that we would see the world,
You tend to have such dreams as a girl.
We both got married and settled down,
But not before we 'painted the town'.
Our children came along and changed our lives,
Our husbands changed and gave us trouble and strife.
Divorce brought an end to a lot of our dreams,
What followed was only subterfuge as schemes.
We picked ourselves up and tried again,
All that brought was responsibility and pain.
This went on for a great many years,
Then came her cancer and a lot of tears.
I lost my friend at 53, I was lost,
What became of me?
I carried on in life without my friend,
Her good sense and counsel came to an end.
It left a void, a gap, no one to fill it,
Are there any answers, I would try to fill it.
To will her back, to ease my mind,
Because friends like her are hard to find.
I miss her terribly, selfish I know,
But I ask myself daily, why did she go?

Ellen Spiring

Parents

Honour your father and your mother,
Help them out when they get into bother,
You know they'd do the same for you,
They'd bail you out of Kathmandu!
You only ever get one of each,
I know they lecture, I know they preach,
But they only want what's best for you,
To get the most from life, it's true.
But I'm sure whatever you decide to do,
There's no doubt they'll love you, your whole life through.

Christine Nolan

Hope

Hope is a word that's not understood
It's hard to see this if enclosed in dense wood
When no pathway is seen and the branches are thick
When mud is around you and you're feeling sick

By looking up to Heaven and seeing a star
You can but walk on for He'll know where you are
He'll guide you and lead you to a pathway that's light
Have hope in your heart that things will come right

No branch is too thick not to find a way round
No forest too dense that you cannot hear sound
The birds make their homes in such places as these
They know of the wisdom of seeing light through the trees

What they have been given by our Father above
Is provision of food and water with love
Most do live and survive with joy in their hearts
Take a lesson from them and you will then start

To understand hope and understand why
We need to have faith like the birds and not cry
For that which He sends is precious indeed
It's His love in our hearts and a hand that will feed.

Sue Brooks

Hope

When you are gripped by a feeling of isolation,
In the midst of your despair;
When you feel that you can no longer bear your pain,
And that life's no longer fair;
When things are at their bleakest moment,
Hope's there, to nudge you and offer out a hand;
To reassure you that there will be brighter days
In this green and pleasant land.

Indeed hope is our journey's friend;
A companion on a long and winding road.
Though at times, lest we forget,
Whispers will remind us, we are here to share your load.
When we feel that we are lost on the rapids of life,
Hope is there to guide us back safely to a sense of fun;
To remind us of the good we've already found,
On this road called Life, and that the journey's still not done.

So much love.

David Barnett

Libido

Urge glitters like the stars.
Unknown are hidden scars.
Passionate kisses reveal sensuality
as vulgarity accompanies verbosity.
Reality drowned in the senses.

Watch out for that burning desire
that sets many hearts on fire
making roses grow in the desert
where all is arid and dead.
Illusion takes the place of reality.
Caution thrown to the wind
man thus develops wings
to fly to where none have ever been.
Vice is all he gets as company
as he unveils in his county.

He readily signs away cheques
giving away all without checks.
In just a split second, with a heavy sigh
he sees that he cannot build
all he lost in that sweet second.

Magdalen Ogundu

Release

My step is waiting for me
I cannot rest my head
My thoughts are all a-tumbled
In the silence of my bed.
In waking I bring sorrow
To a mind so full of woe
Too much to feel and dwell on
So very far to go.
Of fortune, I think little
Of travel, I think much
I cannot go on living
In a tiny rabbit hutch.
My captors have released me
But I've not ventured far
To the edges of my mirrors
To the land of Oubliar.
I want to go on thinking
I need to feel my fire
But more and more I'm sinking
To the shadows of bizarre.

Cherry Hullock

Reflections

(December 2004)

Christmas again, hip hip hooray!
I wish this time would fade away.
Turkey, pudding, crackers too
Season's greetings to all of you!

Phew, the dreaded day is past
Back to normality at last!
But then the news began to break
All these lives lost in a quake!

Season of goodwill to all and sundry
This news has brought the blackest Monday!
It overshadows all the celebration
How can we, when there's all this desecration?

I thought my life was at a low
Seeing these images now I know
My plight is just a dot on the horizon
These people will rise again like Orion.

Yes, I'm not at such a low
They've taught me to get up and go
My problems seem so insignificant
Their spirit has been *so significant*.

I'll forge ahead, as they are doing
No more sitting back, and boohooing
I can be strong, they have shown me how
You have got to fight for the here and now.

When push comes to shove,
You haven't much clout!
Nature takes over
You take what's dealt out!

M McBride

Hymn To Spring

Spring has come once again to this land that we love,
Proud trees raise their arms to the clear sky above.
Daffodils' golden heads looking toward the sun,
Reincarnation of dead earth, new life begun.
Within the heart, a new stirring of the blood,
After the cold of winter, life again feels good.
There's so much to behold, to make one hold one's breath,
With all things being reborn, it's hard to think of death.
Yet all things must die, to once again be born,
As sure as after the dark night, comes the new day's dawn.

Gwladys Mills

This Girl

It's plain to me
And perhaps all can see
This girl has a hold on me
For her innate beauty
Has transfixed me
Her very nature
Draws her closer to me
How I long to be the one
She chooses to love forever
To spend a lifetime beside
And never lose her from my side
Can my dreams be realised?
Every day I pray to the sky
You see now
The hold she has on me
I have fallen for her personality
As well as her never-ending beauty
She has it all you see
Hence her hold on me
Her name is my heart's key
Her name is . . .
Now you tell me.

Matthew Holloway

The Little Things

Life is short-lived
If you're not aware
Of the dangers lived
So take time to care

The little things
They aren't so trivial
Every moment brings
Something memorable and special

The things you share
Through full moon or sunrise
They are precious - if you care
You won't close your eyes.

Jane Limani

Worth In Action

Human nature; everywhere,
chain and fetter, forged to snare,
our mind and heart, misery gained,
squeezing truth, the lie ordained,
divide and rule, a vileness who,
splitting classes, me and you,
against each other, stop the wrong,
of hollow word in basest tongue,
foulness born of wretched mind,
greedy monsters, counting wind,
profit's clock of moneyed yield,
stolen riches, wealth to wield,
the axe of doom, on wishes fine,
all the hopes for thee and thine,
who declares? It must be so,
titled rogues, who turn and go,
steel away, in stealthy flight,
at darkest hour of feeble light,
bite the hand that feeds and clothes,
so how can you not then suppose,
might is right, by force of arms,
we dictate from labour's palms,
hand is clenched, fist is raised,
to power's worth, for future days,
read thee not, the written book,
who wrote this? The ones who took,
all your land and all your work,
laws for us, for them to shirk,
convenient, I hear you say,
did you not then learn the way?
United bond, a worthy stand,
ousts the thief from all our land,
if we be true, ourselves to try,
treasured gain, so vast the sky,
for everyone and all the hours,
action's deeds, are ever ours.

C Thornton

Nature's Garden

Wandering along a city street
A solitary policeman on his beat
Dead-eyed windows everywhere
From empty buildings seem to stare

Nothing here to catch the eye
Except a stray cat slinking by
When, round a bend to my surprise
A sight most pleasing to my eyes

A grand old house from yesteryear
From a time when there was land to spare
A plot left here, forgotten by Man
Where time and nature had made their plan

By old stone walls, wild roses grew
Honeysuckle, honesty and feverfew
Convolvulus and Russian vine
Climbed high above wild columbine

So here was a garden not fashioned by Man
But a moment of pleasure for everyone
A tiny oasis suspended in time
Away from city noise and grime.

Doreen Gardner

Stingy Gaffer

It's blooming hard if I say so myself
Putting up this wonky shelf
Blinkin' gaffer, he's to blame
Crikey, the spirit level's gone all lame!
How can an entrepreneur do the job
With shoddy tools at a couple of bob?
He even skimped at his daughter's wedding
Her dress was made from cotton bedding!
And the bouquet made from discarded blooms
And as for the Mercedes that was the groom's
His idea of romance had a lot to be desired
He'd woo the lasses then have them fired!
I'll wager the moths have sought abode in his pocket
Jeepers! Best continue or my wage, he'll dock it.

Caroline Dean

Tsunami

Paradise islands - peaceful sea-girthed strands,
Clothed in shimmering dresses of sparkling golden sands,
Echoing to the carefree laughter of visitors' revelry,
Kissed by the warming sun - caressed by an amorous sea.

Suddenly, touched by adverse fate, the Earth began to shake,
Foretelling the onset of a catastrophic seismic quake,
Far away beneath the ocean in a belch of gas and fire,
The bowels of the Earth erupted in a surge of savage ire.

The revellers played on - life was furious - life was fun,
Ignorant of the terror unleashed, they had no need to run -
Few noticed the horizon . . . how the ocean began to swell,
That they would soon all be engulfed by a cauldron brewed in Hell.

It came! In minutes it was over - their paradise was lost,
The visiting holidaymakers had paid an awful cost,
For the indigenous islanders - the effects can ne'er be rated,
Everything . . . men, women, children . . . all just obliterated!

The tsunami has left those now deserted debris-littered beaches,
But for the world, there is a lesson its aftermath teaches,
Compared with nature's forces which are mathematically inestimable,
Humanity's efforts to negate them are hopelessly ineffectual.

Yes, the tsunami has left many a devastated, savaged shore -
Left whole populations dead atop a ruptured ocean floor -
Left humanity heartbroken and shattered - left with nothing but to cry . . .
'Dear God, why did You let it happen . . . why . . . why . . . why?'

F R Smith

Old Fools

I thought it wouldn't hurt as much
As I grew older.
I thought perhaps my blood would run
A little bit colder.
I thought the words I'd want to say
Would be readily spoken.
And I didn't think my tough old heart
Could be easily broken.
But, as they say in the song,
I was wrong.

Lesden Chance

A Fish Out Of Water

I'm bored now. What can I play?
It's no fun being left here alone all day.
I've plucked her new curtains and sprayed on the wall,
Torn his newspaper and popped his football.

Waiting now. Where can they have gone?
They left here at twelve, now it's twenty to one.
Then I couldn't wait - I needed the loo.
I just had to use her new high-heeled shoe!

Hungry now. What is there to eat?
Those fish in that tank would go down a treat.
I knocked the tank over, it fell to the floor,
Now they won't see the puddle I made there before!

Fishes leapt from the tank as it flew through the air,
Bounced off the table, right into my chair.
They looked so delicious, I'd just have a taste . . .
Pity to see them all go to waste!

Thirsty now. What is there to drink?
I know where there's water, but can't reach the sink.
I tried to drink tea, they'd left in the pot.
It fell from my hands - didn't know it was hot!

There's an awful smell from that shoe on the rug.
I'll just take this sweater and give it a hug . . .
It reminds me of Mother, so warm and like silk.
If I suck the buttons, I might get some milk!

Tired now. Where can I doze?
Outside in the sun would be best I suppose . . .
Back through the cat flap, as quiet as a mouse,
They won't even know I've been inside the house!

Wendy Preece

God's Garden

God's created a garden of fragrant blooms so rare
The flowers so exquisite their fragrance fills the air.
Faith, a delicate pink flower, its petals soaked in dew
With head held proudly on a stem so strong and true.
A small blue flower lifts its head shyly, this is hope of things yet to be
A happier future in the world, for you and for me.
Pure white petals look up to the heavens above
Their blooms in abundance, this one God called Love.
Many other flowers are in this garden here
Various colours and perfumes which last throughout the year.
But faith, hope and love outshine all the rest
For God created these to be the very best.

Jan Ford

Gorgeous George

Georgina was a lady of ninety-five
A poet, singer and oh so much alive
With a warm winning smile 'neath her soft white hair
She was a charming character extraordinaire
As she went from room to room her effervescence
Filled each one with her very presence

Often around the upright piano
In vocal majesty, this grand soprano
Would go into song and before very long
She led everyone in a sing-a-long
But when she sang the song of her choice
She filled every inch of the room with her voice

It was a treat I will never forget
When we sang 'Sweet Sixteen' in duet
She said, 'You, my dear are a beautiful baritone
With a nice voice almost as good as my own
You've had it trained,' she grinned with a knowing nod
'But a voice divine, one like mine, comes free as a gift from God!'

Now I am seldom stuck for a word
But there is absolutely no answer to that assertion!

Bill Campbell

The Tsunami Or, Anguished Thoughts

Through latticed branches the full moon shone in aqua sky
Tranquil morn, far from those who had to die,
Two doves preened, a feather gently floated to the ground
The rose-tinted dawn silently awoke.
Children orphaned, whole families lost and drowned
Anguished thoughts I cannot revoke.

The tsunami swept down all in its watery embrace
Death kissed and wiped Mother Earth's saddened face.

A wave of emotion swept over me
And I was drowned in deep sorrow.
For them, no more dawn, no tomorrow.

June Coral Dye

Healing Hands

(An ode to Mr Kanaegonkar)

There are hands that caress,
 and those that repel.
There are hands that can bless
 and those that teach well.

There are those that fight,
 and those that pray.
There are those so white,
 and those old and grey.

There are hands full of love,
 and some point the way.
There are those in a glove,
 just hidden away.

There are hands that write music,
 so gently they sway,

But the hands I admire,
 I can see you all nod,
Are the hands of a surgeon,
 that were touched by his God.

Len Hynds

Harmony

When I feel the sunshine on my face
I forget about everything else
It makes me feel warm all over
And at ease with my inner self

It spreads a calm all around
You can even hear a pin drop
It lights up all the meadows
And rays down on all the crops

I want it to stay forever
And hang onto this sea of hush
I close my eyes and don't want to escape
This tranquillity not to be rushed

I drift off somewhere peaceful
My mind swims with the fish
I dream of all that's beautiful
And always make a wish.

Donna Wyles

Urban Daffodils

(With sincere acknowledgements to William Wordsworth)

I drove along the city roads,
The traffic was unrelenting,
When coloured splashes caught my eye,
A golden display presenting.
A hundred trumpets' soundless blast
Proclaim that winter's gone at last.

Beside the shops 'neath tower blocks,
Where sparse soil and drab space allowed,
Daffodils heralding the spring,
A sheer delight to city crowds.
Clump on clump they tossed together
Rejoicing in the mild weather.

No lakeland waves joined in their dance,
Flowers chorus-lined on their own,
Small servings of the countryside,
Planted amongst concrete and stone.
A joy to see such beauty there
Verging the pavements grey and bare.

My winter-weary spirits soared,
At this most unexpected sight,
Their nodding golden heads outshone,
The flashing amber traffic light.
The red light bid me stop and stare
Behold the beauty all could share.

Oft imprisoned by snow and ice,
And shiv'ring in the winter chill,
I wait with patient eagerness,
To glimpse the urban daffodils,
Beside the shops 'neath tower blocks,
Beauty surviving life's hard knocks!

Pat Heppel

Insecticides

The wise old owl sat in the tree
Shuffling his wings and blinking at me
He hooted once, he hooted twice
Then off he flew in search for mice
He quartered here, he quartered there
But alas the field was bare
Insecticides had done their deed
Tonight, the owl will have no feed.

Neville Saveall

So Still The Night

So still the night,
The stars are bright,
Up in the evening sky,
Alone I stare,
Through twilight air,
And watch the night go by.
Above the trees,
Are memories,
Of all I left behind,
So far away,
My heart does stay,
You'll never leave my mind.
I shed a tear,
For you, my dear,
That I miss so much,
Yet in my dream,
You always seem,
To be in constant touch.
So still I wait,
And contemplate,
On all the love I knew,
As night-time goes,
My sweetest rose,
Will turn the sky to blue.

A Blakemore

Tsunami

When Mother Nature gave a sigh
That raised a wave ten metres high
On tropic seas, its far-flung reach
Vented ire on palm-fringed beach
Destroying many thousand lives
Little children, husbands, wives
Innocents 'neath a friendly sun
Some at work, some having fun -
What awesome power, an engulfing flow
Devastatingly to show
How insignificant we mortals are
Who treat the Earth with low regard
And on this planet hitch a ride
Like ticks upon an elephant's hide.

Robert E Fraser

A Child's World

A child's imagination
Is an ocean full of dreams
A place they can drift into
Where nothing's as it seems

A child can act out many roles
True to life or fantasy
Policeman, fairy, dragon, nurse
Are some they choose to be

Just find a group of youngsters
And watch them as they play
You'll see their imagination
Come to life throughout the day

You might see a shopkeeper
Or a hairdresser around
And a doctor or nurse
Are sure to be found

There may be some policemen
Putting robbers into jail
Or a couple getting married
Complete with hats and veil

Maybe you'll see a princess
Locked up in a tower
Or a super action hero
One with an awesome power

Their world is an adventure
No rules to lead the way
They can let their imagination
Lead them daily into play

A child's imagination
Is not a thing to hold them back
It's a quality in adults
That we find we often lack.

J L Preston

Alesha Rose

She has a very cheeky smile,
With a cute and freckled nose,
She's genuine and loving,
My sweet Alesha Rose.

She can always manage
To put a smile upon my face,
Her eyes are bright and shiny,
Demure, but full of grace.

Her hair is long and flowing
As it sparkles in the sun,
Strawberry blonde, her natural colour,
Surrounds a smiling face of fun.

Although Alesha Rose
Is only a very young girl,
Her heart's so big and loving,
She leaves me in a whirl.

She can always make me laugh so much
When times are very bad,
With a smile so wide and wonderful
And a kiss for her own grandad.

I know I'm very biased
And I am sure you would be too,
'Cause I haven't got just Alesha Rose,
But also Courtney Lou.

Ian Hardwick

Two (Failed) High-Flyers

When Icarus flew near the sun
Aviation had not yet begun
But gravity had
And it clobbered the lad
Who'd have thought it? He hadn't for one.

A 'wannabe' rock star named Blair
Clandestine canoodles did share
Which drove his wife bonkers
Because of that plonker's
Cantankerous chargé d'affaire.

Ron Beaumont

Toast To Sunday Roast

Still echo the bells of the morris men
That dance every New Year's Day
On the 'King and Tinker's' frontage
Riders pass on dappled grey
Slowly I walk on by this scene
Passing Whitewebb's, where golfers roam
It was occasionally here that plotters
Planned carnage of the English throne
Fragrances from the Sunday roast
Emanate from the 'Rose and Crown'
A pint or two in the 'Fallow Buck'
Clear lager not that nutty brown
Windy path through Hillyfields
The bandstand playing jazz
Old gentlemen doze in deckchairs
Others seated on arid grass
There's the bark of Rover returning
His master's well-chewed sticks
The ice cream vendor plies his trade
Cream dripping from children's lips
From Brigadier Hill supporting
Homes ten storeys high
The London skyline seen
In distant, misty sky
There's Centre Point, The Gherkin
NatWest's lofty pile
Majestically they stand
I watch for just a while
Smile a contented smile, before I start heading down
To my home there in the suburbs, dear old Enfield Town.

Clive Goldsmith

Life

Life is a journey of pain or joy,
life is a miracle of a girl or boy.

Life is a plant or a thriving tree,
life is a creature from the sea.

Life is an animal which can be
wild and free.

Life is a bird flying high in the sky,
life is a journey of pain or joy.

Marina Smith

All I Ever Wanted

Now my hair has turned to grey
and those summer days are so far away
and I have seen many seasons come and go
watched those autumn leaves fall
more times than you will ever know

And I still remember you
in your summer dress
there in your room, late on a
summer's afternoon
all I ever wanted was your love

Now my hair has turned to grey
and those summer days are so far away
and I have seen many seasons come and go
watched those autumn leaves fall
more times than you will ever know

And I still remember you
in your summer dress
there in your room, late on a
summer's afternoon
all I ever wanted was your love.

K Lake

The Path Of Life

Life is a gift precious to us all
In many ways it helps when we call.
Following a path we all must tread.
Everything a challenge when we use our heads.
Life lets us choose which path we take.
It is not responsible for our own mistakes,
For down every path, Fate awaits.
Every soul's own saving grace,
Life is meant to be all mapped out,
It never runs smooth or without a doubt,
For some are lucky, some are not.
Everyone should hope and pray a lot.
Life is too short for those who may suffer.
Is always full when we help each other,
For many, sweet with beauty and love all around,
Especially complete when we search and have found.

Sue

My Wish

My wish, for me, is impossible,
Would like to move about without pain, that can be terrible.
When you are getting old,
It's nearly always there I'm told.

Poly-Arthritis, I have, there is nothing you can see,
But it has a dampening effect on me.
Want to walk out shopping, enjoy the sun and rain,
Painkillers ease the pain.

Others are much worse than I am,
Try to carry on, as though I don't give a damn.
If only it would lift, give me a free day,
Then I could enjoy it my way.

If one day my pain would go,
Would be so happy then, I know.
Lucky I can write poetry,
In a way it sets me free.

Can still walk when I try,
The effort nearly makes me cry.
Will never give in,
That would be a cardinal sin.

Count my blessings, one by one,
Especially when I can sit in the sun.
With my poetry too
My life is only a little blue.

Olive Young

The Dawn Chorus

Just as it was getting light,
Before the ending of the night,
I heard a joyous thing,
A blackbird began to sing,
And as its notes climbed higher,
Other birds joined in the choir,
Here a chirp and a twitter over there,
The dawn chorus filled the air,
I wondered at this joyous thing,
Whatever the weather it happens every spring,
Blackbirds, thrushes, robins, sparrows, birds large and small,
Sing together, one and all,
It seems all are welcome.
None drives the other away,
As they welcome the new day.
If we human beings could harmonise like birds in song,
How much better we would get on.

Eileen Tarr

Binary

(Monsieur Jean-Dominique Bauby)

A wink is yes, no wink is no
Through the alphabet we will go
Letter by letter, make a word
I dictate my book, how absurd

What can I do? Blink my left eye
Tell you my tale, lay and say 'Aye'
No brain stem link, so just a blink
All I can do except, I think

I am still myself, just can't live
But I have a message to give
This massive stroke has shown to me
The glory of friendship to see

I read your letters, words of care
Deep things of life, you want to share
The reason for life, don't be blind
Show pity and love, just be kind

What matters? Your soul is yourself
When you die, its state is your wealth
The mystery of existence
Nurture your soul with persistence.

Derek Norris

BST

We'll go at 8 o'clock,' she said.
'That service leaves us all the day
to ready get for all our folks
to spend an hour with us or stay.'

Come Sunday morn I early rose
and took my spouse a cup of tea:
we walked together to our church
in pensive mood and leisurely.

The door was shut, no lights shone forth
but soon the verger hove in sight,
you're early for our choral 'do',
and soon we knew what caused our plight.

We'd read it in the daily news,
maybe we'd seen it on the box,
we'd gone to bed without a thought
to change the hour on all our clocks.

Owen Edwards

Spaces Friendship

A new day begins,
when old day ends,
let's visit new spaces
and make new friends.

A friendly word,
a smile on your face,
a gesture of warmth,
for the human race.
It's cold outside,
but warm in here,
nothing to hurt,
or bring a tear,
make love rule today,
what do you say?

To share our thoughts,
to open our hearts,
though we're far apart,
over land, over ocean,
we come to know a new friend.

If you feel lost,
or just out in the cold,
come visit these spaces,
where friendships unfold,
there's always a welcome,
a story to share,
and people from spaces,
to comfort you there.

Thomas D Green, Pauline Beames, Susan Russell-Smith & Eth Holmes

Sunny Days

Ice lolly melting in my hand
dripping, dripping in the sand
splashing, splashing is the sea
water, water wetting me
scorching sun shines on seaside
nowhere for the sun to hide
not a drop of rain in sight
much to everyone's delight
oh no . . . it seems, it's time to go
for the sun is getting low
kids shouldn't feel any sorrow
for they will be back tomorrow

Emma Orlando (10)

The Tsunami

On an island paradise,
The tsunami took them by surprise,
A volcano erupts out at sea,
And giant waves it caused to be,
People floating with the tide,
Houses pushed from side to side,
Rubble floating with the waves,
Some just stood in shock and daze,
People fighting for their lives,
Sons and daughters, husbands, wives,
Children running from the beach,
For their parents they can't reach,
Some tugged from their parents' grip,
They just had to leave them slip,
Waves came crashing onto shore,
Buildings, shops, are there no more,
People clinging on to trees,
Others brought down to their knees,
Twelve islands hit by giant waves,
And sent thousands to their graves,
The numbers we shall never know,
As some are lost for evermore,
With the shock and devastation,
As it touched the hearts of nations,
For it seemed to be unreal,
The world sent out for their appeal,
People's kindness shone above,
As they searched for ones they loved,
That sad day we shall remember,
The twenty-sixth day of December.

May Rigby

Unfound Blessings

Sanctified within decay,
Of all in all of all we pray,
A swift breeze stealing all away,
The simple sight of a new day.

For the wind has all within but naught,
But naught of all enfolded caught,
For truly what impression taught,
Is what of life indeed is sought.

Transformation of anticipation,
To barely beings of expectation,
Leaving all but all of conversation,
Of doubting hearts and condemnation.

Sarah Heptinstall

Turn My Brain Off, Please!

One o'clock in the morning and I'm finding it hard to sleep
so many questions left unanswered and so many secrets to keep.

Have you seen the cause of the flaws of life around this crowded place
the insufficient lacking hunger that's left without a trace?

Where did the light go that burnt my cigarette
the one that intoxicated my body, where the risks were met?

I can hear the ticking of the clock, the sounds of cars passing by
but God help me I need some sleep, I have a comfy place to lie.

To jump up in the morning, everything's all right
and I answer, God yes I was tired and got some sleep last night.

I get up in the morning and it's like coming to
after having an operation that you were never meant to.

You brood, you sink, you think and think
it's never going to end, never away, always a link.

What could I possibly need? Tell me what more I want!
Tell me, tell me, tell me, tell me, God, I hate this font!

Things seem to swirl around me, the screen . . . it's doing a dance!
Soon sleep doesn't exist and at daytime I'm in a trance.

I imagine being you, waking up refreshed and well
having energy to jump and sing and dance and never dwell.

Well sleep doesn't seem likely again and I've tried everything
perhaps I need to find a CD to calm me and let me sing.

Sing, sing, sing, sing, God please, please let me close my eyes
let me get all snug, I know I can, this bed is a good size.

Let me sleep, let me dream, let me go to gaga land
let me breathe a breath of relief and show me that you understand.

Just close my eyes, just calm my brain, just let me feel like I'm here and me again.

Christina Earl

What A Load Of Rubbish

On the way to work today, I took a look around
Empty cans and sweet wrappers, strewn upon the ground.

An armchair here, a table there, a mattress ripped and damp
Two worn-out tyres, old petrol can and a rusty metal ramp.

Thrown in the road, a rubbish sack, the contents spilling out
The carcass of a chicken, a teapot with broken spout.

What will it take to keep our streets clear of such a mess
More leaflets from the council and wheely bins, I guess.

Taking more care of where we put our rubbish every day
Or very soon, as usual, the environment will have to pay.

Stop factory chimneys churning toxic fumes into the air
Rivers being poisoned, killing fish without a care.

Education is the answer and together we must try
To make our world a cleaner one, with an unpolluted sky.

Recycling is something we all can do every day and never shirk
We all must do our very best if we're to make this work.

Elaine Fearn

07/07 - The Day London Died (And Lived Again)

It was a Thursday of the week of the 7th July
On the buses, riding the tube train, people walking by
Someone planned an evil deed, to blow up London Town
So nearly did it work, as innocents were brought down
The bombers did not have a chance, they died just the same
A murderous, cowardly act, to try it was insane
To say this was a holy war, many would not agree
No god would justify this, but use a hanging tree
People of this island, have had worse enemies in the past
Still walking tall, and working, not cowed by a blast
Fifty-odd people died that day, it is so very sad
Not to be forgotten, like the bombers who were mad
We have to be on our guard, as the enemy is here
They walk and talk the same as us, to the things we hold dear
Salute our police and army, and all forces who are brave
And put these brainwashed spawns where they belong, in a grave.

(This is our land of hope and glory, our mother of the free.)

Robert Henry

A Special Ruby

I look up at the clock on the wall
It's nearly three and the day is done
Except for me, cast out from the group
My day has just begun.

I dread the school bell ringing
A mad rush to get out the door
But, I sit quietly alone in the corner
Staring at my books that were thrown on the floor.

I gather my belongings and composure
And walk with dragging feet to the gate
I don't lift my head to look forward
As I know the 'in crowd' lay in wait.

My crime is a 'ruby-red' birthmark
That marks the side of my face
My punishment is abuse and ridicule
To push me to the ground in disgrace.

'Hello dear how was your day?'
'OK Mum,' I promptly reply
It would break her heart to know I suffer
So later in bed I'll lay and cry.

As I lay here and think of tomorrow . . . ?
And clasp my hands to my face and pray
Oh Lord, help me through Friday
Please don't let it be like today.

Dad calls me his 'precious wee jewel'
He sees beyond my 'ruby-red' mark
I'm a person, a someone with feelings
But . . . the 'in crowd' still pull me apart.

They don't care, race, colour or creed
Or what the outcome is going to be
And I know there are a lot more 'prisoners'
Who suffer in silence, just like me.

Irene Reid

The New Flood

After such joy and jubilation,
Came events to stop celebration,
Scenes of truly mass destruction,
Beamed to the world by TV station.

The Earth unleashed a mighty earthquake,
Two tectonic plates began to shake.
This epic event, a dreadful tale,
Measured full nine on Richter scale.

The nations were shocked by the awful sight,
And Man at once ceased to fight.
Thousands of lives had been shattered,
Parties and presents no longer mattered.

The bloated bodies and floating wreckage,
May be seen as a 'holy message',
For Man to stop his evil deeds,
Consider for once others' needs.

The wave took lives and coral reef,
And the world united in sadness and grief,
Began to give and must go on giving,
To ease the suffering of those left living.

The Asian folk in coastal nations,
And those in idyllic holiday destinations,
Will need our help for years to come,
Before to dreadful diseases they succumb.

We pray, Lord, that all the world might be,
United in love and compassion from Thee,
Help us to raise a world war-free army,
Bringing relief, after the tsunami.

Kathy Johnson

The Wherewithal

When I was young and cocky
I loved a game of hockey.
I'd jump and hit and shout
And throw my weight about.
But now, you see I'm eighty-four -
So I haven't got the wherewithal to do it anymore.

I'd dive head first into the sea
And swish about with glee.
I'd ride the highest wave
To show that I was brave.
But now, you see I'm eighty-four -
So I haven't got the wherewithal to do it anymore.

I'd join in all the dances
(And get admiring glances).
All those naughty boys I'd treasure
Because I knew it gave them pleasure.
But now, you see I'm eighty-four -
So I haven't got the wherewithal to do it anymore.

I always liked to be with boys
And treated them like toys.
And whether they were short or tall
I'd seduce them one and all.
But now, you see I'm eighty-four -
So I haven't got the wherewithal to do it anymore.

Mary Baird Hammond

Live For Today

Tomorrow is for nobody
Live only for today
Who knows what each day will bring
And what will come your way
Live for all the sunshine
The laughter and the rain
The moonlight and the stars above
Frost upon your windowpane
Children playing in the park
The smiles upon their faces
To share your life with somebody
Warm cuddles and embraces
For all the lonely people
With no one left to love
So why wait until tomorrow
For it may never come

N Carruthers

Evil

No physical form
It only can harm
If Man does its will
To go out and kill.

In dark corners it hides
Forever taking sides
When we are all one
Under the sun.

I won't leave you at sevens
'Cause there's good in the heavens
More so that the bad
So don't feel sad.

There'll be a time in the future
When darkness won't nurture
Any fear for us free
No conquering democracy.

Goodwill to all kind
Let's keep it in mind
That we are now free
If you'll let it be.

Robin McGarry

He Stares Into His Cap

He stares into his cap,
a luckless pool unchanged
by our busy days' remains.

Too many starless nights alone
aground between the glass and stone.
Lives unseen by little means
on streets swept clean of simple dreams.
A roof, a bed, a fire, his own,
a kinder place to be at home.

Toss a coin, wish him well,
braves a face sparing tales.
Looks cold, pale.

Across the city's careless pride
he cracks a goodbye smile so wide,
so true, we turn aside.

He stares into his cap,
a luckless pool unchanged
by our busy days' remains.

Tyrone Edwards

Blind Love

If love is blind,
How can it see,
This heart full of love,
That I carry for thee?

How can you cure,
This emotional affliction?
It's torment and torture,
A desperate addiction.

Tend me, with touches,
And lashings of time,
My heart's encased,
Your love is my shrine.

Wrap me in rapture,
And let loose the beast,
Whose hunger and anguish,
Fuel an amorous feast.

Open my heart,
And plunder wholesale,
Blast forth emotions,
Heed the soul's wail.

But love is blind,
So you do not see,
The Heaven and Earth,
That I offer to thee.

Alvin Creighton

To See Ourselves As Others See Us

Mirror, mirror on the wall
Please be kind to me
Sleepless nights with a little one
Have taken their toll on me

My hair is a little frazzled
My clothes are stained with wee
Even the bags under my eyes
Are now plain for all to see

But can you see my happiness
Or that I'm as proud as I can be?
That this little bundle of laughter and joy
Has definitely improved me.

Lynn Greer

Progress And Poverty

Technology is wonderful, it really makes you see
What progress has been made to date, through the twentieth century?
From medicine to computers and aeroplanes to cars
People landing on the moon, taking photographs of Mars
Moving forward at amazing speed, not knowing what comes next
Analysing hieroglyphics and deciphering ancient text
Forensics discovering DNA, solving murders from years gone by
When they thought they'd got away with it, putting justice up on high
Yet still some nations suffer, through selfishness and greed
While their rulers live the high life, there is no food to feed
Many thousands of poor people, who are dying through starvation
Children suffer mostly, from malnutrition and deprivation
So while we're spending millions, keeping up the cosmic pace
Let us spend a fair amount, on the starving human race
Can't we blend the two together, linking progress with poverty?
With new inventions making money, feed the starving families
Banish soldiers; topple rulers, who abuse the power they hold
Let the United Nations help, fight the enemy 'be bold'
Teach them irrigation, how to cope on rough terrain
Growing food in monsoon seasons, so they'll never starve again.

David Cameron

Between

The dark bird flies into the sky,
Out of sight into bright eternity;
It soars with speed, and does not move a wing;
It makes no sound, and neither does it sing.
So do we lie in bed, outstretch a hand,
Touching the fringe of some other land.
We do not wake there, neither do we sleep;
It is no laughing place, yet we do not weep;
Not overgrown with trees, yet not wholly bare;
Not beautiful, yet we might think it fair.
This, the dim-lit island of our mind
From which, on awakening, we find
Only a half-dreamed tale we cannot recreate,
Something evanescent, yet leaving in its wake
A strange impression, a curious star-touched view
Of something old, yet being first time, new.
These are the things our wandering mind does shape
When, folded in sleep, it dares to make escape.

Paul Gardner

Faded Old Bag

I've got a bag that I constantly hold,
Inside are the tales that will never be told.
I'll carry this bag, till my body is cold,
And the stories inside have all faded.

This bag that I have is leather and red.
Inside is a book that is very well read.
Its pages contain things I dream when in bed.
When the light has gone out and all faded.

Oh the weight of this bag at what is inside.
Where the lovers and haters inside reside.
Tales of war, and love been denied
And dreams that came and then faded.

This bag withholds things so that people can't see.
Things that this world could never be.
Ambitions and plans not thought up by me.
But these heroes have now all faded.

This bag's been to places that most wouldn't go.
Seen tales of poverty, famine and woe.
They've grown from the seeds that we should not have sown.
Once-great nations are rapidly fading.

I'll carry this bag for the rest of my days.
But, I hate this bag in so many ways.
Everyone hates it, but nobody says.
The leather, it has faded.

And when I'm old, when I'm finally dead,
I'll swallow this mouthful of questions that never got said.
I've walked this life and my legs are like lead
And my body into dirt is has faded.

Darren Scott

Tsunami - December 2004

It was just another body washed up on the sandy shore
Surprised by an angry monster who attacked with a mighty roar.
It was only one woman of thousands whose life light dimmed and died
And soon others would replace her, this sad victim by my side.
And yet she was somebody's mother - a daughter, companion, friend
Who shared hardship, joy and laughter and gave comfort without end.
There was no time to bid 'Farewell' - no time to hold her hand
No time to say that with her love a future life was planned.
Oh frightening, enigmatic sea! Oh cruel winds that blow!
Oh shifting rocks and changing skies that threaten us below!
Lord, let us treasure all we have and value those most dear
Respect this wondrous world so vast and know that You are near.

Eileen M Pratt

Man Oh Man!

How sick I am of being a drudge
Fifty-five years of nursing this grudge
Of scrubbing unmentionables stuck to the floor
Cleaning the loo pan - detestable chore
Picking hairs out of plugholes (not even mine!)
Gagging at rubber gloves covered in slime
Cleaning round taps with a toothbrush that's old
I would use his new one if I dared be so bold
He'd apply it with gusto, unaware that it's been
All around the loo rim and other places unclean
I'm fed up with washing that needs ironing when dry
Back and legs aching so much I could cry
Then it's something for lunch, something different for dinner
I would live on salads if I wanted to be thinner
Then it's time for some gardening with weeds to uproot
If he was my gardener - I'd give him the boot!
He gets out the strimmer and chops all in sight
My astilbes and bluebells, hellebores and the like
Nothing is sacred when he's on a run
He wouldn't know a weed if it stung him on the bum
He can't boil an egg, let alone cook a meal
Never says sorry - just 'it ain't no big deal'
Sits down at the table for food to appear
Seldom remarking - 'That wasn't bad my dear'
He's not domesticated in any way at all
He does just what he wants - he's having a ball
So I'll continue to slave for him until I drop

Unless of course, one day - *I give him the chop!*

Pam Tucker

The Unexpected Guest

It's always the same on a Sunday,
We have lots of guests,
They are uninvited
And some of them are pests.

But I have found a seat
Where I can be,
I can see the house,
But nobody can see me.

So every Sunday I go
And sit there and then,
I see the guests arrive
And walk away again.

Jenny Bosworth

The Priest's Hole

Lying here with these mossy stones,
a man who now is only dust and bones.
A learned man was he, devout and true,
the doctrine in Latin well he knew.

Oppressed by many foes, was driven to hide,
and tremble at the baying hounds outside.
He listened, as they smashed the wainscot and the floor,
in frenzied search to find his secret door.

With brutal threats his gentle hosts were pressed,
but none betrayed the presence of their guest.
The servants too were faithful to their Lord
and nothing gave away by glance or word.

The captain of the soldiers gave the word
and all the household perished by the sword.
The hall with straw and faggots soon was stacked,
a blazing torch the final barbarous act.

The priest with none to heed his earnest cry,
soon overcome by smoke was left to die.
And though the years have passed he still remains
a victim of our Church's growing pains.

Janet Cavill

The Child Within

Crying, desperate to be held,
The inner child will rarely tell,
The secrets of its broken heart,
Clawing, wanting to be part,
Of the glorious life you think you lead,
But really all you want and need,
Is to be with the child that yearns for you,
The child you forgot but once you knew,
Who is now abandoned and alone,
Just waiting to be found and carried home,
And become again a part of you,
To laugh and be silly like you used to do,
How carefree and happy you used to be,
Being that child that now yearns to be free,
These things merely begin,
To describe the child within.

Jessica Shakespeare

The Picture

The soldier found the Bible, while resting weary from the fight
In a bombed and blackened ruin, his refuge for the night
Someone's home just days before, how many dreams had died
As shells rained down, Death's messenger called, there'd been no time to hide

From the gold-edged leaves a picture fell, to rest face down on the floor
He reached, then stayed his hand in doubt, as in his mind he saw
Another home, another book, with pictures there inside
Each pasted in with loving care, his home, his wife, his child

On that cold night his thoughts drifted back to what seemed another world
Of a little girl in party dress, dark hair in ringlets curled
Proud mother checking tables before first guests arrive
He reached and turned the picture, then unashamedly cried

Proud parents with their babies, held in their loving arms
Stared back as though condemning, the fact he'd brought them harm
It wasn't he who dropped the bombs! He took orders and obeyed
But deep down in his heart he knew. And with the Bible clasped he prayed.

Don Woods

Remembering

I'm not that far away so please don't you cry.
I'll be watching over you from up on high.
My precious one I'll always walk by your side.
Because deep down in your heart I will abide.

We had good times and we also had some bad,
But there is no need for you to be so sad.
I'm in a place where there is no pain
And from this experience I hope you'll gain.

A deeper understanding of why we love
And grief shouldn't wipe out that gift from above.
To feel joy we also have to feel sorrow,
But then there will be a brighter tomorrow.

Be brave and then you will be able to cope.
You'll be happy again and filled with hope.
Remember me and the life we once shared
And never forget how very much I cared.

Ann Blair

The Soldier

'If it's what you want lad
Then you must go
It's your life, I have no hold.'
That's what my ma said
Three months ago.

Now look at me, a soldier bold
Boots that shine like polished coal
My uniform a sight to behold
Hair slicked back, I stand so tall
This is my life and now I go.

Walking down a street destroyed
Buildings battered, families scattered
Dogs and cats run wild and free
Yes, this is the life for me.

With my rifle oiled and polished
My queen and country I defend
To restore and not demolish
I will fight until the end.

Yes, my children will have a future
But first I must find a wife
My gift is freedom, happiness, laughter
This will be my legacy, your life.

A shot rings out and then he falls
Pain like fire fills his lungs
Eyes glazed look, in disbelief
As blood and mud spread around his feet
Rainfall like tears mingle with his own
Ma. Ma. No life at all.

Barbara Brannelly

Forever Lost

One flew over the cuckoo's nest
White ribbons weave though my mind
Tracing the route of insanity
They tie themselves up inside
Amidst the paths of normality
Only a few remain
My memories run here for safety
Before they end up erased
Lost in a world of silence
Calling out your name
A padded cell, my conscience
That helps me to restrain
From hurting myself any more
As it cushions every blow
I stretch out my hands for forgiveness
But there is no one here to show
The scars that remain upon my skin
Have slowly healed with time
But underneath my blood runs cold
I fear I will never find
The answers to my questions
Written upon these walls
Haunting are their scriptures
As I feel my spirit fall
One day you might remember me
For who I really was
A girl who never lived this life
For in this life I'll be forever lost

Lisa Jane Mills

A Mouse Called Potty

I know a mouse that's potty,
He climbs the festive tree,
And hangs down by his lengthy tail,
With a smile, for all to see.

He chats to the distant fairy,
At the very, very top,
Yet even though, she won't reply,
That does not make him stop.

He eats the candy walking sticks,
And blows out all the candles,
He winds up all the clockwork toys,
And hides in people's sandals.

He nibbles at the parcels,
In case there's cake inside,
And when somebody's voice is heard,
He'll always run and hide.

He's very, very cheeky,
And wears a few disguises,
He borrows clothes from toy and bear,
In all sorts of shapes and sizes.

One day he'll be a soldier,
And then he'll be a ghost,
He looks very, very silly,
But it's the one I like the most.

So, if you hear some noises,
In the middle of the night,
Don't be afraid or startled,
Because it's Potty wearing white.

On Christmas morn, he's up at dawn,
Before we get a look in,
He wants to know what gifts we've got,
And if the breakfast's cooking.

I don't know why he does this,
As he only yearns for cheese,
And as we're having eggs and ham,
He will be hard to please.

This year is like no other,
As I dress for the day, I know,
That Potty will be in my shoe,
Where my foot's supposed to go.

But, although he's often trouble,
And a naughty mouse at that,
I'd miss his late night visits,
If we ever got a cat.

Hilary Ayling

The Argument

'Mum calls you a drama queen!'
'Well thank you very much.'
'And you've got food all round your mouth!'
'Don't you like the extra touch?'

'Eugh! You're so disgusting!'
'Don't use such harsh words sis . . .'
'I wish you would just go away!'
'Now I won't give that a miss . . . !'

'Hey. I haven't finished.'
'But you just told me to go off.'
'Don't you act all smart with me!'
'Ha! I'm not the boff.'

'Well, I'd rather be dead brainy . . .'
'Than a dumb person like me.'
'You really should try harder sis.'
'Oh look, Mum's calling us for tea.'

'Why aren't you listening?'
'Hey! Give me back my cup!'
'You really should just learn to share.'

'Will you two just *shut up!'*

'Yes Mum.'

Stephanie Wilkins (14)

The Word-Bee

The leaves in the sunshine boost up the flowers
And bees, in slow motion, zoom to their trade.
The queen allows bees to raise from her powers;
Rise to the peep-show; seize the arcade.

The flowers are colours with nowhere to run
And they love a small bee that squeezes its knees;
As true as all beings ingesting the sun,
Splendorous blossom will drop in the bees.

My words rattle, bee-loud, pretending to know;
Flying from mind and insistent as hell,
That it's not good to stay; that it's safer to go
And play in the sun with the lies that we tell.

My world is a creature that gets in a scrape;
As a spirit from nowhere in warm vapour showers:
A burp of intent; a small cry that escapes
And dances away, like a bee, to the flowers.

John Lavan

My Gran

I visited my gran three times a week
No matter the weather, rain, hail or sleet
She'd hold out her arms and embrace me tight
I'd ask the same question, 'Gran can I sleep here tonight?'

We had this bond, as a small child I sensed it
It made me feel good, secure and protected
I didn't realise then what a precious gift it was
To be loved and forgiven, no matter the cause

Gran fell out of bed and broke her hip
It happened when I was away on a seaside trip
I had bought her presents of a two-foot comb
A flashing red nose and a seashore snow dome

Gran went downhill fast after the fall
We could only be there and do nothing at all
She had lost her hearing at the age of three
And now her sight was failing as fast as could be

Death came for my gran like a thief in the night
She was too weak and was gone by daylight
All that was left was the smell of the dead
The scent of lilies of the valley and a small
Crumpled-up pink bed sock lying in an empty bed

Anne Jenkins

Here I Stand

Here I stand . . . alone and sick of love,
I watch upon the emptiness of space.
In vain awaiting for the whiteness of the dove
To bless me with its wisdom and its grace . . .
Divided lovers . . . what a spell was cast
On our brows? The fate has envied us!
Lands and seas would mock with hideous laugh
And their hungry evilness triumphs.

Each drop of blood in me your name repeats . . .
Each morning robs the light within my eyes
But I will kneel, accepting my defeat
For I was blessed when even love denied:
For I could see you . . . I could hold your palm . . .
And I could taste your lips, my master Kent,
And I could listen to the most elusive psalms
As we made love on mystic foreign sands . . .

In darkest blue . . . into the depths of ocean
A craving will be drowned day after day . . .
Guarding precious moments and emotions
A silhouette upon the empty shore would fade . . .

Eliza Kokanova

Hanging Baskets

In summertime with sunshine complemented with showers
When many gardens are aglow with the colour of the flowers,
Begonias, impatiens, nemesia, pansies too
Geraniums, petunias, marigolds with golden hue.
They grace many a garden border with colours all ablaze
In backyards and on patios, planters' beauty they amaze,
In many a town and city hanging baskets filled with bloom
They brighten up town centres lifting up industrial gloom,
Filled with diasia pink, surfinia blue and tamari bright
Trailing fuchsias, million bells and bacopa flowers of white.
Alas now faceless wonders say hanging baskets must be banned
Removing many coloured blooms from towns across the land,
They say that hanging baskets may fall on someone's head
Giving them a headache or at the worst stone-dead,
And when they water baskets they are so terrified
If water seeps in lamp posts they could be electrified.
Fifty years of making baskets, hanging and watering all
I have never known one from its bracket, to the ground to fall,
Indeed these silly petty rules cause me so much frustration
Whilst lawyers rub their hands at the thought of litigation.

David A Garside

After The Tsunami

The children's faces we see on the screen
Should be smiling, happy, carefree and serene.
But all we see are worried eyes,
Looking and pleading to the skies
'What do we do now?' in fear they ask.
'Rebuilding our homes is a mammoth task.
Our homes, our families - we have lost all.'
Oh God please help them - hear their call.
The rest of the world is doing their best
To speed the recovery, but it's a massive test
Which You have given now to this world of Thine,
Just why, oh why, does the sun fail to shine?
At times like these we have sadness to share,
Why do You give us these horrors to bear?
You must have a reason - has our world done wrong?
All the sin we have committed as we've gone along.
Please help, please help Thy world before long repent
So that You'll make us far more content,
And then we'll be at peace once more,
With no more tsunamis knocking at the door.

Jean C Pease

Colourful Emotions

Black is the colour of death,
Taken away the last breath.

Red is the colour of love,
Yet, it may be as beautiful as a dove.

Yellow is the colour of peace,
In this world it is the least.

Pink is the colour of pleasure,
Something that has been lost in great measure.

Blue is the colour of despair,
Whether you're sad or angry, you always know it's there.

White is the colour of matrimony,
The love shared between two, then they are no longer lonely.

As I feel most of these colours,
I can't help to feel for others.

Without any parents,
Uncles or aunts,
Sisters or brothers,
Friendships or lovers,

Without water or food
Trying to be in a good mood,
Still sharing everything they can afford
These are the people I have adored.

Even in despair
And nothing to wear
Feeling pain
And no self-gain
Living in the rain

These are the people that I do show shame.

Alysia Alida Becker

Smile

Think forward, think 'care',
Someone needs you out there,
Give them a smile, never a frown,
For they may be feeling rather down.

Your smile will make much easier the load,
As one walks along life's bumpy road,
Continue to smile in the way that you are,
Then they, too, may send their smile afar!

P Phillimore

Wild Dogs

I see the young impala there,
Eyes wide frightened as she stares;
My jaws of death, wet, gaping,
Drooling wet saliva as I keen.

The sticky mess of matted hair:
My eyes with no compassion stare,
Moist, unblinking, without care for death.
We roam the land with stinking breath.

But you who make the atom bomb,
Sarin gas and all that's wrong:
We kill to live not live to kill
To that alone is how we thrill.

The black night hides Death's worst rôles
While humans trade their very souls.
What you were once, so now are we
Small part of God's big family.

The shades of dark have many a hue:
Midnight black to midnight blue.
But ours is red, with blood of innocents.
You and yours just have no sense.

Yet there is one thing we should share
Under this colossal sun of life laid bare:
You keep to yours, we keep to ours.
God judges us at different hours.

John G Weeks

A Blue Day

Can I put into words
Just how I feel, lonely, desperate
And down at heel?

I'm so low today
No one knows
I'll try and smile and hide my sorrow
So here I go.

Does the lady know?
She keeps looking across
How are you dear?
You look at a loss
Does it show upon my face?
Even through my gritted teeth
I try to walk tall
And act with inner grace.

D Sherwood

Winter Storage

Mrs Robin Redbreast was feathering her nest,
For the coming winter months would put it to the test.
Mr Mole, popped out his hole, and cried, 'It won't be long,
I hope you chose a good stout tree, and made it very strong.'

Busy Mr Squirrel scampered up the nearest tree,
'I'm saving lots of lovely nuts for an emergency.'
'You'll need them,' shouted Mr Mole, 'as many as you find,
The winter days are drawing in, and summer's far behind.'

Mrs Prickly Hedgehog hadn't got a clue,
As long as it was warm and dry, anywhere would do.
'Anywhere?' said Mr Mole. 'Anywhere at all?
I know a sheltered little spot, behind the garden wall.'

'If you're giving free advice, then perhaps you could help me,'
Said worried Mrs Bunny, with all her family.
Mr Mole went quiet, 'Now you've put me to the test,
'You'll need a great big rabbit hole, and a warren for the rest.'

'I know that my good fellow, such a place I cannot find,
With all these baby bunnies, to feed and wash and mind.'
'I'll see what I can do for you, just leave it up to me,'
Said Mole who disappeared from view, as quickly as could be.

He called on wise old Mr Badger, who seemed to know it all,
He sat and thought for ages, 'Ah a place I do recall.
Now you go through Stony Bottom, and down by Dingle Dell,
Turn left by that thatched cottage, with that old wishing well

And there you'll see a field, with grass that's long and green
And the biggest rabbit warren that I have ever seen.'
So Mr Mole thanked Mr Badger, and hurried off to find
A worried Mrs Bunny, with problems on her mind.

'I've solved all of your problems,' said Mole, full of pride,
'A place for all the bunnies,' and Mrs Bunny cried,
'Why thank you, thank you very much, you've helped me so today,
I'll set off now before it's dark now that I know the way.'

Mr Mole popped out his hole, he had to be quite sure
That all his friends were safe and sound, and then he closed the door.
He climbed into his little bed, and turning off the light,
Said, 'Keep them safe through winter,' then wished them all goodnight.

Pamela Popp

Perspective

Wake up, go to work, always the same
Look out of the window, it's raining again
Makes me feel like I just don't care
Living in this country, it's just not fair

> *I live in a village where we get little rain*
> *We get so thirsty it causes us pain*
> *Our chief works hard to cast a spell*
> *Living here is a living hell*

Get up, have a bath or a shower
Clean my teeth, takes only an hour
Put on clean clothes, they smell so fresh
Wash last night's dishes, kitchen's a mess

> *First thing in the morning, walk to our well*
> *It takes an hour barefoot, my feet do swell*
> *Grab my bucket and lower it down*
> *Collect the water, it's muddy brown*

I'm starving, need breakfast to set me up
A pot of tea, pass me a cup
Fruit juice, cereal, maybe some toast
Bacon and eggs I love the most

> *Back from our well, my stomach does hurt*
> *Feeling so hungry I look in the dirt*
> *Scrounge around for something to eat*
> *Someone kindly donated us wheat*

My day is done, I am dying for a drink
> *Dying for a drink is that what you think?*
Go down the pub, meet my friends tonight
> *I've watched my friends die, not a pretty sight*

No one should die, everyone should live
Keep things in the right perspective.

Mike Tracey

A Lasting Peace

So long the complex imagery faired
Setting the call for traditional tasks
The fullest links to drive divide
Holding us all unto the past

With that the troubles made a start
The way of parting to decide
Those so sure showed their mark
And faced the same on the other side

In that context old rituals held
Both said we fight for peace
To strive for belief, to be heard
Each side killed, each side grieved

Progression by attrition ruled
The future stubbed its toe
And stumbled in onward generations
To the present that we know

With a bridge the roads once parallel
In time may merge as one
To end all hate the strong forgive
And face new days still to come

Albert Whiteside

The Teenager

Thank you for the thought you've shown
Thank you for your news by phone
Sorry that you must postpone
Any thoughts of coming home.

Thank you for reminding me
Of the things you want to see
And how great it feels to be
Young, footloose and fancy free.

Yes the months go racing past
Yes I know the world is vast
And you'll have to move quite fast
For this chance could be your last.

Thank you for informing us
That you're going off with Gus
But as you're only thirteen plus
Come downstairs without more fuss!

Betty Nevell

Contemplation

I want to die
But I know I must stay
It would be a tragedy
If another life was thrown away

My life is worthless
My world has gone black
The stars have gone out
And they're not coming back

I'm all dried up inside
No tears flow from my eye
But since you left me
I just want to cry

I can't believe you're gone
You make me light up inside
Why can't I see your smile?
I want to curl up and hide

And I could scream
God took you from me
Our life was perfect together
Why couldn't He let us be?

Now the world is unbalanced
I'm here and you're there
I know it's just nature
But it seems so unfair

And I want to die
But I have to stay
Although you're in Heaven
Why did you go so far away?

Michelle Clancy

Pill Delight

Pills, I take them by the score
Every doctor gives me more
Some for this and some for that
Most are round but some are flat
Some you swallow, some you chew
Some are red, others blue
But they never tell me what they do.

Terry Rowberry

Cometh The Day

Are we masters of the day
Or the dreamers of tomorrow?
We have lost so much our way,
We are time-worn by fatigue and sorrow.
Moonbeams cast their spell on eyes that sleep,
Conflict goes on and many die,
While women beat their breasts and weep,
The question goes on - 'Why oh why?'

We are the masters of yesterday
And proud of the honour and past,
If the Union Flag could speak, what would it say?
'Send me up lads, to the top of the mast.'
Like waves washing a sandy shore,
You do a job - and you do it well.
You know you have nothing to be sorry for,
One always knows, and can always tell.

'Cometh the day' - the decline and time,
Inner man awakens to great remorse,
The soul displays energy of strongest wine
And middle age is strengthened by a stronger force.
There is agitation at advancing years,
Age and rage are competition for one's life it seems.
Indignation may only bring forth a few tears
And the 'day that cometh' a few pleasant dreams.

E S Peaford

The Farmer

A farmer's work is never bland
From dawn till dusk he's on the land
Outside in all kinds of weather
Him and his trusty dog together
Cattle to feed, fields to plough
It's got to be done, no matter how
All year round he's on the go
Cows to milk, crops to grow
He has no time to sit and rest
He always tries to do his best

Greta Forsyth

Children

Isn't it nice to watch children play?
You look at them with glee
Happy, smiling faces that's all you see
Thinking back to when you were a kid
And sat on your mum's knee.

There on the floor rolling around
Jumping off chairs, falling downstairs
Up you get, jump up quick
Come here darling, I will see what I can do
Mum will make it better and put you back on track
And you'll be raring to go
Come on babes, take it slow.

Soon it's time to sit and eat
What can I give them for their lunch?
Oh they are a greedy bunch
I will spoil them and give them something nice
It might be chips and a gammon slice, that's nice.

Now it's time to put them all to bed
So come on my tribe, up the wooden stairs
I tuck them in tight, kiss them goodnight
See you in the morning light
Then we can play all day
Until night.

Madeline Reade

A New Day

Tomorrow is a new day especially for you,
You will not know what it contains
Till the present day is through.
It may bring you joy and happiness,
Love you have never known,
Nice things which you dream about,
Yet have never been your own.
It could change a life completely for the lonely and the sad,
In new friends who may touch your hearts
And leave them feeling glad.
Tomorrow is a new day, yet be mindful of today,
Of the things which please you so,
Which were part of yesterday.
For the past gave you each memory held safe
Within your heart
And they will always be a part of you
Each time a new day starts.

S Quayle

Fond Memories Of Dad

(For my dad)

Your death was so sudden, a reminder to all,
how precious our lives really are.
Your life was so full of everyday things,
to us you were a real star.

Your fishing, your darts and shove penny too,
a team player is what you were.
Your woodwork you took so much pride in,
as we glance, gives memories a stir.

I remember the day to Belgium we had,
you ordered mussels and ate every one.
Curry sauce you had, if I remember right.
'Go on,' you said, 'try some.'

The laughter and jokes you shared with us all,
some dry, some funny, some not.
There'd be days when we'd not take you serious,
they're the days that will not be forgot.

The thoughts and the memories you left behind,
keep us growing in strength every day.
That smile and that twinkle in your blue eyes,
makes our sadness and tears fade away.

A husband, a dad and a grandad much loved,
your family and friends will miss you.
You'll be a bright shiny diamond in the skies above.
Goodnight, sweet dreams, we love you.

Sara Grice

For My Son Joe

If I should tell you what he means to me -
The love I feel when I behold his face,
The need I have to listen to his voice,
The warmth that months of absence can't erase.

If I should tell you what he seems to me -
The way he fills a room that once was bare,
The brightness of his laughter and his talk,
The gifts that show the measure of his care.

If I should tape the measure of my love,
The fear I have that none will take my place
To hold and love him, just because he's Joe,
To know his worth and long to see his face -

If I could write these thoughts and all reveal
The world could not contain the love I feel.

Lilian Perriman

How I Wish . . .

How I wish that there was more
Than twenty-four hours in a day
And that every second of that extra hour
You'd take my breath away
You gave me something precious to hold
Where it will be forever in my heart
In letters of gold
It's something that won't ever die
When we separate or give up on
When it's too late
I love you my darling and I always will
So look for me in the stars above
Because I'll be there baby
Holding on to our everlasting love
And I ask of you not to shed a tear
Or hide away in your deepest fear
But remember me always in your thoughts and prayers
And I wish that one day you'll meet someone new
Who'll show you the meaning of love
That they have inside for you
I hold on for far too long
It's time to let you go
Don't worry, you did nothing wrong
But one thing that I needed you to know
That the only wish that I ever made
Was for me to truly, madly and deeply do
Was to fall head over heels in love with you!

Annamarie Yates

An Experience

Following the brown beetle,
Down the silvery aisle.
The sweet, chemical vapour,
Sickening for a while.

Forgetting the brown beetle,
Rest the polluted head.
The soft, delicious feeling,
Releasing you of dread.

Favouring the brown beetle,
Love the effortless high.
The deep, placatory spirit,
Allowing you to fly.

Tracy Green

When Scars Of Time Run Deep

when scars of time run deep
impatient fingers scramble and creep
reach within to grab a spirit in your dimmed eyes
like the bumblebee's wings as it dies

rainbow dressed crystals shine like tearful armaments
cocktails of disappointments and seldom moments of contentments
inspiration dances on angel's wings so delicate and mild
golden threads of memories of me as a child

stale breath betters a dead chill
statues of muses stalk closer still
creative cognitions just tease and flee
listening to forgotten secrets of the sea

cascades of wishes deceased engulf neural tissue
stagnated to the spot by self-created glue
fairies singing nursery rhymes
wind orchestrates the quiet chimes

time-like mud held in my resentful fist
golden daffodils glow in the morning mist
sweet odour of breakfast made
soul's debts have been paid

inspiration rest your weary head within my soul
I will nurture you like a newborn foal
its warmth will melt the burning frost
return to Mother and you'll no longer be lost . . .

D Trow

Just . . .

Just one more scone, just one more coffee and top it up with cream,
I usually take it black, no sugar, but today's a bit of a dream.
Just a small fruit tart, a vanilla slice and a mini chocolate éclair,
That's three cakes far too many but I guess I just don't care.
Just one more toffee and one more fudge and OK, a lemon drop,
Oh, I really shouldn't have started as now I just can't stop!
A glass of white, no make it red, oh I'll have both, plus a lager and lime,
This really is too much, but I'll try and do better next time.
Then it's cheese on toast, or chicken pizza, no, make it a fish supper,
It might be very greasy, but it will wash down with a cuppa.
So why the banquet, why the feast, why am I being such a hungry lass?
Have I been starved or marooned on an island?
. . . No, I've just left my slimming class!

Lynne Saint

Winter Is Over/Spring Is Begun

You were the winter of my life
But now my spring is here
I'll say goodbye to the long cold nights
For the blue skies are forming near

You held me back and dragged me down
And filled my life with dread
But now a new dawn rises up
To the good years that lie ahead

I became entangled in your weeds
Until I couldn't find the sun
But now your grip's been hacked away
And it's time to have some fun

I remember how you smothered me
How I put up with all that gloom
But I've planted the seeds for my new life
And I can feel them starting to bloom

So now I'll flourish, just watch me grow
And I'll reach up for the skies
By day my heart will bask in the sun
And by night my star shall rise!

Jane Somers

Tsunami

A terrible thing happened on Boxing Day
Indonesian lives were washed away
By the seabed erupting and causing a wave
30-feet high and black - like an enormous cave
It caused great damage to 300 miles of coast
Quarter of a million died, we know of, at most
It happened in early morn, before most were awake
On the Richter scale, 'twas a very big quake
It was heard and seen all around the world
People ran like hell, and some were hurled
Out to sea, and thrown onto land
Amongst debris, homes, and filthy sand,
Bodies were found on top of each other,
Grandparents, children, father and mother
Their homes were flattened or washed away
People around the world wanted to help and pray
500 Britons were known to be dead
They'd gone to Asia (for Christmas) the papers read
Every day more people were found
Some clinging to trees, and some underground.

Jane H M Hudson

The Fens

The Fens some people think are a bore
But me? I'm not so sure
I've lived here man and boy
As my ancestors before

Big skies that kiss the ground
No mounds to be found
Straight drains galore
Great sunsets and more
Then sunrise spectacular for sure

Cloudscapes take your breath away
Thrill you to the core
Barley swaying in the wind
Makes waves
Need you ask more?

Rivers with banks above the land
Strangers think it very grand
Summer days with very brilliant light
No hills to fight
This I love with all my might
Geese in flight
Windy terrain
Ideal for the kite

Go for a walk
Cross the stiles
See for miles
Farmers tending fields
Hoping for good yields
These landscapes we should shield
Nature may reclaim one day
Who can say?

Persi-Vere

Humbled By Death

He moved like a movie star,
Witty and enormous as a displayed boar.
With authority he would roar.
When he bought the brand new car,
He gambled his own life on the tar.
Each day we watched him die, from afar
As we sipped our hard earned cash in the bar.

Nyasha Musimwa

Inspired Portraits

Were I an artist, could I paint His face?
If I wrote volumes, could I tell all His grace?
The King of Kings with a thorn-crowned head
Silent! Yet His voice could wake the dead

Altogether lovely though His visage was marred
Absolutely tender with hands that are scarred
How beautiful His feet that walked God's way
They also were nailed to a Cross one day

Oh the pictures that flash to the mind
Cradled in a manger, unwanted by mankind
Tired and weary, sitting on Jacob's well
Waiting for a samaritan, of Messiah to tell

Invited to a wedding, He attends the Lord Divine
Provider of all things, turns water into wine
The Good Shepherd who gave His life for sheep
By the grave of Lazarus, people see him weep

If all were written the world would not hold
The stories of Jesus, that could be told
But oh, the joy of reading God's Holy book
So many pictures of Him, with life for a look.

Sarah Smeaton

Say It With Flowers

Here we are, all set -
can our timetable be met,
will we do it this year
and bring others good cheer?

The theme, it would seem,
is *healing and reconciliation*.
Now our time of contemplation;
a problem to solve, a plan to evolve.

At last we are ready,
ideas firm and steady.
Bring in the flowers,
we'll be busy for hours!

Eagerly we develop the theme
beyond our prayers or wildest dream;
from *healing and reconciliation* -
worthy of honourable mention -
    is *resurrection!*

Shireen Markham

No Regrets

This year, as I reach eighty-one,
I think of all I haven't done,
And all that I'd still like to do,
Provided I reach eighty-two.
But though I sometimes sigh a sigh,
At all the years that have passed by,
I'd really rather just be glad
Over the happy times I've had:
Two wondrous wives, with whom to share
A life of love beyond compare.

And despite early polio,
Appearing on the radio,
With folk of whom you might have heard:
Dick Barton, or Dame Thora Hird,
Mrs Dale of diary fame,
And many more who I could name.
Although I'm sure as I can be
You've never, ever heard of me!
Which makes me not the least annoyed;
It's only something I enjoyed.

However, now I must confess
That, more than my quite small success,
What brings to my dear wife and me
Much happiness, for all to see,
Is our three sons, of whom we're proud
And wish to sing their praise aloud.
Which means, when my time comes to quit,
Though I might mind it, just a bit,
As I depart this world of strife,
I'll say thank God for a happy life.

Harry Cooper

Simon

Simon is my strength, my rock.
A dependable man, not easy to shock.

He helps me out in many ways,
suggesting things for nights and days.

Although quiet in house and home,
with good wife, Debbie, he is not alone.

I'm grateful for a son like him
and two gorgeous grandsons;
my life will never be grim!

Ruth Markinson

Circle Line Incident

'Customers are asked to clear the station immediately.
We regret the inconvenience.
Normal service will resume as soon as possible . . .'

The jostling platform crowd peers up
To watch the ever-changing sign,
That blinks its silent message down,
'Next train, one minute, Circle Line.'

One odd man out amidst the throng,
Has bought a one-way ticket to
A station called Eternity,
A journey to a life anew.

The clock hands inching slowly round,
In nervous jumps they tick away
The remnants of the shattered life
He plans to end this fateful day.

The loser leaves his launching pad
To lay his life upon the line,
The crowds watch as they would a play,
As if they're frozen hard in time.

His arms reach like a drowning man
To grasp the deadly lifebelt rail,
While one guard springs in urgent haste,
Leaps on the track, the train to hail.

The platform's clear, the station closed,
A few are showing some concern,
But mainly for their own delay,
Frustrated, to the street return.

The odd man's broken yet unhurt,
The failure's failed to seal his fate,
His bleak, unwanted life is saved,
The crowds return through open gate.

Geoffrey Elgar

A Sea Of Tears

O Grief, how you ensnare each moment in your grasp,
Taking to yourself the brightness of the day,
Repeating poignant moments from the past
Restricting all in constant disarray.

These memories you bring, so bitter-sweet,
Of joys and sorrows shared throughout the years.
The world around looks grey and incomplete
As life now flounders in a sea of tears.

What holds you Grief, have you no better place to be?
You keep me captive from the love I knew,
A love and friendship many never see,
But your relentless presence breaks my heart in two.

O Grief, stand back and give me space to breathe!
You choke me as I try to gain control;
You desecrate my mind, the way you cleave
And keep obscured the vision of my soul.

I long to see beyond the veil of death
And clear the clutter leading me astray,
But still I mourn your passing with each breath;
O God, I beg you, hasten Grief away!

J M Redfern-Hayes

Sinking Spirit

I've a sinking spirit, it follows me around,
nothing really in it, just a buzzing sound.
Have you ever had that feeling where nothing really gets you,
no happiness or laughter, but nothing to upset you?

Yes, mine's a sinking spirit, I'm numb, can't feel a thing.
Like someone sitting on your chest, stomach tight, lungs compressed.
All is empty, one big hole. Nothing enters,
lonely soul.

I've a loosened spirit, it grabs me in my sleep,
nothing really in it, just the constant creep
of that same tired feeling where nothing quite affects you,
no consciousness or coma, nor any place to get to.

Yes, mine's a sinking spirit, I'm numb, can't feel a thing.
Like someone sitting on your chest, stomach tight, lungs compressed.
All is empty, one big hole. Nothing exits,
lonely soul.

Julia Sutton

Tsunami

Dazed confusion, panic attack,
Are they ever coming back?
Gone in a flash, under the sea,
Thousands were drowned innocently.
The monstrous wave came crashing down,
It wiped out the village and local town.
A coastline changed, lives lost forever,
Mesmerised nations unite together.
A freak of nature, so out of the blue,
There was nothing anyone could do.
An unbearable grief, families in pain,
In our hearts, they'll always remain.
Millions are given to the needy,
No one holds back, not even the greedy.
The world is frozen by this nightmare,
Time to show how much we care.
Wars are forgotten, momentarily in peace,
A minute's silence for the deceased.
Thousands of people from this life are released,
May you always be remembered, may you all rest in peace.

Ciara McBrien

My Granddaughter - Alice - 'As Once Were Mine'

Oceans deep - tranquillity - windows to your mind
you look toward me - without a thought - that I might be unkind.

Pure and clear and empty - untouched as yet by 'life'
no doubts, no expectations - no clouds of pain or strife.

No cause to 'flutter' lids - or hide behind their frown
no question of a need to close the curtain down.

No signs of friction of any shape or form - no light too bright
no need for caution, no anxious escapement from a storm.

Simply two bright pools of innocence - not a ripple, not a stir
two clear windows to your mind - uninhibited, not a blur.

I pray long may they remain angelic - innocent and sublime
reflecting the innocence of the babe - as once were mine.

Tomboy

Dark Illusion

It takes one drop of poison
To spoil the sweetest wine
And create a dark illusion
Inside the fledgling mind

On this devious battleground
The cold weaponry of choice
Are the hearts and minds of others
Suppressing their free voice

Insidious in execution
As they take up your fight
It will one day haunt you
Like a tunnel of dwindling light

Justify the purpose
The vengeance that you seek
Selfishness personified
As days flow into weeks

Wait silently in the shadows
Inner strength will overcome
Barriers of dark persuasion
Built by a caustic tongue

Alan Iddenden

Callous Sweetheart

Seeing my poignant woe senile, she got upset
My patience of utmost virile, she got upset.

I never took her betray'l for grant'd, or perchance
I praised her for her beguile, she got upset

She embraced all those men at a party dance,
I stood next to her for a while, she got upset

She was utt'rly amus'd by my rivals all day long
For once I made her smile, she got upset

I sang to her at love's request, a woeful song,
Her stone heart melted fragile, she got upset

And like always, she turn'd down my hearty plea
Though I wanted to reconcile, she got upset

Alas! The woe is virulent as it could possibly be
The more and more things got vile, she got upset.

Hamza Ismail

Why?

With your back to the wall
No one hears your frantic call
With nowhere to hide
Your nightmares come to life
For you the skies are grey
And it looks like it will stay
Your life has been derailed
And nothing will prevail
The only safety is in your room
But tomorrow is another day at school
Through these dark and dreadful times
Before his spirit leaves this life
This bullied child - who never smiled
Shouts, 'Why . . . ?'

Frank Howarth-Hynes

Time

Always in a hurry
Never have the time
To take in the world around
That really is a crime.

Too busy doing something
Be that work or play
Too busy doing nothing
To see the beauty in each day.

Perhaps tomorrow, or the next
I'll make the time to see
And not be so wrapped up
In all that concerns just me.

Michelle Borrett

Praise Be! I'm Completely Talentless

I heard the vicar speak today,
About talents. He said we all have many,
I'll stake my claim to prove him wrong,
I really haven't any.
I'm not much good at team sports,
I can confidently predict
That, when they pick the teams to play,
I'm the last one to be picked.
Cooking's not my thing at all,
Preparing meals not chosen,
I can provide a decent meal
If it comes ready frozen.
When it comes to speaking in public,
My effort's hard to note,
My mind, alas, won't function, and
A frog jumps in my throat.
My mind is full of good ideas
I'd really like to spout,
But when I try to utter them,
Nothing will come out.
It's sad, but on the talent scale
I remain a total bore,
On the skills swingometer
I can't register a score.
At last I've found a talent
That'll leave my listeners groaning,
I'm not much good at doing things,
But I'm a dab hand at moaning!

Jack Scrafton

Dad

*(Memories of my dear dad, Raymond Bowes, stroke victim
passed away on 23.3.02)*

Late one night the phone did ring,
From the hospital you were in,
Fight for life you couldn't win,
Your body so weak and thin,
Jesus knew you were calling Him
Ten days later He was listening.
Now in Heaven you are strong
Pain and misery now all gone,
And in my heart you belong,
Forever remembered big and strong.

S Ballantyne

Buried Treasure

As I went out this morning
After weeks of cold and snow
My spirit was uplifted
By a sight we all must know.

There on the grass like soldiers
As if hatched beneath the ice
Were scattered upright crocuses
In purple, yellow, white.

I thought of times of sadness
When I wore a happy face
As snow disguises ugliness
And frost will cover waste.

Yet underneath, like crocuses
Deep in my mourning heart
Ready to flower and live again
Hope now has a start.

When spring enfolds the gardens
It spreads beyond, to me
It enters my whole being
So that faith and love I see.

No longer sad and lonely
No longer in despair
As colourful as crocuses
The hues of hope I wear.

Christine Crandon

Upon Yon Grassy Bank

Down a shady woodland path
With thoughts of you I wander,
I heard the burbling river laugh
Rejoicing in my wonder.

The trees majestic, proudly stood
All dappled in the sunlight,
While birdsong echoed through the wood
To add to my delight.

We lay upon a grassy bank
And tenderly did kiss,
Then from the loving cup we drank
A drop of joyous bliss.
Now memories I have to thank,
But you I endless miss.

A J Macdonald

Warnings On The Outside

You want to live a healthy span,
see a doctor, least you can;
But when there's smoke of toxic kind,
danger then should trip the mind!
To do with your life as you please,
all health risks must cause unease;
Addiction that coins more than wealth;
suspects, number one's bad health.
Breathed in deep! Inhaled too long!
what it's doing reads not wrong -
Warning on the outside clear: goes
unread within.
A cough that's not a part of cold,
can start each day of morning rise;
Within those artery walls so deep,
site of hardenings, silent creep;
Restrictive blood flow! Breath that's short!
Increased workload on the heart.
Fingers seen as mustard stained,
with lungs perhaps the same?
Too late! No day should ever come,
when giving up might leave parts numb!
Withdrawal symptoms! Niggling doubt!
Persevere! Stub smoke risk out -
Beneficial turnabout,
Your health from then on no doubt.

David Pooley

Look On The Bright Side

Just look on the bright side
Things may be looking bad
But if you look on the bright side
You won't be feeling as sad

Why don't you look on the bright side
And throw all your worries away?
See, if you look on the bright side
You can enjoy the rest of the day

You may have lost your favourite jewel
But you still have each other
All your family is there for you
Your mother and father, your sister and brother

Because if you do look on the bright side
You'll get along great - I bet!
So why don't you look on the bright side?
Your troubles are there to forget!

Jordan Hatch

Wake-Up Call

Though nature does its raging worst,
In spite of gale and rain and snow,
The shoots of green triumphant burst.

Secure in soil and safely nursed,
As trees and buildings fall and go,
The daffodil is well rehearsed.

The snowdrop too, by poet versed,
As people scurry to and fro,
Rises to greet the new year first.

In vain the wind with blue lips pursed,
Tries to discourage blow by blow,
As larger objects are dispersed.

But bulbs and seeds are deeply immersed,
In nature's nursery below,
Refreshed by rainfall, quench their thirst.

Sifting life's blessings from the cursed,
Knowing the upward way to go,
Their time renewed and reimbursed.

Hope is a messenger diverse,
The birds of spring are in the know,
Earth enriched by life's traverse,
A thrusting, outward, upward show.

Kathleen Mary Scatchard

Old

As winter comes near, I feel such cold.
Old.
My body aches and my life's on hold.
Old.
The pain I feel, anguish can't be foretold.
Old.
Those dreams I had, my search for gold.
Old.
If I chose to stop fighting, life would just fold.
Old.
But the story of my life, has yet to be told.
Old.
I'm too young to die and decay into mould.
Old.
Seasons change, I'll enjoy spring till I'm old.
Old!

Des Beirne

You

Is that you who kneels and prays
Before your god on sacred days?
Who cries to him to hear your prayer . . .
Do you think your god should care?

I was begging on the street
You fed me dust from well-shod feet
You didn't spare a kindly word
You looked away, I knew you'd heard

Was it you in time of war
Denied me entry to your door?
A soldier tore me limb from limb
But still you wouldn't let me in

Are you the one who cries each day
Your life is hard, you've lost your way?
When I must struggle in the heat
To scrape the soil for food to eat?

Was it you said you were poor
When I was lying on the floor?
No human comfort as I died
While you were warm and safe inside?

Aren't you the one who left your home
Whilst I sat in a room alone
My mother dying, father gone?
I'm sure it's you . . . you are the one

I am the one you didn't touch
The weary soul not asking much
The one who hungered while you ate
The one who loved while you still hate

You are the one who comes and kneels
Who says he cares, who says he feels
'Be in my heart dear Lord,' you pray
I came to you. You turned away.

Jane Johnson

Thoughts When Alone

I walk the moorland heights alone,
Sometimes pausing to examine a stone,
Perchance to find a piece of flint,
With chipping around it, just a hint,
Man-made, 3,000 years gone by,
And since then, here, it did to lie.

Close by there is a great earth mound,
Our senses it does so confound,
Was it built at a place much revered?
Perhaps o'er which, the sun it appeared.
How lived these people so long ago,
Who hunted with only an arrow and bow?

Now a brief rest, to enjoy the scene,
Deep breaths I take, of air fresh and clean.
The views grand and varied o'er valley and hill,
Sights from these places always to thrill.
My companions are curlews with strange bubbling cry
And a lark loudly singing, as it soars up on high.

A quarry disused, where once busy scene,
Now overgrown by nature supreme,
Bilberries grow on remains of a wall,
Now used by pipits, as a perch, as they call.
Millstones, unfinished, lie where they were left,
Ne'er to be used, yet from rock they were cleft.

Drystone walls along moorland edge,
Separates field from peat moss and sedge.
Upland farms built of millstone grit stone
Which fits into landscape, with its multi-grey tone.
These views are all free, of 'my' Lancashire land,
Where surely, God in His wisdom, laid on His hand.

Jay Smith

Spring Is In The Air

There's the golden glow of daffodils
And excitement in the air
There's the rainbow and the sunshine
And new shoots everywhere!

There's the buds of blossom waiting
To dress the cherry tree
In pretty pastel shades of pink
A welcome sight to see!

There's the messenger who's eager
To greet the start of spring
And with his rich and fluty voice
He begins to sing!

There's a reason to be joyful
When we hear his cheerful song
Our days will be much brighter
Now that winter's finally gone!

We can rely upon the blackbird
When *spring is in the air*
To bring the news impending
For everyone to share!

Carol Kaye

Moon
(Echo Verse)

Is that you who lights the sky tonight?
echo: Might.
Tell me is it you, the moon?
echo: Soon.
Tell me oh you globe of delight.
echo: White.
Tell me of your wondrous glow.
echo: How?
Tell my why you come and go?
echo: No.
Why not tell me the moon so bright.
echo: Spite.
If you will not tell then I will go.
echo: So?
I will watch you disappear from view.
echo: Do.
Adieu to you.
echo: Adieu.

Gilly Jones

Images Of Autumn

Brown leaves are a-scurrying
Along the roadside as we walk,
All is haste and hurrying
As the wind whispers its talk.

Umbrellas are blown inside out
And trees stripped of their leaves,
The wind makes mischief all about,
A-tugging at our sleeves.

A time to get inside our homes
And shut the dark night out,
To sit beside the warm hearthstones,
As fire flames dance about.

Black cat by black window sill,
An orange pumpkin's grin,
Moonlight's magic, silent, still,
And candlelight within.

Broomsticks, and the firelight glow,
As midnight witches fly,
Taking their black cats on tow
Across the autumn sky.

My heart leaps every autumn,
The season of my birth;
Its madness and its magic,
Its mischief and its mirth.

Brenda Maple

Kisses To Treasure

To me it really is sheer bliss
When our two lips they meet and kiss
For when our two lips meet and touch
Our kisses are wonderful and enjoyed so much
For your two lips and mine it's true
Kissing is wonderful for me and for you
For when they meet and touch we're blessed
With kisses that really are the best
They're kisses that give us so much pleasure
Our kisses forever we'll always treasure.

Royston Davies

A Tale Of Magic And Derring-Do

His car went lame, as horses do
Whene'er their time is o'er
When charged and ridden out of view
Long chases to endure

It coughed and spluttered, lungs well dry
No lights to see his way
The thing just clogged and stopped hard by
The track where fortune lay.

The gold he told himself was near -
The magic man had said -
A great big coffer full of cheer
When be the monster dead.

The faithful steed he left alone
To cough and splutter solo
The many ventures left undone
Because the car went sparko.

He reached the canyon where he knew
The monster, Zot, lay dormant
Until such time as he awoke
The monster with his torment.

'Come fool,' he said out loud,
'Spit into me your venom,
I shall not cease 'til run the clouds
Where'er the gods should send 'em.'

Great Zot, he heard these loudsome tones
From such a small advers'ry,
'Come hither fool, and say what's up -
You want my precious treas'ry?'

'Yes, yes loud oaf, oh puff of smoke
I'll get it all together
Because, you see, I'm free, I'm free,
And you are slave to weather.'

'Oh yes, indeed, come on then feed
My pleasure with your death.'
'My death,' said he, 'oh no, not me
I'll not come near your breath!'

'My breath is poison to your soul
So come on man, be brave
And when you get to pots of gold
I'll blast you to your grave!'

'Such boasting, ugly monster, Zot
Such loud, all fire and temper
You sound your gruff voice
Like a dog, now dying from distemper!'

Then out from dark and dingy cave
Came Zot, alive with fire
The great cloud burst, the rain did come
And turned Lord Zot to mire.

The treasure now came into view
It glittered, gleamed and shone
But little man, so brave, so true
Said, 'I am having none.

Of this large fortune I aspire
But so does half mankind
I'll leave it safe in cavern dark
'Til its true value find.'

Brave humans all, when this great fool
Named Zot came out the cave
The moral should have been to talk
Not dig the monster's grave.

For reasons only known to God
His treasure to transpire
Mankind must learn to love and trust
And to their god aspire.

Doreen Weller

Then And Now

The old church bell rings out its merry chime,
To our wedding I'll make you mine.
For five long years of going steady,
You held my hand and said you're ready.
Slowly down the aisle, it seems so hot,
Hope there's nothing I've forgot.
Vicar welcomes you and me,
My stomach churning, I want to flee.
Outside weather has turned out nice,
But been forbidden to throw any rice.
It's with such pride I'm fit to bust,
I'm the one you placed your trust.
Memories we both now have plenty,
Without them all my mind would be empty.
Looking back over more than forty years,
We have had lots of love and so few tears.
So please dear Lord when it's time to rest,
Tell the world we tried our best.

E J Fensome

Loneliness

Loneliness can hold no fear
When, Thou art to me so near.
In my Lord's presence so blest
No fear could e'er disturb my rest.

Contented in His love for me
Life's most blest security,
I now only wish to share
His most ever-loving care.

If I could make all people see
When lonely just to turn to Thee,
If only, His love they would try
And to His loving arms would fly.

If His dear love you would try
When life no more can satisfy,
It has so often then been found
Life without Him is not sound.

You will then feel more secure
Than ever you have felt before.
No fear will ever touch your mind
With one so gentle and so kind.

There is no loneliness in Thee
Only Thy blest security.
No arms could be more secure
No love could ever be more sure.

Edith Kinloch

Age!

Don't be sad about your age
Remember you have knowledge of many a page
When you still have health to fit a shelf
And time to spare to mend a tear
You can still alight with the lark
Covering life to make your mark
Helping others for a start
Adding another page
So don't be sad about your age

If you have a family to call and care
Who love you dearly, and are always there
Remember you are blessed doing your best
Accept life at this stage
And don't be sad about your age.

B Lockwood

Moving Gnome

I've sat here through each season,
Through every day and night.
I must have been here at least ten years
And never had a bite.
Now I really am fed up.
I'm not staying here anymore.
They think I've got no feelings,
I'm totally ignored.
Besides there's somebody next door,
I'd really like to get to know her,
But I am in such a mess
Where they've bashed me with the mower.
Tonight I'm going to do a runner.
First I'll nip into the shed
To do a quick touch up job,
And scrape the birds' muck of me head.

I mustn't lose my nerve
Now I've reached the dividing wall,
And whisper, 'Hello darling,
Shall we have a ball.'
I hear a little giggle
And a positive reply.
I bet you didn't know,
That happy gnomes can fly.
I've landed right beside her,
She gives me a knowing nod,
And says with a saucy smile,
'I really like your rod.'

Marlene Parmenter

I Missed You

I missed your cheeky smile this morning
I awoke to find an empty space
I missed the way our bodies touch
I missed the way you stroke my face
I missed the way you squeeze me tight
I missed your kisses all through the night
I hope you had a good night's rest
To start your day feeling your best.

Nikki Jackson

The Prodigal

I wish I could have given you a rainbow
So you could see the Father's smile into your heart,
Hear Him tell you how much He loves you, every minuscule intimate part.

I wish I could have given you the stars
So you could see how special you be,
Know the seasons are here for your pleasure, cycles rotating to your life's soliloquy.

I wish you could have held the promise
To save you from all the pain,
I wish you didn't travel that journey, even though it brought you back again.

I wish that your eyes didn't see
Where your soul should never have dined,
But now you know in the depths, it's always His love you will find.

I wish I could have given you a rainbow,
I wish I could have given you the world,
I wish you could have seen the Father pine for His little girl.

I wish I could have given you a rainbow
To promise all those hurts away,
But I couldn't and prayed for your safe return,
I knew you'd come home some day.

Welcome home.

'Amaka Okeke

Family Love

'Tis hard to watch the young you love, grow up and move away.
They make a new life - take a husband or wife
And seldom come to stay.

But comes the time as they grow old, when your love for them you share
With their little ones - some boys - some girls
For whom Grandma is someone to care.

And Mother then becomes Grandma and the miles that are between
Mean you just hear a voice on the telephone
No cuddles - no games - they're unseen.

Although I've made a brand new home and live in another shire,
I know that the mother's love I took - and give - will continue to fire
The family love that will carry on for many a year to come.

And if I can teach my grandchildren the meaning of love so true,
That is always there when you need it (as I learnt myself from you),
Then the miles that come between us will be easily overcome -
And I can hear more often, those magic words - that's Mum!

E Winifred Garland

Religious Mountain

I am mortal, I quiver and shake at thunder,
In a sea of debt, doubt and worry,
Sink slowly - I sink, until I go under.

Profound is my guilt a mountin',
Under red barren skies, I bend to the cries,
For my roots are not strong,
I always do wrong,
And quick to admit the twit that I am,
I am no religious mountain,
Just a pathetic, human being, poor species of man.

I shoulder along,
A rough, jagged, twisted terrain,
Under a huge mountain of sin,
I search and I scan,
Till my eyes become hurt, my vision blurred,
And finally, fatefully, wilfully, give in.
To the ludicrous and absurd,
And believe in the emptiness of loneliness,
Mankind's abyss,
Where nothing is heard,
Except the silence of violence,
Not even a word.

I am no religious mountain, not even a rock
I am a sinner, unfortunately born of Satan's stock.

Glenwyn Peter Evans

My Angel

We swam like buddies
Pummelled through ornate pillars, Tuesday's wild
Crouched beside rolling thumbs, fallen smiles
Like liquid life, sun beading down
Kissing angels slow your heart
Like valid spring
I threw a twig and clipped your wing
Sadness grew in the forest bloom
I mustered wind to pine for you
In nightly glade I mourned
On the hue she glistened new
I'd scared my angel

Colin Beck

If You Love Me . . .

The hospice is pleasant, set among trees, with a view.
I drive in and park, 'Such a nice spot and so handy.
They're wonderful up there. The staff are so very kind.'
Though why the view, now you are nearly blind?

I walk in through Sunday hush, peaceful with potted plants,
A jungle of greenery, and cool artworks that soothe.
I love you, so I dread what is lying on the bed.
All those tubes, a mad skein feeds you, and deadens the pain.

I dress the same, blue jeans, white shirt, hair loose, the same scent.
It's so that you can recognise that I have not changed.
You were beautiful, but now your dear face is hideous
Like Elephant Man. The tumour distorts loved features.

The once mad mop of chestnut curls is grey, short and dull.
The tumour grows, despoils the nerves that lead to eyes and ears.
I sit down on the bed and hold your hands, thin and cold.
Hour crooked thumbs blindly stroke my strong, warm skin.

It hurts you to speak but you say, 'Hair,' and touch my hair.
I can see your skull through matted grey crew cut locks.
I sit and chatter of mundane things and memories.
I say, 'We'll always have Paris,' and you try to smile.

Dreadful cancer stench prevails, I feel my stomach clench,
Their synthetic perfumes have no power over that smell.
Some kind domestic brings me tea. I gag, but smile and say,
'Thank you, so much. Please put it on the table, I can reach.'

You grasp my wrist, 'Hug.' I hold a bag of bones,
I wipe my tears on my hair, 'Love you,' you gasp,
'I love you too. Oh dear, the time, I must go.'
Outside is clean and cold, I breathe deep.

   'If you love me, why are you doing this to me?'

C M Welch

Tide

The harmony of the tide of the sun's true mirror
Shivering, washing away lonely sand from the shore,
Unheard, undisturbed, untroubled it rolls into the deep,
Rolling through, rolling over the coolness of its sleep.

Oritsegbemi Emmanuel Jakpa

Just Her

I just love her voice and the things she says
Just hearing her is as welcome as warm sunrays
I just love her; she's the one I choose
For it is her and only her, she is my muse

I could be with her, hear her speak her mind for hours
On topics she comes alive with like budding flowers
I just love her; she's my one true passion
For it is her and only her, my inspiration

It's true we don't always see eye to eye
We love to spar, it keeps our nature wry
I just love her; she is my soulmate
For it is her and only her, my life's fate

The geography of her expression, smiling at what I've said
The small, white scars joins wrinkles on her soft forehead
I just love her; how I long to explore
For it is her and only her, that I adore.

Mark Cunliffe

A Summer's Day

If I need inspiration, I just watch as time goes by,
I sit here in a field of green, beneath a pale blue sky,
The sun in all its glory, warming up the still cold air,
As I just sit in silence, all the creatures stop to stare.
The whitest clouds are overhead just passing in the breeze,
The sound that breaks the silence is the rustle of the trees,
Our world in all its splendour, yes it is a wondrous place,
The birds so softly chirping puts a smile across my face.
The minutes turn to hours as the dusk just dims the light,
All animals and insects disappear out of sight,
Whilst evening time approaches then the moon comes out to play,
I have my inspiration on this special summer's day.

Robert Basham

Be Happy

Why destroy what is given in kindness
Why bring hurt to the friendship of love
Why bring pain without forgiveness
Without remorse for something not done.
Why when the world it loves you
Why when you are all things
The body of all future life
The tenderness to calm as loving wife;
Can the party not go on
Through the still of night?
Is the noise too late for all to hear
For a ready soul to date?
The price to dance the night away
Never fearful of the swooning moves
Understanding action without much thought
Automated so natural as if you're taught
The ways of the self are real
And it's your love within I want to feel.
Who is unnatural to their self
By placing what is may be a burden
Chained and stoned, hung and starved
If you're not happy for life
You'd be the roast that's carved;
Dead and served with gravy
For flavour of such nourishment
Not walking, soaking, full of life
Be happy, and not with strife.

Anthony Rosato

A Summer Day

Snow-white clouds
and soft veiled grey
Resting on a summer day
on sky madonna-blue
Eyes delight at such a view.

A world that's bathed
in sunshine yellow
Stirs the soul
in joyful mellow
Singing God be praised -

For such a summer day.

Opal Innsbruk

Time For A Moan

My back is in agony
My legs are too!
My hands won't do
What I want them to do!
I can't turn my head
Without feeling pain
Oh why must I go through
This over again?

The simplest tasks
Take forever to do
To walk anywhere
Takes an eternity too!
My body is shattered
My brain is confused
I'm feeling completely
Battered and bruised!

When I'm shaking and numb
And my body won't go
How do I cope?
I really don't know!
But I carry on going
Although I am sore
Until my body screams . . .
'Please! No more!'

Melinda Penman

Can I Help?

Are you hurting?
Has the day been unkind?
Have they hurt you?
Have they tortured your mind?
Can I help you?
I will just hold your hand.
Can you feel how much I understand?
Be silent or tell me what has hurt you so much.
I sense it, I see it.
Take comfort in my touch.

J W Whiteacre

The Jurassic Coast

(Of all England's counties, just Dorset can boast a world heritage site, The Jurassic Coast)

Travel with me, if you dare, through time
As I walk the shore, between Eype and Lyme.
Together, we'll stroll along Charmouth beach
And seek an age that is out of reach.
Among the pebbles and in the sand
Ammonites, belemnites, come to hand.
For here, between the cliffs and foam
Is the land, where dinosaurs once roamed.
Maybe today, is your lucky day
As you split the stones, made of hard blue clay.

You'll shout with joy and pure delight,
When first you discover an ammonite.
This fossilised find, on the Lyme Bay shore,
Will make you eager to look for more.
You'll return to a time, so long ago
Who knows what wonders will be on show?
From Golden Cap to black, Black Ven
Your mind will see them walk again.
No! Not for real, but you'll feel their ghost
As you walk along the Jurassic Coast.

When you've had your fill of walking the shore
Visit Charmouth Museum - (it's on the first floor).
You'll learn of the history throughout the years
From the friendly wardens and volunteers.
Books to study and maps of the bay
All this, and more is on display.
Sea creatures and monsters, the years have spanned
Now fossilised form, to hold in your hand.
Transport yourself, to that time long ago
By sharing, with others, the video show.

Tony Fuller

Over The Border

Where will I go? When I want somewhere to go -
With you - no longer there.

Where will I go? When I need somewhere to go -
Waiting for you to appear.

Where will I go? Just to have somewhere to go -
Without you being near.

Where will I go, when I need somewhere to go?

When you are over there . . .

Anita Richards

With The Memories Laden

The curse of February so loathed and proud
Does fill the sky with heavy cloud
And from the warmth inside the coach
We feast on scenes our eyes do poach
Outside the windows the snow falls hard
Covering the Pennines like a Christmas card
Through the Arctic blast and dubious thought
The intrepid coach still heads to York
But beyond the hills the blizzards wane
In York the snow has turned to rain
The drizzle employed by the eerie mist
Does welcome the tourists who still exist
The spirit of York does wrap its arms
Around the souls of its historic charms
Nursing the centuries that are so defiant
York Minster looms like a Gothic giant
The tourists assemble for the sights they seek
Navigating their way down each cobblestone street
And shoppers refreshed from afternoon tea
Converge on the shambles for more therapy
They're too busy to notice, too busy with life
To notice the past in the peripheral light
To hear the faint echoes of another time
Of the Roman soldiers marching in line
Some saw the Viking village time did condemn
But not the ghosts walking next to them
Some visited the river but others did not
With time being the enemy now we cannot
With the memories laden the coach soon departs
This day in York has touched all hearts

David Bridgewater

Christmas

C hurch bells ring to start the day,
H allelujah as one does say.
R ays of sunlight reach the ground,
I ndescribable it is found,
S now resting on the land,
T rees and shrubs as they stand.
M aking the scene a master for all,
A nother period to rest and recall.
S himmers of light from the star,

D uring the birth beside the bar.
A n indication for all to see,
Y our Saviour is here; find your key!

James Stephen Thompson

The Perfect Gift

I planned to buy the perfect gift
To show my love was deep
The shops were packed, the queues were long
The prices rather steep
But still I'd find that perfect gift
To place beneath the tree
I'd battle on and choose with care
No quick whiz round for me!

That perfect gift, I'd seek it out
It had to be the best
The most exciting present
Far more pleasing than the rest
It might be dear, this perfect gift
Well, nothing cheap would do
I couldn't show my love without
Financial pain - could *you*?

The perfect gift proved hard to find
I searched with all my might
The shelves were laden, overstocked
Yet nothing seemed quite right
It wouldn't *be* the perfect gift
Unless it warmed the heart
Received with joy and eagerness
Gift shopping's such an art!

The perfect gift, that's all I asked
That's all I wished to find
But dreadful fears and worries
Started preying on my mind
Suppose I picked the perfect gift
And all misgivings fled
Then what if - well, it went down like
A lead balloon instead?

The perfect gift - what *can* it be?
I *have* to know for sure
I don't care what it costs, but doubts
Like this I can't endure
The perfect gift! They had it easy
Back in days of old
A lamb, perhaps, some frankincense
A bit of myrrh or gold

Some people claim the perfect gift
Is love itself - it's *true!*
But what a cop-out! Just be *nice!*
How hard is *that* to do?
The perfect gift? Love can't be bought
And wrapped for all to see
It's *free!* Well, *I'm* no cheapskate
No, it's back to town for me!

Helen M Clarke

St Catherine's, Penrith

Here is a church in Drovers Lane,
St Catherine's it is called by name.
It's to this church I make my way,
There, with the good people, kneel and pray.

George and I, books in our hands,
Back of the church we both stand.
As all the people come into Mass,
We know them all to the very last.

It's really great to see them here,
These people we love and hold dear.
Our congregation here I find,
Are good friends, loving and kind.

At the altar Fr Jerome stands,
Welcoming us with outstretched hands.
From here we hear the good news read:
To love the Lord, and the Devil dread.

We all come to this parish church,
Where for Jesus we came in search.
Leaving God's house we have to part,
Saying our goodbyes right from the heart.

When a baby to St Catherine's I came,
In this church I was given my name.
It's here I'll end up when I die;
In front of the altar I will lie.

Then, when I am dead and gone,
I pray memories will linger on.
Here in this church in Drovers Lane;
St Catherine's it is called by name.

Francis Allen

Great Budworth Church

One of England's ancient piles,
Great Budworth church, it still stands.
From its tower, view for miles
O'er Cheshire's lovely countryside.

Much of history has been written
(Cromwell's horses were stabled there).
Since church first allied with Witton,
And strange customs were observed.

Through wars, famine, she's stood firm;
All kinds have passed through her doors.
Life can only go its term:
'Neath lychgate coffins have rested.

Her strength doesn't rest on stone
But on people who tend her needs.
Man doesn't live by bread alone,
Nor a church survive without love.

She'll not be left in the lurch,
This massive brown sandstone pile
With the name Great Budworth Church,
All that makes history is there.

Taken up are gravestones rubbed bare,
O'er which, in the aisle, we once walked.
Long have people worshipped there,
My ancestors are buried there.

How many times in history's twirl
Have people been called upon
To help to save the old girl?
Many more, no doubt. *She's survived!*

J Millington

Cock Peter

In Catmose vale lies Oakham town
its spired church the jewel in crown
whilst atop the steeple Cock Peter stands
silent, watcher of the surrounding lands.
From wooded hill and sheep-filled dale
the views across this pastoral vale
focus on the Heaven-pointing steeple
where Cock Peter high above the people
has rotated come wind and rain
for aeons, this medieval weathervane.

Alistair L Lawrence

Forget The Past

Forget the past,
It's gone and forgotten.
Think of the good,
Forget the rotten.
Relax for a change,
Ease up on the shrew
Forget the evil,
That certain men do.

Forget the past,
It's under the bridge.
It's out of sight.
It's over the ridge.

Forget the past,
That's what you should do.
Do good unto others,
Hope good's done to you.
Look for the future,
Forget the past.
It's evil that's rotten,
It's good that will last.

Forget the past,
Look to the dawn.
Keep hope in your heart
And anger won't spawn.

Forget the past,
Remember to smile,
To do otherwise,
Is bloody futile.

Look to the future,
Wise up, use your brain.
To do otherwise,
Is bloody insane.
Forget the anger,
Forget the pain,
Have hope in your heart,
They won't come again.

A Power

Tom

Over dark pines, a silver moon
and in west, tremulous star
and soothing sweet mellow tune
of church bells ringing afar

Listless, her daily tasks done
standing at rose-wreathed door
sending her thoughts to sun
and a land she'll see no more;
roses rioting in their bloom
and curtains moving in pain
while an old piano shines in room
waiting for her touch again

At last, her hands touch keys
with pleasure and delight
a sad song from overseas
goes crying long into night;
she sings a song full of pain
of life transcending art
homely, deep, a celestial strain
swansong of a broken heart

I come along the railway track
an old dog whose day is done
I pass, then pause, then come back
I listen, her audience of one;
golden voice with passion fraught
she charms my listening ears
trembling, and she knows it not
down my cheeks roll my tears

Silence. Stillness as if to pray
she stops. Stars still burn bright
now, her lover Tom goes his way
and only a ghost cries into night

T Webster

First Entry

Waving sea of lands lost true
regret unfound and force unto
how weave we not to seek the day
that finds the one within the fray
I hear the sound of long-lost love
I see the sight of truth above
to temper these the force of leaves
how whisper they throughout the breeze

S L Brooks

An Ode To Sharlett Street

When we were young, very young
We'd grab a bag and go with Mum
We'd wait a while for a bus
A car cost too much for the likes of us

To Commercial Road we would go
And see the lights in shops all aglow
In Samuels we would see beautiful things
Necklaces, bracelets and diamond rings

But the real reason we went that way
Was to go to Sharlett Street on market day
It really was a grand affair
Seeing the barrow boys trading there

There was a man, selling meat
Like from a butcher's shop
And for that skinny dog
Always catching something he'd drop

The fruit was arranged in contrasting lots
Looking like a picture on a chocolate box
The tradesmen were calling two pounds for one and nine
Yes it was shillings and pence at that time

At Christmas you could buy a Christmas tree
Mistletoe, holly and all things Christmassy
Bananas and tropical fruit was short
But we had a great time with the things we bought

We'd leave Sharlett Street, with bags loaded down
And catch the bus back out of town
But they've moved the market and it's not such a treat
Oh how I wish it was still in Sharlett Street

Pearl Williams

Silent Friends

Books as friends some do not see
Yet they are truly so to me
In quiet solitude I seek
From those who in their pages speak
Escape to days now long past
That enthral, excite and hold me fast
An outlet for my hopes and dreams
Away from the mundane it seems
And there too within its exciting cover
So many things I can discover
Knowledge, excitement, it never ends
Books truly are my silent friends.

Brenda W Hughes

Nottingham's Child

A majestic being upon its throne
This monument to days gone by
Standing proud, yet not alone
Giving joyous beauty to the open eye.
This is our castle, Nottingham's child
We are blessed with this building so grand
No sign of meekness nor anything mild
This vision of grandeur we hold in our hand.
Those Normans great and builders proud
Brought forth this edifice of sandstone mix
To govern its people, their heads all bowed
In the year of our Lord 1066.
On sprawling land it took its place
Its turrets guarding through the years
Protecting all from invasions faced
Calming hearts and quelling fears.
A tower of strength to those who have gone
Past and present through hallowed halls
Secure to all it looks upon
Within its mighty gated walls.
Sumptuous greenery and leafy surround
Paths that meander and wind
Hundreds of caves running deep underground
Waiting for more of mankind.
Museums and artwork dictate its inside
Sweeping staircases carry you on
Through rooms that are high and so equally wide
Filling footsteps of people now gone.
Concrete and cobbled, sloping and straight, parts that are both new and old
You should visit our city, come see Nottingham's child, 'tis a wondrous sight to behold.

Linsi Susannah Sanders

Moonshine, Moonshine

Is it time to brew the moonshine tonight.
See the stars shine glistening bright.
Hot whisky for breakfast, sour mash on the boil,
Only a gallon of whisky after all this hard work and toil,
Tested by me for specific gravity,
Checked, a PH test or three,
Checked, 'Are you sober enough to go?'
Checked, is your head still laying in the snow.
Footnote:
Please remember, don't forget,
Never drink the first few drops from a still you get,
Or for the rest of your life you may regret.

Karl Hermanis

Slemish Mountain

Oh Slemish Mountain by the Braid, how peacefully it stands
Midst pastures of an emerald green, a lovely scene commands;
The loaf-shaped mountain fair and high, it seems to reach the sky;
Its slopes and foothills fresh and steep gives beauty to the eye.

This mountain like a mighty rock is seen for miles around
From Cullybackey and from Larne and Ballymena town;
From Tully Brae near Portglenone and near the River Bann
Even from my own front door and right across the land.

An ancient landmark Slemish, a volcano at a time;
The spot where Patrick herded swine and offered prayers sublime;
The soft grey mists upon the slopes just like a ghost appears;
The fresh spring rain the summer sun it's stood for years and years.

How beautiful this mountain looks upon a winter day
With frost and snow upon its brow, a picture card I'd say;
In summer sun it's lovely blue, in autumn silvery grey;
One of Ireland's oldest landmarks, or so our fathers say.

James McIlhatton

My Village

My village is simply called Liphook
It looks like a picture in a book
The focal point is our general store
It holds the post office and much more
They serve us all with pure delight
And are open from morn to night
The village pub dates from bygone times
Has links with Nelson and ancient rhymes
When you are hungry and could eat a horse
Where else to go but to our pub of course
Village events are run throughout the year
Our annual carnival brings forth a tear
Sporting activities to suit everyone's taste
Most sportsmen enjoy this fun-loving place
We offer all the amenities in the book
So come along now and enjoy Liphook.

L A G Butler

Friends Disunited

Would you like to be in touch again with friends from long ago?
What has happened to them, all those years? Would you like to know?
Do you have the same warm feelings towards people whom you knew,
And presume (naught to the contrary) they feel the same for you?
Electronic gadgetry can offer some success
(But my ability in using it could hardly be much less).
A 'Friends Reunited' scheme is on the Internet,
Very popular, according to the media, and yet
Its success is in sharp contrast to my sad experience.
In attempting to revive the past, I've found indifference.
That's over now, say people by their failure to reply.
One actually said it. So cold. I wonder why.
We got on well. What factors have transformed their attitude?
Once we were so friendly. Why are they now so rude?
After several such 'lessons' one might think I'd had enough.
I have, but being friendly I am open to rebuff.
The world I've found is frequently a superficial place,
Its shallowness concealed behind an amiable face.
This is true not just of people I remember distantly,
But also of some who were colleagues much more recently.
After I had lost my job through no fault of my own,
Some I thought were more than mere colleagues left me alone.
One did telephone me, in fact he did so twice,
In later years, but on each occasion wanted free advice.
Disillusionment and disappointment are the things I share
With you, lest you think friendships survive; there may be nothing there.
Feed the new, revive the old ones, if you wish to try,
But (as to the response you get) don't set your hopes too high.

Anthony Hofler

Janice

We have a new warden in our sheltered flats
A wrench it will be, old age sees to that
We tend to be settled in so many ways
Changes make us anxious - like the same every day

Her name is Janice - a nice name that
She looks quite OK, neither thin nor too fat
Soon we look forward - I believe this to be true
We'll get on together, sharing our views

Now she's turned out OK
A treasure indeed
Aiming to satisfy
Our every need

Dolly Harmer

Kisses And Cuddles

She breezed into the cardiology
waiting room like the first crocus of spring.
Mummies, embalmed in glaciology,
felt life returning and began to sing.
'Kisses and cuddles,' she cried.

Came wafting in, an angel, three years old -
pink anorak, trainers with twinkling heels,
a ribbon in her hair, flax of spun gold.
Her mum and gran hearkened to her appeals.
'Kisses and cuddles,' she cried.

Came bouncing in on flashing heels like strobes.
Sunlight around her head, an aureole,
warmed up the corpses wrapped in flimsy robes
and roused them from their dark night of the soul.
'Kisses and cuddles,' she cried.

I, sitting nearest, bent to hear her prate
about her brother, William, and their dog,
discussed her picture book, tried to translate
her contribution to our dialogue.
'Kisses and cuddles,' she cried.

Addressed, the waiting room wrinkled its eyes.
And, when she waved goodbye, we who remained
forgot our flimsy robes and smiles, with sighs
over a glimpse of paradise regained.
'Kisses and cuddles,' she cried.

Norman Bissett

Elevenses

Sipping my coffee, I sit and ponder,
of what goes on, in that blue sky yonder?
We are surely not alone,
with our satellites and telephones.
What is going on, out there in space
perhaps another human race?
A race that lives in harmony, regardless
of colour, creed and the odd one.
Chasing each other, in and out of the stars
some we have names for, like Jupiter and Mars.
Perhaps one day, we'll bump into each other,
say hello, like sisters and brothers.
My daydream is over, over too soon,
I doubt I'll get a trip to the moon.
My coffee is cold, my feet on the ground,
out of space, is still out of bounds.

I D Welch

All You Need Is Love

Someone's whispering in my ear,
The voice is familiar, and the words are clear,
All you need is love.

Come follow me in the name of love,
Spread the word about the kingdom of God,
All you need is love.

Give all you have as I give to you,
And keep good faith in everything that you do,
All you need is love.

'For I am the bread,' He said,
Come follow me, for I have shed My blood,
And paid the price with My love.

'I am the bread,' He said,
'Come follow Me, for I am the bread of life,
And My word is alive.'

Someone's whispering in my ear,
The voice is familiar, and the words are clear.
All you need is love.

Judith Arden

The Reunion

Past pupils assembled and greeted each other.
Some are friends which remain to this day.
Others recognised by a look or a name.
Though now older, the years rolled away.
The babbling began, we were all girls together,
Sharing memories happy and sad.
Remembering schooldays, the laughter flowed free,
We all had a tale we could tell.
Wide range of interests, professions galore.
Family stories we're proud of it all.

Teachers attended, still shown respect,
We cherish the dedication they had.
Giving us guidance, a true sense of worth,
Which moulded and equipped us for life.
Then 'twas back to the present, farewells, give a cheer,
Our schooldays - we loved them,
So here's to next year.

Alice Turner

Sensible Shoes

I'm a middle-aged woman in sensible shoes.
My hair is too long, my skirt is quite plain.
I'm drinking my coffee in a cafe forlorn;
While others do likewise, avoiding the rain.

There's a little fair boy in the opposite seat.
His jersey is blue, reflecting his eyes.
He's digging for treasure with a silvery spade,
Then samples with relish his creamy surprise.

There's a picture book open of animal folk.
He points to a page, then growls like a bear.
He is shaping his mouth for a pussycat mew,
Then manners returning, sits up in his chair.

I'm a middle-aged woman in sensible shoes.
I'm glad of them now, the puddles are cool.
There's a little fair boy in his wellington boots,
He's choosing a bag for nursery school.

We're waiting with others in a miserable queue.
Their voices are grim, they spare not a glance.
'I'm a lucky boy, Nanny,' he smiles like the sun.
My sensible shoes are ready to dance.

Alma Shearer

Up Through Life

When I was small it was my mum
Who stopped my life from being glum
She made sure I was always well
And never wore a pungent smell

She told me to come in at night
As strangers hold a nasty fright
She warned me never to take sweets
As she would give me ample treats

She helped me to do well at school
And took me to our local pool
I learnt to read and write with her
She taught me never to wear fur

She washed and cooked and cleaned for me
And every night she cooked my tea
But now I know the tricks of life
I'm taken care of by my wife

Terry Lander

My Dogs

I have two dogs, Gucci and Tia.
What they have brought to this family you just have no idea.
A fantastic pair of characters in their own right.
They keep us all entertained night after night.

We have watched them grow and develop since they were pups.
You could enter both of them for that dog show Crufts.
Gucci is a follower of J-Lo as she has a large behind.
Tia is totally the opposite I find.

But both great fun and joy.
Just to watch them squabble over a toy.
One is full of bravado, the other takes a back seat.
Everyone loves them, whoever they meet.

They can make you smile any time of day.
Without them our days would be grey.
The love they give is unconditional and pure.
If we had a larger house we would have more.

Gucci is 10 months older than Tia but it's Tia whom leads the way.
She is a brave little soul and she always has her say.
It's beautiful to watch them sleep and lie together.
All cosy and snug indoors, out of reach of the weather.

Dogs are life changing, they really are.
I love to watch them both looking out the windows of the car.
But most of all just have them around.
They have a way of keeping your feet on the ground.

Tom Roach

Sleeping Rough

I'm like a fine rich earl newly fallen in love
Reading yesterday's Herald, sun shining from above.
I'm keeping closely in touch with the world, its mother,
With this and that, such and such and news of Big Brother.

I'm here outside, (did you guess?) stretched on a wooden seat,
Feeling I'll make a success - my crossword nigh complete.
These long green benches, I vow, make resting sure, OK;
Help smooth out that furrowed brow and chase the glooms away.

My sharp thinking turns to mist, my mind plays games of fun,
My head feels it's being kissed and stroked by burning sun.
Now, I cannot recollect the answer to the clue;
This snag, I did not expect, this mind-fog from the blue.

'Mummy,' queried a wee lass, 'who is that hairy man?'
('Twas like I'd had sleeping gas), 'Don't worry my wee lamb.'
(the voice I heard was now but a faint distant tinkle),
'That old man you see sleeping, why, that's Rip Van Winkle!'

Ken Millar

This Was During My Wife's Illness

If I had control over time,
I'd wish that time would stand still,
If I had some influence over time,
My wife she wouldn't be ill.

If I could turn the clocks back,
Thru one score year and ten,
It would be about the time we met,
I was working for a living then.

If I was given just one wish,
It would be for Annabell's health,
I wouldn't wish for money,
Cos there's more to life than wealth.

If I was given a second chance,
To live my life again,
There's only one thing I would alter,
That's the disease in Annabell's brain.

If I had control over time,
I'd want Annabell to be well,
But what God has in store for us,
No one can ever tell.

Lee Brooks

Love's Reward

The air is full of birdsong,
The sky is full of light.
My heart is full of happiness,
My womb is full of life.

I am filled with awe and wonder,
I'll keep our secret a little longer.
I'm going to fly for a moment or two,
While I teach my baby how to dance on the moon.

In time you will know my little treasure,
How precious you are to me and your father.
I wish you a life with much joy and pleasure,
And you'll never want for anything ever.

We'll give so much love, you'll have love to spare,
And I know some day when your turn comes . . .
You will teach your own baby
How to dance on the moon.

M C Barnes

Elements Of Love

Twisting and turning in the breeze
The aged oak tree bends
The long green grass adjacent
Bows in its small defence.

The creaking branches bending
The bright red poppies fade
The young white swans are battling
Against the forceful wind.

The ripples widen on the water
The clouds form in the sky
The rain starts gently falling
The thunder rumbles nigh.

The flashing of the lightning
Like daggers stabbing the sky
The crashing of the thunder
The rain pours from on high.

The barren earth is sodden
The animals scurry forth
The smell of wet grass deepens
The storm just wields its wrath.

The calmness arrives so suddenly
The stillness and quietness around
Nothing at all is moving
There are no longer sounds.

My heavy heart is still beating
My thoughts are still so new
And all I can hear around me
Is the quiet breath from you.

Margaret Luckett

The Inseparable Pair

There they go this inseparable pair
A dog and his master both full of care
Side by side they go on their way
Out in all weather, every week, every day
Big brown eyes looking up at his master
Both getting on, they can't go any faster
They live for each other and in each other they trust
They've been for their evening stroll and now it is dusk
True and faithful each other they defend
They say a dog is man's best friend.

Hazell Dennison

Life And Love

I see the dawn break through.
The sun is shining high.
I see the colours that shine through,
But then I start to sigh.

I cannot hear the thunder.
The things that life can bring.
Wishing I could hear again,
But then you start to wonder.

Why I cannot hear
And things I'd love to say,
But life is what is brought to me
And wishing that one day.

I still believe in miracles,
Hoping that I'll find
A day when I awake,
Believing in my mind.

A miracle will happen.
I live within my dreams,
That I could hear the noise
Which life could bring to me.

When I awake at dawn each day
I see the light shine through.
The sparkle that I see,
I live in dreams of you.

M B Tucker

Grandad's Garden

In my mind's eye I will always see
Grandad's garden as it used to be,
His flowers growing for the show
Standing straight, like soldiers in a row,
Gladioli and chrysanthemum,
Carnations, pinks and delphinium.
A greenhouse growing fruit, bright red,
Part of it used as a potting shed,
Veg for the table down the bottom,
A pile of compost, smelling rotten,
A well dug deep, that we must avoid
Or Grandad would be very annoyed,
A seat to rest when the work was done,
A time of peace, in the dying sun.

Doris Green

My New Pony

Clipperty clop, clipperty clop
I've bought a new pony, saddle and crop
I've found a stable with plenty of room
To muck him out I'll need a bucket and broom
A trough for his food and plenty of hay
For when he's inside on that winter day

I'll sit straight and tall as I ride him out
When there's not much traffic about
My hard black hat I must always wear
And those jodhpurs, I have a spare pair
My riding boots now shine like new
From up here you get a great view

Home again and the work must begin
Muck him out and give him a good grooming
His mane now like a lady's long hair
His tail plaited with a ribbon there
Bridle and stirrups will shine so bright
They will twinkle silvery in the light

His tackle has all been spit and polished
The floor is clean, any smells abolished
He is cosy in his socks and warm rug
And tucking greedily into his grub
One last chat and a cuddle before bed
I think it's about time that I was fed

Janet Gomersall

Saints And Sinners

Like a reoccurring nightmare,
You penetrate my defences,
And move in for the scare,
Leaving me shocked and tense.

Like a ghost that haunts me,
You loop around me in the shape of a sphere,
Blocking my vision and all that I see,
Emitting from me colossal fear.

Alarm bells ring in my head,
Hands go to my neck and I gasp,
Unease revolutionises into dread,
I feel your sting, like that of a wasp.

With haste your hands leave,
My saviour has arrived and I am exultant,
My melancholy mood goes and I am free,
And I look upon my saviour as a saint.

Kimberly Harries

The Ancient Oak

The old oak tree stood alone
Shivering, shaking, stripped to the bone
Leaves all gone with the autumn air
Winds had blown, left him bare.
Men had come in the early morn
Talk of old wood, new wood to be born
Came with their axe, came with their saw,
Strong rubber boots and bright jackets they wore.
All around him decimation occurred
The oak tree stayed silent, not saying a word.
They came to him at the end of the day
Needed to fell him to earn their pay
They sweated and toiled but try as they might
The old tree was blessed by an ancient rite.
As darkness fell they laid down their tools
Wise of the ways the men were no fools,
Stood back in respect and bowed to the tree
Put on their jackets, went home for their tea.

Jan Hedger

Odyssey

If I could escape the pull of this Earth,
I'd race to the heavens for all I was worth.
Exploring the limitless space that's out yonder,
Exceeding the height of the high flying condor.
Flitting about 'mongst the billions of stars,
Jumping off t'moon and landing on Mars.
Enjoying the role of celestial flitter,
Eager to learn what makes the stars glitter,
To see if close study then could explain us,
What we don't know of, what lies on Uranus.
I'd keep zooming about, with much to be done,
It's a pity that Mercury's close to the sun.
High on my list, amongst other things,
Is to find time to look inside Saturn's rings.
People would see me as some sort of loon
If I said I'd had words with the man on the moon.
I'd need more than one lifetime to see things I've read,
Yet it doesn't take long, fantasising in bed.

Bill Austin

Half Truths And White Lies

They say vote for us
And you cannot lose.
We are the only party you need to choose.
We will give you this
Then again we will give you that.
We can pull the economic rabbit out of the hat.
You will have more money
In your pocket to spend.
This is a truth on which you can depend.
This is a promise
We will deliver if selected.
A promise we can only make good when elected.

Is it cold words
That always make me shiver,
When these political parties promise to deliver.
Deliver Heaven
To us here on Earth.
What are their promises really worth?
Too many questions
With not enough answers,
From these party political politician dancers.
Waltzing around the issues
With their little white lies,
But the truth can be seen in the whites of their eyes.

Keith Tissington

Despair

Living in a world full of despair,
Events occur that seem so unfair,
Life isn't priceless anymore,
And a spark of unrest, leads to a war,
Road rage, wrong colour, or speaking your mind,
Can lead to acts so cruel, and unkind,
School bullying is rife,
What has become of human life.
Hoodies and yobs that kill just for fun,
Making life miserable for everyone.

People say that the world has gone mad,
It's not the world, but the people in it,
That's what makes it so sad,
Using religion as an excuse to kill,
Hurting the innocent, which makes it worse still,
Where will it all end, does anyone care,
Or will we now exist forever, in a world of despair?

Maureen Arnold

Those 70s Fashions!

High-legged boots and hot pants tight
Velvet, shiny, colours bright.
Puffed sleeve blouses and sequinned tops,
Girls *and* boys with long-haired mops.
Gentle flares, embroidered jeans,
Bell-bottoms worn by all the teens.
Trevira suits or check-flared skirts,
Tank tops with butterfly collar shirts.
Sheepskin coats with fur trim - *or* -
Chunky cardies like Starsky wore
Trendy waistcoats, scarves like Dr Who
Footless leg warmers and pop socks too.
Feather cuts and crombi coats
With pockets full of 'Love Is . . .' notes.
Big Afros and tongued hair flicks
Worn by guys as well as chicks!
Halter-neck jumpsuits made in white
Lycra vest tops to catch the light.
Reflecting lights on satin jacket,
Men with medallions were all the racket!
Broderie Anglaise petticoat hems
Peasant style skirts and pretty gems.
White, creamy tights with black patent shoes,
Six-inch platforms were headline news.
Ponchos briefly made their mark,
A bit like that film about a shark!
Oxford bags and two-tone loons,
Dancing to the disco tunes.
Pins and chains and all sorts of junk,
Were really in if you were punk!
The 1970s had fashions to hate
But boy the music sure was great!

Kim Kelly

All Cock - No Bull!

A farmer once married a wife
Who'd not been on a farm in her life.
At breakfast one day:
'Just one egg?' he did say.
She replied, 'Yes; the hens gave me strife!'

The farmer whose surname was Moody,
Smiled kindly at his new wife, Judy,
'Oh dear; oh my,
I think I know why:
It's that cockerel again - he's gone broody!'

Roger Williams

A Spell In School

Mr Cook, he is our head
And every day he'll bore me
With the very same old words
Said a million times before.

'I'd enjoy school while you can!
One day you'll be a full-grown man.'

He saw me play the fool in class
As by the window he did pass,
He frowned and banged upon the glass
And always, always those same old words!
(He's really getting on my nerves!)

'I'd enjoy school while you can!
One day you'll be a full-grown man.'

He wagged his finger, then he said,
'You've got some brains inside that head!
Don't waste your life, don't jest and joke,
It'll only upset all your folk.'
I rolled my eyes, my jaw was set,
Those words: they had to come forth yet
And then he said the immortal verse,
'You're only young, life could be worse.'

'I'd enjoy school while you can!
One day you'll be a full-grown man.'

Said I to Cook, 'No, not a man, I'll be a full-grown wizard.'
A magic wand, a puff of smoke and now Cook is a lizard!
I chucked him in my school bag and turned to leave the room,
I heard a noise: *vroom, vroom, vroom, vroom!*
Mum had landed on her broom!

J A Solly

Only One Chance

If your life is filled with confusion
Work it out there is a solution
Everyone's life is just a big gamble
So take what you can if you are able

If you are not happy with what you have got
Turn a new corner and change the whole lot
Because as you get older you live with regret
Do what you want and do not fret

It is a free country, so live life with ease
The world is your oyster, so do as you please
Talk to someone that you can trust for advice
You don't have to take it but it'll make you think twice

J L Chapman

This Month

An autumn drive through the forest,
She's been at work the seasonal florist
Turned summer's shades of green leaves,
Into multitude of coloured trees.
It never seems to be shut,
The little tea hut
Of worldwide motorcyclist fame,
On the gentle bend of the forest lane,
Hammed by silver birch.
Pass the Holy Innocent church,
Its spire upwards reaching,
Overreach by great whopping beeches.
Autumn leaves in the breeze falling,
Fallen leaves cover all.
A postcard setting off the fall.
Rich reds, golden browns,
Litter the forest grounds.
Pastel autumn yellows of silver birch leaves
Are the first to leave their trees.
Common oaks russet leaves drop,
Before the fast growing turkey oak crop.
As far as one can see,
A sea
Of beeches' grey trunks.
Dead leaves crunch
Under the long horn cattle's hooves.
Beauty in abundance this month,
Cannot help being moved.

B G Clarke

One Wish

If there was one wish for me,
I would wish for peace and harmony,
where you walk or who you are,
does not leave a lasting scar.

I would close my eyes and wish so bad,
how I hate when you are sad,
I wish that war was not of hate,
but the war of love and fate.

If my wish was on a mountain high,
I would climb till I reached the sky,
if my wish could only come true,
sadness would not be the colour blue . . .

Hasina Rahman

Touched By The Stars

Before dawn's light there is no better time to see the magic that is theirs at night.
So I stood and gazed towards the heavenly stars to view and wonder
at their God-like light.

And as I looked in awe at the greatness of the stars a hand unseen and silent
reached down into my very being.
It drew me to a place I did not want to go, but a place only I, alone, was seeing.

There I met my ghosts of days gone by, hidden for years and shrouded in pain.
I saw my past come through that hand, a past I never thought to ever see again.

His smile was there and so too was his cross, his anger and his love submerged in one.
I felt confusion and the love and hate that went to make my life and loss of John.

I saw his cross that both of us had shared, a cross not asked for but sent into our lives.
It had, at times, brought sadness and despair, but had also brought great passion
and deep sighs.

I knew then that these ghosts were very real, that I in this life had left so much unsaid
I need now to stretch out my hand as well and heal the chasm that my ignorance has fed.

A new beginning beckoned me that night, a direction that I hoped would rectify
My head hidden in so many clouds, but now, with hope, would see a clearer sky.

And through the confusion of that night, a calmness settled where had been such pain.
My life from now would tread a different path, and those I love would feel my love again.

Kathleen Furlong

Loneliness

I sit in my flat gazing into space,
The unhappiness of being lonely shows upon my face.
The days are monotonous and no one rings on the phone,
I'm trapped in this hellish nightmare of being all alone.
The internet is my companion and my only soulmate,
It relieves my feelings of emptiness and despondency that I hate.
Depression and negative thoughts creep slowly into my brain,
If someone were to cheer me up, I'd never feel like this again.
I look outside my window at the happy people on the street,
I wipe away the tears with tissues and throw them at my feet.
I feel suicidal at times as darkness clouds my soul,
Only friendship, happiness and excitement can make me feel whole.
I hope that one day all these feelings will become a thing of the past,
And I'll have lots of friends and a life of purpose to occupy me at last.

F Buliciri

'It's The Way You Tell 'Em Grandpa'

'Tell me a story please,' young David said,
'You must keep the promise that got me to bed.'
I said, 'It's no use, I can't think anymore,
I can only repeat what I've told you before.'

'In that case, dear Grandpa,' said David, said he,
'I'll tell them to you as you told them to me.
Whether they're true, legend or fable,
They excel all the tales from King Arthur's Round Table.

During the war, a Spitfire you flew,
In fact, you were the first of the First of the Few.
Yet I can't quite see just how it would work,
At the same time you brought out the troops from Dunkirk.

And then in the desert, you gained Monty's thanks,
For blowing big holes in old Rommel's big tanks.
You commanded destroyers with consummate ease
Ensuring Brittania kept rule of the seas.

After the war when you captained test cricket,
You scored most of the runs and took every wicket.
When talking of football you got me excited,
When you won the cup for Manchester United.

I've just worked it out that in the Gulf War,
You flew a Tornado when aged sixty-four.
You said at my age you were awfully bright,
But it was me who helped you with my homework tonight.

And so it goes on, these tales about you,
Of romance and danger and brave derring-do.
Your tales were exciting, enchanting and bold,
As good as the stories Sheherazade told.

But I've loved every one, their memory I'll keep,
And they've achieved their objective,
They helped me to sleep!'

Joseph Brough

Dedication Lost

O for the love of Marguerite
Wouldn't life be so sweet
When I first saw you I was in a state
It wasn't so long ago that I had lost my soulmate
Ever since that first glance
My heart began to dance
To be so close to the one I adore
How could I dare ask for more
Just to see your wonderful smile
Makes my life seem worthwhile
Whenever I see you my heart skips a beat
Was it fate that decided we meet?
I've known for such a long time
You're the one I would like to make mine
The feelings I have for you are so strong
To deny these feelings would be wrong
Will my feelings for you ever fade away
Not ever, even when I'm old and grey?
I've tried in vain to endear myself to you
While deep in my heart of hearts
I knew there couldn't possibly be a me and you
Although at this moment in time
I can only dream that you will be mine
If only dreams could come true
I would never again have to be blue
If something so wonderful could happen to me
I would be grateful for all eternity
As for the future all I can see
Is a life of loneliness for me
As my sad and lonely life drags on
My dreams of you will still carry on

A Reilly

King Canute

Old King Canute, we've all heard of the name,
He once was a king of great maritime fame;
He built sea defences but they wouldn't stand,
And neither did he when he spoke from the land.

He sat on the beach, told the sea to go back,
But sadly to say the waves wouldn't change tack;
So then with a towel his feet did he rub,
Then put on his shoes and went off to the pub.

Bernard Johnson

Charlotte Brooke

On Thursday morn on 7th of July
Our 'Charlotte Brooke', arrived
And after all the restless nights and heartburn
My Rachael had survived.

She swept into our lives
And turned them inside out
From piles of dirty washing
And sleepless nights, I have no doubt.

She made my daughter a mother
And me into a gran
Instead of my PC in the hall
She's given me a pram.

My home is full of baby things
And happiness abounds
From gigglings, to cries and laughs
The house is full of sounds.

'Thank you,' Marc and Rachael
For bringing an angel to our door
And thank you, 'our little angel'
For giving us so much more.

Veronica Barnett

Rivers Of Blood

Before my eyes a field of corpses
Rotting flesh, both man and horses
Lying in a quagmire of mud
Where days before ran a river of blood.

But this is just one field of many
Where a soldier's life costs just two-a-penny
Unknown men with unknown faces
Forgive me mate while I take your boots and laces.

Before my eyes a field of horses
No more death and no more corpses
And playing in a puddle of mud
Little children, unaware of the rivers of blood.

Mark Hutchines

What You Are To Me

A blue patch of sky on a grey, rainy day
A best friend who always knows what to say
A smile to cheer you up on a day you are down
Company that never lets you frown
A laugh so hearty it brings a tear to the eye
A long awaited hello after the last goodbye
A familiar voice that you love to hear
A hug that seems to cure all your fear
A bright star in the sky on a dark, lonely night
A flicker from a log fire that gives a room light
A warm bed on a cold winter's morning
A promise on the truth that means a new dawning
The warmth from the love that you feel
A look that tells you that this is real
A kiss in the rain that makes you happy to be there
It's cold in the rain but you don't care
A message on your phone that you read many times
A trust so deep you never have to read between the lines
A weekend off so you can just be you
A touch that leaves you not knowing what to do
A relative that you're always glad to see
A companion that lets me be me
All the things and more that make my life so filled with love,
No matter how long you're with me it's just never enough
I am blessed to have you by my side
You make me strong and I never want to hide
Thank you for being the person you are
You're my hope, my strength, my shining star.

Zoë Thompson

Nana And Grandad

I brought some flowers
to your grave today,
I was standing there
thinking of words to say.

I felt silly talking to you
knowing you weren't there,
it just made everything
much harder to bear.

Everyone has missed you
and the times we shared together,
you will always be in our hearts
forever and ever.

Louise Chafer

All Saints' Church Choir, Peterborough

(A poem dedicated to the hard work of All Saints' Choir)

Now here's a choir, men and boys,
Who have fun and make loads of noise,
Some happy and some sad,
But the quality of the singing is not bad.

On a Friday, the boys have fun,
It doesn't matter about the sun,
But the fun does not always last,
So they reflect upon the past.

Rochester, Chichester, we've all been there,
We did have time to look and stare,
But there was work that had to be done,
Before we could relax beneath the sun.

They sing in services every Sunday,
But they believe it is a fun day,
Anthems, psalms and hymns too,
They sing them all just for you.

So remember there is a choir,
Always there for you,
From boys eight and onwards and men too.
So come to see All Saints' Choir in Peterborough and see what is true,
We're always there and here for you.

Matthew Willbye (17)

Easter Parade

The green flag is flying
The spirit, reborn
The dreamers are dying
A nation is torn
There's bodies a-lying
Along Sackville Street
There'll be many more
Till this sad isle's complete
This grim fight for freedom
Will run to its end
The land of their fathers
They're born to defend
Let not foreign rifles
Deter or dissuade
Liberation will come
From this Easter parade

John Robinson

My Family

My sister is always on the computer
She's never out at her tutor.
She reads her emails all day long,
And she's never even sung a song.
When I call her down for tea,
She's always in a mood with me.

My brother is always out with his mates,
He's never going out on dates.
My brother goes to a cricket club,
And then he's off to the pub.
He always likes to have lots to eat,
You can tell by the size of his hands and feet.

My big sister lives down under,
Why she's there I sometimes wonder.
She's tall and dark and very pretty,
She lives by a beach next to the city.
Her fiancé, Jack, likes to play cricket,
He's very good and has never lost a wicket.

My grandad was a fine sailor,
He never has been a failure.
He sailed across many oceans,
And washed his hair in many lotions.
My grandad was in the war,
He never knew such a world before.

My dad is always on the phone,
He tells us to leave him alone.
We spy on him if we can,
But he is a very cunning man.
He also likes to cook the tea,
And makes up his own recipe.

My mum likes to bake cakes,
She never makes mistakes.
My mum does it to perfection,
She never has to do a correction.
My mum bakes all different kinds,
She uses anything she can find.

My grandma likes to call me pet,
Though I'm not used to it yet.
It's still a cool name,
It's just our little game.
I still love her so,
As she will know.

Sophie Roach (11)

Awaiting That Grandson
(Thoughts of a mother awaiting her daughter's firstborn child)

Blue to celebrate a boy
Bells to ring and brings us joy
Due to come in Feb 05
Join us then and be alive!
Now you're waiting to be here
Moving hard to make it clear
You're a boy without a name
But, for this, you're not to blame!
Wonderful it is to me
That you'll join my family
Grandson mine is what you'll be
Proud of your hereditary
Now we all await the day
As together we all pray
Safe and sound you'll come our way
Joy for all on your Birthday!

Christopher Head

My Darling Daughter

I wished for a child, perfect and true
And you came to me, straight out of the blue
But you were not perfect, problems undefined
But despite all of this, you can be loving and kind

As a baby you rarely slept and constantly cried
So many doctors, diets, pills and potions I've tried
I wish I knew how to grant inner peace to you
Life doesn't give you a handbook to say what to do

People avoid or abuse you, they just don't understand
Sometimes in life all that is needed is a helping hand
I fear for the day when I can't shield all of your knocks
So I guess I'll wish now that I can freeze all the clocks

Jeannie Ashplant

Where Has It All Gone?

Where has it all gone?
We were two now I'm one
The love we had for one another
Were we too busy to become Dad and Mother?

Did we spend too much time apart?
When I think back it breaks my heart.
The laughs we had, the shows, the walks by the lake
The picnics, oh how my heart aches.

I love you so much, where did it go wrong?
We've been together for so very long.
I don't know how I will survive
Now we are no longer husband and wife.

Why did it happen? Was it me, was it you?
Or was it the intervention of someone new?
God gave us feelings we cannot control
They can make you happy and glad or destroy your heart and soul.

Where did it go, the happiness we shared?
All the things you did showed how much you cared.
When did it happen love, please tell me, I need to know.
Please tell me love, before I go.

And when I'm gone and you're on your own
Maybe then you'll think what have I done?
Maybe you'll regret it and want me back again
And maybe you will feel like I do, full of pain.

It is so sad that we are no longer together
When we promised in church it would be forever.
I pray to God we will find happiness some day
Even if we go our separate ways.

Was I blind and could not see
How you'd changed, especially towards me?
How you were away a lot of the time
And I couldn't see it was near the end of the line.

How do I begin to start again?
How do I get rid of this awful pain?
How do I make a new home without you?
Buying for one when it used to be two.

And now I think it's the final goodbye
I will try to be brave and not to cry,
At least 'til I'm out of your sight
And pray to God to make it all right.

I love you still
I think I always will.
I hope you find what you're looking for
And may God bless you for evermore.

So take care, look after yourself, sort yourself out
And if one day you feel any doubt
Call me and see if I feel the same
And see if we can relight that wonderful flame.

God bless you.

Felicity Pigtails

Wishful Thinking

I'd like to visit the pyramids of Egypt,
I'd like to go to Niagra Falls,
I'd like to sip champagne in a gondola,
And I'd like to visit The Wailing Wall;
I'd like to visit The Grand Canyon,
I'd like to visit Athens and Rome,
I'd like to see lots of shows on Broadway,
And visit the Millennium Dome;
I'd like to gamble in Monte Carlo,
Shop at the salons of Milan,
Go on a round the world cruise,
And go to Paris to see The Can-Can;
I'd like to ride on The Orient Express,
See The Hanging Gardens of Babylon,
Ride a horse by The Swiss Alps,
And visit the city of Bonn;
I'd like to cycle by The Rockies,
Water ski in the south of France,
Swim in the Atlantic and Pacific,
And in a café in Brazil do Latin dance;
I'd like to go walking in Austria,
Visit New England in the Fall,
Go on safari to Kenya,
And go to The Ritz when there's a ball.
Instead, I'm stuck in a small flat,
The rain beats on the windowpane,
My mind wanders off again,
And I imagine myself on a beach in Spain.

Sarah Sidibeh

It Really Hurts . . .

'It really hurts,' I yell to Mum
'There is a pain inside my tum.'
Mum just looks and shakes her head
And pulls the quilt right off my head!
'Oh no! The pain it's in my leg,
Please don't send me to school I beg.'
But Mum ignored my woeful plea
And made herself a cup of tea.
'Oh no! The pain's inside my head.'
'Oh no it's not,' Mum quickly said.
'I cannot move my fingers and toes,
And something horrid's coming out of my nose!'
Mum ignored me anyway
And said I'm going to school today.
So after breakfast off we go,
I tried to walk really slow.
'Come on hurry up or you'll be late!'
She said pushing me through the rusty school gate.
The bell rang out my last chance now
I hugged my tummy and shouted, 'Ow!
The pain is worse, I think I might die.'
Mum just laughed and said, 'Nice try!'
I sighed and wearily walked away
I suppose it won't be a very long day.
Mum waved me in with a cheery smile,
And said she'd see me in a while.
The day at long last has come to an end
Mum took me to the park with my friend,
And as for my aches, have they gone away?
No, I'm sure they'll be back another day!

P Hoddinott

The Power Cut

Today we had a power cut
My kitchen was no good,
Of all the things I have in there
They won't work as they should,
I cannot boil myself an egg
Or make a cup of tea.
What would happen without power
Is very plain to see.

Betty Mason

Bees In The Basement

There are bees in our basement
In a long-forgotten tin,
On a shelf beside the boiler
And an old recycling bin.

There is junk down there aplenty -
Broken toys with missing eyes,
That bicycle of Grandad's
And that tin of bee surprise.

Old records from the seventies,
A bed with missing springs;
Ornaments and window blinds,
A tin, jam packed with stings.

Down there in the basement
The dust will make you sneeze,
While somewhere in the darkness
There's the buzz of angry bees.

There are bees in our basement,
But I'm not concerned at all.
We've a *tiger* in the toilet
And I need to pay a call!

Tim Harvey

A Pile Tale

When good old Farmer Johnson died
It made his lawyer smile
When reading out his will
Said nephew John was left a pile.
John thought of piles of bank notes
With lots of cash to spend
And knew to whom his uncle
Would leave it in the end.
We'd all be poor relations,
He'd buy a Rolls Royce car,
And every night at dinner
He would smoke a big cigar.
He prattled on and on about
The things he meant to do.
A world cruise on his own fine yacht
Were only just a few.
But we all grinned behind our hands
And wisely held our tongue.
We knew the pile he'd been left
Was a massive pile of *dung!*

Margaret B Baguley

Babies

I hate Mother Nature, she played a cruel trick
She made me want babies, and I spent weeks being sick
I really was broody, I just couldn't wait
And so I was caught and then 'twas too late!

I grew up believing that breeding was easy
Till I woke every morning feeling all queasy
Pregnant and glowing sounded a cinch
Until I expanded and needed a winch!

Oh labour's a doddle, a walk in the park
Those evil midwives kept me in the dark
I splashed in the birthpool and groaned through the pain
And spent half the night screaming, 'Never again!'

I actually thought babies slept through the night
And discovered perhaps when they're thirteen they might!
The hourly feeding and pacing the floor
I seethed while watching dear hubby snore.

Whatever's this red angry thing
It's loud, constantly yelling, making our lugholes ring!
I just can't believe it, it's all such a shock
Living each day by the hands of the clock!

I'd dreamed that my babies would be 'apple of Dad's eye'
Again he's gone 'AWOL', 'I'm busy,' he'd lie!
He seems to be 'missing' when babe is being fed
And by magic appears when baby's in bed.

Who said that girls were pretty and pink?
While mine was all grubby with a permanent stink
'Oh boys are so loving and lots of fun'
Well, this doesn't seem to apply to my son!
Mealtimes are a warzone, but bedtimes are bliss
Small chubby arms hug you, to give you a kiss!

With junior asleep, the house very quiet
I survey the house thinking *when was the riot*?
As I sink in the sofa dreaming of rest
Hubby is winking, oh God he's a pest

I take off my 'tent' and gaze down at my belly
Dismayed as it looks like a red strawberry jelly
My boobs are like melons, but hubby is happy
Maybe it's him who should be wearing the nappy!

It really is tragic, how on earth could I know
My 'bits' would be butchered from ass to elbow
Just walking was painful, no one said a thing
How I'd spend the next fortnight perched on a rubber ring!

My bottom resembles a giant baboon's
I'm informed I must live on diet of prunes
I assumed my dear figure would snap back with a twang
And have to admit now that everything 'hangs'!

As time passes by bad memories fade
I think it's a wonder *any* babies are made
I hate Mother Nature, oh how could this be?
My test kit's confirmed we shall have number three!

Julie Trainor

A Soggy Flop

She woke up one morning
Determined to make creative use of her time;
She thought of the cookery lessons she'd had -
Neglecting them was a crime!
She chose a good recipe,
Wrote down a list of everything she would need,
Then put on her coat and her gloves and a scarf
And went into town with speed.

An hour or two later she walked up the hill
With all that would be required -
The load was quite heavy,
Her arms ached a bit and soon she was rather tired;
But still, with a will, back at home,
She began preparing to mix and bake -
(How happy the family would be
To behold a bona fide home-made cake!)

She weighed her ingredients, sloshed in the eggs
And added some chocolate, too,
Then threw in some kirsch for more richness
(Although she wasn't supposed to do!)
Then something went wrong with the oven, it seems -
The mixture remained a 'slop'
'What happened?' the children asked,
'Had you no time to go to the baker's shop?'

Rosemary Yvonne Vandeldt

Grand Designs

A famous architect boiled his eggs
He liked them very underdone
All soft and wet and squishy
But eating them was really fun.
For when he banged them with his spoon
To try and reach the inner yolk,
They splashed all over everyone
And gave his shirt and suit a soak.
So off he'd hurry to his work
To design tea shops and art schools,
In a suit all covered in whitish streaks
And lots of little yellow pools.
His mum despaired and to end his plight
Bought him a raincoat in which to eat
So he could splash as much as he liked
But his suit would still be nice and neat.
And so it worked successfully
He was protected from his food
Until he married and moved away
and left his eggs at home for good.
His mum then threw the coat away
She didn't want to have it packed
For when she tried to fold it up
It didn't bend in half - it cracked
The bin men who collected it
Picked it up and said, 'Oh gosh,
Do you know what we've got here?
It's Charles, Runny MacIntosh!'

Russell Adams

Beautiful Strangers

We could move into another room
where all the beautiful strangers litter
the lamplight with jewels of conversation.

Their words dance across carpets to a tune
that only lovers hear (and maybe friends),
tapping on the door like invitations.

Whispers circle around the ceiling,
draw pictures on the wall in smiles that blend
with meaningless topics and good company.

Most days we only talk in silence
like strangers wearing coats, about to leave
a room without being hugged by a cloud of words.

T Stephen Williams

Teacher's Bloomers

The day it happened I'll never forget,
Below the hem the bloomers had crept.
Jim Coyle and I sat smirking and grinning,
We saw the potential right from the beginning.

Pointing with eyes and pointing with feet,
Soon titters and giggles from every seat.
All over the blackboard a lesson in chalk,
Disaster was looming the further she walked.

With every step the bloomers descended,
Shocking pink, my word they were splendid.
Pencils were dropped for a different view,
Swinging off chairs like chimps in the zoo.

Around the ankles the bloomers dropped,
The teaching and writing instantly stopped.
She turned around with a sick little smile,
What a beautiful day, let's go out for a while.

Go out to the yard, start weeding the rockery,
Oh, and Gerry my boy, I want it done properly.
Up to the windows we clambered like monkeys,
Just to steal a glimpse of teacher's auld donkey.

Poor innocent children, what a terrible sight,
For ages thereafter we had bad dreams at night.
The bloomers were awesome, as large as a tent,
Had we paid for the view, it was money well spent.

GFB

Tea With The Vicar

I'm invited to the vicar's for tea
He's invited you, he's invited me
I've never been to tea with a vicar before
I hope he doesn't think I'm a terrible bore
I must say thank you, I must say please
Shake his hand, don't give it a squeeze
On this occasion what should I say?
I want to follow Jesus, please show me the way
I have tried to be faithful, I've tried to be kind
I've looked after the sick, I've helped the blind
I love my neighbour as I know I should
And given a kind word whenever I could
I'm looking forward to my tea and cake
And a good impression I hope to make.

Muriel Turner

Supermarkets? You Can Keep Them!

I hate shopping at my local supermarket,
The trolleys seem to have minds of their own.
I go up and down the gangways walking crabwise
Bumping people, I'm a walking danger zone.

Why don't people see that I am coming,
Most of them seem to go out just to chat.
In groups of two, three or four, they block the blooming floor
Giving dirty looks if I should prod a back.

And why do staff have to change the lay-out?
As the things I need are no longer there.
I get in such a flap, as I start another lap
Searching, ever searching, makes me swear.

Then, when it's my turn at the dreaded pay point,
Which is when the till roll's had enough.
Sally isn't able, and has to call for Mabel,
She puts it right, and leaves her in a huff.

Of course, I'm the one with something minus bar code,
And the queue of eyes behind me start to bore.
If I had my own computer, my shopping list I'd booster
Then I wouldn't have to go there anymore.

A shopping trip for me is not a pleasure,
There are things or places, I would rather be.
Somewhere nice and sunny, if I only had the money,
Or watching TV, sipping cups of tea.

Gone are the times when you could write an order
For the corner shop, alas, who is no more.
I have a master plan, 'bring back that little man'
Who aimed to please you - and, delivered to your door.

A G Revill

Friendly Monsters

With spindly legs and body all hairy
No wonder we're considered scary
Big men quake in our wake
Women scream when we are seen

But in every home you'll find us living quietly
Behind the curtains or under the settee
In hidey-holes all over the house
Places too small for any field mouse.

Dad lives behind the washing machine
He prefers a place that's super clean
Sometimes he emerges late at night
Just to give the cat a fright.

My brother stays upstairs in the bath
Keeping nice and fresh and cool
Forgetting when the water runs
He'll be washed away, silly fool.

Mother reclines in the bedroom
She says she loves the décor
Taking a little wander around
When the inhabitants start to snore.

I've taken over the lounge
Being the busiest member of the clan
Weaving sticky webs all around
Catching as many flies as I can

One member of our family travelled from Ghana
Hitched a lift on a bunch of bananas
The police were called out, what a palaver
As they escorted him back to Ghana.

Humans look upon us as monsters
But we only aim to please
Without our skills as trappers
Homes would be full of disease.

Spiders are environmentally friendly
Weaving a magic spell
So next time you see us
There's no need to scream and yell.

Rachel McKie

Loch Ness Monster

'Mighty serpent, sea fare foul,
Where I wonder do you prowl,
Why indeed no bathing towel,
    Where on earth your undies?'

'I keep them fresh for Santa Claus,
In my ancient chest of drawers,
I guard against the moth of course,
    And fetch them out on Sundays.'

'Writhy serpent, wriggle and hiss,
Wot you not will come of this?
Wist you not it much amiss,
    What will say the rabble?'

'To Loch Ness depths I'll glide and grope
Under a wrong-way telescope,
They'll see a wriggly worm I hope,
    And then my myth will travel.'

'Wily monster, coiled and cute,
What'll you do if they find thee oot?
Mickle of men will heave a boot,
    Mony a lass will snigger.'

'To bottomless depths I'll slither and slide,
'Til Hogmanay I'll there abide,
Then wriggle up quick and flash my hide,
    Sarongs will be de rigueur.'

Terence Belford

... A Secret Place

Inside my structured world
Is a place where I rest
Where no one can
Find me
Or
Chase me out.
I sit all curled
Like a sleeping mouse
Where nobody can reach me
Or
Shout.

Gillian Twaite

Visiting Time

The full moon reflected the frosted paths,
Shimmering like sparkling jewels.
Leafless trees, gnarled fingers, accused me,
Blaming, whispering ghouls.

The old hospital abandoned, unearthly.
Victorian asylum, unchanged.
Icicles hung from the window sills,
The faces above them, so strange.

The shadows crept out from the bushes,
Unkempt, and grasping at me.
It's five years today, I last saw her,
I had to come back, just to see,

If her memory of suffering still lingers,
Like the tormented souls, all around.
Forsaken, rejected, most wretched.
Confused, violated, earthbound.

The moon illuminates the stark frozen earth.
And my sister that I couldn't save.
Memories of her, supposedly safe.
Bleak, cold as her grave.

Karen Fedrick

Blueberry Kill

Woken with a jolt
In a land of cloud,
I find myself nude
But for a white shroud.

Befuddled, I wander
To find my head
But soon realise,
'Oh, b****r, I'm dead!'

Just forty years young;
Not a chance to grow old.
Never to walk with a stick,
Lose my mind or go bald.

How was I to know
It was riddled with mould?
How was I to know
It was ten days old?

I remember the warnings
Of under-cooked stuffin',
But who would've thought
Death by blueberry muffin?

Neil Outram

Memories Of A Pottery's Lad

Sitting patiently waiting in a traffic jam today
gave me time to reflect on times far away.
As a lad, on the main A53 I would play football
Sundays were best, hardly any cars at all.

Now and again we would have to stand aside
to allow past a family, off to the seaside.
An Austin Cambridge, maybe a Mini or a Maxi
every hour a PMT bus or posh people in a taxi.

When it was raining we'd watch the TV screen
Rawhide, Bonanza and Dixon of Dock Green.
No colour in those days, just black and white
Psycho from Hitchcock gave us all a fright.

Saucepans on the boil, potatoes for mash,
brisket in the oven, to spin out the cash,
spring cabbage and gravy made with cornflour,
enough coins in the meter to last for an hour.

After tea we'd polish our shoes ready for school,
make a tank from an old wooden cotton spool,
put dubbing in our football boots ready for games,
pump whitening on our plimsolls with sewn in names.

Clutching sixpence pocket money to the sweet shop we'd run
have a lucky bag, contents unknown, just for fun,
six penny chews or would it be a sherbet dab?
Those were the days, no jams, absolutely fab!

Carl Nixon

Tasteless - A Sonnet

I won't tread on eggshells for anyone,
Nor swallow my words to feed your ego.
Can't bite my tongue till bitterness is gone,
But I will let those juices of truth flow
So you may taste your hollow, boring words.
Is it hard to chew and swallow that fat?
Like Little Miss Muffet you eat your curds,
But see that spider creeping where you're sat?
I hope its poison clears you of your lies
Which you spread like a plague, or a disease.
And your error? Your sin which I despise?
Your uncompromising desire to please.
If only there was a vaccine to rid
The world of those who keep their hearts well hid!

M F James

Spring Is In The Air

There's the golden glow of daffodils
And excitement in the air!
There's the rainbow and the sunshine
And new shoots everywhere!

There's the buds of blossom waiting
To dress the apple tree!
In pretty pastel shades of pink
A welcome sight to see!

There's a messenger who's eager
To greet the start of spring!
And with a rich and fluty voice
He begins to sing!

There's a reason to be cheerful
When we hear his cheerful song
Our days will be much brighter
Now that winter's finally gone!

We can rely upon the blackbird
When spring is in the air
To bring the news impending
For everyone to share!

Carol Kaye

Beautiful Butterfly

Butterfly fluttering near and far,
you flutter where your country companions are,
your wings are so detailed to perfection,
you flutter around in every direction,
among colourful flowers,
red, pink, white, orange and blue,
there's no other creature
more graceful or as gentle as you,
you enjoy quality time in
the warmth of the sunshine,
as summer's breeze comes blowing in,
you flutter your wings of soft satin,
you mesmerise, beauty you emphasise,
a brief life you live,
all the joy you give,
nature's beauty you discover,
you're so unlike any other,
you participate,
in spring and summer,
where we all celebrate.

Joanna Maria John

Cop, Skip And Dump

We hired a skip last Saturday,
And mega bucks we had to pay,
To take in rubbish, just a few,
A wash basin, an ancient loo,
Some broken tiles, and mats well worn,
And other things, all old and torn

Sunday dawned, to our surprise,
The rubbish had begun to rise,
By Monday morning, dry and bright,
The rubbish level was in sight.

On Tuesday evening; in the dark,
Someone thought that for a lark,
It was time to ditch some junk,
So to our half-filled skip they slunk

By Wednesday morning, it's no laugh,
The skip was filling, nearly half,
Muffled figures, in the night,
Creeping up, well out of sight,
With bags of rubbish, just to tip,
Into our half-empty skip.

When Thursday came, quite cool and damp.
A BBQ, a reading lamp,
A washing line, some cardboard strip,
Had found their way into our skip.

Friday morning, it's no lie,
The rubbish level was so high,
It wobbled way above the top,
We thought the time had come to stop.
The workmen, with impending gloom,
Would find there wasn't really room,
For what the skip was rented for -
To take away our cloakroom floor.

And other things we'd thrown away,
And didn't want to have to pay,
To have things taken to the tip,
Why bother, when we have a skip?
It seems that others of our kind
Had the same idea in mind!

Derek H Tanton

The Green Hill

(Dedicated to Ron Bryning)

The green hill has seen so many scenes
As it stood on the edge of Dartmoor.
The Stone Age men were the human feet
That first trod the slopes to explore.
Today we see traces of field systems laid
We can only guess how the children laughed
As on the green slopes they played.
Soon progress came to the plains below
And minerals were found on the ground
And on the hills of the moor,
Miners came as never before
The Miners Charter was granted to Chagford
In thirteen hundred and five.
When Chagford was made a stannary town.
From then, the community thrived.
Tin was the metal found on the moor
And with sheep and rabbits
The town lived and survived.

And now the hill hosts all manner of things
Like the bonfire at time of Armada.
Enacted once more in the wind off the moor
And the beacons lit on strict order.

But most famous of all, is the Two Hills Race
When the hill puts on its most colourful face.
A ribbon of runners dressed in every hue
Climb up that steep green face
And anxiously waited down at the club
For the results of the race.
The tannoy rings out, here comes the winner
My word! what a good pace!
The last of the runners compete to the finish
And cheers ring out o'er the hill.
The cups are presented, there's smiles and tears
The hard work over and done.
Congratulations all round for a mission accomplished
Now everyone join in the fun.

Christine Youd

Step By Step

When the sun is darkened by a cloudy haze
And you have a steep mountain to climb
Don't falter at the journey ahead
Just take it one step at a time.

Though the mountain has a tortuous path
With obstacles all around
You will overcome them one by one
With a new strength you have found.

Sometimes the summit seems further away
No matter how quick your stride
But as you journey on you will find
A helping hand is by your side.

But if sometimes you stumble
And the journey seems too much
You will be lifted up again
By a firm and gentle touch.

If in the silence of the night
You feel you don't want to go on
Look back down the mountain
And see how far you've come.

Do not feel disheartened
Let your doubts and fears, be few
For loving care is all around you
Always there to see you through.

Each footstep is a triumph
And with each passing day
You will see your goal draw nearer
Because you have found the way.

And when you reach the summit
And your weary journey is done
You will feel a peacefulness and joy
At a battle bravely won.

Patricia Madden

Connections

An interview has been arranged
The first time round we all feel strange
How shall we approach the other people
Don't worry you are not asked to climb the church steeple
A few deep breaths, a silent prayer
Will give you the incentive to get there
I caught the bus, the driver receives me well
And when I look worried by my face
He can always tell
I arrive at my destination
And ring the big brass bell
A young girl opens the door
Her face I know full well
I go to the reception room and give a tentative knock at the door
'Come in,' said a voice.
This is the right room, based on the second floor.
'I'm afraid Mr Brown is off sick today
How may I help you, do tell me I pray?'
'I've come for a job as an assistant teacher to work,
In a school, I am not a preacher.'
'What experience do you have?' said she,
'Have you read science or chemistry?'
'Neither,' I replied, 'my subject is English
And have obtained an MA degree in the university,
Could you get me a job today?'
'What's an MA?' asked the girl at the desk.
'Master of arts,' I replied with unrest.
'Come back when Mr Brown is better
In the meantime I will send him a letter.
Such short staff in the world today.'
'People don't know their job anyway.'

Y Rossiter

Moment Of Truth

Cold, crisp, clear blue sky
My breath is taken at the sight
As cobweb glistens, shimmers bright

Betty Batchen

Eight Up

A child from a simple family was I
Born in foreign climes,
In a country known as Canada
A typical child from the times.

At three months old, tragedy came
Striking from out of the blue,
Fever took my mother
In another four days took my father too.

A family of teachers
In small house we blended,
But the time had now come
Days of Bolingbrooke ended.

With poor Mrs Thomas
And four children did wait,
Next with Mrs Hammond
And her children, all eight.

That is my life
From zero to eight,
For what follows on
Read the next book or wait.

Ramandeep Kaur (17)

Music Of The Muses

Pulse and ripples of sound -
Mozart, magical composer,
a singer's jewel;
all instruments delight
in his pure melody and soul.
Here we are celebrating
a joyous 250 years.
Yet, he wrote many gems
while human suffering
and personal anxieties
pursued him deeply.
We rejoice in his gift
to all musicians,
enabling us to touch his art
and share music and humanity
with a wider world.
A gift transcending all the years,
perfection in harmony,
bathing us in melody and soul.

Margaret Ann Wheatley

Dr Jekyll And Mr Hyde

His presence fills me like warm sunlight
And replace it with darkness at night
At daybreak he smells like fresh spring morning
But later his brawling breath has my blood boiling.
His gentle voice makes me pay attention
But with moonlight his sounds I cannot mention
And to his swinging moods we must abide
Because we are living with Dr Jekyll and Mr Hyde

Calm, collective, caring and capable man
Becomes abuser, accuser, refusing love oozing from his clan
A supporter, motivator when amongst our friends
But pessimist, critic, toxic when the day ends
Who will tell, who will know
That the life we live is just a show?
Will they believe and grieve if they receive our side
That we are living with Dr Jekyll and Mr Hyde

Middle-management post, a company car
But miserable, unhappy family we are
Knowing that we do not come first in his life,
Not his children, the church or his wife,
But a liquid so powerful, the One to obey
And certainly he will be absent on Monday
At night this lion will with his cubs collide
Because we are living with Dr Jekyll and Mr Hyde

Cheryl Gordon

Loneliness

The beauty of it
The ugliness of it

Nurturing me like I saw Mama cat lick her kittens' shivers
Yet lingering through my immense void like the hot desert sun

Strangers on the colourful beach, all smiles and salutes at my obvious bliss
Failing to notice the absent shoulder, that I must lean on should I feel blue

Oh the joy of concerning myself with only what I dine on, or not
But at the kitchen table I must speak aloud, to myself

Hogging my large bed, spread like an eagle that owns the airspace
Nobody to scoop my waist and spoon their warm body next to mine

Oh loneliness,

Friend of spontaneity
Enemy of rib-cracking laughter!

Kageni Pierce

The Quiet Woman

Dark Horse,
You call her
Secretive
Mischievous
The Quiet
One
But silence
Is golden
And much
Is gleaned
From
Those who talk
Without thought
Loose lips
Can you hear
Yourself?
Knowing
Do not say
Saying
Do not know
All talk leads
To treachery
Eventually

Lauren McCarthy

Epitaph

'Twas life,
To strive,
And thrive,
As known,
Outgrown,
Renowned,
From womb,
To bloom,
This tomb.

Raymond A Uyok

Says The Child

I want to play
I want to laugh
I want to cry
I want to explore
I want to learn
I want to love
I want to be accepted

Adult, my desires cost you nothing.

Love me.
Hug me.
Comfort me.
Teach me.
Grow me.
Encourage me.

I want to be somebody.
I can be somebody.
I am somebody.
I will be somebody.

Don't demean me.
Don't stunt my growth.
Don't clip my wings.
Don't ridicule my dreams.

I am the future.

Rufaro Ruredzo

Love That Is . . .

Love that is a moment still,
Love that is a while until,
Love that time is her glance,
Love that's worth a second chance.
Love that burns a candle bright,
Love that climbs above the night,
Love that turns, so turn again,
Love you are, you are my pain.
Love that is a flower sweet,
Love that lips a kiss would meet,
Love that stays where still I roam,
Love you are, you are my home.
Love that is a promised heart,
Love that you have played a part,
Love that who, or I have seen,
Love, 'O' love, my love has been.

Christopher W Wolfe

Demons

I'm still looking
For something I cannot find
I've looked in shadows and darkness
The torment of my mind.

I'm still asking
Why and was it me?
And will I ever find my peace
From my thoughts to be free.

I'm still waiting
To walk into the light
To find my inner peace
Sleep peacefully through the night.

I'm still longing
For love to make me whole
To put my thoughts away
Ease the torment of my soul.

I'm still hurting
Captive to the pain
Trapped between insanity
And images in my brain.

I'm still fighting
As someone told me to
These words were written
Especially for you.

Suzanne

Sadness

In a single moment lives were changed
For evermore rearranged
A terrible disaster came around
Pulling people to the ground

Families torn apart that day
How will people cope?
Missing people far away
Do they have any hope?

Bodies lying all around
Reminds me of the badness
People's faces never to smile
To me, this describes sadness.

Perry James McLeod (11)

A Visit To The Garden Centre

As we sat in the garden on a summer's day
Pottering about, my brother was heard to say
'Let's go to the garden centre at Brookside
It's not very far, just a ten minute ride.'

Off we went with spirits high
Not a cloud up in the sky
Said my sister-in-law, 'I've never been here yet
When it hasn't rained and I got soaking wet!'

As we pulled up to the car park
The sun went in and it all went dark
Ever hopeful we made our way
To the lovely plant display

The heavens opened, we caught the lot
As we belted to the garden shop
We patiently waited in our refuge
As it turned into a great deluge

We made a dash back to the car
What luck we hadn't come too far
Back home we couldn't believe our eyes
Everywhere dry and clear blue skies

Washing dried out in the sun
Dogs playing, having fun
As we looked at each other and laughed,
I know it all seems crazy
What us gardeners will go through
To buy one bedraggled daisy

Sheila B Fry

Love

Love can mean so much.
The soothing comfort when you touch.

The desires to be close and be as one
A fulfilling and complete being has begun.

An uneasy pain whenever you are apart.
Reunited you find a happy comfort you felt from the start.

Good times or bad, love is there to help you through.
They come and go, only because of you.

Kevin Clark

Dark Deed

Dyeing! At last I will be rid
of this drab, dreary looking thing.
For so long I've been too timid,
it's time to rebel, have my fling!
Monday I considered means,
not too messy, safety vital -
I didn't want to stain my jeans,
or finish up in hospital.
Tuesday, when I bought the potion,
with which to do the daring deed,
I did feel some *slight* emotion,
but, even greater was my need.
Thursday and my courage faltered;
should I perhaps keep my old foe,
once done, it could not be altered.
Decided no! All systems go!
It's today! There'll be no reprieve.
I'll have my way. The die is cast,
and I don't think I'll ever grieve,
for dyeing my grey hair, at last.

Salmagundi

Aqua And Aquatics

In a wild whipped up frenzy
Shoals of tuna go barmy
'Tis sharks I adore
When they are offshore
Dolphins and hatpins
Brooches and cufflinks
Let them be
And swim away free
Far, far away into the sea
For it is honourable
But also immeasurable
Then painted as a Constable
Leonardo Da Vinci smacks his lips
Maybe berries on his fingertips
A cave another painting
No bloodshed is taunting
For our very idea of hunting
Says the Bushman recollecting
A trance is what it is depicting!

Hardeep Singh-Leader

Island View

Set amidst still waters,
Like a jewel within a crown,
Showing forth a beauty,
To all the world around.

Where shores are bathed and sparkle,
By an ocean green and blue,
With a sun whose pink and gold rays,
Light arrays of wood to view.

Where you find a winter daffodil,
Sweet birds to see and hear,
Each ripple of the water,
Its sound is ever near.

In winter can it cover,
Or take away your glow,
How can you hide such beauty,
With the loveliness of snow.

As if a piece of Heaven fell,
Then landed in the sea,
God thought it looked so beautiful,
A taste of things to be.

Even darkness cannot hide you,
As the moon just makes you shine,
And the stars bend down to kiss you,
Like a new and true love find.

Peter Siggery

Milly And Molly

Milly and Molly were two little girls.
Milly had straight hair, Molly had curls.
Milly was dainty, pretty and small.
Molly was big, very plain and tall.

Milly had lived in a big house with chimneys so tall.
Molly's house was cosy, happy but small.
They both swapped places and nobody cared,
Molly lived in Milly's house and Milly in hers.

Milly and Molly were two little girls.
Milly had straight hair, Molly had curls.
Both were as happy as happy could be.
They each invited the other to tea.

Angela Dolphin

Is It You Or Is It Me?

You listen to my every word,
But you never really hear,
You know that I am petrified,
Yet you cannot sense my fear,

You're talking very loudly,
With nothing much to say,
You know I'm in the greatest pain,
But fail to help me anyway,

You know just how I'm feeling
But could you be so blind,
Your taunts and cruel put-downs,
Are messing with my mind,

You say you see a person,
Did you ever try?
Because you say you know me
Yet I feel you just pass by,

Was I ever important?
Do I play a part?
Or am I just a joke to you,
Laughed at from the start,

So herein lies a story
And all of it is true,
It says an awful lot about me,
Now take a good look at you.

Chantay Speed

Loneliness

Loneliness is an unhappy state
Like staring at an empty plate
In a crowd you can be quite alone
The sad feeling of being on your own
Looking out of your window at people passing by
Wishing you were part of them, in your heart you cry
Hoping someone will give you a ring
Or maybe a letter the postman may bring
Where are all the people, you knew
They now seem to be very few
It's hard if you have just lost your husband or mate
You sometimes think, *what will be your fate?*
Promises of, I will give you a call
Or we'll go out and have a ball
True friends are precious to everyone
I wonder where they have all gone

Jenny Parker

Some Joys Of Tranquil - Sailing In England

Come to Birdham Pool, 'midst Chichester harbour's bends;
Or, to Bisham Abbey on the beautiful River Thames,
Or, to Oulton Broad, near Lowestoft's fishing port,
To enjoy tranquil sailing, a most relaxing sport.

In a dinghy, or small cabin boat,
You feel at peace when you are afloat
Steering gently, by tiller, as you glide along,
Entertained by birds singing their beautiful song.

In the gentle air of a light summer breeze,
The craft quietly glides with the greatest of ease,
While the beauty of the pastoral scene
Is reflected in the waters on either beam.

This gentle sailing is so easy to learn,
With life jacket on, you sit in the stern.
The small sail is simple to hoist and belay,
While the tiller steers you on your way.

The sail's mainsheet powers your boat,
You now can enjoy the full life afloat.
All your cares are left behind;
Water ripples under your bow are much more kind.

At the end of the day, watch the sunset sky,
As red-tipped clouds drift gently by.
Your boat is berthed, your sail is furled,
You've enjoyed the most relaxing sport in the world.

Wilfred John Parker

Preparation

We went shopping for your gown.
We really went to town.
The fun we had, we went quite mad.
Each gown you tried, was quite supreme
When I looked in your eye, I realised why!
A sight I'd never seen,
The love reflected way up high guided us by and by.

Transformed into a bride, today, then we went on our way.
With looks from others, 'Are you mad?'
We laughed and laughed, and darling, I'm glad
The fun we had will live forever,
As you take your steps together.

So beautiful you are, my daughter dearest.
The fun will live forever.
To see you as a wife to treasure
Brings life's meaning all together.

Dawn Taylor

The Use Of Time

Time not ours to squander,
Ours to ponder,
Not to wander
More to do along life's way.

Warnings leap our way,
To do our part in all we can,
Overcoming all that
Points our own way.

Wisdom of all that's best,
Food for the soul,
As the tried and true,
Who go all the way,
To keep to His way.

So little of time, so precious
None spare to save,
Beyond the here and now,
Though some we squander
In various ways.

Opportunity waits not,
Much of what's precious
Spills in with demand
Distracting into waist
By a none mighty source.

Rachel Taylor

Anticipation

On the drive home
Listened to the radio
Looked in the mirror
Saw cars in a row

They were staring
Curiously alert, wot
Unbeknownst to me
My car had levitated up

No longer in the past
Though memories remain
There were promises
Of an adventurous gain.

Anita Marie Shirk

When I Am In Heaven . . .

When I am in Heaven . . .
I will run like a Kenyan and never get tired,
I will be just as fast as those men I've admired.
Haile Gebrselassie will no longer impress me,
Past Radcliffe and Holmes; I'll be running alone!
I will leap like a leopard and chase like a cheetah,
Bound through each mile as if it was a metre.
With a spring in my step and a bounce in my tread,
Running will no longer consume me with dread.
They will call me The Express!
I'll be as fast (more or less)
As the greatest decatheletes the world's ever seen;
Everyone will bow, including the Queen
And say, 'Goodness that girl has learnt to run quick!'
It makes me feel faint!
It makes me feel sick!
That puppy fat dunce with a D in PE?
Can it really be her?
Can I trust what I see?
Oh that man Linford Christie
Will be glad to have missed me;
His illustrious career will look rather weak
In the face of my triumph and competitive streak!
When I am in Heaven . . .
You had better beware -
I am already honing my sprint finish flair
So Seb Coe and your friends
Do not rest on your win;
It's only in Heaven that the race will begin!

Emily Woodhams

Always Blessed

No matter what goes wrong,
No matter how bad it seems,
You always have hope,
That blesses your dreams.

Each little thing,
Is a gift from God,
The birds of the treetops,
And the tadpoles of the pond.

When dolphins clear the water,
And dogs fetch toys to play,
You and I are blessed with love,
Each and every day.

Emmeline Michelle Cambridge (14)

Love Poem

Awake in the midnight hour
Feeling low, sick and sour
Thinking of your emptiness
With me in this wilderness

I begin our life to reminisce
A fond embrace, our first kiss
Holding hands, fingers entwine
Lovingly, yours and mine

A fleeting thought, something to share
Like the stroking of your hair
A whispered endearment in your ear
'I love you!' so sincere

Wind blown hair, smiling face
A silly moment, each other chase
Across the park? Along the sand
Running with outstretched hand

Close my eyes, this vision I see
So clear it is reality
And voices, oh! How this to pen
Like an echo in the glen.

Catch me, hold me. Catch me, hold me
Love me, keep me, love me, keep me
Together, together, for evermore
Together, on Heaven's eternal shore

Oh! How I miss you
Long for you, ache for you
Please, my hungry arms to fill
Please, my beating heart to still

Darling, dearest, please be mine
Our empty arms evermore entwine.

A Quinn

Great, Great Aunt Mabel

(A Clerihew for those who knew)

Great, Great Aunt Mabel
was so great she'd hardly fit at the table,
but when she arose,
she came up to my nose.

Kate Williams

Barnby Restoration

How could we restore our church?
Form a committee - several people led!
Could we begin a drama group
A dancing troop to train?
It seemed we could - even without much brain!

Pantomime was favourite
More than twelve produced.
Then comedy plays and thrillers
Were often introduced.

Our tiny country village
With its river, marsh and lane
Became a real community
Adding pride to its name.

We worked hard together
And nearly everything was done
With all the money raised
While we were having fun.

Lastly, on the list
Our run-down village hall
And soon we would be celebrating
With a thanksgiving ball.

We had a brand new kitchen
An extension added on,
So to all the village people
Who helped in any way,
Feel very pleased and proud
This thanksgiving day!

Pauline Burton

Speechless

Thoughts, feelings, emotions
All written together as one,
For the young, elderly and all,
Even ones that are gone,
A poem from the heart,
To remember those who are dead,
But no matter what is put down,
It's never enough said.

T Pickup

My Mood A Medium Blue

There is a need for me to be linked with the living,
For the task of a medium can be so unforgiving.
Reflecting life elsewhere in an ultraviolet hue,
What hope do I have?
Whose heart do I grab?
When I place only the dead onto empty chairs.
I stare into the great blue yonder,
To treasure and measure the past.
Cast my net into the empty air.
A gift maybe yet not really living.
To the many, much comfort giving.
But the strangeness of my vocation,
Sees me treated personally as a pariah.
So in truth, in this reality, I am lonely
And feel in the depths of dark despair.
Does anyone around me really care?
I stare out of my bedroom window
At the ceaselessly pouring rain,
For within me there lies only pain.
I need someone to lift my spirits,
Yet I seemingly talk to the empty air.
Then I become aware of the rippling,
Soft shadows about me now shifting,
As into the twilight gloom I stare.
Then I want to cry out loud,
As more and more spirit folk,
Into my bedchamber crowd,
My room aglow with their kindly light.

Julia Pegg

Poetry

P erhaps today the rain will come
O r the sun will shine
E ven if either come my way
T oday I'll make it mine
R eason is today, you see
Y es, it's my birthday, yippee!

Mavis Gould

Stormsong

bruising bracing chafing gypsy wind
buffeting dead ear with doleful song
whipping skipping havoc-wreaking stuff
mischievously scattering along
scathing scourging prancing phantom rain
spattering bowed head denied reprieve
hounding pounding spirit-sapping tough
mercilessly battering the eaves
surging searing raging whoreson chill
blistering raw skin with ragged claw
haunting taunting unrelenting sting
pitilessly shattering resolve
huddled hooded wretched pygmy man
cowering grotesque distorted form
whinging cringing genuflecting king
impotently flattering the storm

John C Traynor

Tour Of Egypt In October 2005

I flew from London to Cairo by plane,
Pyramids, sphinx and a camel ride gain,
Cairo to Aswan overnight by train,
High Dam, Lake Nasser, temple, Nile's source main.

Next by Felucca cruise down River Nile,
Two days and two nights sailing mile by mile,
Temples at Luxor and Karnak awhile,
Swam in hotel pools and photos to file.

Coach police convoy, Dahab on Red Sea,
Suez, Mount Sinai, deserts, palm tree,
Diving and snorkelling, swimming for free,
Dinners by moonlight with coffee and tea.

Then Cairo Museum, mosque and bazaar,
Flew back to London from Egypt so far.

Susan Mary Robertson

Untitled ...

Why is your heart so lonesome?
Have you fallen by the way?
Come home to me my comfort,
Enter and love me now this day.

Yesterday I don't want to know,
Though my heart cannot forget,
The ugly scene inside my heart,
For the love I could not get.

A weeping man I am inside,
Where my heart is deepest set,
Loneliness I have had abundant,
My dream of happiness upset.

Please excuse this angry voice,
As it passes like a storm,
Give me love at breakfast time,
Melt the cold and keep me warm.

He who knows the rights of man,
The cure who kills the disease,
Enter in revealing truth,
Will you never leave me please.

Where is my love from yesterday,
Show the face you hide away,
Come home to me tomorrow,
And invade my life that's grey.

Reach out and hold a hand so brave,
Awaken me from this nightmare,
Tell me words to break my fears,
Please show me love galore.

The turning of the tide has come,
Compassion wins the day,
Love for every man on Earth,
Is homeward bound today.

The age has passed when darkness ruled.
Now man can see beyond,
He has left the roots of evil,
In Hell where it belongs.

William Archibald

I'd Like To See Much Less Of Me!

(In twenty-zero-six)

I'd like to see *much* less of me
in twenty-zero-six -
a down-sized version of myself
built from beans and carrot sticks.

To be a less . . . complete, less rounded me,
ah, what noble new year aims!
A weight-loss queen who can fit between
her mirror's narrow frames!

And *yes,* I'd love a world at peace,
leafy homes for the chimpanzee,
our crops not mutating in some science lab
and our hens all roaming free.

And *yes,* I hope the ice caps hold
and our shores don't break and flood
and our kids can swim in clear-bottomed
lakes - not acrid swamps of mud!

And *all* these things I wish for us
though I know we'll never see
the wonders of a pristine world
as it was meant to be.

But the greatest woes on Earth today
are *nothing* to those I face -
beating radioactive dumping
and that rubbish they've left in space!

For I'd *really* like to see . . .
much less of me,
this year and many more.

And over my boobs,
finally get to see
the tiles on my shower floor!

Maree Teychenné

Once In A Lifetime

Once in a lifetime, if luck is on your side,
Your true love will find you; you'll have no place to hide.
He'll never try to change you, or turn you into someone new,
He'll give his love completely, just because you are you.
He won't see the fine lines that appear upon your face,
He'll never ever care if your hair is out of place.
If ever you feel troubled, or you're just feeling low,
Just one look into your eyes, and instantly he'll know.
You won't have to tell him, or ever say a thing,
He knows the way you're feeling; it's instinctive to him.
He'll wrap his arms around you, kiss away your tears,
He'll keep you safe forever, and banish all your fears.
The love that he gives you, you will never doubt,
The love that he gives to you, you could never live without.

Once in a lifetime, if luck is on your side,
Every time you're with him, your heart will swell with pride.
You'll get a funny feeling, whenever you hear his name,
The life that you knew once before will never be the same.
You'll feel your heart a-pounding, when he walks in through the door,
You'll know deep inside your heart that you'll love him for evermore.
You might just be wondering, how I know these things are true,
Well luck was on my side, the day that I met you.

Jan Cash

Dance To Freedom's Music
(For Ian - 02/10/03)

We met in the autumn years, laden with our guilt and tears,
Confidence gone, faith broken, licking wounds from words spoken.
Warily skirting round the truth, shamed, revealing past abuse.
Talked all night of the darkness - reality's harsh starkness.
Facing the forest of fear, cut down at last, hope is near.
To live again, you have to trust, shed suspicion in the dust.
Life is love, but you must choose, take the risk or always lose.
Cross the falls of faith once more; it will not be in vain,
Climb the hills of happiness; you will not fall again,
Memorise the spoken lies; bury them by graveyard wall,
Listen to the tongues of truth; the lies were lies - that's all.
Leave misfortunes far behind, in the past where they belong,
Life is so short, sing future's song - take a chance and carry on.
Now we dance to freedom's music, boundless loving - no regret.
Now we touch without measure, giving all that we have left.
Now intertwined, we lose our souls in the land of laughter,
Now wholly given to each other - in the light of love thereafter.

Leigh Crighton

By The Way

And by the way, where have you been all my life?
You took your time in coming round.
Looked for you before I settled as a wife
and mother - you would not be found.
As years trickled by I wondered if you knew
the sound my heartbeat makes in sleep.
And how tender, silent kisses searched for you
with love and laughter, warm and deep.
It took so long - could you be too far away?
No maps, no compass, faintest calls
that touched your dreams, dissipating into day,
returning only at nightfall.
I waited still - listening for your footsteps near,
heart pounding as I heard their beat.
Softly, softly, closer, louder - can you hear
the music made by lovers' feet?
Door wide open - blankets warming by the fire
and my heart's embers start to glow.
Come in, come in - let's surrender to desire.
This love, my love, the one I know.
So by the way, I know the answer to my quest,
Souls eternal have no heed of time.
Aeons seem shrunk to nanoseconds now you rest,
Soul-searching over, hearts entwined.

Gabrielle Gascoigne

A Small Boy's Lament

I can't find my mum anywhere!
And my dad is not always there!
I can't find my nanny, she's nowhere about.
My brother and sister have also gone out!

The dog's torn the sheet on my bed!
Oh! I know that my mum will see red!
So I've combed down my hair, packed my teddy bear
And I'm going to Granny's instead!

I tried phoning Gran, but she's old
And can't hear it ringing I'm told!
I know that she'd fetch me, if she only knew how!
Gran did ride a bike, but she can't ride one now!

So, I won't come home ever again!
And I'm thinking of catching a train!
But I'm in such a muddle, and needing a cuddle,
And just want my mummy again!

Greta Gaskin

Your Love Is Like Water

Did you know that the grass still grows,
even though the rain may not fall?
Did you know that a bird still sings,
even though his world is torn?
Deep in their souls,
they find the reason to grow and grow.
They're touched by the hand.
They drink the water that makes them whole.

Did you know that I see your face
in every ray of warm sunlight?
Did you know that every drop of rain
makes me bask in your delight?
I'm feeling your pain,
but I can still sing the sweetest refrain,
because a flower won't bloom
without the water to make it swoon.

Your love is like water.
You lift me up.
Your love is like water.
I drink from your cup.
Sustains me and still,
I thirst for a sip,
of your water.

I'm free as a bird flying high in this world,
on a river of joy and bliss,
this happiness.
You're lifting me higher and higher,
I'm a bird in the sky so high.

Greta Solomon

Strength

There is a hero in each
And every one of you,
Walking out on the abuse
Was one of the hardest things to do.
Your children have or will see
The hero in you,
Stopped repeats of abuse,
They could have suffered too.
Though times have been hard,
We all still pulled through,
Just remember
There is a hero in each
And every one of you.

Laura Jennings

My Children, My Happiness

The very best times of my life,
Are the ones I spend with you,
When we sit together in the sun,
And laugh about the things we do.

Our conversations mean so much,
Because I feel such love inside.
Knowing the two people you've become,
Brings me joy and pride.

The very best moments of my life,
Were as I watched you grow.
My time was filled with purpose,
In teaching you all I know.

Our house overflowed with toys and books,
Laughter, quarrels and tears.
I often wish I could turn back time,
To those rewarding, fun-packed years.

The very best days of my life,
Were the ones when you were young.
Your childhood dreams were unrevealed,
And your songs were yet unsung.

Through all of our experiences,
In dreams lost, or come true,
The memories that I treasure most,
Are the ones I've shared with you.

Lorna Lea

7th July - The Day I Found It Hard To Be A Christian

Somewhere out there are terrorists - proud of the havoc they caused
They ruined the lives of strangers - they killed and destroyed without thought
They left bombs on the trains and the buses which exploded and many died
Innocent, ordinary people - not those on particular sides.
Somewhere out there are those terrorists - free to go their own ways
Somewhere out there are the brains who set out to kill and to slay
How can they live with their conscience? Perhaps they're completely insane
We can only hope that the good men will stop them repeating again.
These wicked men are evil - they work for the Devil we fear
But God will support his people, and those murderers will suffer for years
No one will want to help them and they'll shrivel away and rot
They've cut themselves off from society, and I hope that their hell will be hot.

Doris E Pullen

Night Music

Last night a little moonbeam
Came creeping over the hill,
'Til he reached my open window
And jumped up on my sill.
He poised there, light and airy,
I watched him as he danced.
He fluttered like a fairy,
I was dreamily entranced.

Then a cloud, dark and heavy,
Enveloped his mother moon,
And my little friend the moonbeam
Was called away too soon.
All the raindrops gathered,
Falling down in playful shower,
To play music on my window sill
And to nurture every flower.

Then came the distant rumble
Of nature's percussion band,
As thunder, loud, and lightning
Rolled over all the land.
Suddenly the symphony ended
And I could hear that rain,
Chuckling and gurgling
As It jostled down the drain.

Then as I sat there watching,
Much to my delight,
My little friend the moonbeam
Came stealing through the night.
He climbed up on my window sill,
Flickering his tiny light,
Pirouetting on his toes,
First left and then to right.

Patricia Adele Draper

Losing The Battle

Sometimes when I'm feeling blue,
I shop for clothes until I'm through
And when I've bought something new,
Friends say that looks good on you.

But when I'm feeling in the pink,
In the wash they begin to shrink.
At least that's what I like to think,
It's not about what I eat or drink.

So I expect you will surmise,
That I have started telling lies.
It shouldn't be a big surprise,
To hear I bought a smaller size!

Now I've really got the hump,
As in my armchair I slump.
Forever destined to be plump,
Looking like a heavy lump.

Nothing ever stays the same,
I've only got myself to blame.
That I feel this awful shame,
Maybe I can change my game.

Today's the day I'll strike,
Aiming to be sylphlike.
I'm going on a long hike,
Taking a ride on my bike.

Now my feet feel like lead
And I've pains in my head,
I feel like I must be dead,
So I'm going back to bed.

Rosemary Davies

The Asian Tempest

There was a momentary three-minute pause
For the Asian adversity
And its mysterious cause.

So many lives have gone
And can't be named
But we will remember them - just the same!
As they did try to gain
God's grace for the joy of living together.

So let the vital spirit
Of the brightest of the oriental faiths be recast,
Through our generosity of giving them back
Their future with trust.

Sammy Michael Davis

A Smile In War

No enemies, a casualty of war
Easy to label, she cries no more
Orphaned, the forgotten child
Alone, starved, yet smiles

A statistic in a crisis
Scratching the dust for food
A life of innocence, oblivious
To the destruction and death, she cannot elude

The soldier, the peace keeper
Can do nothing to save a life so young
The irreversible damage war has done
Observing from a hilltop camera in hand

My whole body trembling trying to understand
The unbelievable images of my camera's eye
Now I must follow this devastation of death
To show the world that smile

A child's last breath.

R S Wayne Hughes

Hidden Treasures

Memories are like treasures
We dig so hard to find
It can easily be lost as the passing of time
It's only then we realise that memories are really divine

Age with all its reason
Flitters our dreams away
Living your life
Trying to recall
Is a dreadful price to pay

Some live in the present
Others recall only the past
Whatever they can hold onto
Their momentous treasures will last

So do not take your memories for granted
For the brain outlives the past
Try and remember where your treasures are planted
For the future will come with a blast.

Angela Nevo Hopkins

Cross On The Moor

On the moor it stopped me
shattered in the rocks.
Scattered was its reverie
and sadness was its shock.

Guardian of the ancients
gargantuan in guile.
Its architect with one accord,
said, 'Talk to me awhile.'

Its sermon shivered in the mist
from skeleton to soul.
My heart entombed in hope and prayer
mortal man made whole.

It held me as a helpless pawn
and opened up my check.
The King was written on the wall
with all my forces wrecked.

It carved a gaunt and Godspeed glance
edges glaring wet.
I mourned for many a mile askance
my maker had been met.

Sean Kinsella

The Gurkas

It's good to read of valiant men
Many fought and died
They all served our country well
And did it with much pride

They served for nigh 200 years
Their battle honours many
It's sad to see how they have fared
Now pleading every penny

Their bravery shown, beyond the call
The stories do unfold
And they need support from everyone
Now they are getting old

To fight for king and country
They were not alone
But to dedicate such bravery
When a country's not your own

It's something that we all should know
And be made aware
Even in this day and age
Show that we do care

Bert Knight

Why Bother

Feeling sad, don't know why
Only know I want to cry
Got up this morning no one there
Same old silence down the stair.
Rattling about in an empty house
Hearing neither man nor mouse
Can't get used to being alone
All I do is moan and groan
No letters ever come for me
Never had a family
Neither daughter nor a son
Seems I wasn't a chosen one
But I had love from someone dear
And I miss him every year
The days are long the nights are cold
I never wanted to grow old
Not on my own with no one there
To comfort me and wipe my tear
We were meant to be together
With a love so strong forever
But I'm left here on my own
I know myself how tired I've grown
And that my thoughts are sometimes grim
It's hard to smile without him
Better off I know I'll be
When this old life sets me free

Elizabeth McNeil

Weighing Things Up

A look in the mirror gave me a fright
Something was certain, I needed advice
Would it be easy? No, just sacrifice
If I wanted rid of my cellulite.
I hadn't noticed my clothes getting tight
Stretchy waistbands allowed another slice
From that day, on salad I would suffice,
To be strong-willed and curb my appetite.
I couldn't believe the size of my rear
So the only answer was exercise
I'm not saying I didn't shed a tear
But getting on the scales won me the prize
So now it's only compliments I hear
With my healthy look, for I've dropped a size.

Shirley Pinnington

Amen

Swiftly like Mercury it flew through the clouds,
A chariot of fire, from the sun it came down.
The brightest of beings with flames all around,
People amazed at what they were seeing.
Their eyes on the skyline, would it land here?
What could it mean? Was the world going to end?
Or was this a dream without any end?
It's possible one day in this world's frantic race,
Circulating in orbit to meet its true fate.
Would we be ready whatever it demands
To stand up and be counted as the Lord might command?
It's all speculation, your word against mine,
All people are different and not all divine.
God can be different for each one of us,
Depending on concepts and whom we can trust.
Parents do influence their standards on us
And we follow their religion or whatever seems just.
The one true religion born here on Earth,
Taught us about mercy which we all should extend.
Give unto others what you would desire,
It would not be hatred to which some people aspire.
Love is the key to open all doors,
With faith, hope and charity, I could want nothing more.

Joan Prentice

Faces From The Past

The face you remember is fastened in time,
It's just as you saw it last,
No wrinkles or scars the whole of it mars,
It's just as it was in the past.
You tend to forget the passage of time
And the possible journeys it's borne;
Though kingdoms may fall, the face you recall
Still stays the same as before.
No wonder you don't recognise it
As you gaze in the mirror each day,
And you're faced with the truth that the face that was youth
Is now looking aged and grey.
Is it so with the friends you grew up with?
Are they showing signs of old age?
It's queer; aye, it's strange, how nature can change
What is fastened in history's page.
To you they're the faces of youth;
Their image is there in your brain,
Though in truth you may find that they're nowt of the kind
It's as boys that they'll always remain.

John Benjamin Freestone

Tamworth Castle

After the Norman conquests in the year 1066,
William I then owned it, so the story did depict.
It was granted to Robert the Bursor, a Doomsday tenant-in-chief,
As he died with no heir, and no one to share, his ownership was quite brief.

So the land was shared between families, Beauchamp and Marmion be,
Robert Marmion being the stronger was granted it yet not for free.
His quest was to be royal champion to honour and fight for the king,
In armour he stood against others, all enemies' trouble would bring.

He lived in the castle till 1291 as this is the way it was told,
Also when Philip, last baron died and passed the castle he just couldn't hold.
Lady Jane took his place but not for too long, as an heir still wasn't to be,
Sir Alexandra de Freville, was the next in line, as a branch from the family tree.

The husband of Lady Jane's fine young niece was chosen by Edward I,
Appointed to be his last champion, and not wanting to ever be cursed.
At Edward III's coronation, he was dressed in armour so proud,
In the year 1327, imagine the cheers from the crowd.

The line of de Freville diminished, so the castle was passed on the same,
To a man who married a Freville, Thomas Ferrers of Grosby, his name.
In the year 1423, life settled back down for a while
But passed down again by marriage, to the Shipley's Charley with style.

Compton, the Earl of Northampton, was another to live in this place,
How this castle was passed through the ages, fine people of breeding and grace.
By the early 1700s now the Townsends made this place to live,
The castle remained with the Townsends, a family with so much to give.

Apart from the late 19th century, when an auctioneer he did appear,
A Mr John Robins of London would sell it without any fear.
But the castle to this day is standing, looking just like it did way back then,
And the ghosts that now walk the building have no fear of women or men.

So when you are visiting Tamworth, a town with a heart of gold,
Take time to visit the castle and share with the memories of old.

Betty Hattersley

The Hungry Sea

The Earth gnashes, opens its under sea plates to gouge plight.
Crescendo of sea doomed, now out of sight.
The sea's waves boiling, to savour its fight,
Unleashing its fury, travelling so fast, gaining its might.

The wave orbits its destination, it will attack.
Hell is bent on its destructive paths, who's on the rack?
People's curiosity watches in awe track,
The tsunami grabs the sun-kissed shores.

Washing the beach, no discrimination is in store
Grabbing people, their objections, they are not valid,
Houses, cars, people, trains, boats, now squalid.
Screaming people swamped like tiny ants.

The sea is reaping its wrath,
Realising destruction, villages and towns are beset
Ripping up homes in the wall of water's path,
Throwing trees, trains, battleships afar.

Indian seas are trespassing its squalid war,
The aftermath must be borne,
Hundreds of thousands boiled in the ocean's pot,
Bodies are wrapped up, starting to rot.

People own the Earth on paper, but God says not,
All is lost, people gaze and stare in awe,
As bodies are washed up upon the lagoon's shores,
Bodies in bags line the streets' floors.

No one is left but just a few to cry,
Nature has now made known who owns this Earth,
Pyres are burning, all over this barren waste.
Quicksilver acts like this only dictate.

Lay waste, God's land, beautiful but very old,
We will try again this land, wonderful our homes!

Derrick C A Bright

On My Desk

Beyond the faxes, somewhere amongst the mess
There is the prettiest picture on my desk
My four-year-old daughter in her school uniform
With her piercing blue eyes and smile so warm
With all the hustle and bustle around me
Those sparkling eyes will always find me
When I look into them deeper and deeper
Suddenly my surroundings seem to disappear
I drift into a world solely for us
A reminder of the rewards of fatherhood
I remember now that she is four
She's a little person, not a toddler anymore
With different hairstyles and bobbles every day
And always something new and clever to say
How can this miracle be?
As I try to teach her I find she teaches me
And I am forever living the dream
I blink for a second and I'm back at work
With a smile on my face feeling loved and refreshed
My message to everyone the world over
Sitting there with a treasured snap on their desk
Take a minute to look deeper and deeper still
For these treasured moments are what we love best
Proving beyond all doubt we are truly blessed.

Paris Powell

Foolish Heart

You said goodbye ten years ago,
Besotted by another.
Left me to break the news to
family and Mother.
Broken hearts and many tears.
Grandchildren missed you so.
Love in abundance.
Why did you go?
Money invested in a new home.
She sold the house,
Leaving you alone.
Your assets gone, you're rich no more,
Not even rich in love,
Which you had before.
Children have welcomed you back.
Gone to Heaven, has Mother.
Your hope of living again, with me,
'Tis sad,
For now - I love another.

Janey Wiggins

Oceans Apart

The rains came - the floods rose
drowning everything in their path
No roads left - only rivers and river craft
displacement - fear - aftermath within.

The wave came - it grew and grew
what would be left no one knew
the aftershock was felt around the world
as the disaster began to unfurl

The landslide came and in its midst
gathered everything - with no resist
what a miracle no lives were lost
now disbelief - and the clean-up cost

The loss of - friend - partner - family or other
what for the future - a coat of many colours
loss of wildlife - security - but never hope
if we all pull together as one - we'll cope

The ebb and flow of tides - is life
the uncertainty for the future lives
yesterday's gone - tomorrow might never be
we'll all take one day at a time and see

The time has come - to follow the flickering candle
the time to draw a line under what's past
The time to look into the horizon - to see new shores
the time has come to pass and to move on.

David Charles

The Body Of Norma Jeane

Pearl-white teeth
Ruby-red lips
Alabaster bosom
Rounded hips

Wiggle in the walk
Clenched-in waist
Giggle in the talk
Picture-perfect face

Eyes of blue
Hair of gold
Figure fashioned from
A perfect mould

Won't see her like again
Best ever seen
The incomparable body
Of Norma Jeane.

S Beverly-Ruff

Just Another Day

Sometimes we cannot understand
Our world in its plight today
Yet we must remember
That love finds a way
Should we smile
And have a kind word to say

We improve our world
With an act of kindness
As you smile and go your way
Then truly your world
Is made a better place to stay

Suddenly the world smiles back
As your kindness helps
You heard their prayer today
Someone, somehow
Shows you kindness pays

As you lighten your step
And go your way
You know you've found another friend
Prepare another smile
And greet another day.

Anne Marshall

Ode To Three Skylarks
(Dedicated to Father Patrick McAuliffe, Holy Family Church, Rathcoole, Co Dublin)

Thrice blessed was I, that magic autumn day,
In Holy Family Church, having chanced to stray;
Such wondrous singing floated sweetly round my ears,
A Gaelic dirge that surely had me very close to tears.

The source, three little girls, each aged around eleven,
The quality of their sound, as if direct from Heaven;
Their mentor, Father Paddy, at the organ sat nearby,
Playing - and inspiring that sad, poignant lullaby.

Had Percy Shelley happened upon that simple, striking scene,
I stop to wonder what his thoughts precisely might have been?
My guess - *This gives me new perspective down life's timeless road*
Perhaps the hour is ripe, to recast my precious, ancient ode!

The impact of that October '98 first day lives as of yet,
I clearly well remember, choosing not ever to forget;
God keep you, Father Paddy, ever tapping that rich, rich seam,
E'er inspiring all-Ireland winners like Catherine, Marian and Noreen.

George D Conlon

If The Prize Was You

In this life there are many winners.
Seeking each and every prize
From seasoned performers to raw beginners
Limelight dazzling their wide eyes
But in my humble estimation, adulation, capitulation
I'd consider such a coup
Would be to start anew
If the prize was you.

If the prize was you I'd skim the rim of the Grand Canyon
Then I'd swim across Lake Mead
Each and every night at Disney
Main Street parade, I'd lead
I'd blast off in a rocket ship without a thought
Explore the vast universe as an astronaut
There is nothing I could not do
If the prize was you.

If the prize was you I would be the greatest athlete
And at each and every Olympic game
Come first in every entry
Be the carrier of the flame
I'd chisel out a face at old Mount Rushmore
Till my hands were bleeding and were sore
Then sit and enjoy the view
If the prize was you.

If the prize was you there'd be nothing more for me this world could hold
I'd sell my soul, trade my heart, for that pot of gold
Say you love me and I'll spend eternity crossing the desert sand
Take my hand
Understand
I'll be happy my whole lifetime through
If the prize was you.

S Beverly-Ruff

Parting From A Friend

I fear this last goodbye is final
That we will not meet again
I hope the future holds good things for you
That life will bring you little pain
I do not wish to say goodbye
The parting hurts, and I am sad
For I've been happy in your company
And grateful for the good times we have had
And so we part regretfully as good friends should
For I must take the journey, you must stay
And I would stay beside you if I could
Who knows, we may well meet again one day.

Gordon Andrews

Our Struggle

There's nothing but the cruel Earth;
Empty, heartless and bleeding,
Where we struggle from our birth
Always hurting, craving, needing.
People torture, murder, lie;
Everyone wanting to be the best,
Not caring how many they cause to die,
Failing through ignorance, the real test.
A learned man once did say,
'By the quality of our mercy are we blessed'
But mankind sees mercy as in the way;
His true nature has he then professed.
    I fear I cannot be a part
    Of a society completely lacking heart.

Barbara A Yeager

25

I've searched for years to find my mind
or at least a piece to last this life
I've found this year and will make it mine
reach my goals and pay my fines
I've taken this bull by its horns
I feel success and the weather warms.

I'll work so hard with the knowledge that
we all have our chosen path.
This year brings change and the prospect that
I'll right my wrongs, can't change my past
and past mistakes, I've said and made
won't leave me sitting in the shade.

A fantastic year, my twenty-fifth
I've been lucky enough to heal some family rifts
I got a decent job and some self-respect
the present has no regrets.
So bright my future now it seems
I've harnessed the power of my dreams.

So happy we are, me and my girl
she is the centre of my world.
To be the best man I can be
because me and her are destiny
this year we start the rest of our lives
I'll hold her close, she is my light.

This year I am twenty-five.

Adam Miller

Just Think Over

The scars of starvation,
The fears of isolation,
Both when prey on poverty
A trail of death without mercy
Would be left behind
To pounce perpetually.

The showers may welcome soon,
Crops may flourish like a boon.
Yet, poverty flourishes to torment
All through ages, without vent.
The thirst of death doesn't end,
Till an alternative to hunger is found;
Possibly by the mercy of the rich.
But, who has time to think it over?

Hunted by death, tamed by hunger,
Poverty governs the fate of poor.
In askance, if one thinks over
Where do the merciful strings dwell?
Are they at the doorstep of the rich?

Cursed by fate,
Accursed by destiny;
The plight of the poor
Like a common phenomenon,
If ignored in the routine,
How can poverty be eradicated?
How can the poor cope to survive?

T Ashok Chakravarthy

Sunday Lunch

'What's going on?' she says,
'Nothing,' I innocently say,
wondering why my aunt is talking to me this way.

'Your dinner is in the oven,
I've had mine,'
I protest, 'It's not yet lunchtime.'

Suddenly it dawns, the clocks went back last night,
and for her this was an oversight,
it went clean out of her head,
she'd been left wondering where I was instead.

I rushed back from a friend's to eat my lunch,
except for the hard roasties I happily munched,
grateful my aunt had cooked me lunch.

Julie Marie Laura Shearing

The Great Exploiter

The dog, we say, is Man's best friend,
For master and home he'll defend,
But Man's best friend - workwise of course
Till modern times has been the horse,
Though Man's been no friend in the least
To this manipulated beast.
Throughout mankind's grim history
This fine creature, born to run free,
Has frequently been harshly used,
Overworked, beaten and abused.
With brutalness that should appal
We've held this noble beast in thrall;
Forced iron bars between his jaws
And spurred him into bloody wars;
Condemned him to a man-made hell;
Torn his flesh with sword, lance and shell;
Driving him on till his last breath
To an excruciating death.
In more recent, enlightened times,
We immured him in Hadean mines,
Down in a subterranean hole,
Blindly dragging truckloads of coal.
Kept in the bowels of the earth -
Nevermore to tread soft green turf.
This is the way Man treats dumb friends,
Exploiting them for his own ends.
Could any philosopher refute
That Man has been a callous brute?
Deny that one of our worst features
Is the way we use other creatures?
Though perhaps that's not surprising -
Really doesn't need surmising,
When we see, as we daily can,
The way Man treats his fellow man!

Arthur Allen

Ode To Mitzie

(12.08.95 - 06.07.05)

We said we were only going to look when
We visited Gamston kennels that day,
But two big brown eyes changed our minds,
The little darling came to stay.

Black mask face Pekingese, with coat of white, fawn and cream,
A treasure that we have now possessed beyond our wildest dream.
We found she had a heart complaint, so treated her with care,
She loved to sit and let you groom her long and silky hair.
Mitzie was so photogenic, that was very plain to see,
As soon as she saw the camera her eyes lit up . . .
'Please take another of me'.

Nearly ten years of our lives have revolved around our pet,
Now I must tell you her real name, oh no I shall never forget.
She was registered as Elrosa Glorette,
But that was too much to say,
We christened her . . . 'Mitzie',
It suited her . . . in a way.

The last days of our faithful friend's life
Were sad and painful to bear
Alas her poor little heart stopped beating,
And is now sleeping in God's loving care.

Pauline Vinters

Unseen Anger

Fire, fire, set the liars on fire,
the night sky is bright when the campsites are burning,
it's civil unrest and the tables are turning,
there will be fights over travellers' rights.

We pay our way,
day by day, we're forced to pay,
we pay to be victims of political betray,
we will always lose, never win
never choose or even begin
to live the life we all deserve,
we only get what's kept in reserve.

The guilty are free and the victims are tagged,
and our freedom of speech is criminally gagged.
The upper class huntsman thinks it's his right,
to kill, how he chooses, foxes on sight,
and in force they will stand to make their demand,
and yet they won't let rip as the government dip,
into land ownership, for new roads they need,
they can count on *their* greed.

Rick Oak

When You Awake Tomorrow

When you awake tomorrow to face your fate upon this Earth
Will you see the awful horror, to which the Lord has given birth?
Will you switch on a wireless to hear news from a foreign land
Or will your thoughts be careless, because you do not understand?
Will you question your allegiance
To the leaders without credence
Who demand your obedience
And carry on in blindness, with the blood dripping from your hand?

When you awake tomorrow, will you turn on a plasma screen?
Will you watch those that follow, each sack of flour or soya bean?
Will you be busy making war, or drilling holes to drain the oil
Or will you just close the door and stick a flagpole in the soil?
Will you question your direction?
Can you alter your perception?
Can you see through the deception
Or will we suffer more and more,
As you make sure the cauldrons boil?

When you awake tomorrow, as the counting goes on and on,
Will your stomach be hollow, because you lost your only son?
Will you be safely hiding, as the pyres raise another soul
Or will your heart be aching, to achieve a much greater goal?
For pity's sake, the time has come
For something different to be done
Before this world is overrun
By those intent on making Earth, just a *bloody great black hole!*

Vernon Norman Wood

King Of The World

I'm the king of the world, just look at me!
After the election it's time to put through my policy.

My mouth speaks the word of God,
If you disagree I will beat you with my rod.

'I' am the one, so I hate countries whose names begin with 'I',
Iraq is done, and now it's Iran that I'll poke in the eye.

Ireland and Iceland had better watch out,
Or change their name to Eire and Eis before I shout.

The world's a safer democratic place after my toil,
It's all done in the name of freedom not for a barrel of oil.

Dick Whitehouse

Porcelain

Hide the sun; hide your shame
Time proves things just don't change
She can hide her face behind the clouds
But decisions bruise her with their stones
Lose control; lose your head
Where's the dreams she once had
She could try to mingle in the crowd
Maybe she's slept too long to have known

Wild tigers ran with urban lions
During those dark days of July
Relying on conversation
While the sun fought storms coming by
She's still running with the tigers
Ain't gonna let those lions in
But someday she'll finally see
She's tired of being porcelain
Dwelling on those second chances
Asking questions about the past
Learning a thing about choices
In relationships that don't last
But time has its own price to pay
And when she wants to let them in
The lions will have run away
From tigers made of porcelain

She didn't want people to see
Things she never wanted to be
Things she found out about herself
The pain that she found underneath
She found herself while she was gone
Found herself wanting to belong
Wild tigers made of porcelain
Wanting to prove the lions wrong
New moons mean that moods modify
Evening lasts in the warm dark sky
There's still a chill felt on the soul
During those dark days of July
She's improved on her defences
Mended emotional fences
Wild tigers made of porcelain
She knows she's going to be a woman some day

Steve V Morris

Brummy In The Desert

(Indicative of the nostalgia which is probably felt by men serving abroad, are the following verses written by one of 'Birmingham's fighting men' which were sent to the Evening Despatch, by Private H Dyer of the Dorsetshire Regt - Private Dyer unfortunately was killed in Germany two weeks before the war in Europe came to an end, and is buried in a military cemetery in Germany)

From Alamein to Tripoli there's nothing else but sand.
It stretches miles before me, and miles on every hand.
As I doze upon me carrier 'neath the chilly desert sky.
I can hear the gyrating grinding, as the tanks and guns go by,
And I dream I am back in Stirchley, with the shop fronts all alight,
And I am riding on a thirty-six, with me girl on Saturday night.

I have seen the sights of Egypt, the pyramids and sphinx.
The jostling crowds of Cairo streets, and I will tell you what I thinks
That I would swap 'em all, and willingly, for a sight of all the folk,
A-strolling down the Bristol road from Bournbrook to the Oak.
I will give 'em all free and gratis, every blinkin' sight,
Just to glimpse the good old High Street, with me girl on Saturday night.

I have seen the date palms waving, feathery tops in scented breeze.
I shut me eyes and straight away, I am back among the trees
That crowd the slopes of Lickey, or perhaps in a dream I am sent,
To stand by Frankley Beeches, and take a look at Clent.
Or I see the Evesham orchards, a foaming mass of white,
And I am peddling home on me tandem, with me girl on Saturday night.

I have swum the Mediterranean, the blazing sky beneath,
But I would swap for the five chill minutes in the Lido at Rowheath.
And oriental odours - well they soon begin to pall,
Give me a whiff of fish and chips, and you can keep them all.
Swaying camels look *romantic*, but I would make a bigger fuss
To go around the Outer Circle, on a swaying yellow bus.

I have seen the mosques and minarets, and of course I thought them fine,
I have seen the Holy cities on me leave in Palestine,
But the new Jerusalem's golden street, with angels fair to see,
Can't beat dear old dirty New Street, full of Brummy folk like me.
So we gotta keep on moving, till the foe gives up the fight,
Then we can all go walking with our girls on a Saturday night.

Frank Baggaley

Mother And Me At The End

Mother, breathe easy.
You who can no longer breathe alone,
Who cannot cough or spit,
Who cannot even vomit on your own,
I stand near.

Mother, come look into my eyes.
Together we encompass all of it.
Together, without words,
In holy silence we are a prayer
Beyond the reach of fear and lies.

We banish all but now and here.
Time is but an endless end.
All unreels again and again.
Nothing moves - there are no directions.
Neither a gyre, nor a spire,
None can divide eternity into sections.
Time is a wonder - cuts the mind asunder.

Eternity
In the hiss of a cat.
I say this, and you say that.

In the beginning was the word.
Beginnings and endings need not be heard.

Do not speak of the living or the dead.
All that counts cannot be said.
Mother, it does not matter what we know.

Come, let us wait hand in hand.
My fingers in yours point like Noah's great dove.
In silent prayer I touch your soul,
Shared now forever in quiet love,
Eternity in every grain of sand.
Everything else is beyond our command.

Keith Alan Deutch

Bereavement

To lose my father, at the age of twelve
My innermost feelings, hidden, withheld
Father, I used to tremble and shake
You made me feel like a big mistake

So many times, you would breathe down my neck
I would sit in the chair a nervous wreck
This would often lead up to a smack or a slap
You would always continually be on my back

Everything I did, was never good enough
You made my life miserable and tough
When I was a child, I would lie on my bed
Sometimes, I wished that you were dead

I couldn't believe, when you had finally departed
I was hardly dejected or broken-hearted
To be perfectly honest it was such a relief
I will not apologise, for this belief

I was haunted by images of you for a while
Woken by nightmares, hideous and vile
I would literally wake up in a hot and cold sweat
A vision of you breathing down my neck

Andrew Nokes

?Who

Hanging over the butcher's shop
Is a sign with, ?who
As well as proclaiming he is a butcher
And what he can offer you
The meat he sells is the finest
From rump steak to pigs' feet
All on display on the counter
While he stands awaiting to greet
His customers all seem to be faithful
The same ones day after day
Then suddenly you find he's not there for a while
The stand-in is starting to say
He's had a slight slip of the chopper
And a digit came off by mistake
So a rest at home while it heals
Is what he's been ordered to take
I have always wondered about the sign
Now I know the question mark who
Did his finger end up in a sausage?
If so, who ate it, me or you?

Daphne Fryer

A Day To Remember

My father, born 1907 (died 1980)
Lived his young life in the city.
I live - 80 miles south of London - 1988
Home care visit, I mustn't be late.
Such a nice man, much overweight.
I help as he struggles from bed to chair,
Strapped to his leg, a calliper.
In conversation, I ask,
What was your work?
Furniture, my father's factory, north London.
My dad was a French polisher, Islington.
Silence - then my dad's name was a guess.
He knew he was right
As I stumbled a 'yes'.
My dad, as a lad, was his dad's apprentice.
It was strange to hear him say,
My dad was sent to collect him
From school every day.
A chance in a million
A coincidence, so rare,
Fate brought us together,
Our memories to share.

Janey Wiggins

Aim For The Head

Bullets whip up sky
This is more than meat pie
The aim is low
And also high
Into the bread basket
Plenty more ammo in the casket
Far from the heralded muskets
Popping heads like a gasket
So you want to groove
Be like water and move
People and 'Men of Arms'
Stay out of harm
Blasted to be they are
To grind bones afar
Keep off the bars
Bam, bam, bang
Rat-a-rat-fang.

Hardeep Singh-Leader

Timmy

My darling Timmy was very sick
From birth he hadn't a chance
Nature decided to play cruel games
I the tree, he the decaying branch
What a lesson in patience, kindness he taught
Put us fit ones to shame
Always in pain and nearly blind
He never moaned or complained
We travelled the world Timmy and me
His dad, adored, long gone
We searched for help, for a miracle
To mend, to ease those aching bones
Those clever medical people
Sympathised - did their best
No miracle was forthcoming
Their advice - get plenty of rest
My faith was tried and tested
How frustrated and angry I felt
In my lonely bedroom the tears would flow
A safety valve - my anger began to melt
To be replaced by the constant worry
What if something happened to me?
Who will love and take care of
My precious boy, cuddled on my knee!
The love of his life, his passion
Was Sunderland football team
He could see the bright red and white stripes
As he watched them on the TV, he would dream
He was their brilliant striker
Scoring goals by the score
Carried shoulder high by his team-mates
Listening to the famous Roker roar
How tragic it could only be a dream
Even going to a match was rare
Tickets were impossible to obtain
Especially when we needed a pair
The season was coming to an exciting end
The first division trophy within their grasp
That crucial final deciding game
Those Sunderland lads had a daunting task
'Just one more point Mum,' my brave boy whispered
He was praying so hard for them
I thanked God for giving him an interest
Away from this sadness and pain

I picked up the envelope from the doorway
'To Timmy', was scribbled there
'Two tickets to Roker Park on Saturday,'
And a note saying, 'Have no fear
We'll pick you up and take you
You'll have a wonderful day.'
We were both in a state of delicious shock
Couldn't find anything to say
Miracles happen, even today
My dear son will remember that kindness
And the excitement and thrill will stay
In his heart, through the greyest of days
The treasured memory of the time
He watched his beloved heroes at Roker Park
Win that magnificent trophy
Even brought it to him, happy as a lark
So he could touch it and shake hands
With that famous defender
Who smiled at him and shared
Such an historic moment, yet so tender
That ticket the donor will never know
How much joy he caused that day
For ninety minutes, Timmy was in a magic world
Pain and misery far, far away.

M C Armstrong

Please Don't Tell

Please don't tell the world my secret,
Please don't tell I care.
Please don't tell the world my secret,
My secret love I can't declare.
For you are wed to another
With vows that keep us apart,
So my love I must smother
And keep it locked within my heart.
I saw you pass across the way
Alas! What could I say
But to wish you good time of day
And watch you as you walked away?
I'm so sad when I'm alone,
I brood and then I cry.
My secret love I would disown,
But then again I lie.
There is no hope for me I know
When Fate against me stands,
You have a wedding ring to show,
My secret love it bans.

A J Macdonald

Lips Entwined

Lips entwined, sat here looking at how it was
Listening to our song, feelings that I cross
A sharp stabbing, like a knife in my heart
I thought that I was coping with this loss

The days pass by, I feel a little stronger
Then I fall back down, with just a little push
See all the reminders, photos, people and places
Hear the songs, the noises, hush!

The brave face I put on, I paint each day
To hide my feelings, the hurt I feel
The pain you put me though, all of this
Will my broken heart, ever heal?

I want you to feel my pain, like I am now
I want to show you, how you have hurt me
Feeling pain, deep in this pit, aching, rising pain
All this I'm feeling, you don't save me, you leave me be

How could you be so heartless, and not have a soul
I love you with all my heart, forever and ever
And yet you hurt me, broke my heart, through and through
You tricked me, broke me, you think you're clever

I've lost everything, I really have
And you just don't care, you'll tell me 'whatever, just go'
My body, my temple, you used it and abused it
Physically and mentally ruined me, used me like your ho

Don't you worry, you will not win
You will not get away with this, no not at all
Your day will come
You won't rise in the end, you will trip and fall!

G Steele

No Clay Piping Here

They will rue the appointment of the municipal museum curator -
A certain 'Captain Carruthers' with the deign of a dictator.
He has a peculiar penchant for stuffed domestic cats
And ships in bottles and politically incorrect hats.
His latest exhibitions are on 'Glass Eyeballs and Their Makers'
And 'The Fifty Greatest Russian Beetroot Pickle Recipes' - any takers?
He has beguilingly high hopes for 'Milk Bottle Tops Through the Ages'
And 'How to Build a Matchstick Battleship (in 15,000 stages)'.
There's his substantial sacred collection of 'Virgin Mary' pens
And an atmospheric montage entitled 'Foggy Days in the Fens'.
The municipal museum curator is a curious, cantankerous fellow,
Intolerant of talking, but rather inclined to bellow,
'Come educate your offspring! Come marvel one and all
In my idiosyncratic idyll, at the rear of the Town Hall!'

Emily Woodhams

What Do You See?

Look into the depths of a fire
What do you see?
Devils fighting
Demons biting
That is what I see.

Peer down through the ocean
What do you see?
Merfolk playing
Sea horses swaying
That is what I see.

Gaze at the clouds above
What do you see?
Fairies prancing
Angels dancing
That is what I see.

Search through the soil below
What do you see?
Serpents gliding
Landslips sliding
That is what I see.

Look at the elements around you
What do *you* see?
Words soaring and diving
Imagination thriving
That is what I'll see.

Rachel Gleavy (15)

Night Walk

Up to my ears I tug my coat collar,
Turtle my neck in and tuck down my chin,
A dog's plea I hear, he begs *let me in.*
My hands in soft wool gloves nestle encased,
Cats run, seek the hearth of a warm fireplace.
I walk past gold windows with draped frilled lace.
Feet hurry, soles crunch in rigid water
As pools and puddles splinter then shatter
While a polished moon in a blushing sky
Shines down on lurex dusted rooftop tiles.
Diamond flecked cars dazzle both my eyes,
Suspended ghosts of speech float in the air,
My thick coat grows thin, I almost despair,
The door opens, amber warmth tints my hair.

Ethel Oates

A Poem

This thing of mine I am talking about,
Although it is quite old,
It does perform remarkably well,
So I am always told.

'I wish I had one as big as that!'
The men quite often say,
'Me and my girl could play with it together,
During days of inclement weather.'

The favourite place to demonstrate
Is in the attic on high,
On the floor things take place,
The watcher's comment, 'Oh my, oh my.'

Once it gets really wound up
And starts off on its way,
Never seems to have enough,
With a rock and roll rhythm and sexy sway.

You think of me being horny
And talking of nothing but sex,
But what it's really about is my Hornby,
My old grandfather's Hornby train set.

W H Stevens

Going Home

(Written for a friend who passed away)

I'm going on a liner, crossing the wide, wide sea,
Starting a new adventure to a place I've yet to see,
You're waving me off at the quayside,
You're sad to see me go,
It's a journey in time we all must make,
For that is surely so.
But when I arrive on the other shore,
There waving and cheering me on,
Will be my friends and family
And people I have known.
So don't be sad at my leaving,
It's not as tho' I can write.
But think of me as the dawn breaks,
As the darkness turns to light,
Think of me as the sweet smell of flowers,
And the birds that sing on high,
And remember with your kindest thoughts,
That no one ever dies.

Sandra Garrod

Front Line

The 'Poetic Truth' has at last arrived
When MI5 took over at Ally Pally WW2
The first thing he did was absolutely 'Bang On'
He confiscated all office typewriters, pens and ink
All BBC admin archives including my promotion salary
To prevent Moseley's black-shirt spies at BBC breaking security
The very thing Goering's spy-ring wanted 'our radar frequencies'
They did not get them.
But I lost my promotion pay rise instead purely by coincidence
But why take sixty years to unravel Aunty's bloomers
With 'British Intelligence' red tape giving me war-psychic rumours
All I am asking now is for MoD to pay up
What more could a back-room poet ask
Unless it be to make all my poetry lines rhyme
That I will do if they pay up on time.

Paff

Moments

What is it that
You dream at night
That sharpens your view
Of the world in sight
That makes you so far removed
From the struggle and the daily fight?

What is it
That you can see
When everyone else
Is oblivious and free
From the hidden trauma
Kept inside you desperately?

What you hide
Behind your face
Undisplayed in public
To evade any disgrace
Haunts you at night
In that dark, lonely place
Unrelenting in vividness and pace
You're paralysed beyond repair
Emotions cold and thoughts laid bare.

K Jenkins

Menopausal Season

Body sweating, hormones you fight.
Toss and turn, no sleep at night.
Bedclothes on, then off again,
Windows open, life's getting a pain.

Your mood swings, sometimes good,
Happy, carefree, as it should,
Then your tongue, cutting like a knife,
Anger, sadness, trauma, running rife.

No rose-tinted glasses to see life through,
The next one to cross you, you threaten to sue,
The doctor, just another prescription he'll write,
Pills to help with your hormonal fight.

No one listens when you shout and scream,
People think you're just letting off steam.
Thought deep inside you want the world to know,
That this hormonal thing is not just for show.

Despairing and despondent, you're on the brink,
Your mind riddled, unable to think.
No outward signs, but, for nature's reason,
You're a woman, in her menopausal season . . .

Alan J Morgan

Time

What do I see?
Time has changed without me
So look at the world around us
It can change dramatically

So much so our museums overflow

Memories of the past just come and go
Because the people help it change itself
Don't you know?

So when you wake in the morning
It's not the same
But who really cares
You and me have it so easily
So break the clock
Break its face
Yes! Old Father Time knows his place

Debbie Storey

The Mother's Bond

There's always something special
About the love of Daughter and Mum,
I believe it started long ago
When Babe was in her tum.

From the day that Baby's born
She recognises Mum's touch,
And by just one little look
The love is felt so much.

Shannon is my daughter
And I know our bond is true,
Our closeness is so special
The love just grew and grew.

Mum and I also have that bond
A mum, best friends, that's right,
She manages to care for me
Even when I'm out of sight.

I hope that when Shannon's a mum
This friendship is passed down,
A bond is special between us three
It's not often that we frown.

I'm thankful that we have this bond
Of friendship, love and fun,
I just wish I could tell the world
How three of us make one.

Andrea McDermott

I Got Life

They say you must have hope to live a dream
And push beyond belief to be redeemed
But I want to live life the most; my way
And not live by the rules you tell me each day.
I'm told right from wrong each day and night
Preventing me from succeeding in my plight
I got life for now but will that always be so?
If not please tell me when I must let go.
We all have our own place as we travel this road
That we call life, as we dedicate each ode
And I got life, what more is there?
Well I don't know but I sure do care
I got life, I got dreams and hope
My only wish is that I can cope.

Graham Connor

Hidden

Now I am getting older I sit and reminisce
About the past - those long gone - friends I sorely miss
But one was much younger - so closely knit were we
Our houses faced each other - both very near the sea.

She often used to speak of her far-off youthful days -
Then there'd be a silence - she'd fall into a daze
As if closely hidden lay a deep recurring fear
Calling for my help - but the words I could not hear.

What memory caused that silence? Why was I not more bold
To ask if I could be of help - would she then have told
Her innermost longings to me - what power could they hold
To make me feel so useless and left out in the cold?

Her children loved to come across for an hour or two
Often staying for their tea - they called me Auntie Prue
I enjoyed their company so very, very much
Being a wee bit lonesome - I liked to keep in touch.

Then sadly I had to leave my home upon the hill
And go across to Ireland - my mum was taken ill.
I was there for several months just sitting by her side
Leaving my home empty until after she had died.

I returned to Dorset on a cold December day
Much later, in the evening, I saw that something lay
On the doormat - a scribbled note - it was from my friend
Just full of grateful thanks from beginning to the end.

Then only in the postscript did things become more clear
The reason why they'd left their home so cosy and so dear
'Work has not gone well of late' and then I felt her pain
As I read in small writing 'Joe's hit the bottle again'.

G E Bray

Tell Us A Story Dad

Tell us a story Dad
Before we go to bed
One that we can laugh at
Not cry ourselves to sleep in bed.

Tell us a story Dad
About when you and Mum were young
Of all the tricks that you pulled on people
That were highly strung.

Tell us a story Dad
About life on the farm
Make it sound more life-like and real
Not like any old yarn.

Keith L Powell

The Knock On The Door

That knock on the door
Was waited for.
We knew it would happen, and prayed it would not.
The pain that it raises is too high a cost.
Your brother was battered and still bears the scar,
He trembles at the knock on the door.

To protect him is the only way,
Even at the cost of your father to be.
You are so tiny, a life anew, you'll not understand
The fear and flight that was caused on that night.
Your brother, he loves you, and we do too,
But the knock on the door carries the scars for you too.

He has found you at last, nothing anew.
The fears of the battering and life shattered through.
The anger that happened, and the pain too,
Is something we share in the love of you,
And daily we know you must never be found,
Protecting you both is all that we pray,
To keeping that knock on the door at bay.

Dawn Taylor

Dreams Of A Hidden Desire

In the valley of dreams, where we meet
Garlands at our feet
The tendrils of our love
Entwined in passions sweet

In the valley of dreams
Where we meet

Holding, touching, caressing, loving
Under a multicoloured sky
Showered by warm-scented beams
Of love's sweet cry

The delights of love's sweet
Mysteries unfold
In delights of fantasy untold

The ebb and flow together brings
Like the softness of a butterfly's wings
As rising passions complete
In the valley of dreams where we meet

David Stuart

Golden Chain

My heart is bound to yours
it's tied with the fetters of love,
an amazing golden lock and chain
neither one of us could break,
this entwining golden manacle
joins your heart eternally to mine,
our love and devotion is the strength
this precious chain feeds upon.

The more we love each other
the stronger it becomes,
it holds fast our hearts,
this wondrous chain of gold,
and with time it will flower,
becoming deeper and more bold.

Anthony and Cleopatra had one,
Queen Victoria and Albert too,
Romeo and Juliet in their time
are to name but a few,
and like their love, ours will
blossom and bind us together,
it's cast its spell, this golden chain,
has us locked and shackled forever.

Greta Forsyth

Not Ready

Not ready for old lady voice
or the age-related stoop.
Blue-rinsed, bed-socked,
tea dancing, with the
over sixties group.

Not ready for the knee ops
or the failing sighted eyes.
I want to do some travelling
and hang out in the skies.

Not ready for these wrinkles
and the sagging of my chin.
Fed up with apologising
for not being wafer-thin.

Not ready for the care home
with the daily happy pills.
My bodily functions all recorded
to keep me from all ills.

Not ready for the favours
of the patronising crowd.
Inside I'm still that woman,
who's vibrant, young and proud.

Ann Potkins

Esther

Esther, an orphan, was born as a Jew
And brought up by her cousin when young
A maiden of beauty unlike any other
Lived with women in the palace harem.

She was trained and taught in many of the arts
And told not to reveal her identity
The king embarrassed by his wife not attending
At a banquet she behaved as a nonentity.

The king liked Esther more than the others
And soon he named her his queen
Two guards decided to murder the king
Finding out, she told what she'd seen.

In the king's eyes Esther could do no wrong
She revealed to the king who she was
And of the plot to kill the population of Jews
To intervene and stop the great loss.

The king revoked all orders against Jews
Her people were allowed to live
Esther could ask anything from the king
For her he would always forgive.

C Armstrong

Silence On The Beaches

It is silent now across the sea and the sun bleaches the sand
The fishing boats are now manned by ghosts that will set and trim the sails
A small child waits just to say goodbye and then gently waves his hand
As the fishermen slip their anchor, a warm southern wind prevails
Silently he turns away and sighs
Gently wiping tears that stain his eyes
As the wind catches forever his cries

Alone with memories of his dad, he turns back to face the sea
The white swollen sails are fading now, that the wind has turned at last
Great swirls of spray now cloud the ocean, where he knows that he should be
And he is lost forever in thought, of the disappearing mast
While seagulls squawk and face the deep
The ghouls aboard the boat will sleep
Till he turns once more to weep

He cries out, seeking his mother's womb, to feel the life she gave him
He knows that she cannot hear his call, for she too has been taken
As the water laps around his feet, his senses begin to swim
The fishing boats have all gone to Hell, and he has been forsaken
He sees the demons from the sea
Then walks to meet them happily
To join his loving family.

Vernon Norman Wood

Celebrating Women

'Oh, you are just a housewife,' they say
But do they realise
What you have to do
And how you have to be very wise?

You have to know how to handle money
So a banker you become
Be a cook and a cleaner
And of course know how laundry is done.

Know how to cope with babies
What else is there to tell?
Learn how to garden, change batteries
My, aren't we doing well.

Be a mother and wife
Nurse and playmate as well
Drive a car, be a lover
Does all this ring a bell?

You learn to sew on a button or a dress
Emulsion walls and ceilings also
How to work around others
It really is all go.

So if someone says, 'Oh just a housewife,'
You can point out all these things
Saying, 'Oh I am very proud
Look at all of these I have been in my life.'

H Dormand

Divided By A Common Language

Can you distinguish
American from English?
Americans say, nevertheless
I can't *second guess*
(Instead of *predict* or *anticipate*)
So we'll just have to wait!
Instead of *suppose*, they say *guess*
(Something they need to redress)
And instead of *tap*, they say *fawcet*,
(It rhymes, you can see, with corset).
In their renditions
They omit prepositions,
They mix the superlative
With the comparative
And, it is absurd,
Use adjective for adverb
So, can you distinguish
American from English?

Catherine Blackett

Anchor Books Information

We hope you have enjoyed reading this book - and that you will continue to enjoy it in the coming years.

If you like reading and writing poetry drop us a line, or give us a call, and we'll send you a free information pack.

Alternatively if you would like to order further copies of this book or any of our other titles, then please give us a call or log onto our website at www.forwardpress.co.uk

anchorbooks

Anchor Books Information
Remus House
Coltsfoot Drive
Peterborough
PE2 9JX

01733 898102